Working Alternatives

CATHOLIC PRACTICE IN NORTH AMERICA

SERIES EDITOR:

John C. Seitz, Associate Professor, Theology Department,
Fordham University; Associate Director for Lincoln Center,
Curran Center for American Catholic Studies

This series aims to contribute to the growing field of Catholic
studies through the publication of books devoted to the historical
and cultural study of Catholic practice in North America, from
the colonial period to the present. As the term "practice" suggests,
the series springs from a pressing need in the study of American
Catholicism for empirical investigations and creative explorations
and analyses of the contours of Catholic experience. In seeking to
provide more comprehensive maps of Catholic practice, this series
is committed to publishing works from diverse American locales,
including urban, suburban, and rural settings; ethnic, postethnic,
and transnational contexts; private and public sites; and seats of
power as well as the margins.

Working Alternatives

AMERICAN AND CATHOLIC EXPERIMENTS
IN WORK AND ECONOMY

John C. Seitz and Christine Firer Hinze, Editors

FORDHAM UNIVERSITY PRESS
New York   2020

Fordham University Press has no responsibility for the persistence or accuracy of URLs for external or third-party Internet websites referred to in this publication and does not guarantee that any content on such websites is, or will remain, accurate or appropriate.

Fordham University Press also publishes its books in a variety of electronic formats. Some content that appears in print may not be available in electronic books.

Visit us online at www.fordhampress.com.

Library of Congress Cataloging-in-Publication Data available online at https://catalog.loc.gov.

Printed in the United States of America

22 21 20   5 4 3 2 1

First edition

Contents

Working Alternatives

Introduction

JOHN C. SEITZ AND CHRISTINE FIRER HINZE

This is a book about experiments. It documents efforts among a diverse cast of scholars, activists, institutions, and businesses to test out significant, alternative models of economic thought, value, organization, and practice. Some of these experiments happen right here, in the pages of this book: authors outline and test hypotheses, tweak variables, document results, venture conclusions. Other experiments happened in the past and are brought back to life here, elevated, revived, and examined for the lessons they offer about the deep roots and stubborn challenges of economic transformation.

Taken together, *Working Alternatives* is not just a book *about* experiments, but is itself a kind of experiment. Collectively, the works gathered here assert a hypothesis: economic theories, systems, and practices— ways of conceiving, organizing, and enacting work, management, supply, production, exchange, remuneration, wealth, and consumption—rely on basic, often unexamined, presumptions about human personhood, relations, and flourishing. Foundational conceptions of what people need, how they thrive, and what they owe to others help determine the contours of economic life in a given time and place. Those conceptions, in turn, are embedded in and shaped by the specific material and cultural contexts in which people undertake economic activity. Efforts to analyze and critique economic arrangements and practices, or to envision viable alternatives, thus must contend with both the particularities of those contexts and the (descriptive and normative) assumptions entrenched in them. Those who are advancing transformative economic agendas must also offer their own explanations of the consonance of their proposals and what they posit as basic human needs, responsibilities, and capacities.

The crucial correlate of this hypothesis is the idea that thorny problems of material provision, survival, and well-being demand scholarly analysis that transcends disciplinary boundaries as they have taken shape in the modern academy. The unusual collection of scholars joined in these pages—they come from the areas of business management, religious ethics, and history—transforms the book from the assertion of a hypothesis into the testing of it. The ultimate results of this test, of course, await the readers' judgment and any creative thought and action their reading provokes. But we have found that the task of enriching our economic and business imaginaries benefits from the creative prodding of multidisciplinary conversation. As we discovered in our meetings with one another in the production of this volume, these conversations have stubborn, jagged edges. Different methods, competing assumptions, varying levels of tolerance for tragedy and hope, these held strong. But like the spines of a burr that sticks to your socks long after the hike has ended, these prickly differences offer persistent reminders about the various terrains to be accounted for in the pursuit of alternatives.

In keeping with our interest in foundational conceptions, the essays in this volume engage extensively with religious thought and practice. For all the talk about a modern separation between "secular" and "sacred" realms, religious thinkers and actors have never felt particularly constrained by such boundaries from applying their ideas about what human beings need, who we really are, or what we owe to others. The purportedly "secular" has never been free of religious actors, arguments, and framings, just as the realm of religion has always been infused with practical questions of survival and flourishing. This volume boldly acknowledges that reality and goes a step further: religious histories, ideas, and ethics can help crack open stubborn problems by offering fundamental ethical and existential reorientations to basic economic questions as well as provocative stories of radical experiment rooted in alternate conceptions of what, at bottom, truly matters.

But religious thinking, histories, and practice are not offered in this volume as simple cure-alls for ailing economies. Religious commitments have just as often undermined economic health as they have promoted it. These essays are not blind to that reality; in fact, many of the contributions to this volume take shape as assessments of disputes *internal* to particular religious communities or traditions concerning economic questions. Religious arguments have no special authority simply because they are religious. But religious thinking and practice offer one arena of action in which human beings try to respond to the immediate circumstances and mysterious forces into which they are thrown and through which they must make their way. For many of the authors of this volume, certain religious thinkers and practitioners have offered particularly compelling responses, which seem to do justice to reality and expand our imagination and capacity to respond to it effectively. To varied degrees, they see possibilities for positive transformation through serious consideration of theological ethics, histories of religious experimentation in realms of economic exchange, and conceptual recalibrations rooted in certain kinds of religious imagination. Religious ethics, history, and theology are valuable interlocutors, not to be shunned in order to perpetuate outdated fantasies about the neutrality of the secular realm or the pure science of economics.

In April 2016, an international conference was held at Fordham University called *Building Good Economies: Interdisciplinary and Practical Perspectives*, recognizing modern Catholic social teaching (CST) at its 125th anniversary. This "CST@125" gathering provided a context for the authors of this volume to meet and undertake this project in the light of critical and multidisciplinary reflection on this particular, durable, and dynamic tradition of teaching, thought, and practice.

Rooted in two millennia of Christians' reflection on the implications of faith for their social, political, and economic circumstances, "modern Catholic social teaching" sprang from efforts by nineteenth-century Catholic leaders and laity to grapple with the impacts of industrializing economies on the lives of workers, families, and communities. One fruit of this concatenation of ecclesial thought and activism was a new papal foray into public engagement, Pope Leo XIII's 1891 encyclical letter, *Rerum novarum*, "On the condition of the working classes." Speaking directly and urgently on behalf of just business practice and equity for vulnerable workers, using language meant to appeal not only to Christians but to all reasonable people of good will, Leo's widely discussed letter inaugurated what is now a 125-plus year tradition of official church teaching addressing contemporary economic and social matters, and the conversations, debates, and actions this teaching has evoked.

Centered on the God-given personal *dignity* of each and all, realized within an interdependent *common good*, modern CST promotes a holistic, "solidary humanism." Its multi-associational vision of communal life stresses both *subsidiarity*—the value of locating power and decision-making at appropriately local levels of organization—and the role of *governmental authority* in ensuring the shared well-being of citizens and communities. From Leo forward, CST has singled out economy and work as crucial sites for moral reflection, positing, in varied and evolving ways, several key themes. These include *the universal purpose of created goods* (the claim that God intends the resources of creation to serve the well-being of all), which requires equitable sharing and use of the world's resources; *the dignity of work and the rights of workers* to just remuneration and working conditions; a conception of *authentic, integral development* that sets directions for inclusive human progress while caring for and respecting the integrity of creation; and an insistence on *solidarity* and a *preferential option for the poor and vulnerable* as keys to combating inequities and abuses of power at both local and systemic levels. In considering policies surrounding work, popes from Leo to Francis take their cue from CST's normative understanding of economy's inclusive, provisioning purposes, and on the primacy of persons over their labor, and labor over capital. Many of the authors in this volume engage directly with this modern Catholic social tradition. Other essays echo or dialogue with its themes and leitmotifs pertaining to work and economy; our meeting and conversations in the light of Fordham's CST@125 conference helped shape the project as a whole.

Other forms of religious and nonreligious thinking and practice factor in the volume as well. Alison Collis Greene's study of a particular Protestant history of activism and struggle for economic and racial justice offers the possibility for comparison. The interdenominational Protestant "Social Gospel" that animated the figures Greene studies arose around the same time as the first social encyclical emerged from the Vatican. Like Kathleen Holscher's essay about Catholic nuns, Greene's account of Protestant activists and their Protestant opponents demonstrates the ways Christian social thought ran up against racial and ethnic boundaries it did not always know how, or perhaps even desire, to overcome. Historian Kirsten Swinth observes late twentieth century US feminist activism around questions of "care" work. Seeing the activism of the women distinct from particular religious affiliations offers both critique and complement to the religious arguments around the same issue featured in other essays. Sandra Waddock offers a different approach, extending the tradition of modern Western curiosity about non-European religious categories. Waddock's adaptation of "shamanism" offers a reminder of

the endless range of religious resources that might be put to use in fostering alternatives. What kinds of possibilities does the idea of "shaman"
open up that might not be evident if leadership is imagined under the
rubrics of priest, patriarch, minister, saint, or martyr, just to name a few
that have dominated in Western thought?

Taken together, the essays create a body of work within which Catholic forms of engaging with economic questions come into conversation
with one another and with non-Catholic experiments in economic
thought and practice. In a global context within which economic disparities persist and in some cases are expanding, where women, people of
color, and people of the global south remain at a severe economic disad-
vantage and are frequently exploited or disregarded for the advantage of
the few, we are compelled to do whatever it takes to rethink foundational
concepts.

The task of defining foundational concepts remains a challenge. In this
volume, the question "alternative to what?" has to be answered in con-
textual ways. Economic systems impinge locally and with different
effects. The varying historical and social sites of our authors' engagements means they identify particular foundational concepts to which
alternatives were or need to be articulated and enacted. That said, we see
rough contours of the kinds of problems our authors address in the Catholic forays into economic thinking, including Rerum novarum and the
substantially more progressive revision of that approach in 1931 with
Pope Pius XI's Quadragesimo anno (Forty years after [Rerum novarum]).
To be sure, these documents and the thinking they spurred were focused
on their own era, and specifically offered alternatives to what the popes
saw as the two dominant economic options of their times—unfettered
market capitalism and statist socialism.

It should not go unnoticed that attunement with the foundational
issues of their times gave their approaches traction. Just to take one
example, already by the 1910s Father John A. Ryan, an economics professor and moral theologian, had applied CST to help advance minimum
wage laws and the idea of a "living wage." By the end of the decade Ryan
helped the US bishops draft a plan for post-World War I US "reconstruction," which called not only for a minimum wage but also for old age

insurance, unemployment insurance, local health clinics, and greater representation of labor in management. Although such proposals did not yield immediate results, they spoke to their times and gained momentum, especially as a post-war boom gave way to a catastrophic global depression. CST was in the mix as the United States sought a way out of the tragedy. Catholic historians are fond of pointing out the excitement generated among Catholics when in 1932 the Democratic presidential nominee, Franklin Delano Roosevelt, aligned himself and his economic proposals with *Quadragesimo anno.*

These observations do not constitute a judgment of the successes and failures of the New Deal or its actual alignment with the encyclical Roosevelt name checked. Instead, they provide a kind of dual lens for reading the essays in this volume. First, the example the late nineteenth and early twentieth century CST encyclicals demonstrate is that, when attuned with their times, the proffering of alternatives to foundational concepts and practices can make a difference, even if it is temporary or riven with complexity. Ideas once ridiculed as hopelessly naïve, even those consigned to the dustbin of history can sometimes revive and break through to change things for the better.

Second, CST articulated a set of concerns with modern economic practice that continue to circulate. Although these are and should be contested categories, the CST articulations of the universal purpose of *created* goods, *the dignity of work and the rights of workers, authentic, integral development,* and *solidarity with a preferential option for the poor and vulnerable* suggest the dominance of their opposites, the established systems they seek to replace. The world's natural resources still funnel to the privileged; work too often remains undignified, and workers suffer for lack of rights; development is frequently exploitative and unsustainable; and class interests and white privilege trump effective solidarity, with the least bearing the cost. This broad outline of the status quo does not require that meaningful progress be dismissed: when things moved toward a closer approximation of CST's key themes, our authors say so. But we also share the sense of dis-ease with the ways the world's economic systems perpetuate or exacerbate conditions at great distance from these ideals.

It is often remarked that scholarship and university faculty operate in "silos." Although tense university politics mean that sometimes it seems otherwise, scholars generally operate under the premise that the metaphor refers not to bunkers housing missiles ready for launch but towers housing grain ready for use. For our part, the editors and authors of this book are not hostile to silos, at least those in the agricultural model; it pays to put scholars tested or threshed through similar disciplines together. But silos, it should be noted, are never meant to be shut off permanently from the world. Not only do they need ventilation, they are designed to open, to pour out their well-stored goods: functioning silos flow. This book facilitates that flow in the hope of producing multigrain thinking and action toward change in economic practice. We are aware that this is only a beginning, that crafting new economic imaginaries demands this but also demands other kinds of flow, different grains. Disciplinary diversity is only one kind, and perhaps not even the most significant context for creative combination. To be sure, our focus mostly on Euro-American and Christian contexts offers the virtue of certain shared discursive frames, but at the same time it presents limits that call out for expansion by future researchers.

Our method for advancing our modest forms of flow relies on a framework developed by early twentieth century theorists of Catholic Action—a movement (in light of the church's slipping temporal power) for structuring everyday Catholics' contribution to the advancement of the church's mission in the world. Catholic Action leader and founder of the influential Jocist or Young Christian Workers movement, Belgian priest Joseph Carijn, promoted a tripartite framework designed to delineate, concisely and concretely, the dynamics of Catholics' moral engagement in the world: see, judge, act. First, see: look at the situation honestly and analyze its parts rigorously. Second, judge: evaluate what you have seen, weigh its merits against its limitations, use the standard of compassion set out by Jesus of the gospels to assign value to various practices. Last, act: work to bring the world you see more in line with the world you hope to produce. Although most essays in this volume include (or study) all three of these moves in some measure, they tend to prioritize one or the other. Inspired by this legacy, and in order to facilitate comparison and reflection, we cluster the essays under three rubrics: "Seeing Differently: Alternative Visions of Economy and Work," "Valuing Differently:

Challenging Work and Business As Usual," and "Practicing Differently: Creating Alternative Ways of Working."

Seeing Differently: Alternative Visions of Economy and Work

The first cluster of essays in this volume explore what might happen if we approached economy and work with new eyes: what have we not seen and why, and how might things change if we look more carefully or remove certain blinders? For theological ethicist Sandra Sullivan-Dunbar, the hidden realities have to do with both the categories of work and the gender of the workers. Her essay is less about the implementation of an alternative economy than it is about the *recognition* of an alternative economy, one that has been in place since long before "markets" became the dominant metaphor of economic activity. The care economy, as Sullivan-Dunbar calls this set of practices, includes all human efforts oriented toward "sustaining life and promoting basic well-being." The care economy is alternative in the sense that it has been "written out" of everyday conceptions of economics and thus under-theorized as a part of any remedy to broken systems. Sullivan-Dunbar aims to add back the care economy into economic theory, particularly the economic arguments laid out in Pope Benedict XVI's *Caritas in Veritate*, a document with promising interest in the normativity of economics and the importance of "gift," but little attention to unpaid care work and its entanglement with gender. When care work is taken into account, especially unpaid care work that takes place in the home, it becomes clear that women "already demonstrate more economic participation than men, they simply get paid less for it, and get paid for less of it." Feminist economics offers a way to enhance CST by recognizing the material needs not only of those receiving care but also of those giving care.

Borrowing from recent papal documents, Michael Naughton elaborates on an "integral ecological" approach to economic activity. At the heart of this approach is a more robust recognition and embrace of the horizontal connections across social institutions. Strong primary institutions—the "basic cells" of culture—radiate outward and inform other facets of society, including business and the state. CST, as manifest in encyclicals like Pope Francis's *Laudato Si*, the short, targeted talks of Pius XII to particular professional associations, and the Pontifical Council for Justice and Peace's *Vocation of the Business Leader*, highlights these interconnections among different institutions. Wages, for example, are not just an economic exchange but are also a personal relationship affecting a family. Ignoring this personal relationship in favor of a strict market logic detaches business from the centers of human vitality it is supposed to advance. A limit on business hours, to take another example, means an opening to other kinds of human activity, which in turn make business itself more connected to human goods. Gathering as a church can offer "breathing space" in communion with the transcendent, creating a context for gift relationships and leisure while upending familial insularities. Integral ecology for Naughton entails careful recognition of the institutional intersections that can either fertilize or poison the economic environment.

The parties in Nicholas Rademacher's historical study include US Catholic radicals who, drawing on the social encyclicals of Leo XIII and Pius XI, were already experimenting in the middle decades of the twentieth century with ways of working and living that later popes would dub "integral ecology." As an historian drawn to plumbing the particularities of concrete narratives, Rademacher proposes that a study of their history, including their disagreements and failures, as well as their common "theological and spiritual legacy," can advance contemporary efforts to replace a technocratic economic model with new modes of ecological and social organization in "rhythm with nature" and in prayerful communion with others and God. Their models of transformation were not rooted in traditional parish life or family structures. In fact, the institutions of family and parish were partially at odds with their ambitions. Too often, they argued, family and parish in practice were products of insularity and status quo economics as well as an acquisitive, worldly oriented "bourgeois mind." Likewise, these critics debated the degree to which the traditional university and its intellectual life were compromised by dependence on existing economic orders. Rigid models of family, church, and university risked elevating barriers to more expansive social arrangements within which cooperative economics could flourish.

As a result, these radicals—Peter Maurin, Dorothy Day, Paul Hanley Furfey, Thomas Merton among them—turned to monastic models, particularly the practices of simple and communal living close to the earth, whether in urban or rural settings. The Benedictine tradition of *ora et labora*, the disciplined interplay of prayer and work, make possible a "contemplative disposition" which could serve as the root of a new spiritual vision. Such discipline is unlikely to flourish, these radicals argued, so long as people remain entangled in ordinary institutional structures— the insidiousness of the technocratic paradigm demands a more radical break, symbolized and manifest in the history of monasticism and radical communal experiments that follow their lead.

Business scholar Sandra Waddock maintains that proper thinking about business must situate it "in the context of economies, which themselves live in societal and, ultimately, planetary contexts." Building on Fullerton's core principles for creating a healthy, regenerative capitalist system, Waddock foregrounds the need for "generative businesses" whose focus is not on growth and profit-maximization, but "on goals of vitality at multiple levels, with operations based on principles of renewal, restoration, and resilience." To shift from the neoliberal status quo will require both "new memes and a new narrative" (reshaping "the stories that we tell ourselves about what businesses do and how they do it") around the purposes and goals of businesses "that better harmonize business activity with ecological and social constraints."

Limning a nonreligiously specific spirituality that can sustain the messy, long-haul work toward needed changes, Waddock imagines business leaders as modern day "shamans"—community-serving visionaries devoted to "healing, connecting, and sense-making," who "gather new information by crossing into different realms (functional, organizational, social, or disciplinary)." These shamanic leaders take a spiritual-ethical posture of respect for the intrinsic dignity and value of all aspects of the world. By taking a humble, experimental approach toward the complex interconnectedness of economic, social, and natural systems, such change agents help reorient economic activity toward "resilience, renewal and restoration," in service of a common good that comprises personal, communal, global, and ecospheric well-being. This notion of vitality-fostering business could offer a new "dominant story," an essential precursor to the basic mental shift the times demand.

Valuing Differently: Challenging Work and Business As Usual

The essays collected in this section of the volume raise questions of judgment: whose work and what kinds of human activity are accorded value? How might value be measured differently? According to the history unearthed by Kirsten Swinth, feminist activists have established a strong foundation upon which religious ethicists like Sullivan-Dunbar can build. Swinth's history documents the successes and unfinished business of US second-wave feminists' efforts to enshrine household labor on a level with other kinds of work, both in terms of compensation and social respect. The refusal of domestic worker organizations and radical feminists alike to accept prevailing notions about household work—the idea that household work is innately a matter for women and innately less valuable as a part of the economy—led to remarkable legal and political efforts and achievements in the mid-1970s and beyond. Lobbying, strategic alliances, publication, and protest brought about significant change, forging alternative economic arrangements out of the will and determination of women to be counted as equals to men.

Victory was not entire, of course. Despite winning some legal protections, domestic workers remain profoundly vulnerable in the broader economy. Men, who may now be more likely to tolerate the *idea* of an equal division of household labor and family wealth, continue to lean heavily in practice on the feminization of care work. Another abiding challenge came from within the movement itself. Swinth documents the ways the movement occasionally fractured over different ways of talking about homemaking. White, affluent feminists wanted to emphasize the filthiness of homemaking responsibilities in order to extract them from the romantic glow cast by the idea of innate feminine selflessness. In contrast, domestic workers, often economically disadvantaged people of color, wanted to emphasize the technical challenges of the work and thus boost recognition of their unique professional expertise. Here it may be that the Catholic language of "dignity," along with CST's consistent emphasis on all work and workers (paid and unpaid) as dignity- and rights-bearing, could play some mediating role. Perhaps the idea of dignity can be molded to accord value to people absent gender and accord value to work in keeping with its necessity and difficulty.

Gerald Beyer elevates another arena in which labor has been strategically mislabeled and significantly undervalued. As Naughton does with businesses, Beyer urges universities, particularly those with a Catholic heritage, to own up to their implication in a wider ecology of value. Using the language of contamination and disease, Beyer argues that a destructive idea of human personhood has infected universities. The triumph of *homo economicus*—the idea of human beings as essentially self-serving, independent, and only implicated in others' lives through temporary transactions—blinds universities to the real effects of their policies. University decisions, about the use of adjunct instructors or about assessment and the categories of faculty productivity, damage the wider ecology when they are made under the sign of a fundamentally *asocial* understanding of personhood. Beyer sees the possibility of ethical decision-making through conversation and testing of ideas under the light of *homo relationis*, a notion of personhood emphasizing rights, inviolable dignity, and responsibility as "member[s] of an interdependent family." Beyer's use of CST wagers on the rational persuasive power of CST's ideas alongside others in a public discourse made up of individuals from all kinds of backgrounds, religious and irreligious, married and single, churched and unchurched alike.

A reading of evolutionary biology and philosophy allows Michael Pirson to offer a challenge to business management strategy. Management theory, he argues, has failed to incorporate the ways human survival and flourishing have depended not on competition in pursuit of individual "wants" but on a relational tendency toward long-lasting, workable connections with others. This conclusion allows Pirson to recognize "human dignity" ("which escapes the price mechanism and has intrinsic value") as a category of primary value for business management. But both "economistic" (focused on wealth creation) and "humanistic" (focused on well-being creation) models for business may either neglect, protect, or promote dignity. Thus, "enlightened economism"—which captures a range of "doing well by doing good" business philosophies—protects and promotes dignity in the interest of maximizing performance and wealth. By contrast, "pure humanism"—which resonates with the aspirational visions of both Waddock and modern Catholic social thought—promotes dignity as contributing to its ultimate bottom line of maximizing well-being. Pirson provides specific business cases (Grameen Bank, Unilever, and Tesla) to illustrate and advance his theoretical argument. In addition, he articulates ideal types and frameworks (which also can serve as aspirational and action guides) for evaluating a business's relative proximity to purely economistic versus purely humanistic management thinking and practice.

Practicing Differently: Creating Alternative Ways of Working

Expanding on examples like those suggested by Pirson and recalled by Rademacher, the authors in the final section of this volume consider in more detail specific cases within which people have acted by experimenting with alternative ways of working. These experiments have not always succeeded, nor have they been free from the kinds of ambivalence Swinth exposes among second-wave feminists. But in their struggles and ambivalence, they witness to possibilities and expose the challenges that come with putting new plans into practice. Like Sullivan-Dunbar, historian Kathleen Holscher focuses attention on the tendency of Catholics to fashion the home and motherhood as institutions "apart from the money economy." Whereas Sullivan-Dunbar notes the gendered disparities that such renderings of family promote, Holscher explores the ways the idea of a distinctly feminine, home-based, and extra-economic sphere actually worked—at least in part—to elevate women in one historical setting.

The setting of Holscher's investigation is mid-twentieth century Santa Fe and its surrounding villages. It was there that a group of Medical Mission Sisters began a midwife training school, the Catholic Maternity Institute, which trained and employed sisters as midwives to serve the needs of the mostly poor and Hispana Catholic population of Santa Fe and its surrounding villages. Their ministry was based on the goal of providing professional and medically sophisticated care while preserving the "dignity" due to women in the process of giving birth, a dignity they saw sorely missing from the institutional, impersonal birthing practices of contemporary hospitals. For over twenty years the sisters offered low cost, attentive, and professional nurse-midwifery, often in the home, for women who might otherwise have not received proper care; in the process, Holscher concludes, they "saved the lives of economically disadvantaged women and infants." These efforts were not without their complications, however. The project relied on assumptions about Euro-American superiority as well as distinctly Catholic ideas about women's dignity as rooted in their difference from men. Although this latter assumption helped situate birth outside of the male-dominated medical world (and, arguably, empower both the midwives and the mothers they served), it also further entrenched both the sisters and the women in their care in narrow and gendered realms of value. In this particular historical setting, Catholic economic and social teaching was double-edged, and produced "layered effects." Documenting these layers offers one means for adding suppleness and creativity to new efforts to revise theories about what counts as economic.

Alison Collis Greene documents the history of another set of efforts to address economic and social inequalities through experimental cooperative institutions. Greene's subjects found inspiration not from CST but from the nineteenth-century Protestant Social Gospel tradition, particularly the rural church movement and interwar articulations of Christian socialism like those of prominent theologian Reinhold Niebuhr. Like Beyer's witness to the entrenched interests guiding university decision-making, Greene's study of the efforts to put cooperative economics in practice in the rural south reveals the intersectional difficulties facing any effort to overturn or reform the social order. The post-Reconstruction economy of the rural south was dominated by white elites, who protected their stake in land and capital through violent repression of workers' organizing efforts and enforcement of Jim Crow economics. This entrenched an unequal wage system for black and white workers while simultaneously pitting poor people of different races against one another. Local management of New Deal projects meant that economic opportunities provided under the system in the rural south generally "preserved a white supremacist, patriarchal, and capitalist social order." Greene documents the struggles of the liberals and radicals gathered under the organization of the interdenominational Fellowship of Southern Churchmen to respond to these tremendous challenges.

The challenges facing these new institutions were less about the purity or coherence of their theology or policy than they were about the resistance they faced from entrenched southern power structures. Good southern white men, proud members of their churches and the patriarchs of intact nuclear families, saw fit to attack these efforts with every tool at their disposal, including on occasion the threat of violence. Like Rademacher, Greene sees value in the witness provided by these bold experiments toward a more just economic and social order in an unlikely setting. But more than simply offering a "model," these stories also provide a "note of caution": the experiences they recount offer a stark reminder that new ideas, however compelling and however courageously tested, face daunting obstacles when market and social structures are arrayed against them. Efforts to enact working alternatives cannot proceed effectively without trenchant understanding of the complex layers of power intersecting within the particular social worlds in which they aim to implement their change.

Vincent Stanley, longtime executive and chief officer at outdoor gear company Patagonia, concludes our volume with stories about formative events during the company's early years that shaped Patagonia's core understandings of their company's ecological and social responsibilities. Stanley relates on-the-ground experiences by which owners and employees undertook the "royal pain" of switching to organic cotton for all its products. The process became a company turning point. He shares that "our success became a source of confidence and pride that permeated the business culture," and cultivated a shared ethos that has underpinned the company's forty-year-plus commitment to an alternative narrative to the typical, shareholder-profit-maximizing business story line. Patagonia's working alternative for business is captured in its mission statement: "Build the best product, cause no unnecessary harm, use business to inspire and implement solutions to the environmental crisis." Describing the interrelated economic, political, and ecological dysfunctions that make this "a time of crisis," Stanley draws on business, philosophy, and CST to point toward a different path. This alternative path involves changed business strategies, but more fundamentally, it demands people and institutions with changed ways of seeing and valuing, marked by "urgent and patient" (Pope Francis) commitments to protecting and advancing the tangible economic and social well-being of people, communities, and the planet. The volume ends with this account of an actual business trying to implement actual changes not because Patagonia has cracked the code or achieved perfect success but because Stanley's recollections and engagements signal the kind of experimental and deeply reflective endeavor that will continue to be necessary across economic realms.

––––––––––––––

The title *Working Alternatives* aims to speak on multiple levels about the ambition and structure of this book. On one hand, the phrase "working alternatives" in everyday English connotes the implementation of stop-gap measures that can suffice while the original practice recovers from a breakdown. There is value in this way of thinking about the book because it offers a reminder that alternatives need not be perfect or seamless in order to work. There will be problems with the implementation or articulation of ideas rooted in CST, humanistic business management, the Social Gospel, feminist solidarity, and other alternatives. The experiments we witness here are not perfect alternatives, in other words, but *working* alternatives worth a test. The original practices have certainly shown enough breakdown to warrant such experiment. In this same vein, we put emphasis on the word "working." Like a stiff new baseball glove, alternative economic practices need to be worked in.

As various essays show, this working-in process has not always gone well. Social forces and established power dynamics too often prevent new practices and ideas from seasoning into supple and dynamic systems. Moreover, the practice of alternatives is demanding, and usually means sacrifice and a tolerance for less among certain privileged communities. This is work. In light of this reality, *Working Alternatives* also makes a point of identifying sites where experiments worked for a time or are working, or at least working relatively well in comparison to previous models. In place of a grand, encompassing vision, the book offers evidence of pockets of provisional success, where companies, institutions, and communities have accounted for harmful systems and responded with less harmful alternatives. Highlighting small-scale successes (and learning about the forces arrayed against them) may stimulate the broader spread of change. Finally, *Working Alternatives* also speaks to the idea of "work" in a positive sense. The economic sphere is a valuable site of human creativity. Work—differentiated, perhaps, from toil or drudgery—is the effortful expression of that creative energy. Although this is perhaps rarely the case, it can be personally gratifying, socially constructive, and even energizing. We conducted this experiment with a vision of a world where work matched this ideal. May the work that went into this book by its authors, but mostly by its subjects, stimulate the kinds of changes that make the work of the future a channel of creative energy, a supported and sustainable site of productivity, and a source of joy.

Part I: Seeing Differently

Alternative Visions of Economy and Work

The Care Economy
as Alternative Economy

SANDRA SULLIVAN-DUNBAR

This volume seeks to examine experiments in "alternative economies" and the conceptions of the human person that undergird them. In my contribution here, I will focus on an enormous and pervasive alternative economy that has existed for longer than the market economy: the care economy. By care economy, I mean human activity that is oriented toward sustaining life and promoting basic well-being, whether that activity is paid or unpaid, and the material goods that are devoted toward this task, whether or not those goods are mediated through the market. In one sense, it is not appropriate to call the care economy an alternative economy; as I will argue, our contemporary conception of the economic must be broadened to incorporate care. Nevertheless, the care economy can be seen as alternative because it has largely been written out of the discipline of economics and of everyday conceptions of economy. A volume exploring alternative economies cannot be complete without attention to this under-theorized economic activity. When we begin to think of the economy as incorporating care and other work oriented toward sustaining life, we find that many fundamental assumptions about human motives and the human good that underlie contemporary economic theory come into question.

In this essay I explore the care economy. I document its erasure during the development of classical and neoclassical economic theory. I track recent work by feminist economists and development theorists to reincorporate care into conceptions of the economic, taking account of the proportion of overall economic activity that care represents and the implications of care relations for our understandings of the human person and social relations. To think of care as economic is to disrupt the theorization of economic activity as motivated primarily and predictably by self-interest. Care work is very often unpaid, so establishing caregiving as economic activity signifies that the economy is not coextensive with the market. At the same time, a significant portion of care work is paid, which shows that market activity can incorporate relations involving other-regard and self-gift. Furthermore, paid and unpaid care are deeply interrelated with one another, often coexisting within the same caring practice. These facts have implications for our understanding of the economic as well as for social welfare policies and development policies.

Pope Benedict XVI's 2009 encyclical, *Caritas in Veritate (CV)*, calls for a more integral understanding of development, and for a *"further and deeper reflection on the meaning of the economy and its goals."*[1] One of my primary theses is that there exist suggestive parallels between many of Benedict's concerns in this encyclical, and concerns expressed by feminist economists addressing the care economy. These include challenges to sharp binaries between the market and the state and affirmation of a spectrum of motives driving economic activity. Benedict and feminist economists also share a critique of an anthropology that highlights autonomous choosers and ignores aspects of our existence that come to us as gift, as well as a concern for economic development that addresses the holistic well-being of all persons. These parallels, coming from what might be seen as very different perspectives, suggest that contemporary economic theory indeed holds a far too narrow understanding of economic activity. The parallels also suggest that some of Benedict's own concerns might be addressed via engagement with economists studying caring labor. However, Benedict does not draw on feminist economics at all, nor does he so much as mention the care economy. The practical impact of his ideas is seriously curtailed by this omission. Dialogue with scholarly work on the care economy would provide Catholic economic thinkers with additional, powerful tools to press the central concerns expressed by Benedict but would also challenge these thinkers to accept a more complex and pluralist account of the appropriate social organization of caregiving than Benedict appears to presume. This dialogue would help developers of the Catholic social tradition to embrace more embodied and material dimensions of "the astonishing experience of gift" that is a central theme of *CV* and to articulate more clearly a role for

---

1. Pope Benedict XVI, *Caritas in Veritate* 32, Encyclical Letter, Vatican website, June 29, 2009, http://w2.vatican.va/content/benedict-xvi/en/encyclicals/documents/hf_ben -xvi_enc_20090629_caritas-in-veritate.html (italics in original).

the state in supporting the care economy.[2] This chapter begins that dialogue.

The first section of this essay will briefly trace the history of the exclusion of care from conceptions of economy during the evolution of classical and neoclassical economics, as well as of the sharp bifurcation of altruistic and self-interested motives within economic theory. The second section will turn to *CV*, pointing out some initial parallels between Benedict's central concerns in this encyclical and concerns raised by feminist economists in their treatments of the care economy. The third section will address efforts by economists and development theorists to reincorporate caregiving into economic analysis, including methods to measure the scope of the care economy, and will discuss the role of the state in supporting the care economy. The fourth section will address concerns about the "commodification" of care and attend to the complexities of motive in the care economy. Throughout, I will place Benedict into conversation with scholarship on the care economy, arguing that we can only make progress toward the vision of development outlined in *CV* if we take into consideration the pervasive economy of care.

How Care Was Excluded from Economics: A Brief History

Caregiving was not always considered to be outside the scope of economics. Before the Industrial Revolution, the economy (or "oeconomy") was understood in terms of stewardship of resources to assure subsistence and well-being. Writing in 1769, Sir James Steuart connected economy in the household with political economy:

> Oeconomy, in general, is the art of providing for all the wants of a family, with prudence and frugality. . . . The object of it, in a private family, is . . . to provide for the nourishment, the other wants, and the employment of every individual. . . . What oeconomy is in a family,

2. Within the tradition of papal writings on economics, I focus on Benedict because he addresses neoclassical assumptions in original ways that suggest points of intersection with writings on the care economy—for example, in his call for juridical frameworks to facilitate hybrid forms of commercial activity, and in his affirmation of a range of legitimate motives within market activity.

political oeconomy is in a state . . . The principle object of this science is to secure a certain fund of subsistence for all the inhabitants, to obviate every circumstance which may render it precarious; to provide every thing necessary for supplying the wants of the society, and to employ the inhabitants . . . in such a manner as naturally to create the reciprocal relations and dependencies between them, so as to make their several interests lead them to supply one another with their reciprocal wants.[3]

Steuart's vision of "oeconomy" was embedded in a thoroughly hierarchical and patriarchal understanding of both family and government. Still, feminist economists have suggested that we recover this notion of economics as "provisioning," as an important ingredient alongside economics as the study of market behavior.[4]

How was this notion lost in the first place? Economic historians have traced the erasure of the domestic economy from the scope of the economic, beginning with the work of Adam Smith. Smith's *Wealth of Nations* was written in the earliest stages of the Industrial Revolution, as production increasingly moved outside of the household into small "manufactories." Interested in the economic growth that new production processes could generate, Smith distinguished productive from unproductive labor, defining the latter as labor aimed at capital accumulation, which would increase the productivity of future labor.[5] Unproductive labor was valuable, but only in the sense of maintaining subsistence in the here and now: "A man grows rich by employing a multitude of manufacturers. He grows poor, by maintaining a multitude of menial servants."[6] Smith did include "the acquired and useful abilities of all the inhabitants or members of the society" as a form of productive labor, resulting in "a capital

3. Sir James Steuart, *An inquiry into the principles of political oeconomy*, Edinburgh: Oliver & Boyd for Scottish Economic Society, 1966 [1770]).

4. Julie A. Nelson, "The Study of Choice or the Study of Provisioning? Gender and the Definition of Economics," in *Beyond Economic Man: Feminist Theory and Economics*, ed. Marianne A. Ferber and Julie A. Nelson (Chicago: University of Chicago Press, 1993), 23–36.

5. Adam Smith, *An Inquiry into the Nature and Causes of the Wealth of Nations*, vol. 1, ed. R. H. Campbell and A. S. Skinner (Oxford: Oxford University Press, 1976; reprint Indianapolis: Liberty Fund, 1981), 330.

6. Ibid.

fixed and realized, as it were, in (the) person."[7] This included the labor of teachers and masters of apprentices. He did not, however, include straightforward caring labor, such as child-rearing, within the scope of productive labor.[8]

Indeed, the analytic tools that Smith developed could not easily be applied to caregiving relations. Much caregiving activity is aimed precisely at subsistence, at the value of living well here and now within embodied limits. Caregiving is not an activity that lends itself to ever-increasing productivity. Unlike Smith's pin factory workers, increasing production through the division of labor, caregivers must be generalists, engaging a wide and varied range of activities within their caregiving practice. Furthermore, care frequently involves deep attachment and attention to very particular needs and circumstances. Economists presume a certain degree of fungibility in the labor supply, allowing them to predict wages and labor mobility. But for many types of care, if caregivers are treated as fungible, the care recipient cannot thrive. Recognizing this, caregivers do not act according to predictable laws of self-interest in allocating their caregiving labor. And although care for children might be theorized as an investment in later productivity (and it is this, though this is certainly not all that it is), care for the elderly or for persons with severe disabilities is aimed at the present end of living well here and now, not at later productivity.[9] Care escapes Smith's frame because it often involves a range of motives: care cannot be good care without some degree of other-regard, of placing the needs of the care recipient over one's own needs some of the time. Yet care can also be deeply rewarding, and caregivers must find ways to care for themselves in order to continue caring for others.

Nancy Folbre and Heidi Hartmann suggest Smith gave little attention to the domestic economy in part because complex motives undermine predictability. We can predict what fair but self-interested persons will do within exchange relations with strangers. We cannot so easily predict the outcome of economic activity embedded in intensive relations

7. Ibid., 282.

8. Michelle A. Pujol, *Feminism and Anti-Feminism in Early Economic Thought,* (Aldershot, England: Edward Elgar Press, 1992), 18.

9. Susan Donath, "The Other Economy: Suggestions for a Distinctively Feminist Economics," *Feminist Economics* 6:1 (2000): 115–23.

imbued with affection, self-interest, inequality, and power relations.[10] Additionally, Smith could ignore the caregiving economy, because he assumed that care would occur: women were presumed to be naturally suited to it, and their love for care recipients was presumed sufficient and reliable motivation for such labor. In Smith's work, therefore, self-interest drove economic relations outside the home; affective relations and other-regard were located inside the home.

In the second half of the nineteenth century, as the industrial economy increasingly became a commercial economy, the discipline of economics evolved further toward an emphasis on market and exchange processes. The "marginalist school," what is today known as neoclassical economics, defined the value of commodities as the price at which supply meets demand.[11] Economic activity that occurred outside the market—including unpaid labor—posed a problem here; without a price, how can the value be determined? Alfred Marshall, author of the classic *Principles of Economics* that was first published in 1890 and remained the standard introductory textbook for decades, asserted that "(t)he most valuable of all capital is that invested in human beings; and of that capital the most precious part is the result of the care and influence of the mother."[12] Still, he argued that "gratuitous" (unpaid) services should be "left to be accounted for separately."[13] Marshall argued for the inclusion of salaries for domestic servants in calculations of social income, and noted the "inconsistency in omitting the heavy domestic work which is done by women and other members of the household, where no servants are kept."[14] However, he did nothing to address this inconsistency. Marshall's followers quickly enshrined the exclusion of unpaid domestic labor from

10. Nancy Folbre and Heidi Hartmann, "The Rhetoric of Self-Interest: Ideology and Gender in Economic Theory," in *The Consequences of Economic Rhetoric*, ed. Arjo Klamer, Donald N. McCloskey, and Robert M. Solow (Cambridge: Cambridge University Press, 1988), 198, n.2.

11. William Stanley Jevons, *The Theory of Political Economy*, 2nd ed., ed. R. D. Collinson Black (Baltimore: Penguin, 1970); Carl Menger, *Principles of Economics* (New York: Free Press, 1950); Leon Walras, *Elements of Pure Economics* (Homewood, IL: Irwin, 1954).

12. Alfred Marshall, *Principles of Economics: An Introductory Volume*, 8th ed. (New York: Macmillan, 1948 [1890]), 564.

13. Ibid., 524.

14. Ibid., 80.

economic calculations, and failed to pursue the separate accounting that Marshall suggested.[15] Thus, nonmarket labor, production, and exchange simply disappeared from the subject matter of marginalist economics.

In addition, the marginalist school further sharpened the bifurcation of self-interest from other-regard, and the assignment of these motives to sharply separated public and private spheres. Outside the family, "preferences" were theorized as "inscrutable." In other words, we have no way of determining what and how much a particular person desires except by observing his choices in the marketplace; we cannot access another's internal experience.[16] However, within the family, preferences are "soluble" and family members hold a joint utility function. That is to say, family members are fully aware of the preferences of all other family members and desire things as a unit.[17] The family is altruistic, noncompetitive, and family members know each other intimately. Thus, the family is the mirror opposite of the self-interested, competitive marketplace. In either case, there is no objective account of the goods to be sought through economic activity. Preferences, either observed through self-interested choices in the marketplace or perceived through an intimate altruistic concern, are the only indicators of appropriate economic purpose.

Benedict does not engage this history of economic thought in *CV.* However, we will see that his conception of economics incorporates many elements that were deliberately banished from the discipline during the course of this history.

Caritas in Veritate

Benedict XVI's 2009 encyclical is framed as a reaffirmation of and reflection on Pope Paul VI's 1967 encyclical, *Populorum Progressio,* and like his predecessor, Benedict focuses sharply on the perceived causes

15. Pujol, *Feminism and Anti-Feminism,* 134.

16. For a historical account of debates among economists over the ability to discern others' preferences or utility functions, see Drucilla Barker, "Economists, Social Reformers, and Prophets: a Feminist Critique of Economic Efficiency," *Feminist Economics* 1, no. 3 (1995), 26–39.

17. Paul Samuelson, "Social Indifference Curves," *Quarterly Journal of Economics* 70, no. 1 (1956).

and remedies of global poverty and inequality. Benedict offers a conception of *caritas* as necessary to the "integral human development" advocated by Paul VI. Integral human development addresses all aspects of the human person: material, social, and spiritual. For Benedict, *caritas,* or charity, is connected to an objective moral order (charity in truth) and must infuse all levels of politics, economy, and society. Furthermore, *"authentic human development concerns the whole of the person in every single dimension,"* including the transcendent dimension of the person, the dimension that is destined for eternal life.[18] Benedict describes integral human development as a vocation, which "involves a free assumption of responsibility in solidarity on the part of everyone."[19]

Benedict also takes aim at what he perceives as an exaggerated emphasis on autonomy: "Sometimes modern man is wrongly convinced that he is the sole author of himself, his life and society."[20] To counter this false sense of autonomy, Benedict argues that we must be open to "the astonishing experience of gift."[21] Benedict elucidates this experience in terms of nonmaterial realities: truth, hope conscience, *caritas.*[22] Without contesting these spiritual forms of gratuity, I suggest that he ought to attend to an embodied, material form of gratuity that is essential to human life, particularly in an encyclical on economics. This is the gratuitous experience of care, a care that we must receive to survive and grow into adulthood, and require in periods of disability, illness, or frailty. This care is profoundly material. It is care for embodied persons, and requires material goods to meet material needs. We must view the transcendental, spiritual dimension that Benedict highlights as existing in and through a material, everyday other-regard such as that called out by dependent care relations.

The development of classical and neoclassical economic theory deliberately excluded normative considerations to make economics appear more scientific; for example, neoclassical economics deliberately excludes any account of the goods to be sought through economic activity, other

18. Benedict XVI, *CV* 11 (italics in original).
19. Ibid.
20. Ibid., 34.
21. Ibid.
22. Ibid.

than the preferences expressed by autonomous choosers in the market-place.[23] In contrast, Benedict insists that economics is normative to its core. Benedict insists that the economy "needs to be *directed towards the pursuit of the common good*."[24] Its primary purpose is holistic human well-being, where "holistic" includes, especially, a transcendent aspect. Economic activity that damages human persons and communities thereby subverts its own ends.[25] Furthermore, in language that echoes Alfred Marshall's assertion that the most valuable capital is invested in human beings, Benedict declares that "the *primary capital to be safeguarded and valued is man, the human person in his or her integrity*."[26] In its emphasis on well-being and on the development of human persons rather than just on products, Benedict's discussion here recalls the care economy, but he appears unaware of this parallel, and his emphasis on the spiritual aspects of well-being are not balanced by attention to the embodied needs attended to within care relations.

Caritas in Veritate also engages the relationship between the state, the economy, and civil society. Initially, Benedict describes each of these sectors as driven by unique motives or "logics": the economy operates according to the logic of exchange; the state operates according to the logic of duty and compulsion.[27] Having articulated these sharp distinctions, Benedict then declares "this exclusively binary model of market-plus-state" to be "corrosive of society."[28] The "logic of gift" is most at home in civil society but must also infuse the economy and state. He advocates a plurality of forms of political authority and economic activity, arguing for a spirit of mutuality and solidarity from the most local level to the highest and most inclusive.

In the market economy, such an infusion can be expressed through "hybrid forms of commercial activity," or organizations that aim both at profit and at broader social goods.[29] These organizations reflect a "wide

---

23. For more on this, see Sandra Sullivan-Dunbar *Human Dependency and Christian Ethics* (New York: Cambridge University Press, 2017), 56–69.

24. Benedict, *CV* 36.

25. Ibid., 32.

26. Ibid., 25.

27. Ibid., 39.

28. Ibid.

29. Ibid., 36.

range of values," not simply self-interest.[30] Benedict encourages the development of fiscal and juridical frameworks for the development of a range of such enterprises.[31] He asserts that "authentically human relationships of friendship, solidarity and reciprocity can also be conducted within economic activity, and not only outside it or 'after' it."[32] Of course, if we conceive of the economy as incorporating care, then economic activity that expresses a range of motives and values appears to be the norm, rather than the exception, and the neoclassical assumptions that Benedict is resisting are already in trouble.

The state too must be infused with a "principle of gratuitousness."[33] Benedict's first encyclical, *Deus Caritas Est* (2005), cast state-sponsored care as bureaucratic and impersonal, lacking the "look of love" that occurs through personal encounter.[34] But *CV* seems to show an evolution: here, Benedict asserts that the state must be a channel of charity, and that individuals must express their charity politically: "This is the institutional path—we might also call it the political path—of charity, no less excellent and effective than the kind of charity which encounters the neighbor directly, outside the institutional mediation of the *polis*."[35] At the same time, Benedict notes that the forces of globalization have weakened the sovereignty of the state, and suggests that the role and powers of "public authorities" must be "prudently reviewed and remodeled" in light of the forces of globalization.[36]

Interestingly, Benedict does not explicitly include the family in this discussion of social institutions. Though some scholars have suggested that the family should be considered as part of civil society,[37] Benedict's discussion of civil society remains undeveloped in this document. Though earlier documents in Catholic social thought describe the family as the

---

30. Ibid., 41
31. Ibid., 46.
32. Ibid., 36.
33. Ibid.
34. Ibid.,18.
35. Ibid., 7.
36. Ibid., 24.
37. See, for example, Lisa Sowle Cahill, *Family: A Christian Social Perspective* (Minneapolis: Fortress Press, 2000).

"cell of society" and assign the family a social justice function,[38] Benedict does not pick up these themes in CV. References to the family occur in two primary contexts. First, Benedict repeatedly references the human race as a family,[39] and even titles one of his chapters as such.[40] His point is that the globalization requires that we be concerned for the inclusion of all within the scope of integral human development, but he gives little attention to the local kinship networks that constitute family in the everyday sense of the term, and that serve as the concrete locus for material relations of giving and receiving, of care, and of subsistence. Rather, Benedict refers to the usual kinship-based family of parents and children primarily as the locus of sexuality and procreation, and the protector of sexual morality—the second primary context under which "family" is considered in CV.

Although Benedict's silence on the economic importance of unpaid care work is striking, it is perhaps not surprising. Official Catholic social documents assume that most care should be given in the home, and presume the primary financial support for families should come from a (male) breadwinner. Benedict's predecessor, John Paul II, affirmed women's access to public roles as long as this did not endanger their most central vocation, that of motherhood. Although John Paul II urged that "the work of women in the home be recognized and respected by all in its irreplaceable value," it is clear that he considers this work to be *women's* work, and that women and men have "different vocations."[41] Though John Paul II at one point suggests the state provide "grants to mothers devoting themselves exclusively to their families,"[42] Benedict does not emphasize the need for state support for caregiving relations even in this

38. Pope John Paul II, *Familiaris Consortio* (http://w2.vatican.va/content/john-paul-ii/en/apost_exhortations/documents/hf_jp-ii_exh_19811122_familiaris-consortio.html), 42–44.

39. Benedict, *CV*, 8, 13, 33, 50, 73.

40. Ibid., chapter 5, "The Cooperation of the Human Family" (*CV* 43–67).

41. John Paul II, *Familiaris Consortio*, 23.

42. John Paul II, *Laborem Exercens*, 19, Vatican website, September 14, 1981, http://w2.vatican.va/content/john-paul-ii/en/encyclicals/documents/hf_jp-ii_enc_14091981_laborem-exercens.html. This suggestion, to my knowledge, was not repeated by John Paul II in later writings.

limited respect, infused as it is with assumptions about traditional gender roles. As we shall see, development theorists who attend to the care economy see state support for caregiving as essential to effective development policy.

In sum, we can see how Benedict seeks to introduce into our conception of the economy some elements that were quarantined during the development of the discipline of economics. These include a range of motives that may be expressed in the same economic practice, a sense of indebtedness and gratuity that precedes and limits our autonomy, and a normative conception of the aims of economics. He also addresses the role of the state, the market and civil society in development, and critiques impermeable divisions between them, but his discussion of the role of kinship and family in development is seriously underdeveloped. In the next section, we will see feminist work on the care economy aiming to reintegrate some of the same elements. But this feminist scholarship is more thorough, pluralistic, nuanced, and sophisticated than Benedict's generalities. In part, this is a function of the genre of the papal encyclical, which seeks a certain level of generality and avoids technical policy prescriptions. But I suspect that Benedict avoids scholarship on the care economy because even as it offers a path toward more successful development policy, it would challenge his gendered understandings of care and the family.

Bringing Care Back into Economics: Recent Feminist Work

As we have seen, care was excluded from increasingly specialized and "scientific" economic theory in part because it would have been more complex and difficult to predict caring behavior, as opposed to market behavior. Not surprisingly, then, the project of integrating unpaid care work back into the scope of the economic is challenging. Arguably, however, it is no more complex than other developments in economics that stretch the neoclassical model to address areas outside the market, such as the valuation of public goods like clean water or the cost of carbon emissions. In fact, there has been a great deal of work, particularly over the last two decades, to conceptualize care as a portion of the broader economy.[43]

---

43. Riane Eisler argues for a broader conception of economics—one that incorporates both care and natural resources, in her *The Real Wealth of Nations* (San Francisco: Berret-Koehler Publishers, 2007), in a way that is accessible to a popular audience.

Even before the last two decades, some economists (even those teaching within the neoclassical fortress that is the University of Chicago) analyzed the domestic economy. In the mid-twentieth century, Hazel Kyrk focused her work on household consumption, and developed a concept of economic waste as the diversion of resources to "whims" before basic needs were met.[44] Clearly, such an approach presupposes a normative account of the goods that economic activity should seek to further, a departure from the orthodox view. Kyrk's student Margaret Reid developed methods to measure the economic value of household production and unpaid domestic labor.[45] More recently, Nancy Folbre is one prominent economist attending to the economic valuation of caregiving and domestic labor.[46]

Efforts to theorize the microeconomics of the household are complemented by work to incorporate unpaid domestic labor into macroeconomic analysis. A substantial body of scholarship has shown that a failure to attend to care, unpaid work, and women's work (distinct categories, but ones that overlap significantly), leads to counterproductive development policies. Given that *Caritas in Veritate* is focused primarily on development, it is striking that Benedict did not engage this work, much of which was available well before 2009.

In 1988, Marilyn Waring published an extensive critique of the United Nations's System of National Accounts (SNA), a system developed in 1953 to measure economic production.[47] The SNA excluded unpaid domestic

44. Susan van Velzen, "Hazel Kyrk and the Ethics of Consumption," in *Toward a Feminist Philosophy of Economics*, ed. Drucilla K. Barker and Edith Kuiper (London: Routledge, 2003), 40.

45. Margaret G. Reid, *Economics of Household Production* (New York: John Wiley, 1934), 11, cited in Yun-Ae Yi, "Margaret G. Reid: Life and Achievements," *Feminist Economics* 2, no. 3 (1996), 21–22. The work of Kyrk and Reid has, unfortunately, been largely overshadowed by that of another Chicago economist, Gary Becker, the so-called Father of the "New Home Economics." See Gary Becker, *A Treatise on the Family* (Cambridge, MA: Harvard University Press, 1991). While Becker challenged some neoclassical assumptions, the neoclassical approach remains dominant in his work and generates absurd, gendered, and hierarchical accounts of the family. For these arguments, see Sullivan-Dunbar *Human Dependency*, 69–74.

46. Nancy Folbre, *Valuing Children: Rethinking the Economics of the Family* (Cambridge, MA: Harvard University Press, 2008).

47. Marilyn Waring, *If Women Counted: A New Feminist Economics* (San Francisco: Harper & Row Publishers, 1988).

labor from the "production boundary"—activity that would be included within gross domestic product calculations. Other feminist scholars elucidated similar themes. In an important 1992 article, Diane Elson laid out several ways in which male bias structures the macroeconomic analysis that has undergirded much development policy. This analysis presumes that human labor is unproduced—it basically ignores reproductive labor—and that human labor can be transferred quickly and without cost between activities, "in the way that a piece of land may be used for growing one crop one year and a different crop the next."[48] International financial organizations also emphasized the production of goods for trade over goods for consumption inside the country. This practice not only put developing countries at risk should international supply and demand change but also obscured the fact that production for consumption inside the country is largely subsistence consumption.[49] In other words, the analytic frameworks assume that labor will simply be transferred from one activity to another; they do not account for the possibility that overall labor may increase (for example, to ensure continued survival while goods are being produced for export), and that much of the increased labor may be unpaid. In addition, most macroeconomic analysis did not account for the fact that gender roles may render men unwilling to take on labor that is culturally understood as "women's work." To the extent that this sort of work must increase in response to structural adjustment policies, women will often be the ones taking on additional labor.[50]

In response to work by Waring, Elson, and others, the 1993 version of the SNA was amended to suggest "satellite accounts" to measure non-market activities that were not initially included in the "production boundary," including unpaid domestic labor.[51] Furthermore, the platform

---

48. Diane Elson, "Male Bias in Macroeconomics," in *Women and Adjustment Policies in the Third World*, ed. H. Afshar and C. Dennis (New York: St. Martin's Press, 1992), 166.

49. Ibid., 167.

50. Ibid., 168.

51. Other satellite accounts address other important values that are not captured by the pricing mechanism, such as natural resources. In addition to this system of satellite accounts, other systems have been developed more recently to measure economic productivity and well-being in a more holistic sense. The genuine progress index (GPI), developed in 1995, measures a wide range of goods and, in addition, counts certain

for action of the 1995 United Nations Conference on Women in Beijing set forth, as one of its strategic objectives, a call for "developing methods . . . for assessing the value, in quantitative terms, of unremunerated work that is outside national accounts, such as caring for dependents and preparing food."[52] The initial emphasis at Beijing was on recognition of the enormous amount of unpaid work in the economy, and the high proportion of such work done by women. This resulted in the development of time-use studies that were well-suited to the estimation of the overall proportion of work that was unpaid and the development of household sector satellite accounts to better estimate aggregate economic output.[53] Early time-use studies generally did not separate out care work from other unpaid activities like subsistence farming.

Over the intervening two decades, more detailed methods of time-use data collection have been developed. These allow economists to discern, for example, the impact of structural adjustment policies on the amount of unpaid labor done by women, and can support advocacy for greater public support of certain services or infrastructure. For example, detailed time-use accounts might bring to light the significant amount of time spent collecting water or reveal the time cost of cooking less expensive foods, which generally require longer preparation. Time-use surveys can also help track the movement of care back and forth from the paid to the unpaid economy, as when, after the implementation of structural adjustment programs, cutbacks in public-sector health care spending results in increased unpaid care work in the home. Among other loci of research,

---

"bads" as negatives. For example, cleanup from the damage from Hurricane Katrina reflected an increase in gross domestic product (GDP), but the hurricane represented an enormous negative in terms of overall human well-being (http://www.gpiatlantic.org/gpi.htm). The Organization for Economic Co-operation and Development's Better Life Index (BLI, oecdbetterlifeindex.org) and the United Nation's Human Development Index (HDI, hdr.undp.org) both measure well-being in terms of qualitative categories such as housing, education, and nutrition, rather than measuring economic progress by GPD alone. These latter systems measure outcomes rather than labor, productivity, and exchange, but an economic system that recognizes, supports, and rewards caregiving activity is likely to produce better outcomes as measured by the GPI, BLI, or HDI.

52. UN Fourth World Conference on Women 1995: Strategic objective H.3, point (f), published in *Feminist Economics* 2, no. 3 (1996), 125–28.

53. Valeria Esquivel, "Sixteen Years After Beijing: What Are the New Policy Agendas for Time-Use Data Collection?," *Feminist Economics* 17, no. 4 (October 2011), 217.

the United Nations Research Institute on Social Development conducted the *Political and Social Economy of Care* project between 2006 and 2009, compiling both quantitative and qualitative research on how care is provided by household, state, market, and community in a number of developed and less developed countries.[54]

There are complications associated with collecting time-use data on unpaid care, and researchers have used a variety of methods, each with their own strengths and weaknesses.[55] But as Debbie Budlender notes, "There are . . . also far more complications and heroic assumptions associated with the estimation of GDP than most who use this measure generally recognize."[56] Furthermore, research attempting to measure the care economy, whether through time-use studies or other methods, has only begun to emerge in the last two to three decades; given the immensity and complexity of that economy, we should not yet expect fine-grained pictures of variations in care economies that emerge from cultural differences and varied levels of economic development. Despite the challenges and the variety of methods used to assign a monetary value to unpaid care, three consistent findings remain clear across studies: the care economy represents a very significant proportion of the overall economy; a large proportion of care is unpaid care (which, in turn, depresses the wages for paid care); and the majority of care, paid and unpaid, is performed by women, across the globe.[57]

54. For research conducted under the auspices of this project, see http://www.unrisd.org/research/gd/care.

55. See Esquivel, "Sixteen Years"; Debbie Budlender, "What Do Time Use Studies Tell Us About Unpaid Care Work? Evidence from Seven Countries," in *Time Use Studies and Unpaid Care Work*, ed. Debbie Budlender (New York: Routledge/UNRISD Research in Gender and Development, 2010), 2; Debbie Budlender, *A Critical Review of Selected Time Use Surveys* (Geneva: UNRISD, Gender and Development Programme Paper Number 2, June 2007).

56. Budlender, "Time Use Studies," 41.

57. In addition to Budlender's work, see Miranda Veerle, "Cooking, Caring, and Volunteering: Unpaid Work Around the World," *OECD Social, Employment, and Migration Working Papers* No. 116 (Paris: OECD Publishing, 2011), http://dx.doi.org/10.1787/5kghr-jm8s142-en; Mignon Duffy, Randy Albelda, and Clare Hammonds, "Counting Care Work: The Empirical and Policy Applications of Care Theory," *Social Problems* 60, no. 2 (2013), 145–67.

The International Monetary Fund (IMF) and the World Bank have based their lending policies on macroeconomic models that ignore unpaid care; consequently, they have imposed significant cutbacks in government funding for health, education, and public services as loan conditions. These services then are either not delivered at all, or are provided through private channels, primarily without pay and by women. Development scholars who attend to the care economy are virtually unanimous in their view that strong state support for care services is a prerequisite both to gender equality and to successful development policies.[58] This need is dictated by the very nature of the care economy. Care is a public good; it is not subject to ever-increasing productivity, and beyond a certain (very limited) point, pressures to make care more "productive" will dramatically reduce the quality of care.[59]

In the last few years, the World Bank and the IMF have shown signs of evolution in their approach to gender inequality, issuing policy recommendations, including better family benefits, accessible finance and property rights for women, tax benefits for low-wage earners, and increased public expenditures on education, infrastructure, and health. Recent reports have also discussed the division of domestic unpaid labor between women and men.[60] But these emphases stand in tension with the still-dominant neoclassical assumption that productivity and growth are measured by earnings and that "economic participation" by women is equivalent to increased participation in paid labor.[61] Although women's legal and practical access to paid employment is indeed important, this language obscures the fact that across the globe, women do more work

58. Kate McInturff and Brittany Lambert, *Making Women Count: The Unequal Economics of Women's Work* (Oxfam Canada and Canadian Center for Policy Alternatives, March 2016).

59. Duffy, Albelda, and Hammonds, "Counting Care Work," 150.

60. *World Development Report 2012: Gender Equality and Development* (Washington, DC: The International Bank for Reconstruction and Development/The World Bank, 2011); Christian Gonzales, Sonali Jain-Chandra, Kalpana Kochhar, Monique Newiak, and Tlek Zeinullayev, "Catalyst for Change: Empowering Women and Tackling Income Inequality," (International Monetary Fund: October, 2015).

61. Shahra Razavi, "World Development Report 2012: Gender Equality and Development: A Commentary," *Development and Change* 43, no. 1 (2012), 425; Lourdes Beneria, "The World Bank and Gender Inequality," *Global Social Policy* 12, no. 2 (August 2012), 175–78.

than men, when both paid and unpaid labor are taken into account.[62] In the full sense of "economic" advocated in this chapter, women already demonstrate more economic participation than men; they simply get paid less for it, and paid for less of it. Furthermore, although policy papers may create gradual conceptual shifts among decision-makers at international financial institutions, this process is slow and, some would argue, easily co-opted by the dominant neoclassical paradigm; there is no direct link between such papers and the conditions of actual lending agreements.

In sum, there is now an extensive body of work on the extent and importance of the care economy, which even international financial institutions are now beginning to recognize. Benedict briefly criticizes IMF and World Bank policies: "budgetary policies, with cuts in social spending often made under pressure from international financial institutions, can leave citizens powerless in the face of old and new risks."[63] However, he does not connect this critique to discussions of the care economy, and the increase in unpaid care that is consequent upon reduced state spending. Were he to do so, his advocacy of "integral human development" would be more compelling; he could add a powerful voice to those asking that unpaid care be factored into development policy.

As we have seen, Benedict is concerned to avoid a sharp binary between market and state. Here again, scholarship on the care economy could be helpful, as it moves well beyond the binary.[64] Many who study

---

62. Although this is most pronounced in the least developed countries, it remains true in the United States. According to the 2015 American Time Use Survey, while men worked more hours per day in paid employment (4.18 hours to women's 2.92), total work time (paid and unpaid) was higher for women. When combining time devoted to household activities (housework, food preparation, lawn and garden care), direct physical care to other persons, purchasing goods and services, and paid employment, adult women spent an average of 6.94 hours per day working, while men work an average of 6.68 hours per day. See Bureau of Labor Statistics, "American Time Use Survey: 2015 Results" (June 24, 2016), available at https://www.bls.gov/news.release/archives/atus _06242016.pdf. Calculations are made from data on the chart in Table 1, page 9: "Time spent in primary activities and percentage of the civilian population engaging in each activity, averages per day by sex, 2015 annual averages."

63. Benedict, CV 25.

64. Ibid., 41.

care regimes in various countries are beginning to use the term "care diamond" to reference four institutional sectors—state, market, households, and communities—each of which are involved in the provision of care, in unique but overlapping ways.[65] Although the *primary* motives operating in each sector of the care diamond may be distinctive—for example, affection and other-regard may motivate much care within the family, and the expectation of payment is an important incentive for care provided in the market—in fact varied motives pervade all four institutional loci for care provision.[66] This points to an important parallel between care economics and Benedict's conception of economy: both are concerned to demonstrate (and encourage) a more complex account of motives within economic activity than that presumed in neoclassical economic theory.

Fears of Commodification: Can We Mix Love and Money?

The conceptual split between the market as the realm of self-interest and care as the realm of altruism has led many to worry that paid care represents the intrusion of an inappropriate motive into an activity that should be driven by affection and concern. Some care scholars openly worry about and debate the impact of the "commodification of care."[67] Although this worry often seems to operate at the level of intuitive values, some scholars attempt an empirical argument that money taints altruistic love or care. An oft-cited study found that people who received payment for blood donations were more likely to lie about medical conditions and to pass on infections than people who donated their blood.[68] Similarly, in some situations, monetary remuneration has been shown to

65. Shahra Ravazi, *The Political and Social Economy of Care in a Development Context* UN RISD Gender and Development Programme Paper 3, (June 2007), ix; Parvati Raghuram, "Global Care, Local Configurations—Challenges to Conceptualizations of Care," *Global Networks* 12, no. 2 (2012), 155–74.

66. Raghuram, "Global Care," 166.

67. Virginia Held, "Care and the Extension of Markets," *Hypatia* 17, no. 2 (2002), 19–33; Susan Himmelweit, "The Discovery of 'Unpaid Work': the Social Consequences of the Expansion of 'Work'," *Feminist Economics* 1:2 (1995), 1–19.

68. Richard M. Titmuss, *The Gift Relationship: From Human Blood to Social Policy* (New York: Vintage Books, 1971).

"crowd out" altruistic motivations for attending to the needs of others.[69] Such studies have been used to argue for low salaries in caring occupations.[70] However, as Nelson and Folbre point out, studies of the relationship between remuneration and motivation have shown different impact based on the framing of the remuneration. If it is perceived as *controlling* the agency of the person helping another, it "crowds out" altruism; if it is perceived as *recognizing* the intrinsic altruistic motivation of the person, it "crowds in" altruism—it increases other-regarding behavior.[71]

Benedict does not openly worry about these questions because he never discusses paid care. And yet Benedict is eager to inject the spirit of gift into the business arena, traditionally seen as the realm of self-interest. Why, then, does he not notice and embrace the coexistence of monetary payment and other-regard within relations of care? I suspect this has much to do with assumptions about women's natural caring role and about the private home as the most appropriate location for care. When we think of caregiving as economic activity, some of which is mediated by the money economy, we reveal the integration of self-interest and other-regard within the practice of care. We also reveal the ways in which caregiving, even within a nuclear family, is connected to the public and economic realms. These complexities and connections stand in tension with the gender essentialism espoused by Benedict's predecessor, John Paul II, and embedded within much of the Catholic social tradition. John Paul II asserted that women possess a "feminine genius," rendering them particularly attuned to the needs of others and particularly suited to self-gift.[72] Women and men have different vocations, and while women should have access to public roles, these roles should not impede a woman's most

69. Bruno S. Frey, "Institutions and Morale: the Crowding-Out Effect," in *Economics, Values, and Organization,* ed. Avner Ben-Ner and Louis Putterman, (Cambridge: Cambridge University Press, 1998), 437–60.

70. Anthony Heyes, "The Economics of Vocation or 'Why is a Badly Paid Nurse a Good Nurse?'" *Journal of Health Economics* 24 (May 2005), 561–69.

71. Julie A. Nelson and Nancy Folbre, "Why a Well-Paid Nurse is a Better Nurse," *Nursing Economics* 24, no. 3 (May–June 2006), 127–30.

72. John Paul II, *Mulieris Dignitatem,* apostolic letter, Vatican website, August 15, 1988, http://w2.vatican.va/content/john-paul-ii/en/apost_letters/1988/documents/hf_jp-ii_apl_19880815_mulieris-dignitatem.html, par. 30.

central role, the maternal role.[73] The gender binary is mapped onto a public/private binary, and discussion of monetary compensation of care would seem to threaten this binary as well as the self-gift that is presumed to be the particular genius of women.

Even if there is reason to worry about the commodification of care, it is better to worry out loud and debate its benefits and dangers, than to remain silent about such concerns. Some care is already (and should be) commodified, and honest engagement with the care economy demands that we examine and grapple with the benefits and dangers of this commodification. In developed economies, most of us meet our care obligations through a combination of paid and unpaid care. Care receivers sometimes prefer their care to be delivered through a market contract, rather than through preexisting relationships, for a wide range of reasons.[74] Furthermore, we should not assume that accepting pay for care represents the dilution or poisoning of other-regard with self-interested motives. Caregiver salaries are not generally spent to fulfill the insatiable desire for more presumed by neoclassical economic theory, but for the necessities of a decent life: "our very human need for basic food and shelter is at the base of our work 'for money.'"[75] If we think of paid care as serving both the human needs of the care recipient (through care) and the human needs of the caregiver (through monetary reimbursement), then paying for care is not a matter of competing ends, but a way to meet the ends of both parties in the relationship. Paid caregiving relations can involve genuine other-regard, affection, and even love: these motives are not mutually exclusive. This will be unsurprising to those of us who employ paid caregivers for our own family members, and empirical studies have demonstrated their coexistence. For example, a recent

73. John Paul II, *Familiaris Consortio*, apostolic exhortation, Vatican website, November 22, 1981, http://w2.vatican.va/content/john-paul-ii/en/apost_exhortations/documents/hf_jp-ii_exh_19811122_familiaris-consortio.html, par. 23.

74. Rutger Claasen, "The Commodification of Care," *Hypatia* 26, no.1 (Winter 2011), 50–51; Hazel Qureshi, "Boundaries Between Formal and Informal Care-Giving Work," in *Gender and Caring: Work and Welfare in Britain and Scandinavia*, ed. Claire Ungerson (London: Harvester Wheatsheaf, 1990), 68.

75. Julie A. Nelson, "Of Markets and Martyrs: Is it OK to Pay Well for Care?," *Feminist Economics* 5 no. 3 (1999), 48.

study concluded, through both in-depth interviews and four hundred hours of participant-observation, that childcare workers in United Kingdom nurseries find their work rewarding, develop powerful attachments to the children in their care, and perform emotional labor to set boundaries to these attachments.[76]

Thus, paid care is not intrinsically problematic: paid care serves many good purposes. The most pressing problem associated with paid care is not the tainting of care, but the exploitation of caregivers. Such exploitation has, in the United States, frequently been facilitated by the assumption that the "higher" aspects of care are the nonmaterial aspects: the affective or "spiritual" aspects of care. These aspects of care are most likely to be seen as needing "protection" from the taint of remuneration: you can't buy love. And these aspects of care are frequently conceptually separated from the material and often "dirty" aspects of care: washing bodies, feeding, dressing, drawing blood, cleaning wounds. In historical practice in the United States, the "dirty" aspects have frequently been assigned to women marginalized by race, class, and nationality.[77] Christine Firer Hinze argues that such a division of reproductive labor reflects gnostic tendencies, a purity-based attempt to escape our embodiment. She calls for a retrieval of the incarnational elements of Christian faith to combat the deep social inequalities that are reinforced through a purity-based division of work with dirt and bodies.[78]

76. Kate Boyer, Suzanne Reimer, and Lauren Irvine, "The Nursery Workplace, Emotional Labour and Contested Understandings of Commoditized Childcare in the Contemporary UK," *Social & Cultural Geography* 14, no. 5 (2013), 517–40.

77. For studies of this phenomenon in the United States, see, for example, Evelyn Nakano Glenn, "From Servitude to Service Work: Historical Continuities in the Racial Divide of Paid Reproductive Labor," *Signs* 18, no. 1 (Autumn 1992), 1–43; Evelyn Nakano Glenn, *Forced to Care: Coercion and Caregiving in America* (Cambridge, MA: Harvard University Press, 2010); Dorothy E. Roberts, "Spiritual and Menial Housework," *Yale Journal of Law and Feminism* 9 (1997), 51–80.

78. Christine Firer Hinze, "Dirt and Economic Inequality: A Christian-Ethical Peek Under the Rug," *Annual of the Society of Christian Ethics* 21 (2001), 45–62. There is a parallel between these disparate attitudes to bodily caring labor and the disparate attitudes toward housekeeping pointed out by Kirsten Swinth in her contribution to this volume. In the battle for the inclusion of domestic labor under the Fair Labor Standards Act, middle-class feminists painted a picture of housework as tedious and dirty, and remuneration as compensation for tolerating such work. Domestic laborers themselves, who

This discussion of attitudes toward paid care has drawn primarily on examples from the United States and other highly developed Western countries. We cannot extrapolate such attitudes to other contexts (indeed, caregivers in less-developed countries may not have the luxury of distinguishing affective concern from the material, embodied aspects of care in a division of caring labor). However, development policies that have increased the burden of unpaid labor on women have been conceived and imposed largely by persons from the United States and other wealthy countries, who may share in the unexamined assumption that caregiving is properly motivated by love and not money, that love should be infinitely elastic, that true care requires no material support, and is even tainted by it. But the material prerequisites of care, both the goods that meet human needs and the embodied labor of care, are not infinitely elastic; they require support through the state, the economy, and the community. Too often, this material support has been eliminated through austerity policies imposed by international lending organizations. Thus, attitudes that drive injustice to caregivers in the United States are also implicated in development policies that impose suffering in poor countries.

Benedict wants to reintegrate self-interest with other-regard through a range of commercial forms. My discussion here suggests that a significant portion of the economy already displays the range of motives that Benedict encourages within the business sector. This combination of motives is not intrinsically problematic; and who can better speak to the possibility of multiple ends and motives than the professional childcare worker, teacher, or home health aide? These multiple motives can coexist within an overall practice that meets both the needs of the recipient for care and the needs of the caregiver for economic sustenance. Yet this range of motives is often obscured, and this obfuscation reinforces structures of privilege and exploitation, and underwrites a counterproductive approach to development. We must view interest in material return for caregiving labor not as a failure of caring, but as appropriate and necessary motives for this embodied labor. Efforts to humanize the economy must attend to a spectrum of options both for business enterprise and for caregiving arrangements, and must allow for close, critical

---

were often women of color, painted a picture of domestic work as a dignified and highly skilled profession, deserving of respect and wages that reflected professional expertise.

assessment of economic arrangements all along this spectrum, in both the care economy and the market economy. Benedict does not evidence the same comfort with a plurality of caregiving arrangements, as he does with a plurality of commercial enterprise forms. And although Benedict argues for a spirit of *caritas* to infuse a mutually supportive relationship between state and economy, he does not fully address the intersections of all aspects of the "care diamond"—state, market, household, and communities—which are necessary to support a fully incarnational "integral human development," a development that provides material support for caregiving labor.

Conclusion

The domestic economy, including caregiving, was extracted from conceptions of the "economic" during the development of classical and neoclassical economic theory. Current efforts to reintegrate care into economic theory and measurement are crucial for gender justice and for effective development policies and practices. In addition, reintegrating care into economic theory requires alterations to the anthropology underlying economics. Care is an embodied, incarnational practice. As such, the care economy *must* involve a range of motives—care is intrinsically focused on the needs of others, but caregivers are needy beings as well, and must and should attend to their own needs.

Benedict suggests that we need an openness to the transcendent for charity and the "spirit of gift" to pervade our market economy, but he does not turn to the economy of embodied relationships of dependency and caregiving as a site where such charity is already pervasive. Thereby, he devalues the embodied aspects of *caritas,* the work of dealing directly with frail and often messy bodies. A truly incarnational approach to development would also recognize and support the embodied care that necessarily pervades human life. Future Catholic social thought on development would do well to attend to the insights of feminist scholars of the care economy.

An Integral Ecology as the Ground for Good Business

Connecting Institutional Life in Light of Catholic Social Teachings

MICHAEL NAUGHTON

There is little argument today that we need ethical businesses. Where contention exists is over the source of what creates ethical businesses. I make the argument in this essay that an "integral ecology" is necessary to reset the discussion of business in a richer cultural soil with moral and spiritual roots that can yield humanizing policies and practices that respect the human and natural environment we inhabit. Where my argument becomes more controversial for some is that the insights of an integral ecology are rooted in a religious and familial culture that forms the life of business. When this rooted character is severed, we, in the words of C. S. Lewis, create "men without chests and expect of them virtue."[1] We unknowingly remove the ethical organ of humanity, yet still naively demand its function. We erode the moral and spiritual capital, believing that family and religion have little role to play in the moral order of business and the larger society. Particularly in the West, we too often believe that we can escape the deepest convictions of our humanity (faith, family, love) in the sphere of business and still remain ethical. We like to think that doing the good is either merely an achievement of the individual will without deeper changes to the habits of the person and the health of the larger culture, or a task that can be socially reengineered through regulations (state) and incentives (markets). Yet, a business ethic that is founded only on utility, contracts, self-interest, and even duty is an ethic that will always be prone to grow cold and fail to

---

1. C. S. Lewis, *The Abolition of Man* (New York: HarperOne, 2001), 26.

renew itself.[2] Life grinds away too hard for such constructs to hold over a lifetime. These are constructs that are too small for the human spirit, and they do not have the capacity to foster within business the conditions for people to develop in an integral way. Like cut flowers, business ethics premised on this basis may appear to look vital and robust, but they eventually decompose when there is no deep soil of relational or cultural resources to draw upon.

This task of reconnecting and re-embedding economic life in our familial and religious institutions that fosters care for creation is a difficult one at this time in history. Activist/philosopher Wendell Berry explains that there is in contemporary life "a movement of consciousness away from home," what theologian David Schindler calls "homelessness," and what others have identified as a cosmopolitan detachment.[3] As the economic life of production and consumption take up more of our time and space, business life becomes increasingly homeless as well as religionless,[4] isolating the businessperson from humanizing relationships as well as from the natural environment. We have too often forgotten that businesspeople come into the world not through a contract or a market exchange but through a gift. They are born not into a corporation, but into a family, welcomed into a religion, educated at schools, and received into a neighborhood and larger community.[5] Although this cultural context of the family suffers from its own particular challenges and exists in a wide variety of forms, it is, nonetheless, where business leaders are first formed. This cultural formation holds the key to the moral and spiritual

2. See Hans Urs von Balthasar, *The Christian State of Life*, trans. Sr. Mary Frances McCarthy (San Francisco: Ignatius Press, 1983), 30–32.

3. David Schindler, "Homelessness and the Modern Condition: The Family, Evangelization, and the Global Economy," *Logos: A Journal of Catholic Thought and Culture* 3, no. 4 (Fall 2000): 42, quoting Wendell Berry. See also Pope Benedict XVI, *Caritas in Veritae*, 40, http://w2.vatican.va/content/benedict-xvi/en/encyclicals/documents/hf_ben-xvi_enc_20090629_caritas-in-veritate.html.

4. Ferdinand Tönnies explained that "every original cult is bound up with the family and finds its most vigorous expression as a household cult, where in the beginning hearth and altar are one and the same." (Ferdinand Tönnies, *Community and Society* [New Brunswick: Transaction Publishers, 2007], 62).

5. See Jim Wishloff, "The Land of Realism and the Shipwreck of Idea-ism: Thomas Aquinas and Milton Friedman on the Social Responsibilities of Business," *Journal of Business Ethics* 85 (2009): 137–55.

"roots" of business, when it engages the meaning of the human person, and takes the transcendent seriously.

The phrase "integral ecology," as well as its related terms of "human ecology" and "integral human development," has recently entered the corpus of Catholic social teachings (CSTs).[6] Pope Francis, with Benedict XVI, John Paul II, and Paul VI before him, address the increasing fragmentation of modern life that too often results in what they see as division and compartmentalization. It is in this light that Francis and his predecessors are calling for a deeper form of integral thinking and acting through a multifaceted ecology. They have used the words "ecology" and its modifiers (integral, human, social, moral, etc.) to focus our attention on the importance of reality's interconnected and given nature. In particular, they see today's increasing ecological consciousness as an opportunity to articulate an integral relationship between *human* and *natural* ecology. These popes believe that the current ecological conversation can increase our sensitivity to our impact on the natural environment as well as to help us rediscover the moral and spiritual consciousness of *human nature and development* that has been weakened and disordered by what Francis calls a "technocratic paradigm," which disconnects us from nature and from faith and family, and supplants human virtuous action with technique.[7] They believe an integral ecology can "broaden our vision,"[8] and "develop a new synthesis,"[9] that can enlarge our notion of the good and in particular the common good.

6. For an excellent and insightful exploration of integral ecology, see Christopher Thompson, *The Joyful Mystery: Field Notes Toward a Green Thomism* (Steubenville, OH: Emmaus Road Publishing, 2017). As far as I can determine, the first use of the term "human ecology" in Catholic social teachings is found in a talk by Pope John Paul II to Italian farmers and artisans in 1989; see Robert Kennedy, Gary Atkins, and Michael Naughton, *Dignity of Work,* http://www.stthomas.edu/media/catholicstudies/center/johnaryaninstitute/publications/publicationpdfs/dignityofworkpdf/DignityofWork_ChapterIII.pdf, 251. See also *Centesimus Annus,* 38 and *Caritas in Veritate,* 51. See also Erika Bachiochi, "Safeguarding the Condition for an Authentic Human Ecology," which points to the social scientific development of human ecology in the 1970s through the 1990s, http://www.thepublicdiscourse.com/2017/01/18444/.

7. Pope Francis, *Laudato Si,* 101ff, http://w2.vatican.va/content/francesco/en/encyclicals/documents/papa-francesco_20150524_enciclica-laudato-si.html.

8. Ibid., 112.

9. Ibid., 121.

The purpose of this essay is to do precisely this—"broaden our vision" and "develop a new synthesis" by coming to a clearer understanding of this term "integral ecology" and to begin to see its implications within the institution of business. This will entail two animating themes throughout this essay—that nature and human nature are integrally connected and that a transcendent vision is needed.[10] These two themes may seem rather distant to the institution of business, but as I hope to show, such themes are essential to orienting business to the common good. Business is the institutional location where much of production and consumption occurs, and these actions are critical to the challenges of combating poverty, protecting nature, and supporting culture. Yet, within a global and commodity driven marketplace, business often suffers from a lack of integration caused by compartmentalization, the dominance of an instrumental rationality, consumerism, careerism, financialization, and an overconfidence in technology, markets, and process-oriented procedures. Without the cultural insights from an integral ecology that has the capacity to provide deep moral and spiritual roots, business will always be prone to see itself within its own autonomous and utilitarian sphere, failing to connect to the natural and human realities in which it is embedded.

To begin to know what we mean by Francis's phrase of "integral ecology" and its relationship with business, this essay is structured in three

10. Devoting a whole chapter to the phrase "integral ecology," Francis explains that "[w]hen we speak of the 'environment,' what we really mean is a relationship existing between nature and the society which lives in it." (Francis, *Laudato Si*, 139). An integral ecology fosters the link between caring for creation and caring for society and, in particular, its institutions, especially those institutions that impact the deepest convictions of culture. Francis wants to reconnect that the nature "out there" is inextricably connected to the human nature in each of us. He believes that what happens in marriage and the family, as well as in other institutions, such as business, have direct implications to what is happening in our natural environment and vice versa. There is not only environmental pollution but also cultural pollution, and the two are integrally connected. The disappearance of culture, such as marriage, as well as religion is just as serious if not more than the disappearance of the natural habitat (Francis, *Laudato Si*, 56). Harm to one is harm done to another. http://en.radiovaticana.va/news/2014/11/17/pope _francis_marriage_and_the_family_are_in_crisis/1111371).

parts. The first section focuses on the human part of integral ecology.[11] In this section, family and religion and, in particular, the church, are described as the primary institutions of society that frame the meaning of a human ecology. When they are healthy and in good relationship with each other, family and church serve as the institutional center point for the culture that morally and spiritually inform other institutions such as business. The second section explores this embedded relationship of this "human ecology" in its moral and spiritual orientation for business, which describes business as a secondary institution. As the primary institutions of culture, family and religion do two very important things to orient business toward the common good. Family and religious institutions *limit* economic activity so that there is space and time for people to foster right relationships with one another. They also *order* economic activity and remind business of its purpose by connecting production and consumption to its natural and human environments in which business is embedded. The third section of this essay explores some of the operational implications of an integral ecology in relation to the goods of business focusing more practically on its ecological and human implications for the three basic goods of business: good work, good goods, and good wealth.

The underlying thesis of this essay is that an integral ecology helps us to see how things are interconnected and related to each other in relationship to business as a secondary institution to the primary institutions of family and religion as well as to the natural environment. This thesis confronts what *Gaudium et spes* called one of the more serious errors of the modern era—the divided life.[12] Although this divided life syndrome

---

11. Human ecology draws upon the long tradition of the natural law. The International Theological Commission stated in 2009: "There cannot be an adequate response to the complex questions of ecology except within the framework of a deeper understanding of the natural law, which places value on the connection between the human person, society, culture, and the equilibrium of the bio-physical sphere in which the human person is incarnate." (See International Theological Commission, *In Search of a Universal Ethic: A New Look at the Natural Law*, 2009, 82, http://www.vatican.va/roman _curia/congregations/cfaith/cti_documents/rc_con_cfaith_doc_20090520_legge -naturale_en.html.)

12. Pope Paul VI, *Gaudium et Spes*, Pastoral constitution, Vatican website, December 7, 1965, http://www.vatican.va/archive/hist_councils/ii_vatican_council/documents/ vat-ii_cons_19651207_gaudium-et-spes_en.html, sec. 43.

has various manifestations expressed in one's personal life, this essay focuses on the disconnection of institutions from each other and from nature. If you want to ask where the richness of a culture is located in a society, look to its institutional life and how institutions inform, correct, and complement each other. The strength of institutions gives culture its strength. And yet we are faced constantly with temptations to undermine human institutions by reducing them to limited goods that undermine their capacity to serve the common good.[13] One of the challenges of modern culture is the "thinning out" of institutions, reducing them from a vibrant set of integrated goods to one flat good—universities to career credentialing, religion to emotive experience, marriage to sentiment between autonomous individuals, and business to shareholder wealth maximization. This reductionistic temptation deprives institutions from the horizontal connections among each other as well as a vertical transcendent breathing space that can draw upon a moral and spiritual vision necessary to move healthy institutions into the future. The working alternative to this minimal view of institutions is to propose a robust set of goods for institutional life and to see how institutions are integrally connected to each other and the larger environment.

Human Ecology and Its Primary Institutions

Francis has indicated that society has been slow to recognize the human part of an integral ecology in the current ecological crisis.[14] Therefore, the principal focus of this essay centers on the human dimension of the equation of what Francis means by integral ecology. How do humans create environments where they can live and flourish as human persons who respect and care for nature? The key to this question is the "institutions" people participate in. While humanity needs a healthy and sustainable physical environment to survive, people also need healthy and sustainable human institutions to thrive and flourish. It is precisely this

13. For an excellent analysis of modern institutional thinking see See Hugh Heclo, *On Thinking Institutionally* (Boulder, CO: Paradigm Publishers, 2008).

14. Pope Francis, "We Must Foster a New Human Ecology," Address, Humanum Conference, Vatican City, November 2014. http://w2.vatican.va/content/francesco/en/speeches/2014/november/documents/papa-francesco_20141117_congregazione-dottrina-fede.html.

understanding of institutions and in particular the relationship these institutions have with each other that constitutes what we mean by human ecology.

The term "human ecology" borrows from the field of natural ecology its first principle that all living things in an ecosystem are interconnected through networks of relationships. Nature itself is made up of systems that are embedded within systems. Each individual system is an integrated whole and—at the same time—part of larger systems. Just as changes within one physical system can affect the sustainability of other systems as well as the whole, so too changes in human institutional systems such as politics and economics can affect religious, educational, and familial institutions and vice versa.

In terms of a human ecology, the family serves as a primary institution of society. It is primary because it is that institution where our deepest meaning and identity should be formed. John Paul II, for example, states that "[t]he first and fundamental structure for 'human ecology' is the family in which man receives his first formative ideas about truth and goodness, and learns what it means to love and to be loved, and thus what it actually means to be a person."[15] As the first vital cell of society of which economic and political institutions should be embedded in, the family is the "sanctuary of life," a sacred place, "the heart of the culture of life."[16]

The family left to itself, however, is prone to tribalism and parochialism, severing itself from the larger good of society. Like any ecosystem, it is dependent on other systems. Institutions need help from other institutions to flourish. When isolated, they tend to suffocate. The family, in particular, needs a transcendent source to resist its tendency to self-absorption and to connect it to the common good. In CST that source is expressed through the institution of religion and, in particular, the church. Mary Eberstadt speaks of family and church as a "double helix" where the two are linked to each other in mutual interdependence, serving as the basic DNA of social life. When connected to each other, they

15. Pope John Paul II, *Centesimus Annus*, Encyclical Letter, Vatican website, May 1, 1991, http://w2.vatican.va/content/john-paul-ii/en/encyclicals/documents/hf_jp-ii_enc _01051991_centesimus-annus.html, 39.

16. John Paul II, *Centesimus Annus*, 39.

reproduce and strengthen each other, giving society the cultural glue to flourish.[17] The health of one institution strengthens the other, but the decline of one powers the decline of the other. On one hand, when individuals have children, they are more prone to move to faith by the very wonder of new life and their participation in it. They experience in marriage and parenthood the importance of virtues such as sacrifice and fidelity and the need to be rooted in a community, such as the church, that shares and supports such virtues. On the other hand, when the churches move away from supporting marriage and family through various ways, they undermine their base and often see a decline in their numbers.[18]

When the family and church are in right relationship, they generate institutional goods that impact the larger society. Francis explains that "[t]he family is the principal agent of an integral ecology, because it is the primary social subject which contains within it the two fundamental principles of human civilization on earth: the principle of communion and the principle of fruitfulness."[19] The family, with the support of the church, is the primary human environment where couples mature and develop in union with each other and children are born and nurtured.[20] These two goods (communion/unitive and fruitfulness/procreative) are the infrastructure of the family's contribution to the common good. In CST, the family is the principal place where the institutional goods of marriage nurture and transmit an authentic community of persons that serve the common good by allowing the family to be itself. But the family

17. Mary Eberstadt, *How the West Really Lost God* (West Conshohoken, PA: Templeton Press, 2013), 22.

18. Ibid., 139–54.

19. Francis, *Amoris Laetitia*, https://w2.vatican.va/content/dam/francesco/pdf/apost_exhortations/documents/papa-francesco_esortazione-ap_20160319_amoris-laetitia_en.pdf, 277.

20. An integral ecology presupposes a normative and natural way in which the ecological and the human operates. What is clearly problematic for today is the claim of a normative way of being human, especially in terms of a sacramental and covenantal marriage that has been presupposed in this essay. Increasingly as a culture, definitions of marriage are more fluid and range from the normative position presupposed in this essay to where the only standard or normative definition for marriage is that there is no standard and normative definition beyond individual preferences.

is never just for itself. It influences other communities, especially in the economic and political arena.

One of the key qualities of these two goods of marriage, the unitive good of the couple and the procreative good of children, is that they are "diffusive."[21] When they are in good order, they do not remain within themselves, but they become generative, and communicate themselves to other places and institutions. As Charles De Koninck wrote, "For the more a being is good, the more it spreads forth its goodness to beings which are further from itself."[22] The goods of marriage, lived authentically, extend the chain of solidarity that includes not only the couple and children, but they also inform and build up other institutions. In a certain sense, the two goods of marriage contribute to a third good, the good of social order in other institutions. Marriage and family, along with the church, serve as primary institutions for the "foundation of society" informing and influencing the couple's future and the future of society. Where the family goes, society goes. The marriage rooted in the good of children is where the couple exists not only for themselves but where their sincere gift of themselves through children enables them to find themselves, which is the basis of their ability to give of themselves in other parts of society, and, in particular, economic and political life. In light of this interdependent and organic view of institutional life, we begin to see in the family the concrete expression of the common good, that is, goods shared in common, diffusing themselves and informing other institutions such as business and the state. It is precisely this last point that helps us to see that secondary institutions such as the state and business should not be seen as unimportant, but they are not the places people should seek their deepest meaning and identity. By themselves, they are inadequate sources for moral and spiritual formation.[23]

21. See John Paul II, "Letter to Families," Vatican, website, February 2, 1994, http://w2.vatican.va/content/john-paul-ii/en/letters/1994/documents/hf_jp-ii_let_02021994_families.html, 10.

22. Charles De Koninck, "On the Primacy of the Common Good: Against the Personalists and The Principle of the New Order, *The Aquinas Review* 4 (1997), http://ldataworks.com/aqr/V4_BC_text.html.

23. This distinction between primary and secondary institutions comes from a book called *True Leadership* originally published by the Habiger Institute at the Center for Catholic Studies, University of St. Thomas, MN, http://www.stthomas.edu/cathstudies/cst/

Embedded Relationship of Business within a Human Ecology

The Catholic social tradition insists that it takes many institutions in collaborative relationships to foster the common good. It recognizes the importance of the state, unions, and international regulatory agencies, for example, and their collaboration with business. But CST emphasizes an even greater need for the collaboration between business and cultural institutions.[24] The primary institutions of family and church, when they are at their best, do two very important things to orient business toward the integral human development and the common good. First, faith and family institutions *limit* economic activity so that there is natural space for people to foster right relationships with one another, nature, and God. Josef Pieper calls this the process of deproletarianization. He writes in *Leisure the Basis of Culture* that in the face of modernity's increasing

---

research/publications/trueleadership/ (Cluny Media). Although, there is a lot more to be explained concerning this distinction, let me highlight a couple of clarifications. Primary institutions need secondary institutions to flourish. Families will struggle to survive or flourish without a well-functioning government or dynamic business sector. However, when people see the state or business in terms of their primary identity, it eventually results in either idolatrous nationalism or careerism. This view of institutional life differs from contemporary liberal theory, but it also differs from the Greeks and Romans. For Augustine, "membership of the state cannot have the ethical significance attributed to it by Plato and Aristotle. The state, that is, cannot be the matrix within which man, made wise by education and practice, can achieve his distinctive good or end by making rational choices and participating in the common life. Man's final good simply does not lie, and cannot be achieved, in this life." (Augustine, *The City of God against the Pagans*, ed. & trans. R. W. Dyson, [Cambridge: Cambridge University Press, 1998], xxii). Aristotle and Plato made the polis that matrix. Christians, told by God to give to Caesar what is Caesar's, but to God what is God's, effected a revolution in this idea. Modern liberal thought, largely rejecting the theological and familial foundation, have placed human meaning and identity in the self-interest of the individual as the key matrix with the state as the arbiter. The political thought of the ancients, however useful, needs to take into account the fundamental shift in understanding given by Christ and the establishment of the Kingdom of God on earth. Citizenship as an identity is not big enough for the human spirit. By itself it will always be prone to idolatry, e.g., nationalism. This does not mean that there is not such a thing as a healthy patriotism or a healthy view of business or that the family and church do not have things to learn from the political and economic spheres. The point is that there is a priority of the family and church in terms of the meaning of life.

24. See John Paul II, *Centesimus Annus*, chapter 4.

"total work mentality," we must "enlarge and widen our scope beyond work."[25] Judaism does this through the Sabbath, and Christianity through the Lord's Day. Abraham Joshua Heschel describes the Sabbath as resistance to the encroaching claims of production, consumption, and technology. The Sabbath tells us that these activities do not own or completely define us.[26] This limit on production and consumption provided by the Sabbath gives space for human and religious identity beyond our view as just workers, entrepreneurs, consumers, or citizens, or any other identity claim that turns a doing or having into a being. Every seven days provides a renewal of remembering what Francis calls "the rhythms inscribed in nature by the hand of the Creator."[27] We are made to have leisure not merely to sharpen the saw and go back to work more productive, but to rest in the Lord that enables us to heal and reorder our relationships by remembering what Benedict XVI calls the "logic of gift," of receiving and giving.[28] The pattern of this logic goes like this: that we are first created (creation), that the earth is a gift with its own laws and demands (nature), that human beings are a gift and not merely self-created or authored (human nature), and that the world was created for the sustenance and enjoyment of all and especially the poor (responsibilities).

Families also limit economic activity by recognizing the covenantal bond of the couple and its commitment to children that takes time and dedication that cannot be violated by the demands of work. It is in the family that our deepest identity as women and men begin to be formed as sons and daughters, brothers and sisters, mothers and fathers. Short-circuiting these identities disorders our humanity.

Second, family and faith *order* economic activity and remind business of its purpose by connecting production and consumption to the common good and its participants to their particular vocations. Pieper explains that deproletarianization not only goes beyond work but also widens its meaning. As Francis puts in *Laudato si*, "[w]e are called to include in our work a dimension of receptivity and gratuity, which is

25. Josef Pieper, *Leisure: The Basis of Culture* (South Bend, IN: St. Augustine's Press, 1998), 39ff.

26. Abraham Heschel, "The Sabbath," In *Working: Its Meaning and Its Limits*, ed. Gilbert C. Meilaender (South Bend, IN: University of Notre Dame Press, 2000), 261–67.

27. Francis, *Laudato Si*, 71.

28. Pope Benedict XVI, *Caritas in Veritate* 5 (italics in original).

quite different from mere inactivity."[29] Without a deep well of rest as spiritual reflection, it is hard to see how business leaders can resist the dominance of an instrumental rationality that reduces business to one bottom line. For Francis, "[r]est opens our eyes to the larger picture and gives us renewed sensitivity to the rights of others. And so the day of rest, centered on the Eucharist, sheds it light on the whole week, and motivates us to greater concern for nature and the poor."[30]

The family also plays an important role in the meaning of work. As the first school of virtue, the family is the typical place where desires are matured, reason is formed, the will is shaped, and a community of persons is established. Francis explains that as a school, the family grounded in marriage is "where we begin to acquire the arts of cooperative living."[31] This familial formation, which serves as the basic cell of culture, should influence business not to be another family but to be a *human* place of production. This cultural soil of religion and family instills in businesses "a greater sense of responsibility, a strong sense of community, a readiness to protect others, a spirit of creativity and a deep love for the land."[32] This family formation, along with a religious social tradition that places work within the realm of a vocation, will help to see business as a goods-producing institution, which we will examine in the next section.

There are of course many obstacles that disconnect business from family and religion as well as nature. There is also the practical challenge of connecting ideas to practices. As one senior health care executive said to me, "How would I know if the common good bit me?" What he was getting at is that these terms the Catholic church uses, such as subsidiarity, solidarity, dignity, common good, and now integral ecology seem like abstractions and moralisms that do not translate into practical alternatives. One interesting note of history is that Pius XII (pope from 1939–1958) never wrote a social encyclical, but he did welcome all sorts of associations, and gave them short talks that pointed to the implications of faith and the social teachings to their particular forms of work. The

---

29. Francis, *Laudato Si*, 237.

30. Ibid.

31. Francis, "We Must Foster a New Human Ecology," Salt and Light TV, last modified November 17, 2014, http://saltandlighttv.org/blog/featured/we-must-foster-a-new-human-ecology-pope-francis.

32. Francis, *Laudato Si*, 179.

groups he talked to were extraordinarily diverse—businesspeople, bankers, public finance officials, Catholic associations of employers, hotel workers, railway engineers, farmers, petroleum leaders, movie producers and theater owners, food producers, small- and medium-sized business owners, automobile executives, and my favorites, bee-keepers, shoemakers, tramway workers, tailors, and bookstand concessionaires of the railway stations of Italy. What Pius XII did in these talks is to connect the social tradition of the church with people's particular fields of work. It is to this task that we now turn. In the next section, we move to the "behavior" dimension, focusing more particularly on the goods of business and how their operation can and does witness an integral human ecology.

Implications of an Integral Ecology for Business

The Pontifical Council for Justice and Peace (now the Dicastery for Promoting Integral Human Development) 2012 document, *Vocation of the Business Leader,* is an attempt to connect the principles of CSTs to the practical implications of what these teachings mean for business. It offers a framework that moves to a more concrete articulation of the specific implications of an integral human ecology for business structured on three goods of business[33]:

Good Work: organizing work where employees develop their God-given gifts and talents not only for themselves, but for others and the world.

Good Goods: providing goods that are truly good and services that truly serve, goods that go beyond market value and serve the common good.

Good Wealth: creating sustainable wealth that can be distributed justly to all those who create the wealth.

33. Dicastery for Promoting Integral Human Development,
https://www.stthomas.edu/media/catholicstudies/center/ryan/publications/publica
tionpdfs/vocationofthebusinessleaderpdf/FinalTextTheVocationoftheBusinessLeader
.pdf. For further exploration of these three goods, see my book *Getting Work Right: Labor and Leisure in a Fragmented World* (Steubenville, OH: Emmaus Road Publishing, 2019).

Embedded within the primary institutions of family and faith as well as the natural environment, business is beholden to something more than just markets and laws. The language of goods within business begins to articulate a transcendent and noninstrumental view of business that connects its specific activities to a human and natural ecology. Employing this language of goods, I will highlight three particular challenges of an integral human ecology for business and ways to address these challenges: 1) Good Work: the challenge of a created gifted order; 2) Good Goods: the challenge of natural ecology; and 3) Good Wealth: the challenge of human ecology.

Good Work: Challenge of a Created Gifted Order

In a career- and consumer-oriented world, work is too often seen merely in terms of one's own personal preferences, one's own passions and dreams, and ultimately one's own choices. This individualistic orientation all too frequently views the world not as a created inbuilt-order gifted by the Creator with its own logic, but rather a world as simply raw material at our disposal to be manipulated according to our choices and abilities within the boundaries of the written law (logics of the market and contract). This view of work and of leadership instrumentalizes the various stakeholders of business and alienates people from each other, nature, and a deeper relationship with God.

In contrast to the individualism of a career, the Catholic social tradition deepens the view of work and business to a vocation. Francis calls business "a noble vocation, provided that those engaged in it see themselves challenged by a *greater meaning in life*."[34] This greater meaning of life for the vocation of the businessperson, then, is not only about one's choice, but a choice that participates in a received created order expressed in terms of a natural and human ecology. Unmoored in these larger ecologies, the freedom of one's choice by itself lands in an arbitrary place that does not have the staying power for a meaning of life worthy of the

---

34. Pope Francis, *Evangelii Gaudium,* 203, http://w2.vatican.va/content/francesco/en/ apost_exhortations/documents/papa-francesco_esortazione-ap_20131124_evangelii -gaudium.html. See also Dicastery for Promoting Integral Human Development, *The Vocation of the Business Leader,* 6.

human spirit. A transcendent reality is needed. Business, like any institution, finds itself in a natural ecological order as well as a human moral order that is dependent on patterns reflected in creation. As a participation in this created order, work should both develop products and services to make the world more human (objective dimension of work) and at the same time develop the people who do the work (subjective dimension of work).[35] Because work has both objective and subjective dimensions, one's work, seen as a vocation, produces something objectively good for the world and subjectively good for the persons doing the work. For these two dimensions are not unrelated; when they are in conflict they put at risk the common good. Work therefore is not merely an instrument in pursuit of a profit abstracted from a human and natural ecology. Good work has built within its very structure the created order, a natural law, a way in which people develop into who they were created to be according to the way the world was created. Although this is not easy language for an increasingly technological culture, it is the language of an integral ecology.

Key to the subjective dimension of work is the notion of gift and, in particular, the principle of subsidiarity (the objective dimension of work will be addressed in the next section). The word "subsidiarity" comes from the Latin *subsidium,* that is, "to assist or strengthen" the other. It serves as a moral principle that directs leaders to place decision-making authority at the most appropriate level of an organization so as to utilize the gifts of people for their own good and the good of the collective entity. It is both wrong to take away from people what they can accomplish by their own initiative and industry and give it to higher levels of the organization as well as refuse help when individuals and groups cannot do things themselves. When Pius XI introduced subsidiarity into CSTs in 1931, his fundamental concern was the state's absorption of the unique and special gifts of institutions such as the family, education, voluntary associations, and the church. What was at stake was not simply an abstract right to have autonomy but the repression of people's gifts. At the heart of human development is the exercise of each person's God-given gifts. When these gifts are absorbed by higher powers—whether of

---

35. John Paul II, *Laborem Exercens,* 6, http://w2.vatican.va/content/john-paul-ii/en/encyclicals/documents/hf_jp-ii_enc_14091981_laborem-exercens.html.

the state, or business, or education, or family, or the church—they repress and disorder. Subsidiarity at its heart is a gift principle, not an autonomy principle. Here there is a deeper theological claim of what the tradition calls *munera*, namely that God has endowed his people with gifts, and entrusts them to do the work.[36]

Although subsidiarity has not been traditionally applied to the workplace, it is a principle, as Benedict XVI puts it, that helps us to recognize within each person "a *subject* who is always capable of giving something to others," and thus business leaders ought to design and organize work in a way that is informed by these capabilities of giving.[37] Good work contributes to "human development and personal fulfillment" of the person who works.[38] Business leaders, who take "good work," seriously, build organizations that actively draw upon the diverse gifts (talents, abilities, and skills) of all employees in such a way that both produces goods at a profit (objective dimension) and allows workers to develop through the work done. Leaders who wish to orient their organizations toward the principle of subsidiarity face three important institutionalizing tasks. First, they need to *design work* for employees in a way that taps their gifts, talents, and skills and at the same time makes the organization competitive in the marketplace by improving efficiency, quality, and profitability. Second, they need to *develop the people* who they lead. And third they need to *establish strong relationships with employees, beginning with delegation, and moving to trust.*

When work fails to tap the talents of workers, and management absorbs their rightful decision-making, employees become disengaged. Gallup polls point out that on average approximately 70 percent of employees are disengaged and disconnected with their organizations.[39] Although there are many reasons for this disengagement, clearly one

36. See Russell Hittinger, "Social Pluralism and Subsidiarity in Catholic Social Doctrine," *Annales Theologici* 16 (2002): 385–408.

37. Benedict XVI, *Caritas in Veritate*, 57. See also Michael Naughton, Jeanne Buckeye, Kenneth Goodpaster, and Dean Maines, *Respect in Action: Applying Subsidiarity in Business* (St. Paul, MN: University of St. Thomas, 2015).

38. Francis, *Laudato Si,* 128.

39. Gallup, *State of the American Workplace: Employee Engagement Insights for U.S. Business Leaders* (Washington, DC: Gallup, 2013): 5, 8–9, 12, http://www.gallup.com/strategicconsulting/163007/state-american-workplace.aspx.

important dimension is badly designed work and poor leadership and management. One organization able to overcome this disengagement is Reell Precision Manufacturing. The company redesigned its assembly line from a command-direct-control style of management in which managers made all the decisions concerning the assembly area, to a teach-equip-trust style of management in which employees were taught inspection procedures, equipped with quality instruments, and trusted to do things right on their own assembly line. By restructuring the work process according to the principle of subsidiarity, employees decreased set-up times for new products, reduced the need for quality inspection, increased overall quality, and required less supervision. By reducing these costs, the company not only created more humane work but also created the conditions to increase their wage rates for better pay.[40] As Michael Pirson demonstrates in his essay in this volume, humane management practices like those implemented at Reell have begun to spread from business schools to businesses around the world.

Good Goods: The Challenge of Natural Ecology

When properly ordered by a human and natural ecology, business brings into existence "goods that are truly good and services that truly serve" (the objective dimension of work).[41] As an institution, business plays a pivotal role in producing and giving a great number of people access to food, shelter, credit, clothing, communications, transportation, medicine, and so forth, namely, the goods and services that promote our well-being. Underlying "good goods" is what the Catholic social tradition calls "the universal destination of goods and the right to common use of them."[42] For example, in the food industry, businesses like Bimbo, Cargill, Kraft, Aldi, as well as thousands of small- to medium-sized companies and farms, create efficient methods in production and distribution to significantly bring down the cost of food, allowing families to spend a smaller percentage of their income on food. This ability to bring food to

40. See Michael Naughton and David Specht, *Leading Wisely in Difficult Times: Three Cases on Faith and Work* (Mahwah NJ: Paulist Press, 2011). For full disclosure, I am the chairman of the board of directors for Reell.

41. Dicastery for Promoting Integral Human Development, 40.

42. See John Paul II, *Laborem Exercens*, 14. See also Francis, *Laudato Si*, 158.

a greater number of people at affordable prices has served everyone, especially the poor.

Yet, these goods, this objective dimension of work, can directly or indirectly produce negative by-products, such as bland and unhealthy food options that result in widespread obesity, industrialized agricultural practices that cause soil erosion and poor use of water, and concentration of market power in agribusiness that contributes to the commoditization of labor and wreaks havoc on rural farm communities.[43] The full costs of environmental and human degradation resulting from these by-products of production are not borne by producers but are shifted on the wider public, future generations, and often the poor. Economists call these costs "negative externalities," which have the effect of socializing costs of production but privatizing its profits.

Products and services cannot be truly good in a complete way when they violate the good of the natural environment and in particular the people who are least culpable and most affected. One particular challenge that Francis notes is that unlike natural ecosystems, we have "not developed the capacity to absorb and reuse waste and by-products. We have not yet managed to adopt a circular model of production capable of preserving resources for present and future generations, while limiting as much as possible the use of nonrenewable resources, moderating their consumption, maximizing their efficient use, reusing and recycling them."[44] Although we have been commanded, as the book of Genesis tells us, to "till and keep" creation, we have tended to "till too much and keep too little" by shifting costs and problems to future generations and the poor.[45]

The production of good goods has to include ways to address the negative externalities of waste and pollution. Although this problem of developing an ecologically sustainable production system is not easy to

---

43. For a fuller description of these problems and their solutions, see *The Vocation of the Agricultural Leader* (Rome: International Catholic Rural Association), http://www.faithfoodenvironment.org/wp-content/uploads/2016/12/The-Vocation-of-the-Agricultural-Leader.pdf.

44. Francis, *Laudato Si*, 22.

45. Cardinal Peter Turkson, "Protect the Earth, Dignify Humanity: The Moral Dimensions of Climate Change and Sustainable Development," delivered at Vatican City, April 28, 2015, http://www.casinapioiv.va/content/dam/accademia/pdf/turkson.pdf.

solve, some companies provide life-cycle assessments of their products and services and are reducing their waste, finding ways to recycle and decarbonize their energy use. Timberland, for example, creates shoes and boots and other forms of apparel. These products are good goods by providing footwear for the world. But Timberland has also taken responsibility for the effects of how they produce by significantly reducing chemicals linked to human or environmental harm by moving to water-based adhesives to reduce solvent use. They have designed their boots and shoes as a recyclable product (reduce, reuse, recycle) by selecting raw materials that can more easily be reused. They have also sought to decarbonize their buildings and factories by implementing renewable energy sources and more energy-efficient cooling and heating systems that have reduced energy consumption and carbon dioxide emissions.[46] As recounted in Vincent Stanley's essay in this volume, the clothing company Patagonia has likewise led the way in sustainable production in both natural and human terms.

Developing new reducing-polluting technologies and using renewable sources of energy are needed to promote sustainable development within business. Organizations such as Timberland, Patagonia, and hundreds of others are finding creative and innovative ways to harmonize production with an environmental mode of operation. Yet, in the final analysis, we cannot completely rely on a market or technological fix to the environmental problems we face. Ultimately, the causes of the problem are not only technical but also moral and spiritual. Francis has hammered this point home by calling for a lifestyle change that confronts a particularly modern global consumerism that is increasing in cultural dominance and homogeneity. He warns of a consumerism fixated on pleasures, blunting the conscience and leaving no room for others, the poor, children, and God.[47] Our throwaways may be recyclable, but if we have become impoverished spiritually, we may survive but we will not flourish.

---

46. See J. Austin, H. Leonard, and J. Quinn, *Timberland: Commerce and Justice* (Boston: Harvard Business School Publishing, 2004). See C. K. Prahalad, *The Fortune at the Bottom of the Pyramid* (Philadelphia: Wharton School Publishing, 2006), 11. See also Gene Laczniak and Patrick Murphy, "Distinctive Imperatives for Teaching Marketing in a Catholic Business School." http://www.stthomas.edu/media/catholicstudies/center/johnaryaninstitute/curriculumdevelopement/marketing/MurphLacBackground4.pdf.

47. See Francis, *Evangelii Gaudium*, 2.

Good Wealth: A Challenge of Human Ecology

You cannot distribute wealth you have not created, nor should you create wealth without justly distributing it to those who are responsible for its creation. These two dimensions of good wealth, and creation and distribution, which are too often juxtaposed to each other, cannot be understood apart from each other.[48]

In terms of *wealth creation*, business enterprises are the economic engine of society. Francis states that business is "directed to producing wealth and improving our world. It can be a fruitful source of prosperity for the areas in which it operates, especially if it sees the creation of jobs as an essential part of its service to the common good."[49] As a creator of jobs, business must exercise the stewardship of resources in a way that it creates more than what it has been given. This is commonly called margin or profit. Profit, the surplus of retained earnings over expenses, enables an enterprise to sustain itself into the future. Profits wisely used over time generate equity in companies, which strengthens the firm's wealth-generating capacities to build for the future. A business with a healthy balance sheet, for example, simply has greater abilities to build a future than those laden with debt. A profitable business creates the conditions to properly employ the factors of production, which is a necessary means to realize the common good of a society. Yet, profit is like food. You need it to be healthy and sustainable, but you ought not to live for it. Profit makes for a good servant but a lousy master.

Wealth creation brings with it the concomitant task of *wealth distribution*. A *just* distribution calls for wealth to be allocated in a way that creates "right relationships" with those who have participated in the creation of such wealth. Without justice, business becomes organized robbery. Justice in business raises a set of knotty and enduring moral challenges for business. Among other things, businesses need to discern and account for the moral implications of how they make a just distribution of this wealth to employees (a just wage as well as possibilities of employee ownership),

---

48. See Charles Clark, "Promoting Good Wealth: CST and the Link between Wealth, Well-Being and Poverty Alleviation," April 28, 2015, http://www.stthomas.edu/media/catholicstudies/center/johnaryaninstitute/conferences/2015-manila/ClarkBackground Final.pdf on distinguishing good and bad wealth.

49. Francis, *Laudato Si*, 129.

customers (just prices), owners (fair returns), suppliers (just prices and fair terms on receivables), government (just tax payments), and the larger community and especially the poor (philanthropy). Pius XII made the analogy of wealth being like blood in the human body: it needs to circulate to all the parts in order to make the whole healthy.[50] Good wealth depends on a just distribution throughout society; where there is undue concentration, there is most likely disease. Business plays an essential role in creating a just distribution of wealth that both generates authentic prosperity and alleviates debilitating poverty.

Good wealth understood in terms of the relationship between its creation and distribution both enhances a human ecology and is dependent on it. For example, without wealth creation and employment, families often suffer from poverty. Yet, this employment, which is predicated upon a strong political stability within a society and a vibrant entrepreneurial environment of innovation and creativity, is also dependent on the social capital of families to produce such qualities. As several scholars have noted, family structure is too often ignored or discounted when speaking about the economic health of society and in particular business.[51] Besides nature itself, the deepest and most sustainable wealth of a country, which is the insight of a human ecology, comes from the family and its relation to religion—what we called in section one of this essay, the basis of a human ecology.

One of the more tragic consequences of the broken relationship between the family and religion, and economic life is persistent poverty.[52] The causes of poverty and the lack of social and economic mobility are complicated and varied. They entail poor education, inadequate health

50. Pius XII, Letter *Dilecti filii* to the German Bishops, October 18, 1949; quoted in Jean-Yves Calvez and Jacques Perrin, *The Church and Social Justice: The Social Teachings of the Popes from Leo XIII to Pius XII* (Chicago: Henry Regnery, 1961), 149.

51. See the work of Charles Murray, *Coming Apart: the State of White America, 1960–2010*, (New York: Crown Forum, 2012).

52. Faith institutions complement families by becoming a family of families that support each other in times of crisis. W. Bradford Wilcox, Andrew J. Cherlin, Jeremy E. Uecker, and Matthew Messel, "No Money, No Honey, No Church: The Deinstitutionalization of Religious Life Among the White Working Class," http://creed-design.com/NMP/wp-content/uploads/2012/05/Religion_WorkingPaper.pdf. See also Amy L. Wax, "Engines of Inequality: Class, Race and Structure," *Family Law Quarterly* 41, no. 3. (2007): 567, http://lsr.nellco.org/cgi/viewcontent.cgi?article=1219&context=upenn_wps.

care, racism, poverty segregation, inefficient and lack of government programs and regulations, corruption, regressive tax policies, weaker unions,
polluted environment, drugs and alcohol, violence, globalization, and so
forth. Each one these problems and their relationship to each other
deserves attention. But too often their relationship to family and religion
as key dimensions to human ecology, and are discounted and ignored.[53]
Francis captured the significance of this phenomenon when he stated:
"Evidence is mounting that the decline of the marriage culture is associated with increased poverty and a host of other social ills, disproportionately affecting women, children and the elderly."[54] This decline of a marriage
culture and increasing poverty points to the relationship between *economic*
and *cultural* inequality.

In the United States, for example, there is an increasing cultural
divide between lower- and middle-class populations that are withdraw-
ing from marriage and religion, and upper middle-class populations that
have higher participation rates in such institutions. Although marriage
and religious participation rates have declined for all classes since the
1960s, significant divergence started to occur in the 1980s. For the upper
middle class, marriage stabilized during the mid-1980s, and since then
actual divorce rates have started to decline for this group.[55] For the lower
to middle classes, however, marriage participation rates have continued
to slide to the point where a minority are now married. Whereas in the
1960s, poor and rich both participated in religion and marriage at similar rates, today a majority of upper middle-class people marry, and their
children are born into two-parent homes and usually attend religious services. A majority of middle- to lower-class people do not marry, their children are born into single parent homes, and they usually do not attend

53. See *Economic Mobility: Research & Ideas on Strengthening Families, Communities &
the Economy,* ed. Federal Reserve Bank of St. Louis and the Board of Governors of the
Federal Reserve System, https://www.stlouisfed.org/community-development/publica
tions/economic-mobility.

54. Pope Francis, "We Must Foster a New Human Ecology," Address, Humanum
Conference, Vatican City, November, 2014, http://w2.vatican.va/content/francesco/en/
speeches/2014/november/documents/papa-francesco_20141117_congregazione
-dottrina-fede.html.

55. W. Bradford Wilcox and Elizabeth Marquardt, eds. "When Marriage Disappears:
The New Middle America," *The State of Our Unions: Marriage in America,* 2010, http://
stateofourunions.org/2010/SOOU2010.pdf.

religious services.[56] As the "marrying rich and unmarrying poor" move in opposite directions, the traditional working class have become unraveled, preventing them from the economic mobility they once participated in.[57] The relationship of family structure to the other causes of poverty listed above are varied and complex, but an integral ecology approach sees family and marriage as an important factor to the analysis.

What does this mean for business? I want to highlight two implications—one related to wealth creation and the other to wealth distribution. First, wealth creation. New jobs, which are critical to the health of a business sector, usually come not from well-established companies but from entrepreneurial start-ups and, in particular, family businesses.[58] There is significant concern that today's economy in the United States is not generating new jobs as past economies have. New businesses need entrepreneurs who are willing to take risks, who have faith in a future, who have access to credit, and who can operate in a regulatory environment that is not onerous. The macroeconomic environment plays an important role here but so does family structure. Entrepreneurship, and, in particular, family businesses are dependent on healthy families. One study indicates that young adults who grew up in intact families (mother and father and no divorce) work at least 156 more hours per year than their peers from single-parent families. Strong, intact families generate the ability to acquire the skills and habits needed to participate the

56. See Charles Murray, *Coming Apart: the State of White America, 1960–2010,"* (New York: Crown Forum, 2012). See also Reuben Finighan and Robert Putnam, "A Country Divided: The Growing Opportunity Gap in America," in *Economic Mobility: Research & Ideas on Strengthening Families, Communities & the Economy,* ed. Federal Reserve Bank of St. Louis and the Board of Governors of the Federal Reserve System, 145ff, https://www .stlouisfed.org/~/media/Files/PDFs/Community-Development/EconMobilityPapers/ Section2/EconMobility_2-2FinighanPutnam_508.pdf?la=en.

57. See Erika Bachiochi, "The Family: Between Personal Rights and Social Needs," summarized in her blog, "Reflections on My Time in Rome as a Speaker at the Conference Commemorating Popularum Progressio," *Mirror of Justice: A Blog Dedicated to the Development of Catholic Legal Theory,* last modified April 6, 2017, http://mirrorofjustice.blogs.com/ mirrorofjustice/2017/04/reflections-on-my-time-in-rome-as-a-speaker-at-the-conference -commemorating-popularum-progressio.html.

58. Steve Denning, "The Surprising Truth about where New Jobs Come From," *Forbes,* last modified October 29, 2014, http://www.forbes.com/sites/stevedenning/2014/10/29/ the-surprising-truth-about-where-new-jobs-come-from/#7df320e147d9.

economy.[59] Although controversial in its claims, this research suggests that in the aggregate, intact marriages and healthy families simply have greater capacity to teach virtues of justice and courage as well as diligence and industriousness than those of broken or nonexistent marriages. Families are a major determiner of hope in the future—of children, of relationships, of opportunities, of community. This becomes a major point of a human ecology—the health of one institution, such as the family, is dependent on and informs the health of the other, such as business. Children raised in married, intact families are more likely to do better in school, be successful in work and participate in religious institutions.[60] They see their lives through institutions, as builders of institutions. Although various tensions and dysfunctions occur on the way, such as when the success of business absorbs the time and energy of its employees leaving little time for the family, the integral relationship among institutions and their mutual dependency are still critical factors to the integral development of people.

Second, wealth distribution. If business is to support this human ecology, it must pay a living wage. If families cannot live on the wage given to them and need to get two or three jobs to make ends meet, human ecology will be significantly damaged. The importance of a living wage has been long held in the Catholic social tradition. Josef Pieper stated in 1948 that a living wage is the first defense against proletariziation, which, as I stated above, damages a human ecology. Depending on the industry, a just wage can be difficult to attain. Yet, if a business participates in and enhances a human ecology, it begins to see how the deep relationships within the family inform the relationships with its employees. For example, when an employer receives work from an employee, both participate not only in an economic exchange but also in a personal relationship. For this relationship to flourish, an employer must recognize that in their labor, employees "surrender" their time and energy and cannot use them

59. Robert I. Lerman and W. Bradford Wilcox, *For Richer, For Poorer: How Family Structures Economic Success in America* (Washington, DC: AEI/Institute for Family Studies, 2014).

60. Why they do better is often where disagreements occur. See Kimberly Howard and Richard V. Reeves, "The Marriage Effect: Money or Parenting?" *Brookings*, last modified September 4, 2014, https://www.brookings.edu/research/the-marriage-effect-money-or-parenting/.

for another purpose. A living wage, then, is the minimum amount due to every independent wage earner by the mere fact that he or she is a human being with a life to maintain and a family to support. But precisely because the business is a business, pay is not only income for the worker, it is also a cost to the employer and has a significant impact on the economic health of the organization.[61] It is here where the tensions and difficulties occur, but this is precisely where the business leader must engage, and avoid either a market logic that dismisses the tension or a moralism that ignores it.

In summary, the three goods of business when they are in right order play an important role in fostering an integral ecology. Good work is a participation in a created order cultivating and exercising the gifts that were given and not created. Good goods create products and services that serve humanity and mitigate the negative impact production and consumption have on the ecosystem, future generations, and especially on the poor. And good wealth is generated and distributed by healthy marriages and families that serve such families. Even though they are called a secondary institution, businesses, when they promote these three goods, play an essential role in supporting an integral ecology.

Conclusion

An integral ecology within a business context as articulated in this essay has many challenges, although opportunities are all around. On the one hand, we live increasingly in a technocratic culture.[62] We are prone to underestimate the impact we have on both the natural and human environment, believing that somehow we can manage negative impacts through technology. On the other hand, the seeds of renewal are found in the most unexpected places, which today look small but may flourish in the future. Small, entrepreneurial start-ups, family businesses, as well

61. See Josef Pieper, *Leisure the Basis of Culture*, chapter 4, where he distinguishes a wage from an honorarium. See also Helen Alford and Michael Naughton, *Managing as if Faith Mattered* (South Bend, IN: University of Notre Dame Press, 2001), chapter 5.

62. For a description of the increasingly technological culture we are living in, see Russell Hittinger, *The First Grace: Rediscovering the Natural Law in a Post-Christian World* (Wilmington, DE: ISI Books, 2003), chapter 10, "Technology and the Demise of Liberalism."

as the many faith-based movements in business are taking an integral ecology seriously. Some of these movements are the Economy of Communion from the Focolare movement, UNIAPAC, and Legatus, Compagnia delle Opere from the Communion and Liberation movement. Some are small start-ups that have been influenced by economic philosophies, such as distributism, cooperativism, and personalism, back-to-the-land ideas, etc. These companies and movements incarnate, always imperfectly, an integral ecology that creates linkages among the different institutions that provide a working alternative to businesses driven and formed only by profits and law.

Inaugurating a "Bold Cultural Revolution" through Prayer and Work

NICHOLAS RADEMACHER

During his historic address to a joint meeting of the US Congress in 2015, Pope Francis communicated some of the key themes from his then recent publication, *Laudato Si'*, in an idiom that his audience would understand. He invoked Abraham Lincoln, Martin Luther King Jr., Dorothy Day, and Thomas Merton. He chose these four figures because they modeled for their fellow citizens and the world creative ways to build a better future, to persevere through crises with dignity, and to see and interpret reality in new and creative ways.[1] Although Lincoln and King are well-known, the two Catholics on the list are less well-known by the general public. Francis's choice of Day (1897–1980), founder along with Peter Maurin in 1933 of the *Catholic Worker* newspaper, and Merton (1915–1968), a Trappist monk and prolific author, is especially apt given their contributions to the development of what Francis calls an "integrated approach" to the economy, human relationships, and the earth.

Francis encouraged US lawmakers and the people whom they represented to promote global solidarity and to provide hope to those "who are trapped in a cycle of poverty." He pointedly called for a new way of life. Citing *Laudato Si'*, he wrote, "Now is the time for courageous actions and strategies, aimed at implementing a 'culture of care' and 'an integrated approach to combating poverty, restoring dignity to the excluded, and at the same time protecting nature'."[2] Subsequently, he challenged the US

---

1. Pope Francis, visit to the joint session of the United States Congress, Address of the Holy Father, United States Capitol, Washington, DC, Thursday, 24 September 2015. https://w2.vatican.va/content/francesco/en/speeches/2015/september/documents/papa-francesco_20150924_usa-us-congress.html.

2. Ibid., citing Pope Francis, *Laudato Si': On Care for Our Common Home*, Vatican City: Libreria Editrice Vaticana, 2015, 231 and 139, respectively.

to "limit and direct" technology and power in directions that are "healthier, more human, more social, more integral."[3] Acknowledging that the people of the United States are doing some things well, Francis also called the nation to more.

By mentioning Day and Merton in this context, Francis pointed to a working alternative to what, in *Laudato Si'*, he calls the "technocratic paradigm" and "anthropocentrism" that dominate contemporary society.[4] With these terms, Francis signals concern about the dominance of technology and bureaucracy over human needs alongside the exploitation of planetary resources in short-sighted fixation on human beings at the expense of a wider ecological harmony. Francis's reference to Day and Merton is also apt given his reflection on the "correct understanding of work," as *ora et labora*, the combination of prayer and labor, that emerged in Christian monasticism. Experiencing work as "spiritually meaningful," he suggests, "makes us more protective and respectful of the environment; it imbues our relationship to the world with a healthy sobriety." This undertaking, Francis contends, counteracts the regnant technocratic paradigm and anthropocentrism.[5]

A distinctive lineage of social thought and practice undertaken by Day, Merton, and others who have engaged their legacy in the intervening decades comes into focus when read according to the vision that Francis presented in *Laudato Si'*. This tradition adopts and adapts the principles of Benedictine monasticism—that is, a form of monasticism shaped by St. Benedict of Nursia—with its emphasis on *ora et labora*, the combination of prayer and work, and in doing so offers a significant alternative to a cultural and political economic system that denigrates human dignity and imperils natural ecology by rupturing the divine-human relationship. Indeed, this tradition includes embracing personal and communal alternative lifestyle choices like reducing consumption, promoting sustainable agriculture, and integrating prayer and work.

In this essay, I will examine two historical moments that illustrate the development of this radical Catholic tradition of integrated economic

3. Ibid., citing ibid., 112.

4. See *Laudato Si'*, cited above, for Pope Francis on the "technocratic paradigm" and "anthropocentrism."

5. See *Laduato Si'*, 126.

and ecological consciousness in the United States. These moments unfolded in the context of the Catholic Worker movement, a lay-led network of Catholic activists, houses of hospitality, and communal farms that emerged from the efforts of Day and Peter Maurin beginning in the 1930s in New York. The *Catholic Worker* newspaper played host to two significant exchanges around questions of ecology and Catholic life. The first exchange, which unfolded during 1939 and 1940, witnesses to discussion within the Catholic Worker community about the centrality of the "back-to-the-land" movement. A second exchange, constituted by the writings on ecology by Merton nearly thirty years later, reveals the evolution in Catholic thinking about ecology and its relationship to spirituality and social responsibility. Finally, and by way of conclusion, I explore the ways these foundational exchanges provide the groundwork for contemporary communities of women religious and their lay collaborators, who are leading the way in attempts to manifest the ecological ideal articulated by previous generations. As Francis continues to provide global leadership in shaping an alternative ecological and economic paradigm, these Catholics in the United States have been shaping a working alternative of their own. This essay exposes a distinctive strain of Catholic social thought and practice in their work across the decades. Significantly, their alternative encompasses a different way of looking at and engaging in work. Although not uncontested, and far from perfect, their legacy points toward the type of foundational efforts that need to be undertaken perennially, including education, deliberate action, and spiritual growth.

Laudato Si': Care of Our Common Home

Francis's encyclical—or papal letter—provides an organizing framework for highlighting the fundamental continuity in theological and spiritual outlook offered by radical Catholics in the United States across the twentieth century. In *Laudato Si'*, Francis acknowledges the ambiguous inheritance of technology in its capacity to advance human civilization, retard its growth, or even destroy it. The negative capability of technology arises from what he calls a technocratic paradigm—which in turn sustains a technocratic culture—that instrumentalizes human rationality and objectifies the natural world for manipulation to self-serving ends. As theologians Neil Ormerod and Cristina Vanin helpfully clarify, "Such a culture shapes our thinking and imagination to such an extent that we begin to see our world as a giant machine, where people become interchangeable cogs within that machine."[6] The pope sees its dominance in economic and political life whereby it drives individuals to pursue power and profit without consideration of the negative impact that particular initiatives have on human beings and the earth.[7]

Francis recognizes that this paradigm is so pervasive that resistance is difficult, but, he insists, it is not futile. The pope introduces the term "integral ecology" to describe his vision of social justice. This term, theologian Donal Dorr explains, "refers to our responsibility for all aspects of our lives—political, social, economic, and cultural—and with particular reference to how our actions and whole way of life affects the Earth."[8] The pope calls for a "bold cultural revolution" that heralds this integral ecology, one that addresses the cultural, spiritual, and political-economic dimensions of modernity.

The revolution that the pope encourages will entail the adoption of "a distinctive way of looking at things, a way of thinking, politics, an education program, a lifestyle and a spirituality which together generate resistance to the assault of the technocratic paradigm."[9] The integral ecology that he proposes as an alternative to the prevailing technocratic paradigm entails the undertaking of work in rhythm with nature while simultaneously practicing contemplation with the purpose of enriching relationships between and among human beings and God.[10] As noted above, Francis cites the legacy of *ora et labora* in Benedictine monasticism, recalling that their "[p]ersonal growth and sanctification came to be sought in the interplay of recollection and work."[11] This combination leads to respect for and protection of the environment while, at the same time, moderating our relationship with the world. Although Francis is

6. Neil Ormerod and Cristina Vanin, "Ecological Conversion: What Does it Mean?," *Theological Studies* 77 no. 2 (2016): 342.

7. *Laudato Si'*, 109.

8. Donal Dorr, *Option for the Poor and for the Earth: From Leo XIII to Pope Francis* (Maryknoll, NY: Orbis, 2016).

9. *Laudato Si'*, 111.

10. Ibid., 119.

11. Ibid., 126.

not exhorting everyone to go back to the land or to become a monastic, he is encouraging new ways of seeing and relating to the world.

According to Francis's vision, education, personal and communal conversion, and individual and collective action will be necessary to effect the kind of change that he proposes. He challenges all people of good will to step back from "constant noise, internal and nerve-wracking distractions, [and] the cult of appearances" to "recover a serene harmony with creation, reflecting on our lifestyle and our ideals, and contemplating the Creator who lives among us and surrounds us, whose presence 'must not be contrived but found, uncovered'."[12] He encourages people on the individual level to reject compulsive consumerism by living more simply, composting, recycling, and reducing consumption.[13] Indeed, Francis lauds participation in direct political action as well as less formal individual and collective action that converges "to promote the common good and to defend the environment, whether natural or urban."[14] Ultimately, he calls Christians to a conversion brought about through meditation on and participation in the life of the Trinity through their union with Christ in the participation in the sacramental life of the church.

Francis chose well when he identified Dorothy Day and Thomas Merton as exemplars of an American tradition that promotes creative ways to build a better future, persevere through crises, and see and interpret reality in new and creative ways. Both Day and Merton are part of a longer tradition that has grappled with many of the very same questions concerning work, human dignity, technology, and the earth that the pope addresses in *Laudato Si'*. In their own way, participants in this alternative US Catholic tradition fostered an integral ecology founded on a distinctive spirituality. Day and Merton were not "mainstream" Catholics but individuals who engaged in more intensive practice of the Christian tradition. Nevertheless, Francis holds them up as exemplars, "great Americans," who, despite "the complexities of history and the reality of human weakness" built a better future and "shaped the fundamental values which will endure forever in the spirit of the American people."[15] These

12. Ibid, 225; citing his Apostolic Exhortation, *Evangelii Gaudium*, 24 November 2013, 71.

13. See *Laudato Si'*, chapter six, including 202, 206, and 211–12.

14. Ibid., 232.

15. Francis, visit to the joint session of the United States Congress.

hopeful words call out for both support and honest appraisal. If the values of Day and Merton are to endure, we must understand the contexts of their emergence, the controversy surrounding them, and the contemporary struggle to put their ideas into practice.

The Rise of Catholic Worker Agronomic Universities

The Catholic Worker movement was founded in 1933, in the midst of the Great Depression, by Peter Maurin and Dorothy Day. Their movement, whose aim they described in the inaugural issue of the *Catholic Worker* as "an attempt to popularize and make known the encyclicals of the popes and the program offered by the Church for constructing of a social order," which they intended to carry out in action centered on three areas: roundtable discussions for the clarification of thought; houses of hospitality to care for the materially poor; and agronomic universities, to return people to direct contact with the land. As Peter Maurin explained in one of his easy essays, he and other Catholic Worker leaders believed that the farming communes would "help the unemployed help themselves" and "make scholars out of workers" and "workers out of scholars."[16] The *Catholic Worker* emerged as an additional dimension of their work. In the pages of their paper, they shared developments in the movement, disseminated their views on politics, economics, culture, and the church. It was a national outlet for clarification of thought among interested readers.

The agronomic universities rose up quickly. In late 1935, Dorothy Day visited the site of one of the earliest Catholic Worker agronomic experiments. She wrote, "it is perfect—everything we could wish for a farming commune." By 1938, she recorded her positive assessment of their progress on the land: "The farm is progressing well. There is growth. There is every reason to be encouraged. All at the farm are unemployed workers, now busy building for their own and the Common Good." Although the early days on the farm were promising, the long-term reality proved to be far more challenging. In an entry dated August 17, 1940, Day lamented

---

16. Peter Maurin's "easy essays" were short, didactic free verse that frequently addressed a particular social problem to which he would offer a solution along the lines of the Catholic Worker vision.

that when she visited the farm "there are so many problems" and "so much unrest," that everyone expected her to resolve.[17] An early chronicler of the Catholic Worker movement, William D. Miller, quotes Dorothy Day's observation, "There were those whose love of the earth was more academic than real, who found that ideas flowed better while lying in the cool of the shade, rather than hoeing in the heat of the sun."[18]

The farming communes have been a source of debate ever since, especially given their varied fortunes over the years. Scholars who have evaluated the agronomic dimension of the Catholic Worker movement fall into two general camps. There are those like James Fisher who, in an oft-quoted line, describes the Catholic Worker farms as "virtually unmitigated disasters" or David Bovee who argues that the farms have been "too urban-oriented and too small (two to five people) to effect much transformation of society."[19] Differently, there are those like William Collinge and Paul Stock who positively assess the Catholic Worker agrarian vision by taking a long view of its implementation. They acknowledge the setbacks but emphasize its success both in its adaptation across time and its contemporary persistence. Both Collinge and Stock point to the number of Catholic Worker farms in operation today and make special note of the farms that have lasted for decades. Nevertheless, as Stock explains, "the Catholic Worker farm experiment in urban gardening, rural living, environmentalism, and a commitment to valuing life in all its forms" succeeds not by achieving "a point-in-time success" but by "pursuing a larger idea of what the world might look like." For the Catholic Worker, Stock succinctly states, "the process is the outcome."[20] Without muting the serious struggles of the Catholic Workers' farming idea, this essay sides with Stock in emphasizing the bigger picture. What matters is the underlying theological and spiritual legacy of this effort,

17. Robert Ellsberg, *The Duty of Delight: The Diaries of Dorothy Day* (New York: Orbis Press, 2008), 14, 27, 60.

18. William D. Miller, *A Harsh and Dreadful Love: Dorothy Day and the Catholic Worker Movement* (New York: Liveright, 1973).

19. See David S. Bovee, *Church and the Land: The National Catholic Rural Life Conference and American Society, 1923–2007* (Washington, DC: Catholic University of America Press, 2010), 114.

20. See Paul V. Stock, "The Perennial Nature of the Catholic Worker Farms: A Reconsideration of Failure," *Rural Sociology* 79, no. 2 (2014):167.

especially as it relates to earth, work, and culture, where seemingly divergent positions overlap on common ground.

Clarification of Thought Concerning Life on the Land

In 1939, Paul Hanly Furfey, professor of sociology at the Catholic University of America and longtime friend of the Catholic Worker movement, initiated a debate in the pages of that community's newspaper when he challenged their view on the agrarian question.[21] His letter, which appeared in October of that year, criticized a slogan that routinely appeared on the last page of the *Catholic Worker*, namely, "There is No Unemployment on the Land." He struck off a letter to the editor highlighting the contradiction that, in his view, appeared in a recent issue. He pointed out, "Only a few inches below these words in your September issue there is a story about thirteen hundred dispossessed sharecroppers wandering in desperation on the public highways. If they don't represent unemployment on the land, what on earth do they represent? Of course there is unemployment on the land! Everyone ought to know that by now. Indeed, everyone ought to realize that such unemployment is one of our major social problems." In bombastic rhetoric that he frequently deployed to generate debate on a given topic, Furfey accused the agrarians of "refusing to face the fact that every rural district is not necessarily a Utopia." He encouraged them to "get down to earth." He encouraged city people and agrarians to move past debate over the relative merits and demerits of their particular "habitats" in order to "frankly face the fact that we both have parallel problems" in order to open the way that they might "work sympathetically side by side."[22]

The editors of the *Catholic Worker* published Furfey's letter, calling his provocative missive a "controversy for the clarification of thought."[23] The editors invited their readership to participate in the controversy by

21. Bejamin T. Peters discusses the back-to-land debate from the perspective of John Hugo in his *Called to Be Saints: John Hugo, The Catholic Worker, and a Theology of Radical Christianity* (Milwaukee, WI: Marquette University Press, 2016), 171–74.

22. Paul Hanly Furfey, "Unemployment on the Land," *The Catholic Worker* (October 1939): 8.

23. The call for clarification of thought on the agrarian question appeared in *The Catholic Worker* (October 1939): 8. On Day's editorial control, see Nancy L. Roberts,

submitting letters. The response was so great that the editors had to admit that they could not publish all of the letters that they received. For their part, the editors denied that their view was utopian. They acknowledged the hardships that they and their fellow agrarians faced on the land, and reiterated their conviction that the land was an excellent place to fulfill their mission, "to rebuild within the shell of the old, a new society, wherein the dignity and freedom and responsibility of man is emphasized[24]

Among the respondents, John Hugo's letters were prominently featured in the ensuing debate. John Hugo was a priest of the diocese of Pittsburgh who taught sociology at Seton Hill College in Greensburg, Pennsylvania.[25] Ordained in 1936, Hugo had been interested in matters related to social justice from an early age through his study of Pope Leo XIII's *Rerum Novarum* (1891) and Pope Pius XI's *Quadragesimo Anno* (1931).[26] He was radicalized through contact with the controversial Jesuit retreat master Onésimus Lacouture who, as Jack Downey explains, was instrumental in "transfiguring him [Hugo] from a conventional, socially minded liberal into a Catholic barnstormer."[27] Upon his transformation, Benjamin Peters exlains, Hugo strove "to be a part of the American Catholic intellectual discourse of the time and was not afraid to challenge more established scholars."[28] Subsequently, he began to publicly challenge those whom he judged to be conventional and socially minded liberal Catholics to take their spiritual and public life more seriously.[29] His strident rhetoric led him to become a controversial figure within academic circles in the mid-twentieth century.

Although few people who read Furfey's most popular writings in the 1930s would mistake him as a proponent of conventional Christianity,

Dorothy Day and the Catholic Worker (Albany, NY: State University of New York, 1984), 83, 98.

24. Ibid.

25. For a detailed discussion of John Hugo's life and his relationship with the Catholic Worker, see Peters, *Called to Be Saints*. Jack Downey also studies the link between Hugo, Dorothy Day, and the Catholic Worker in his *The Bread of the Strong*: Lacouturisme *and the Folly of the Cross, 1910–1985* (New York: Fordham University Press, 2015).

26. See Downey, *Bread of the Strong*, 142.

27. Ibid., 143.

28. See Peters, *Called to Be Saints*, 173

29. Ibid.

Hugo viewed Furfey's position on Catholic Worker agrarianism as a capitulation to a corrupt economic system. He wrote that Furfey's letter was evidence that industrialization and urbanization had led even some of those people who were friendly to the Catholic Worker movement to "become habituated to economic servitude" and to "[lose] sight of the dignity of human liberty and the human person."[30] Hugo here called into question Furfey's credentials as a radical Catholic, which was quite a claim given how widely respected Furfey was in the community for his early and passionate support of the Catholic Worker movement. For him, Furfey's calling into question the primacy of the land was evidence that living and working in an urban context weakened one's radical commitments.

Furfey answered the editors by proclaiming his allegiance to the fundamental tenets of what he called "sane agrarianism," a position held by what he called "realist agrarians" like himself who took seriously sociological data that revealed what life on the land was really like. He derided "romantic agrarians" for whom, he wrote, the farm was a fetish. He urged romantic agrarians to compare ideal farm life with ideal city life or the reality of farm life with the reality of city life. In both contexts, he explained, there were people who suffered a lack of freedom, toiled in undignified working conditions, and lived in wretched circumstances. Likewise, in both contexts, there were people who found dignity in their freely chosen work and were able to develop intellectually, emotionally, and spiritually.[31]

To balance the view of city work and city life presented by the romantic agrarians, he noted urban dwellers who prospered in meaningful work, including people in the professions (such as clergymen, medical professionals, teachers, and engineers), small, independent business people (grocers, druggists, real estate salespeople), civil servants, and even laborers in the construction industry, especially carpenters who live according to "our Lord's own trade." He argued, too, that holiness can be achieved in the city. He cited the work of his students, Mary Elizabeth Walsh and Sister Christina Schwartz, alongside the German Jesuit

---

30. John Hugo, "Capitalism Impractical," *The Catholic Worker* (November 1939): 8.
31. Furfey, *The Catholic Worker* (December 1939), 7-8.

scholar Constantine Kempf, to demonstrate that the overwhelming majority of saints and beati of the nineteenth and early twentieth centuries lived in cities. He acknowledged his own surprise at the one-sidedness of the results, but he then enumerated the spiritual advantages of the city life with its numerous parishes, Catholic schools from elementary through college, and a multitude of opportunities for cultivating personal piety.[32] In other words, all was not lost in the urban context.

The editors gave Hugo the final response in the January 1940 issue of the *Catholic Worker*. His article took up the entire "page eight," that is, every inch dedicated to "The Land." Hugo said that Furfey had a fetish in his focus on the facts and his insistence on being practical. He was willing to concede that agrarians needed the support of their urban counterparts and of politicians who understood their goals in order to promote the kind of broader social change that agrarians sought, but he dismissed Furfey's positive appraisal of city life by arguing that it did not fit the contemporary reality "of the squalid industrial towns and inhuman megalopolis of the capitalistic era." Indeed, Hugo believed that Furfey's approach—the pursuit of sanctity in the city—was a compromise that merely slowed, and perhaps even offered piecemeal reform, but ultimately would do nothing to halt the inexorable envelopment of modern society in the collectivist state.[33]

Hugo was concerned about the state taking on roles that did not belong to it. As Pius XI explained in *Quadragesimo Anno* (1931), "It is an injustice and at the same time a grave evil and disturbance of right order to assign to a greater and higher association what lesser and subordinate organizations can do."[34] Hugo held that "romantic agrarians" were both realistic and practical but in the best possible way. They were realistic because they recognized what they perceived to be the growing threat of a collectivist state, and were eminently practical because their practice of subsistence farming was a direct response to the state's encroachment.[35] Agrarians, in other words, were taking the first practical step to turn the

32. Ibid, 8.
33. Hugo, "In Defense of Romantic Agrarians," *The Catholic Worker* (January 1940): 8.
34. Pope Pius XI, *Quadregesimo Anno*, 79.
35. Hugo, "In Defense," 8.

tide of the collectivist state they sought by living as if the world that they hoped for, where human liberty and human dignty were respected and protected, was already present.[36]

Although Furfey did not have a chance to reply, it is worth noting that by the end of the year the editors had removed the offending quote, "There is No Unemployment on the Land." The section on the land, in general, did not fare well in the ensuing years. The Catholic Worker continued to address the issue of the land over time but the topic did not receive the consistent attention other matters would, including urban poverty, racism, and war.

Finding Common Ground

In certain respects, the parties involved in this debate were in closer agreement than their rhetoric in this debate suggests. Disagreement seems to have fallen on the relative merits of city life. Hugo and the editors seemed pessimistic about urban life whereas Furfey attempted to split the difference and acknowledge the strengths and liabilities of each. Hugo and Furfey both recognized that the fundamental problem was moral and spiritual. They both sought the transformation of society through direct action. They both acknowledged that cooperation between urban and rural dwellers was necessary to effect lasting social change. An additional underlying area of common ground was the pride of place given to contemplation and the attendant necessity for personal transformation as a necessary condition for social transformation. Francis easily could have cited this debate as a distinctive strain of resistance to the technocratic paradigm and anthropocentrism that he assails in *Laudato Si'* and to which he referred in his address to the US Congress in September of 2015.

The Catholic Worker community encouraged the integration of prayer and work as a pathway to ongoing personal conversion. In doing so, they leveled a searing critique of contemporary society. For Peter Maurin, as biographer Marc Ellis explains, "a society fulfilling an inner dynamic based on profit and materialism could lead only to its own consumption

---

36. Ibid.

and ultimate destruction, for the religious and community values that helped to shape tradition and the history of peoples were being split asunder by the pursuit of the material."[37] Maurin urged social reform based on philosophy (Aristotle) and theology (Aquinas) rather than the social sciences to address the person's relationship with God.

To identify the underlying problem, Maurin adopted Nicholas Berdyaev's critique of the "bourgeois mind." As Ellis explains, bourgeois here referred "not to a social, economic, or ethical condition but rather a spiritual state and a direction of the soul." Ellis continues, "In essence the bourgeois spirit was a pursuit of the material aspects of life and an endless search for the expedient and the useful. The bourgeois was an 'idolator' of this world."[38] In Maurin's vision, the Eucharist was at the center of social reform. As the greatest sacrifice, it served as a model for all Christians to shift the emphasis of their interactions from getting to giving. According to Maurin, the early Christians had successfully implemented such a plan by engaging in personal action "and eventually contributed to social reform through the daily practice of the seven corporal and seven spiritual works of mercy."[39] Likewise, later monastic communities that combined farming, craftsmanship, and prayer were to be emulated.

Communal farms, as adaptations of the Christian monastic tradition, were a way out of this idolatry. As historian William Collinge explains, "At the heart of Maurin's thought was a religious critique of the capitalist and industrialist social order, and farming communes were his alternative to that order."[40] Collinge explains that Maurin saw farms as solutions to social problems in a range of areas, including labor, work, community, education, and agriculture.[41] Further, Jeffrey Marlett says that the Catholic Worker "farm communes embodied the belief that

37. Marc Ellis, *Peter Maurin: Prophet of the Twentieth Century* (New York: Paulist Press, 1981), 56–57.

38. Ibid., 87.

39. Ibid., 62.

40. William J. Collinge, "Peter Maurin's Ideal of Farming Communes," in *Dorothy Day and the Catholic Worker Movement: Centenary Essays*, ed. William J. Thorn, Phillip M. Runkel, and Susan Mountin (Milwaukee, WI: Marquette University Press, 2001), 386.

41. Collinge addresses each of these topics in turn as subheads through the rest of his article.

farming God's creation was a more preferable alternative to modern living in the over-crowded and spiritually-bereft city."[42] Theologically, Marlett continues, they believed that "subsistence farming in community was a precursor to the heavenly kingdom. The more people participating in this only brought that next world closer."[43]

Like Maurin, Dorothy Day was deeply influenced by Benedictine monasticism, particularly the precept to join together work and prayer. They both admired the monastic vocation and attempted to replicate it in their lay movement. Mark and Louise Zwick note the agronomic dimension of the Benedictine model in their discussion of the intellectual and spiritual origins of the Catholic Worker movement, "The monks were farmers and, in addition to their witness to the gospel for the world and the model of hospitality, provided an alternative economic model in the local community."[44] These farming communes, then, served (and continue to serve) as witnesses against corporate and government models that sacrifice human relationships and personal participation in work in favor of scale.

In spite of his seemingly vitriolic rhetoric, Furfey was a friend of the Catholic Worker movement. He was sympathetic with their programs. In his 1936 book, *Fire on the Earth*, he advocated "Catholic village communities" to promote a human-scale economy, one that favored local production, including "raising their own food on their own land," over mass production of goods. He cited the Catholic Worker as a contemporary group then planning such an endeavor.[45] To be sure, Furfey was most impressed with the urban ministry of the Catholic Worker movement and he did not agree with their unwavering commitment to turning to the land. Furfey argued that sanctification was possible in urban or rural contexts without discrimination; neither context was more or less favorable to leading a holy life than the other.

42. Jeffrey D. Marlett, "Down on the Farm and Up to Heaven: Catholic Worker Farm Communes and the Spiritual Virtues of Farming," in *Dorothy Day and the Catholic Worker Movement* , 407.

43. Ibid., 412.

44. Mark and Louise Zwick, *The Catholic Worker Movement: Intellectual and Spiritual Origins* (Mahwah, NJ: Paulist Press, 2005), 54.

45. Paul Hanly Furfey, *Fire on the Earth* (New York: Macmillan, 1936), 125–27.

Yet Furfey joined with Day, Maurin, and Hugo in condemning the materialism of modern society. Furfey focused on what he called the positivistic thrust of materialism. The positivistic society, he argued, was fundemantally flawed because its end was the "success-ideal," one "which preaches decency and respectability but . . . ultimately seeks what is obviously pleasant for self, such things as comfort, security and respectability." He admitted certain advantages of the present order, however limited, insofar as it promoted some benefits for the common good such as "popular education, political democracy, and organized philanthropy."[46]

In contrast to the positivistic society, he favored a society based on contemplation and religious commitment, which is to say a noetic society, one based on deep insight into human interconnectedness on the basis of divine love. More pragmatically, given the challenges of sustaining the noetic insight, he prescribed what he called a pistic, or faith-centered, society wherein a person believed in and acted on God's love even when believing seemed impossible. Contemplation would lead to contempt for the things that this world values, turning away from "honor, riches, power, sense pleasure, to embrace a life of voluntary poverty, not because the things of this world are evil in themselves, but because they are at best only trifles when compared to the really important values of the supernatural order and because they may become actually evil if they distract man from the pursuit of his true end."[47] Its members thus transformed would direct their work to fashion a society founded on cooperation and economic, racial, and national equality would emerge.

Furfey employed scholastic theories of cognition to explain his position. Contemplation upon the mysteries of faith, aided by the sacramental life of the church, especially the Eucharist, he explained, would conform one to the thing contemplated.[48] In this case, one would be conformed to God who is love. Consequently, the person contemplating would love the divine wherever it is found, including in one's neighbor,

---

46. Furfey, *Three Theories of Society* (New York: Macmillan, 1937), 34. See Nicholas Rademacher, *Paul Hanly Furfey: Priest, Prophet, Scientist* (New York: Fordham University Press, 2017) for further discussion of Furfey's social critique. Some of the material in this section is drawn directly from that book.

47. Furfey, *Three Theories*, 188–89.

48. Ibid, 200.

even one's enemies, real or perceived. This love, or charity, would become the foundation for a renewed society. In short, Furfey's and the Catholic Worker's critique of the materialism of contemporary society could be read today as corresponding to Francis's critique of the technocractic paradigm; similarly, their emphasis on contemplation, that is, prayer, joined with work, could be read as corresponding to Francis's emphasis on *ora et labora*, as well.

In this exchange for the clarification of thought, explicit discussion of what today is referred to as "ecology" was not yet a significant concern among Catholic radicals or the general US population, for that matter. The emphasis in the debate among these Catholics fell to human dignity and personal sanctification through work in urban and rural settings with respect to potential social transformation. Two decades later, Thomas Merton would bring to the fore the ecological question as he learned of the growing evidence of the toll that certain human behavior was taking on the earth. Although Merton did not directly engage the 1939–1940 exchange between Day, Hugo, and Furfey, he charted a course that led between their positions. He acknowledged that city life is here to stay, but he also addressed in a more direct and immediate way the ecological concerns nascent in the agronomic movement of prior decades. Like them, he identified spiritual illness as the root cause.

A Deepening in the Clarification of Thought about Life on the Land

Clarification of thought on this topic did not end when the editors of the *Catholic Worker* moved away from this specific debate in their newspaper. The question of the land would resurface from time to time. Thomas Merton was one figure who picked up the question in his wide-ranging writings. Merton, like Day, as a convert to Christianity, was initiated into the Roman Catholic Church after a long period of searching. He continued to grow in his Christian vocation, eventually becoming a Trappist monk, a member of the Order of Cistercians of the Strict Observance, at the Abbey of Ghetsemani in rural Kentucky. Though cloistered, his social consciousness continued to expand through prayer, meditation, and increasingly frequent correspondence with friends and colleauges outside the monastery walls. As a result of his famous experience at the corner of Fourth and Walnut in downtown Louisville, Merton came to a deep realization of the interconnectedness of all people: "They were mine and I theirs, that we could not be alien to one another even though we were total strangers."[49] This profound sense of solidarity impacted his writing on the peace movement, the civil rights movement, and, among other contemporary concerns, the emerging ecological movement.

Several decades after the back-to-the-land exchange, in his 1968 article, "The Wild Places," Thomas Merton introduced a fresh perspective on the question. His ecological consciousness had been developing across his lifetime[50] and this article represents what scholar Patrick O'Connell characterizes as "the most extensive presentation of Merton's developing ecological awareness in the final years of his life, otherwise evident mainly in journal entries and correspondence."[51] The June 1968 *Catholic Worker* edition of "The Wild Places," explains O'Connell, includes the definitive, full-text version of Merton's thought on ecology.

Although he did not directly address the decades-old debate about the back-to-the-land movement among *Catholic Worker* readers, and likely was unaware of it, Merton's essay represents a deepening understanding of and engagement with US radical Catholics' relationship to work, the economy, politics, and the land in light of the spiritual life. Merton's

49. As biographer Michael Mott explains, Merton's experience there "has been given wide importance, both as an epiphany and as the turning point in Merton's life, the movement when he became open again to the world he had rejected in 1941." See Mott's *The Seven Stories of Thomas Merton* (Boston: Houghton Mifflin, 1984), 311–13. For the famous passage in question, see Thomas Merton, *Conjectures of a Guilty Bystander* (New York: Image Books, 2009), 153.

50. Patrick O'Connell traces Merton's ecological consciousness back to Merton's 1938 conversion to Roman Catholicism and his 1949 *Seeds of Contemplation*. Other scholars find even earlier roots, identifying sources for Merton's ecology in his childhood, under the care of his parents. For the former, see Patrick O'Connell, "The Traditional Sources of Thomas Merton's Environmental Spirituality" in *Spiritual Life* (Fall 2010), 154–71; and 155–56. For the deeper roots of Merton's ecological vision, see Kathleen Deignan, "'Love for the Paradise Mystery': Thomas Merton: Contemplative Ecologist," *CrossCurrents* (December 2008): 545–69; Monica Weis, "Kindred Spirits in Revelation and Revolution: Rachel Carson and Thomas Merton," *Merton Annual* 19 (2006): 128–41; Monica Weis *The Environmental Vision of Thomas Merton* (Louisville: University of Kentucky Press, 2011).

51. See Patrick O'Connell's introduction to Thomas Merton's *The Wild Places* in *The Merton Annual* 24 (2011): 15.

focus was not on the relative superiority of the farm over the city or the opposite, though his writing reflects at least some ambivalence on the relative merits of city life compared with rural life. In "The Wild Places," he conceded that "we are firmly established as an urban culture" and emphasized that mass urbanization presented "the problem of ecology ... in a most acute form." This fact, however, moved Merton not to deeper analysis of urban life, but to a broader interpretive frame: the person's self-understanding within the created world at large. Here, he pulled through the foundational emphasis on contemplation and direct action for the common good that guided Day's, Maurin's, Hugo's, and Furfey's contributions to the back-to-the-land debate. Merton channeled this shared emphasis in an additional direction now, namely, toward the ecological crisis that he recognized had to be confronted by personal transformation, both individually, through contemplation, and socially, through direct action.

Merton appropriated the "Greek patristic concept of 'natural contemplation,'" which Patrick O'Connell, quoting Merton, describes as "'a positive recognition of God as He is manifested in the essences (*logoi*) of all things, ... a kind of intuitive perception of God as He is reflected in His Creation."[52] Such an encounter with God would assist those who participated in natural contemplation to overcome their exploitation of the natural world. For Merton, natural contemplation so understood would lead to care for the natural world, "a participation in the creative and redemptive work of Christ." O'Connell explains: "Conversely, the absence of this contemplative perception of the material world, a purely instrumental attitude toward nature, Merton declares, leads in practice to a degradation of creation through an 'impersonal, pragmatic, quantitative, *exploitation and manipulation* of things, ... a demonic cult of change, and 'exchange'—consumption, production, destruction, for their own sakes' (ICM 130)."[53] This contemplative practice leads to a contemplative awareness that leads in turn to a radical transformation of the individual, or as O'Connell describes it, "a rediscovery of authentic personal identity as

---

52. O'Connell, "Traditional Sources," 160.

53. Ibid., 164–65. Emphasis in original. ICM refers to Thomas Merton, *An Introduction to Christian Mysticism: Initiation into the Monastic Tradition*, vol. 3, ed. Patrick F. O'Connell (Kalamazoo, MI: Cistercian Publications, 2008), 122.

reflecting and participating in the divine likeness and of human activity as a way of sharing in the divine creativity."[54] The Christian vocation comes to the fore through contemplation of God's presence in nature.

Monica Weis, a scholar in the area of Christian spirituality, amplifies the contemplative dimension of Merton's conviction that the Christian vocation is "'to be in this cosmic creation, so to speak, as the eye in the body,' a vocation to defend and preserve the 'delicate balance' in nature." Merton, Weis continues, held that "'man has lost his 'sight' and is blundering around in the midst of the wonderful works of God.'"[55] Merton challenged Christians to take and maintain a "'cosmic perspective'—a broad vision that sees all creation as relationship, and human dignity springing from a true sense of our shared creaturehood." Weis places Merton's burgeoning awareness of ecological responsibility alongside his writing on other social justice topics, "racism, the rights of indigenous people, the dangers of atomic energy and technology, as well as the moral imperative for making peace through nonviolent means."[56] Weis's analysis also stresses the link between prayer, in the form of contemplation, and work, in the form of action for social justice, while expanding that vision to include the cosmic perspective.

Thomas Merton's experience, recounted in his writings, reveals that the discipline of natural contemplation and the interior transformation of values from exploitation to cultivation are not easy. Kathleen Deignen points to Merton's Benedictine commitments, including the combination of work and prayer (*ora et labora*), that would lead to a conversion of habits (*conversatio morem*), such as "simplicity, frugality, fairness in distribution of resources, mindfulness in our habits of living."[57] In other words, to overcome the intransigence of distorted values, attitudes, and behaviors, Christians must adopt both a contemplative disposition—*ora*—with respect to nature, to see God reflected in nature, and adopt practices that will gradually transform their way of being in the world

---

54. Ibid., 163.

55. Weis, "Kindred Spirits," 132; citing Thomas Merton's letter to Rachel Carson, 12 January 1963, which appears in *Witness to Freedom: Letters in Times of Crisis*, ed. William H. Shannon (New York: Farrar, Straus & Giroux, 1994), 70–71.

56. Ibid., 133.

57. Kathleen Deignan, "'Love for the Paradise Mystery,'" 558–59.

from passive participation in the technocratic paradigm to one of resistance to it through the pursuit of social justice—*labora*—in God's love.

Carrying Forward a Legacy of the Agrarian Debate

In the late twentieth century and into the present, numerous communities of women religious and their lay collaborators carry on this tradition of adopting and adapting the Benedictine emphasis on *ora et labora*, prayer and work, through their creation of working alternatives. Like the members of the Catholic Worker movement and the example established by Thomas Merton, many communities of women religious are pursuing alternative lifestyle options, both personal and communal, by reducing consumption, promoting sustainable agriculture, and integrating prayer and work. For these women religious, the question of the relative merits of urban or rural life has faded while the core principles articulated through this tradition have remained to the fore.

Ethnographer Sarah McFarland Taylor identifies these women religious as "green sisters," women who "have faithfully and steadfastly taken up the mission to heal and restore the life systems of the planet."[58] Taylor traces the genealogy of their work in part to the Catholic back-to-the-land movement, Dorothy Day, Peter Maurin, and their Catholic Worker movement, and the spiritual and social thought of Thomas Merton.[59] These sisters share many characteristics with their earlier Catholic coreligionists in the United States who have carried this tradition forward across many decades, including a Benedictine spirituality that joins prayer and work, a spirituality that seeks to overcome the technocratic paradigm and anthropocentrism of contemporary society, and concrete forms of resistance from simple living to the development of alternative economic models that are sensitive to human and ecological impact.

Taylor writes that these women religious are "reinhabiting," or "relearning how to live in place," which "has to do with 'staying where you are, repairing the damage and devising new ways of being.'"[60] Some

58. Sarah McFarland Taylor, *Green Sisters: A Spiritual Ecology* (Cambridge, MA: Harvard University Press, 2009), 1.

59. Ibid., among other places, see 9, 31, 36–38.

60. Sarah McFarland Taylor, "Reinhabiting Religion: Green Sisters, Ecological Renewal, and the Biogeography of Religious Landscape," *Worldviews* (December 2002):

of the green sisters have done so by founding farming communes or monasteries while others have stayed within their urban context to repair and heal the earth and to repair and heal fractured communities. They practice voluntary poverty and simple living as spiritual practice in resistance to the consumerism and freneticism that characterizes contemporary US society.[61] Francis would be inspired by the ways in which these women religious have reimagined their vows and transformed their lives in light of the signs of the times: "From diet and dress to modes of shelter, to the use of nontoxic cleaning products, low-impact composting toilets, energy-efficient light bulbs, and other conservation measures, 'green habits'—ecologically sustainable practices and mindful consumption of resources—have become part and parcel of green sisters' vowed life."[62] These sisters are also "standing their ground," as Taylor characterizes their "insider" and "outsider" activism. For example, some sisters promote corporate responsibility through savvy investment practices whereas other sisters practice civil disobedience.[63] A holistic spirituality, rooted in Benedictine monasticism, among other elements of the Christian tradition, is the foundation of this transformation. Prayer and work are expressions one of another.[64]

In the ambit of my own experience, I have been inspired and informed by the ministries of the Religious of the Assumption who join contemplation with action for social justice through community building and respect for ecology.[65] Sister Catherine Soley and her fellow sisters, Reli-

---

230. Taylor revisits the meaning and significance of her use of the term "reinhabiting" in the preface to her book, *Green Sisters*, xviii–xix. She expands on the term in chapter two, 61–63, and elsewhere.

61. Taylor, *Green Sisters*, 72.

62. Ibid., 95–96.

63. See Taylor, chapter two, "Standing their Ground: From Pioneering Nuns to Bioneering," *Green Sisters*.

64. Ibid., 101. On the influence of desert spirituality, see 120.

65. St. Marie Eugénie Milleret founded the Religious of the Assumption in Paris in 1839. The congregation has spread across the globe. The Sisters of the Assumption in the United States are committed to prayer, life in community, and social justice. They are committed to faith formation, ministry to migrants, youth and young adult ministry, parish ministry and pastoral care, and care of creation, among other areas. For additional background on the Religious of the Assumption in the United States, see their website: http://assumptionsisters.org/.

gious of the Assumption, join contemplation with action for social justice through numerous ministries, including the urban garden that they sponsor in Worcester, Massachusetts. With her community, Sister Catherine prays five times a day, including liturgy and Eucharistic adoration. She explains the impact of the rhythm of silence, communal prayer, and work: "As contemplatives, we have a much needed and especially apt perspective. Our sensibilities are formed by time spent looking deeply and listening intently. In quieting our own thoughts and inner voices, we allow the silence to open within us. In turning that contemplative gaze to creation, we recognize the hand of the Creator."[66] This spirituality enables her and her sisters to find God in all things; prayer and work become inseparable. The community garden is a significant prayer space for Sister Catherine and the community. The gardening season is punctuated with liturgy and opportunities for private prayer. Sister Catherine explains, "There is a deep difference when I am in the garden; especially when I am alone. No machinery, no T.V., no traffic. The garden is silent; yet, it isn't. Insects, rain, wind enhance but do not break the silence. In the garden, I find solitude; and yet, I am not alone . . . In touching the sacredness of the soil, I touch a deep peace." Work, prayer, and social justice are bound together in this lifestyle.

This ministry is communal. The garden, called Semillas da Vida (Seeds of Life), was founded by an Associate Missionary of the Assumption and her English as a Second Language students in Worcester.[67] Through composting and gardening, the community participates in the healing of the earth. The community that gathers to garden is diverse: young and old, male and female, rich and poor, from all over the planet: Mexico, El Salvador, the Philippines, Burkina Faso, Algeria, France,

66. Unpublished written reflection of Sr. Catherine on her ministry in the garden. Shared with the author and used with permission.

67. The Assumption Sisters founded the Associate Missionaries of the Assumption (AMA) in 1954. The AMA mission statement explains that young adults serve as AMAs "in collaboration with the Religious of the Assumption in their mission to effect change in society through prayer, education and community building. With the Assumption spirit, the AMA volunteers bear witness to Jesus' love and the Church's love for the people. The relationships that they cultivate transform them as well as the people they serve. They exercise their commitment to service in solidarity and communion, in faith and in trust." See their website, http://www.assumptionvolunteers.org/index.html.

Lithuania, and Fiji, as well as different areas of the United States. As Michelle Sherman, a past director of the Associate Missionaries of the Assumption, explains, the diversity reflects nationality, language, and class. Through community garden, these diverse peoples find unity.[68]

This community garden, although significantly smaller in scale than kindred projects, is part of the broader movement of green sisters. Like her counterparts in other religious congregations and institutes of women religious, this sister and her colleagues are "reinhabiting" their corner of the world, "repairing the damage and devising new ways of being."[69] The Religious of the Assumption and their extended community have remained within their urban context to repair and heal the earth and also to repair and heal fractured communities. Everyone who works in the garden takes home the fruit of the garden, no matter how much or how little one works. They are developing new productive and consumptive practices that resist the pull of capitalist materialism and its ethos. The garden is a model of the kingdom of God evoked by Jesus in his many parables related to vineyards. Aptly, the garden is on a street named Vineyard.

Conclusion: Inaugurating a Cultural Revolution

This urban gardening program and others like it across the United States, extensions of a decades-long movement among radical Catholics in the United States, represent what Stock calls, as noted above, "a politics of possibility related to the dramatic challenges not only of society but also of the environment."[70] They herald Francis's call for a bold cultural revolution that would usher in an integral ecology that takes seriously the link between human dignity, contemplative spirituality, and sustainable political-economic practices. Their work heralds a new "working alternative." The initiatives observed in this essay, and many others not

68. See "Semillas de Vida Community Garden, Assumption Center, 2016," a video by Marie Therese Kane, Mattie Carroll, Tesa Danusantoso, and Xiomara Tenorio, students at the College of the Holy Cross. The video is available on the Religious of the Assumption ("Assumption Sisters") channel on YouTube.

69. Taylor, "Reinhabiting Religion," 230.

70. See footnote 20 above, Stock, "The Perennial Nature of the Catholic Worker Farms," 143.

mentioned, demonstrate the variety and fluidity of these movements. There are urban and rural models. There are models that favor separation from the city to cultivate land on small-scale farms and monasteries, and others that undertake modest gardens in urban contexts. Personal lifestyle choices around consumption and the adoption of a simple lifestyle vary according to context and ability. Social action can include boycotts, lobbying, socially conscious investing, and mindful voting. Taken individually, these initiatives may not seem like much but, as Francis insists, taken together, they can have an impact.[71]

Although there is great variety among the movements that make up this cultural revolution, contemplative spirituality is a common thread that links them all. They agree that, fundamentally, the human race is facing a spiritual crisis that threatens our own and the entire planet's existence. The implementation of the kind of change outlined by the three movements outlined here and in Francis's *Laudato Si'* requires conversion along the lines delineated by theologian Bernard Lonergan, namely, intellectual, moral, and religious.[72] It requires an intellectual conversion according to which, individually and collectively, people become cognizant of the ways in which individual lifestyle choices and the regnant political-economic system contributes to dehumanization and the degradation of the natural ecology. It requires a moral conversion according to which, individually and collectively, people shift their consumption patterns and lifestyle choices from the pursuit of satisfaction to value. It also requires a religious conversion according to which individuals enter into a more intimate relationship with God through contemplation.

For Francis and the tradition of US Catholic social thought and practice described here, contemplative practices undertaken in conjunction with work can provide healing and restore right relationship between

71. Pope Francis cautions against dismissing even simple initiatives for social change: "We must not think that these efforts are not going to change the world." See *Laudato Si'*, 212.

72. For a discussion of these types of conversion, see Bernard Lonergan's *Method in Theology* (London: Dartmon, Longman, and Todd, 1972). See also Neil Ormerod and Cristina Vanin's "Ecological Conversion: What Does it Mean?," in which they define the term "ecological conversion" within the framework of Lonergan's work on conversion and Robert Doran's work on psychic conversion.

human beings and the natural world. As Thomas Merton succinctly explains, "Work in a normal, healthy human context, work with a sane and moderate human measure, integrated in a productive social milieu is by itself capable of contributing much to the spiritual life."[73] According to the tradition outlined here, *ora et labora*, the integration of prayer and work as an essential component of everyday life, emerges as a fundamental condition to initiating and sustaining the kind of social change necessary to save human civilization and even the world.

---

73. Thomas Merton, *Life and Holiness* (New York: Herder & Herder, 1963), 9.

Generative Businesses Fostering Vitality

Rethinking Businesses' Relationship to the World

SANDRA WADDOCK

Generative Business?

How can capitalism change? Like any other system, capitalism is subject to any number of dynamic forces that create constant change—and a constant reinvention through "creative destruction."[1] Though it sometimes appears that today's capitalism, based in neoliberalism and neoclassical economics, is immutable, in fact it is changing constantly. Capitalism, like any other living system, responds to both internal and external pressures, evolving with those pressures. Many today are calling for a complete reform of capitalism to meet the imperatives of a warming world fraught with inequality, violations of human dignity, excessive materialism and consumption, and an overemphasis on financial wealth and growth as measures of success.

This essay offers an approach to thinking about business in the context of economies, which themselves live in societal and, ultimately, planetary contexts. What I will call generative business allows businesses to fulfill their important, indeed vital, roles of meeting needs efficiently by seeking not profitability but vitality in all of their endeavors and practices. In a context in which, as many observers have noted, the current system is unsustainable ecologically, change is inevitable. It could come about because of the constant evolution posted by creative destruction.[2] It could happen because current dynamics push the system beyond ecological or

1. J. A. Schumpeter, *Capitalism, Socialism and Democracy* (New York: Harper & Row, 1962).
2. Ibid.

inequity limits,[3] causing collapse or, minimally, a great disruption.[4] Alternatively, a shift could happen because enough forces interested in creating a more equitable, flourishing world in which there is well-being and dignity for all gather collective energy to enforce change.[5]

A framework for generative business takes into account the constraints that issues of climate change, sustainability, growing inequality, and a global jobs crisis, among other systemic problems, pose. Generative business is a necessary concomitant to what Fullerton calls a regenerative capitalism and is part of a necessary transition toward a sustainable enterprise economy.[6] Generative businesses would focus on goals of vitality at multiple levels, with operations based on principles of renewal, restoration, and resilience.

Such a framework could potentially provide a sustainable basis on which businesses—and humanity itself—could thrive long-term. Although much more could be said about sustainability, inequality, production systems, materialism, consumerism, terrorism, and related issues associated with the dynamics of the current system, others have covered these bases at length.[7] This essay turns instead to preliminary considerations of what a generative business system might look like and how it might enable businesses to continue to be successful in the context of ever-increasing ecological constraints.

As Diamond's work demonstrates, many of the problems human civilizations are facing can be laid directly at the feet of humans themselves—particularly in population growth and use—some might say abuse—of

3. See J. Diamond, *Collapse: How Societies Choose to Fail or Succeed*, rev. ed. (New York: Penguin, 2005).

4. P. Gilding, *The Great Disruption: How the Climate Crisis Will Transform the Global Economy* (London: Bloomsbury Publishing, 2011).

5. See Humanistic Management Network, www.humanetwork.org, for one initiative.

6. John Fullerton, *Regenerative Capitalism: How Universal Principles and Patterns Will Shape Our New Economy* (Greenwich, CT: Capital Institute: 2015), http://capitalinstitute .org/wp-content/uploads/2015/04/2015-Regenerative-Capitalism-4-20-15-final.pdf; S. Waddock and M. McIntosh, *SEE Change: Making the Transition to a Sustainable Enterprise Economy* (Sheffield, UK: Greenleaf, 2011); Gilding, *The Great Disruption*; T. Jackson, *Prosperity Without Growth: Economics for a Finite Planet* (Abington, UK: Routledge, 2011).

7. For example, J. Ehrenfeld and A. Hoffman, *Flourishing: A Frank Conversation about Sustainability* (Palo Alto, CA: Stanford University Press, 2013); Gilding, *The Great Disruption*; T. Jackson, *Prosperity Without Growth*.

planetary resources by today's economic and business systems.[8] This essay, in a sense, takes up where John Fullerton in *Regenerative Capitalism* leaves off. Fullerton sought "universal principles and patterns of systemic health and development," and articulated eight core principles that could create a regenerative capitalist system. Drawing from principles of nature, Fullerton develops eight key, interconnected principles that underlie systemic health.[9]

Fullerton's first principle is being "in right relationship," recognizing that humans are part of, not separate from, the complexly connected natural environment;[10] His second principle "views wealth holistically," as to what creates overall well-being and integrates multiple different forms of capital, such as social, intellectual, physical, natural, not just financial capital. Thirdly, regenerative capitalism is also innovative, adaptive, and responsive, just as natural systems are when they have resilience and diversity, and are balanced and in harmony with each other. Regenerative capitalism also develops what Fullerton terms fourthly as "empowered participation," by which he means that the parts each contribute what they can to the whole, and fifthly, regenerative capitalism "honors community and place," nurturing resilient communities at all levels. Fullerton articulate three other principles of regenerative capitalism, including the "edge effect abundance," which suggests that system edges are where creativity, innovation, and abundance can happen best; "robust circulatory flow;" and lastly, balance. These principles for a regenerative capitalism form a useful foundation for considering what generative businesses could be in the sustainability, global inequality, and "us v. them" context of the world today.

In this context, it is important to understand the dynamics and principles that underlie large system change in complex adaptive systems (CAS) that are fraught with wicked problems, which is what social, ecological, and other systemic problems are.[11] Wicked problems are com-

---

8. J. Diamond, *Collapse*.

9. Fullerton, *Regenerative Capitalism*, 7–8.

10. Fritjof Capra, *The Web of Life* (New York: Anchor Doubleday, 1995); Fritjof Capra and P. L. Luisi, *The Systems View of Life: A Unifying Vision* (New York: Cambridge University Press, 2014).

11. S. Waddell, S. Waddock, S. Cornell, D. Dentoni, M. McLachlan, and G. Meszoely, "Large System Change: An Emerging Field of Transformation and Transitions," *Journal*

plex, interrelated problems, with no beginnings or endings, characterized by dynamism, connectedness, multiple stakeholders with different problem/solution definitions, and unclear boundaries—in other words, most social and ecological problems.[12]

Both CAS and wicked problems need to be approached holistically as they cannot be understood when fragmented or atomized into smaller elements.[13] Like wicked problems, CAS have permeable boundaries at many different levels and across many different types of entities. In socioeconomic systems today, for example, many large organizations are networked to numerous other entities, making it difficult to tell where one's activities begin and another's end. This interconnectivity and interdependence is exacerbated by global communications and electronic technologies, which penetrate many systems in different ways. These interdependencies and the dynamic interaction that they create mean that linear cause-effect relationships are difficult to find in CAS, outcomes are inherently unpredictable, and actions, once begun, are difficult if not impossible to totally reverse.

Such systems tend to emerge as a result of nonlinear past actions and dynamics, evolving and adapting to whatever "is" in coevolutionary ways and interactively reshaping what "is" through their own dynamics. That

of Corporate Citizenship 58 (June 2015): 5–30; S. Waddock, D. Dentoni, G. Meszoely, and S. Waddell, "The Complexity of Wicked Problems in Large System Change," *Journal of Organizational Change Management* 28, no. 6, (2015): 993–1012.

12. H. W. Rittel and M. M. Webber, "Dilemmas in a General Theory of Planning," *Policy Sciences* 4, no. 2, (1973): 155–69; R. D. Stacey, "The Science of Complexity: An Alternative Perspective for Strategic Change Processes," *Strategic Management Journal* 16, no. 6, (1995): 477–95; S. Kauffman, *At Home in the Universe: The Search for the Laws of Self-Organization and Complexity* (New York: Oxford University Press, 1995); S. S. Batie, "Wicked Problems and Applied Economics," *American Journal of Agricultural Economics* 90, no. 5, (2008): 1176–191.

13. For information on CAS, see I. Prigogine and I. Stengers, *Order Out of Chaos: Man's New Dialogue with Nature* (Boulder, CO: New Science Library, 1984); J. Gleick, *Chaos: Making a New Science* (New York: Viking, 1987); Grégoire Nicolis and Ilya Prigogin, *Exploring Complexity: An Introduction* (New York: W. H. Freeman, 1989); M. R. Lissack and H. Letiche, "Complexity, Emergence, Resilience, and Coherence: Gaining Perspective on Organizations and their Study," *Emergence* 4, no. 3, (2002): 72–94; F. Capra, "Complexity and Life," *Theory, Culture & Society* 22, no. 5, (2005): 33–44; S. S. Batie, "Wicked Problems and Applied Economics," *American Journal of Agricultural Economics* 90, no. 5, (2008): 1176–191.

is, systems emerge and evolve in what economist Joseph Schumpeter called a process of creative destruction, in which old ways, practices, and approaches shift toward new ones.[14] This process is inherently unpredictable, though patterns can frequently be discerned. Different actors within CAS tend to coevolve, each changing in partial response to what is happening to others in the system. As we think about shifting the economy and businesses toward generativity, we need to keep these realities of complexity and wickedness in mind. These attributes indicate the complexity of bringing about the type of system change that is needed to foster generative business, and also that the change process can potentially be guided but probably cannot be "controlled" in any real way. Key is shifting the core understanding of the role(s) of businesses in society and how we—and they—view the world. Key, that is, is shifting the mindsets of key players.[15] To do that, we need to fundamentally change the memes—the core cultural artifacts—that surround the idea of business, as I will explain below.[16]

Mindset Shifting

As Michael Pirson, Vincent Stanley, and other contributors to this volume agree, today's system of fragmented and individualistic companies all operating in their own self-interest, with goals of growth, efficiency, and profitability, has created the need for both new memes and a new narrative.[17] A new narrative could shift the purposes and goals of businesses to better harmonize business activity with ecological and social constraints[18] and develop a new mindset to shape the system.[19] The focus

14. Schumpeter, *Capitalism, Socialism and Democracy.*

15. Donella Meadows, "Leverage Points: Places to Intervene in a System," The Donella Meadows Project: Academy for Systems of Change, 1999, http://donellameadows .org/archives/leverage-points-places-to-intervene-in-a-system/.

16. S. Waddock, "Reflections: Intellectual Shamans, Sensemaking, and Memes in Large System Change," *Journal of Change Management* 15, no. 4, (2015): 259–73.

17. S. Waddock, "Foundational Memes for a New Narrative about the Role of Business in Society," *Humanistic Management Journal* 1 (2016): 91–105.

18. Ibid.

19. Pope Francis, *Laudato Si: On Care for Our Common Home*, Encyclical Letter, Vatican City website, 2015, http://w2.vatican.va/content/dam/francesco/pdf/encyclicals/ documents/papa-francesco_20150524_enciclica-laudato-si_en.pdf; I. Rimanoczy and E.

on individual company benefit that is advocated by today's current eco-nomic system is problematic in the resource-constrained context implied by the sustainability and climate-changed context. In fact, emphasizing only individual company benefit/profitability has the characteristics of a prisoner's dilemma,[20] putting the well-being of the system as a whole in jeopardy because each individual enterprise is expected to benefit only itself (and its shareholders) without regard for the societal or ecological consequences of doing so. If each organization, institution, or nation simply tries to maximize its own results, there is little or no consider-ation for the whole, and all end up suboptimizing the whole.[21] The prob-lem now is that because of climate change and the potential for ecological collapse[22] or a "great disruption,"[23] the "commons" at risk now exist on a planetary scale.

Changing mindsets toward a generative business framework is import-ant, albeit difficult. Upton Sinclair, author of *The Jungle*, which exposed horrifying practices in the meatpacking industry in 1906, once stated, "It is difficult to get a man [sic] to understand something, when his salary depends on his not understanding it."[24] People who are succeeding in the current business-as-usual system may well be affected by what Max Bazer-man and Ann Tenbrunsel term "motivated blindness," the tendency to

Laszlo, *Big Bang Being: Developing the Sustainability Mindset* (Austin: Greenleaf Publish-ing, 2013).

20. Prisoner's dilemma situations are frequently discussed in economics and busi-ness. They exist when what seems rational for one individual or business to do to opti-mize results is actually suboptimal for the system as a whole, though if only one individual acts, that individual may benefit. Investopedia describes the prisoner's dilemma as "a paradox . . . in which two individuals acting in their own best interest pursue a course of action that does not result in the ideal outcome. The typical prisoner's dilemma is set up . . . that both parties choose to protect themselves at the expense of the other participant. As a result of following a purely logical [rational] thought process . . . , both . . . find them-selves in a worse state than if they had cooperated with each other in the decision-making process." Jim Chappelow, "Prisoner's Dilemma," Investopedia, last modified May 23, 2019, http://www.investopedia.com/terms/p/prisoners-dilemma.asp.

21. G. Hardin, "The Tragedy of the Commons," *Science* 162, no. 3859, (1968): 1243–248.

22. J. Diamond, *Collapse*.

23. P. Gilding, *The Great Disruption*.

24. Upton Sinclair and Earl Lee, *Jungle: The Uncensored Original Edition* (Tucson, AZ: Sharp Press, 2003).

overlook unethical practices "when [it is] in their interest to remain ignorant." As Bazerman and Tenbrunsel point out, it is "well documented that
people see what they want to see and easily miss contradictory information when [it is] in their interest to remain ignorant—a psychological phenomenon known as motivated blindness." Bazerman and Tenbrunsel are
talking about why executives can overlook unethical behavior—because
its results benefit them. The idea of motivated blindness also applies at the
system level. It is easier to believe that inequality is not a problem or that
climate change is not real than it is to make the tough decisions and
changes that are needed if you understand that the system itself is creating these problems. If you benefit from the way things are currently working—as the 1 percent or, more accurately, the .001 percent, certainly have
over the past several decades, then not "seeing" these problems or not
believing them is the easiest path forward.[25]

The combination of the tragedy of the commons[26]/prisoner's dilemma
and motivated blindness suggests that although there is a significant need
for a mindset shift to achieve system change, it may take a crisis of some
sort (beyond what has already been experienced) to get us there. On the
other hand, Meadows argued that there are nine possible levers for system change, of which the most powerful is mindset change.[27] To change
mindsets requires changing the foundational memes or core cultural artifacts that shape relevant narratives, the stories that we tell ourselves about
what it is that businesses do and how they do it.[28] The current neoliberal
narrative around free enterprise, shareholder wealth maximization, and
the like, is deeply embedded in the psyches of many people—and it is that
narrative that new core memes might shift. This essay is one effort to
reshape those memes in the direction of generative businesses.

By analogy, the current neoliberal narrative or story about the role
of business in society being limited to individualistically serving self-

25. Max H. Bazerman and Ann E. Tenbrunsel, *Blind Spots: Why We Fail to Do What's Right and What to Do about it* (Princeton, NJ: Princeton University Press, 2011), 61.

26. The "tragedy of the commons" is a term popularized by ecologist and philosopher Garret Hardin to describe situations where there are shared resources, in which
any individual acting independently in self-interest exhibits behaviors that spoil the collective resource.

27. Meadows, "Leverage Points."

28. Waddock, "Reflections"; Waddock, "Foundational Memes."

interested needs without regard for the societal, community, ecological, or even spiritual consequences is outdated and insufficient in today's global context of unsustainability and inequality.[29] It is past time for a new narrative that today's shamans—healers, connectors, and sensemakers willing and able to gather information from multiple realms and tell a new story about businesses—can create. As a note, shamans are found in all cultures of the world, including modern cultures. Today's shamans can use a variety of approaches that draw from their own experiences and cultures, without having to appropriate the rituals and practices of others.[30] "Generative businesses" are businesses aligned with planetary and societal needs and constraints. Generative business would be based on a goal of serving vitality that fosters well-being and dignity for all, with core principles of restoration, resilience, and renewal. It is, I believe, the shamans among us who can in their sensemaking capacity help reshape our memes and narratives in productive ways.

A Shamanic Rationale for Generative Business

Let us briefly consider the role of the shaman in traditional societies and apply that role to humanity's present situation.[31] The shaman has three main roles: healer, connector, and sensemaker.[32] As medicine man or woman, the shaman is a central community figure in Indigenous cultures who attempts to heal patients and communities when they are dis-eased or dis-ordered, bringing them back into ease and order. Often healing, the primary role of the shaman can be done when the shaman travels to different realms (typically spiritual realms in traditional cultures) to gather information from which he or she can learn, particularly information

29. Francis, *Laudato Si*.

30. S. Waddock, *Healing the World: Today's Shamans as Difference Maker* (London: Greenleaf/Taylor & Francis Publishing, 2017).

31. S. Waddock, *Intellectual Shamans: Management Academics Making a Difference* (Cambridge: Cambridge University Press, 2015).

32. S. Waddock, *Healing the World*; Peter J. Frost and Carolyn P. Egri, "The Political Process of innovation," *Research in Organizational Behavior* 13 (1991): 229–95. Also, Carolyn P. Egri, and Peter J. Frost, "Shamanism and Change: Bringing Back the Magic in Organizational Transformation," *Research in Organizational Change and Development* 5 (1991): 175–221.

that changes his or her mindset. Traditional shamans operate from the premise that if someone is sick or a community is dis-ordered, it is the cultural mythology that surrounds the community, the stories that people tell themselves about how the world is and works, which are out of order.[33] Gathering new information by crossing into different realms, which in our modern context could be functional, organizational, social, or disciplinary realms, among others, allows for a new perspective, a change of mindset among shamans in their sensemaking capacity. It creates the possibility of telling of a new "story," allowing the patient (or community) eventually to be healed.

Egri and Frost, discussing shamans in a modern context, build on three core principles, which are very related to our business and economic systems as CAS fraught with wicked problems described above. These principles shape their understanding of the change agent as shaman—and by extension, the rest of us as shamans: 1) "there are multiple, co-existing, and interpenetrating realities, including ordinary, symbolic, psychic energy and spiritual"; 2) "everything is interrelated, interdependent, and purposeful in a world of balanced holism", and 3) change is a process over time rather than an outcome. Such a perspective is quite different from believing that "man" [sic] is superior to all other creatures and deserves to exploit the world's resources or that we can somehow "control" a change process in a complex system fraught with the types of wicked problems noted earlier. We can push the shamanic perspective further as we begin to think more deeply about generative business practice.

Further, and importantly, traditional shamans believe that there is spirit in everything.[34] Obviously, this belief extends to other people, and it also extends other living beings, animal and plant, so that a shaman would believe that, for example, a tree has spirit. This belief can also extend to nonliving entities like rocks, mountains, rivers, and lakes—all sorts of manifestations of nature. What this belief about spirit does for the shaman is enable him or her to accord respect for all aspects of the world. In a sense, this belief extends the concept of dignity to all the

---

33. J. Dow, "Universal Aspects of Symbolic Healing: A Theoretical Synthesis," *American Anthropologist* 88, no. 1, (1986): 56–69.

34. Egri and Frost, "Shamanism and Change," 175, 191–203.

world, where dignity means inherent value and worth simply for exist-ing.[35] Indeed, at the broadest level, shamans see the whole world much as Lovelock does, as a living entity worthy of dignity.[36]

Consider the implications for businesses of believing that everything, including aspects of nature, has dignity, that it is worthy of being hon-ored simply because it exists. Such a perspective shifts attitudes about the way people, other creatures, and nature are treated in businesses. For example, if we hold firmly to dignity in global supply chains, we human-ize workers and recognize that they deserve to be treated with dignity just as we might consider ourselves worthy. If applied to nature, includ-ing living and nonliving entities, the idea of dignity radically shifts the way we treat the world around us. Western, or developed, cultures tend to separate mind from body, and human from nature, placing human-kind as the highest evolved creatures and, essentially, making it all right for humans to exploit the earth and its resources for human benefit. If instead we recognize that humans are deeply intertwined with and con-nected to all other parts of the world around—other living beings and nature—that we cannot survive without a healthy and well-balanced interrelationship with earth and her creatures, then we might take a very different attitude toward, for example, how business is conducted. Such a mindset shift would enable the development of a generative approach to business and would help mitigate the climate change and sustainability crises, and also perhaps help us devise economic and political systems that generate considerably less inequality.

By building on life-affirming, generative practices, for example, prac-tices that generate vitality, renewal, restoration, and resilience in the world, businesses arguably could be successful in an economy of societal and ecological balance. Committed change agents can, as modern sha-mans, begin this transition by focusing on new memes associated with generative businesses. Such businesses would focus on goals that syner-gistically benefit the well-being of the whole— people, communities, societies, and planet—rather than simply focusing on wealth maximi-zation for the individual company or simply benefiting themselves and

35. D. Hicks, *Dignity: The Essential Role it Plays in Resolving Conflict* (New Haven, CT: Yale University Press, 2011); Francis, *Laudato Si*; Waddock, *Healing the World*.

36. J. Lovelock, *A New Look at Life on Earth* (Oxford: Oxford University Press, 1979).

shareholders. The exploitation of nature that seems a natural concomitant to doing business would shift dramatically if dignity were really accorded all people and beings and to the world around us.[37] No longer would growth-at-all-costs be the business and economic mantra. Instead, businesses and economies would have to substitute the values of generativity/vitality, accompanied by principles of resilience, restoration, and renewal that constitute generative business practice.

Generativity/Collective Well-Being

Let's reimagine business as generative, that is, with a goal of vitality and well-being for all. Businesses as life-affirming necessitate redefining the purpose of the firm with long-term societal and ecological interests and vitality at all levels held firmly in mind. Generative businesses *serve* the communities in which they operate, creating vitality in the form of connections and community, stable and decent employment opportunities, and a holistic approach to doing business. Current assumptions about the purpose of business, notwithstanding evidence of failures that surround us, are deeply embedded in the neoclassical economics model. Neoclassical economics demands maximized and, in practice, short-term returns to shareholders. Despite advances in behavioral economics, this approach gives primacy to shareholders over other important stakeholders without whom the company cannot exist or survive, for example, employees, customers, suppliers, communities, governments. Add to this grouping the natural environment from which *all* institutions and companies draw resources, whether they wish to recognize that reality or not.

In what is likely to become a seminal paper, Thomas Donaldson and James Walsh argue for a new theory of business that is premised on creating "collective value," with the caveat that no dignity violations to human beings occur.[38] In the current system, the goal of business is frequently and wrongly said to be to maximize shareholder wealth or other

---

37. Michael Pirson, *Humanistic Management: Protecting Dignity and Promoting Well-Being* (Cambridge: Cambridge University Press, 2017); Francis, *Laudato Si*. See also Vincent Stanley, this volume.

38. Thomas Donaldson and James P. Walsh, "Toward a Theory of Business," *Research in Organizational Behavior*, 35 (2015): 181–207.

ways of measuring profitability, with continual growth also assumed.[39] The current system is fraught with abuses of people and nature, which are considered externalities or side effects of the "efficiency" and scale that supposedly result in greater profitability. In other words, businesses exploit nature, people, markets, and sometimes whole nations as much as they can legally get away with (and much of this exploitation is in fact legal) so that they can theoretically at least benefit their shareholders.[40]

"Efficiency," which management guru Peter Drucker once defined as "doing things right," is typically interpreted to mean squeezing maximum monetary profits from the least inputs. Today, efficiency as a core business value results in activities like blowing off the tops of mountains to get at their minerals or energy resources, and dumping the resulting toxic waste in nearby valleys and streams because it is the least "costly" (in terms of profits) way to get them. Efficiency results in sweatshops and environmental abuses in global supply chains, young workers, often female, working with toxic materials to produce goods for the "first world," often in deplorable conditions. Efficiency leads to scale, which in turn leads to the need to advertise and sell many products that lack durability, quality, and good design in the interests of constant product churn resulting in more sales (and profits).

The drive for ever-greater efficiency and scale makes possible activities like fracking for difficult-to-access oil reserves and shipping the resulting oil in pipelines across long distances. It makes clear-cutting rainforests or other forests, dumping of toxins, trawling or blowing fish out of the water, industrial farming and animal husbandry, producing high salt, fat, and sugar-laden "food products" rather than real food, and similar practices seem like reasonable production approaches.[41] Yet the collective value produced using these and related business production methods is largely financial, largely geared toward shareholders, and

39. See L. A. Stout, "Why We Should Stop Teaching Dodge v. Ford," *Virginia Law and Business Review* 3 (2008): 63. See also L. A. Stout, *The Shareholder Value Myth: How Putting Shareholders First Harms Investors, Corporations, and the Public* (San Francisco: Berrett-Koehler Publishers, 2012).

40. See Pirson, *Humanistic Management*. See also Michael Naughton, and Gerald J. Beyer, this volume.

41. M. Moss, *Salt, Sugar, Fat: How the Food Giants Hooked Us* (New York: Random House, 2013).

ignores the ethical, social, health, and ecological consequences and externalities of such methods, which are considered "externalities" and not counted in company financial reports. The efficiency of these methods thus leaves the problematic consequences of production and all their costs somewhere in the system for others to pay, whether in reduced vitality and health, loss of diversity and resilience, or actual cleanup costs.

Imagine substituting what I am calling a shamanic approach, in which dignity is accorded to all for this profit- and efficiency-based system. Imagine substituting the goals of vitality, supporting by principles of resilience, renewal, and restoration instead. Believing that spirit lives in everything (or at least treating everything in that way) would argue for more respectful treatment of other people, other living beings, and nature. People would be viewed as whole human beings, not simply as cogs in a mechanistic production machine that can be used, abused, and then discarded. Though more difficult to measure than profitability and efficiency, vitality/collective well-being with no dignity violations as a goal argues for very different practices toward people, communities, "raw materials" drawn from the land, the land itself, energy production, and animal husbandry practices.[42]

Vitality

Vitality carries connotations of being alive, life-affirming, energy-producing, strong, and active. Vitality is associated with the power to grow and survive in meaningful ways, being lively or energetic, successful. Vitality can be combined with generativity, a term coined by psychologist Erik Erikson, to mean "concern for establishing and guiding the next generation," with implications of caring for the planet in the sense of planetary stewardship.[43] The goal of vitality indicates the need to consider how people, communities, nations, and the planet as a whole, both now and into the future, will be affected by a given practice or set of practices.

Vitality as a business goal suggests that businesses and their leaders need to care about the state and well-being of employees, suppliers and

---

42. Donaldson and Walsh, "Toward a Theory of Business."

43. c.f. John N. Kotre, *Outliving the Self: How We Live on in Future Generations* (New York, W. W. Norton, 1996).

distributors, customers, shareholders, communities, nations, and nature (i.e., the planet and its ability to support human civilizations), not just their shareholders. There is a lot of evidence to suggest that vitality is being drained away from many people, communities, and indeed, the planet today. Vitality implies that all people are treated with dignity and respect, no matter what their socioeconomic status, politics, ethnicity, religion, or station in life. Businesses focused on vitality would ensure that working conditions and raw materials were safe, health-promoting (not toxic), collegial, even democratic. They would be measured and assessed on these factors, not simply on profitability. Products would not include the many thousands of mostly untested toxins that they now include, and advertising would openly and honestly represent what is in the products, and how products are best and safely used. Advertising and marketing that exploit people's psychological, emotional, and physical weaknesses would be gone, replaced by low-key informational ads that conveyed accurate, timely information about truly necessary products, rather than fostering ever greater levels of materialism and consumption. The idea of "enough" or "sufficiency" around acquisition of goods and use of services would be popularized as a new meme, rather than constant acquisition and "more goods."

In a vitality-based approach to businesses, all people would all be treated with dignity, paid a living wage, and working conditions and the work itself would, minimally, be what the International Labor Organization calls "decent." A living wage would allow workers to support their families, live in acceptable conditions, and have diets that were nutritious and satisfying. Work itself might need to be redesigned so that it becomes meaningful, engaging, and worthwhile. People would need to see themselves in the context of the bigger business—and social—system, and learn how their efforts were contributing meaningfully to the betterment of the whole.[44] Vitality suggests the need to build solid, lasting, and healthful relationships among people and within communities at different levels— relationships where dignity is respected and people support each other. Dignity and generativity values would also apply to the relationships between workers and their bosses, generating respect,

44. See Beyer, Naughton, and Stanley chapters on work and livelihood, this volume.

reasonable working hours and conditions, and clean facilities, with support needed for people to experience dignity in the workplace.

Generativity and vitality also apply at the community and societal levels, as well as in workplaces, bringing people together in healthy relationships, enjoying food and products that support their abilities and dreams, and fostering healthful activities of all sorts. Democratic institutions that enable people to participate in governance as they desire and allow their ideas and wishes to be heard are important in such a system. Communities would be designed so that the "village" that is needed to raise children, help elders live meaningful lives, and provide good, stable jobs for working adults, so that families and communities could be kept intact and relationships could flourish and be sustained over time.[45] At the national level, discussions about what public goods are necessary to sustaining a healthy set of communities and the nation as a whole would be supported through equitable tax structures. Such tax structures could eliminate complexity and corruption and enable public discourse about important issues like healthcare, public parks and lands, clean water and air, and other public goods to be made available. As will be discussed below, businesses' relationships to nature and her manifestations would also change radically.

Renewal, Resilience, and Restoration

If the principles of renewal, restoration, and resilience were taken seriously as part of the business agenda, many business practices would shift not only toward people but also toward nature. These principles are highly interrelated, for what creates renewal can often generate greater resilience and vice versa, and certainly these principles apply for human interactions as well as business interactions with nature. It is true that some resources need to be used to create products and services. Some resources may be used up in any production operation. Today, however, we simply "use" nonrenewables and other resources as if they were endlessly available, because of our willful blindness to the impacts of such

45. See Sandra Sullivan-Dunbar, this volume.

practices, which cannot be sustained indefinitely.[46] The principles of renewal and restoration suggest an important shift in how business operates—from using and exploiting nonrenewable resources to focusing on the use of resources that are in fact renewable within reasonable (human-scale) time periods. and then actually ensuring that renewal takes place. If harm has to be done, then restoration to the original (or better) state would be expected, whether that is of the land, a community, or some other entity.

Renewal as a principle suggests new products, built on renewable resources rather than constantly exploiting nonrenewables. For example, in modern agriculture, use of nitrogen-based chemical fertilizers and pesticides replace agricultural practices that actually replenish, rather than deplete the soil, even though the use of agricultural practices is more labor-intensive. Topsoil loss, loss of organic life in existing topsoil, and poor nutritional value in many crops are significant global problems that could potentially be eliminated, with little loss of food productivity and perhaps some gain in nutritional quality. Such a shift in practice would create more jobs, which are desperately needed around the world, would decrease pollution and runoff of pesticides and fertilizers into rivers and streams, and would necessitate less monoculture, creating more plant diversity and resilience, with numerous other benefits.[47] Innovations undertaken with a foundation of biomimicry[48] and natural capitalism would help bring production processes—and goals—more in line with the renewing patterns found in nature.[49]

Restoration literally means returning something to its former condition. In ecological terms, restoration ecology is the return of a landscape or ecosystem to the way it was before it was damaged. That could mean replanting forests or fields with the type of diversity that enables wildlife to return and the forest to regenerate itself. As a principle, it would mean

46. Jackson, *Prosperity Without Growth*; J. Ehrenfeld and A. Hoffman, *Flourishing: A Frank Conversation about Sustainability* (Palo Alto, CA: Stanford University Press, 2013).

47. See M. Pollan, *The Omnivore's Dilemma: A Natural History of Four Meals* (New York: Penguin, 2006).

48. J. M. Benyus, *Biomimicry* (New York: William Morrow, 1997).

49. P. Hawken, A. B. Lovins, and L. H. Lovins, *Natural Capitalism: The Next Industrial Revolution* (Abington-on-Thames, England: Routledge, 2013).

not doing something if doing it means destruction of what exists in ways that cannot be reproduced. Although restoration in this sense is not always possible when people or companies develop a local area, keeping the principle in mind would mean doing as little harm as possible and ensuring that the resources that are being used are used wisely and with as much true effectiveness, in Drucker's sense of the word, as in doing the right thing as possible.[50]

Resilience is directly related to well-being as it refers to the capacity for a being or system to return to an original, presumably healthy state, to bounce back or recover from difficulties (with the recognition that sometimes initial states need to be made even better than they were). Resilience is important at the individual (psychological), community, and ecological levels, as it addresses how much disturbance a system can withstand before it is irreparably altered or even destroyed. Resilience thus defined is essential to well-being, for it suggests that there are both possibilities to use resources—and limits beyond which it does not make sense to go. Many factors can decrease resilience, including stress, life changes, and other problems at the individual levels; destruction of neighborhoods, poor zoning policies, and social disruption at the community level; and pollution, climate change, reduced biodiversity, and human intervention at the ecological level.

The Stockholm Resilience Centre argues that there are seven principles that enhance resilience at the system level, the first of which is to maintain diversity and redundancy.[51] Others include managing connectivity, managing slow variables and feedback, fostering CAS thinking, encouraging learning, broadening participation, and promoting polycentric governance systems. Although all of these principles of resilience are relevant to businesses and their participation in societies, the principle of diversity and redundancy is central, as it argues for diversity and redundancy on a number of levels. One level is institutional diversity, for

50. P. F. Drucker, *The Effective Executive,* vol. 967 (London: Heinemann, 1967).

51. S. H. Simonsen, M. R. Biggs, M. Schlüter, M. Schoon, E. Bohensky, G. Cundill, V. Dakos, T. Daw, K. Kotschy, A. Leitch, A. Quinlan, G. Peterson, and F. Moberg, "Applying Resilience Thinking: Seven Principles for Building Resilience in Social-Ecological Systems," PDF File (Stockholm: Stockholm University, 2014), http://www.stockholm resilience.org/download/18.10119fc11455d3c557d6928/1398150799790/SRC+Applying+Resilience+final.pdf.

example, having many businesses rather than fewer, so that the problem of "too big to fail" that some governments experienced with some financial institutions in the 2007–2008 global financial crisis can be avoided. A second level is avoiding excessive profit-focused efficiency that generates unnecessary products, causing quality levels to be set lower so that items will break and be replaced more frequently, and creating the need for intensive marketing of products people neither particularly want or need but that are somehow made fashionable.

A third level of needed resilience can be seen in the monocultural production of many crops in agriculture and other forms of mass production today, a practice that, for example, leaves crops vulnerable to pests and disease because they lack both redundancy and sufficient diversity. Animal husbandry practices, too, where animals are herded into tight bins with little room to move, fed food they are not meant to eat, and antibiotics to keep them from getting sick because of their lack of movement, poor diets, close quarters, and having to live in their own waste, would have to shift both to find more dignified ways to grow meat products. Processing (butchering) of animals would also shift toward recognizing the sacrifice that the animal is making, and perhaps reduce the amount of meat products eaten, with attendant health benefits for people and planet.

Many other shifts toward renewal, resilience, and restoration might be less efficient and possibly more costly for consumers in the short run. They would, however, carry societal, human, and other benefits, not to mention being better aligned with fostering well-being and generativity, making their actual (internalized, life cycle) costs less overall. For example, allowing forests to regenerate more in their natural state than typically happens when they are replanted with a single crop tree after clear-cutting would generate greater plant diversity and hence more resilience, while still permitting the harvesting of wood products, which could then be done more selectively. Shamanic approaches according dignity to land, rivers, and other natural manifestations would mean that overuse of fertilizer and pesticides and plantings of single crops (monoculture) would need to be replaced with more diverse crops raised through organic, traditional, or biodynamic methods that foster diversity, soil restoration and renewal, and hence resilience. Fishing practices like trawling that devastate the biodiversity of large ocean tracts and sweep whole populations of marine life from the water, along factory "production" of cattle, pigs, and chickens, would need to shift to respect the dignity of the animals, and understand the need to leave enough living species in their territories that population renewal is possible.

The "throw away" culture prevalent in the United States and some other developed nations, also decried by Pope Francis in his encyclical *Laudato Si'*, would have to shift toward a culture that respects the products that are developed, where quality, durability, design, and usefulness take precedence over fad, fashion, and replacement.[52] Companies could design products in such a system so that they follow principles of natural capitalism, focusing on upgrading and renewing still useful products, recycling what is no longer useful, and reusing what has been replaced in other forms.[53]

Naturally, such less efficient methods would create the need to employ significantly more people—and would have far fewer externalities that actually cost society much more than is generally calculated in measures like gross national product or gross domestic product. With more humane work policies than currently exist, companies would have to "spread out" jobs for more people so that working hours, pay scale, and conditions were reasonable.[54] Such practices would create less product demand, and foster the need to produce higher quality, more durable, and easily refurbished products that could be sold at higher initial prices with significantly less waste, fewer disposal costs, and less turnover. Food products would most likely have higher nutritional value, and animals might be eaten less often—but with more respect for their sacrifice if they were treated with some degree of reverence—with considerably fewer deleterious environmental (and health) effects.

The dignity perspective with respect to nature would also mean different treatment of land, mountains, rivers, lakes, the atmosphere, and oceans, for example. Businesses are not treating something with dignity if they are dumping toxic wastes into it. If they approach the earth and its manifestations as something with intrinsic value, not simply something

52. Francis, *Laudato Si'*.

53. Hawken, Lovins, and Lovins, *Natural Capitalism*.

54. For example, J. Schor, *The Overworked American: The Unexpected Decline of Leisure* (New York: Basic Books 2008).

to be used by humans for their own purposes, but something valuable just because it exists, then the idea that it can be "exploited" for your gain becomes less appealing. If extracted materials cannot be replaced because it took nature so long to produce them that renewal or within human-scale time periods are not feasible, then the principles of resilience, restoration, and renewal suggest that perhaps that material should not be used.

Alternatives to existing products (and services) that use nonrenewables would need to be found or invented based on materials that could be restored or renewed. Such a shift could foster even more jobs as a whole new wave of ingenuity and innovation would be needed.[55] Such innovations in business practice could foster businesses that are more humane and in accord with planetary stewardship, while still remaining profitable. Generative business, considered through the lens of vitality with core principles of renewal, restoration, and resilience, is a core element of a humanistic (and shamanic) approach to management that focuses on systemic *and* foundational aspects of the whole, which recognizes physical limitations and limits to growth.[56]

Moving Toward Generative Business

The notion of generative business, with the goal of fostering vitality, and supported by principles of resilience, renewal, and restoration, could be an antidote to today's mass scale, efficient but externalizing, and dominating but not resilient, restorative, or renewing businesses. Taking these

55. T. F. Homer-Dixon and T. Homer-Dixon, *The Ingenuity Gap: Facing the Economic, Environmental, and Other Challenges of an Increasingly Complex and Unpredictable World* (New York: Vintage, 2002).

56. Donella H. Meadows, Dennis I. Meadows, Jørgen Randers, and William W. Behrens III, *The Limits to Growth: A Report to the Club of Rome* (New York: Universe Press), 1972; Graham M. Turner, "A Comparison of The Limits to Growth with 30 Years of Reality," *Global Environmental Change* 18, no. 3, (2008): 397–411; Jorgen Randers, *2052: A Global Forecast for the Next Forty Years* (Chelsea, VT: Chelsea Green Publishing, 2012); Udo E. Simonis, "2052. A Global Forecast for the Next Forty Years A Report to the Club of Rome Commemorating the 40th Anniversary of the Limits to Growth," *International Journal of Social Economics* 40, no. 2 (2013): 181–82.

principles seriously can orient business toward generativity—vitality and what is life-affirming.[57]

Changing the mindsets of people toward businesses and, ultimately, the mindsets of business leaders is a daunting task that starts with changing the core memes that surround businesses, and the narratives or stories that we tell about businesses in society. Creating a generative and collective well-being (with no dignity violations) approach is a first step in making this mindset shift. At the same time, it is important to keep in mind that the system is complex and fraught with wicked problems. Change will happen in multiple arenas, and be fostered by numerous individuals, groups, and organizations, but not all of it will be in the desired direction. The reason that shifting memes is so important is that they provide core guidance that can help people as sensemaking shamans tell much the *same* stories and narratives, guiding change in the direction of greater vitality for all—well-being and dignity.

Not all of the needed changes will be welcomed by everyone. Powerful people and institutions, particularly financial institutes with vested interests in the status quo and who are benefitting from the current system, are most likely to resist. At the same time, people who are not well served by today's system, as well as ecologists, and progressives, are more likely to welcome change. This systemic change will demand a shift back toward the productive economy, away from today's financialized economy and related moneyed interests, because tomorrow's healthy system will probably be more localized (or "glocal," both local and global), with more and varied businesses and other institutions rather than monolithic global ones.[58] Such movement toward greater diversity offers the potential for greater resilience and less need to satisfy anonymous "shareholders" and financial analysts, along with more potential to create collective value, not just financial value for one group of stakeholders (the shareholders).[59]

57. "Leading for Wellbeing" has become WEAll, the Wellbeing Economy Alliance, http://wellbeingeconomy.org/.

58. David C. Korten, *Change the Story, Change the Future: A Living Economy for a Living Earth* (San Francisco: Berrett-Koehler, 2015).

59. Donaldson and Walsh, "Toward a Theory of Business."

The difficulty in this scenario is, of course, the power that is currently held by financial, business, and political elites, whose interests and mindsets are shaped and supported by the current system. Potentially, and most likely, they will believe that they have the most to lose in the significant systemic change that a vitality-based, collective well-being, no dignity violations of people, creatures, and earth mindset implies. In contrast, though, they could think that, indeed, in the longer term, they will still have children and grandchildren who will live on the planet and will need to be able to support themselves in meaningful work, no matter where they live and, it is to be hoped, flourish in communities with others. Since it is increasingly clear that current systemic dynamics cannot get humanity to that place of well-being for all, perhaps it is time to changes our minds, our memes, our values, norms, and business principles and goals so that we acknowledge that we are all living on one pretty small planet that can support humankind only within a set of constraints that need to be met. That planet, our earth, can do so and has done so for the past ten thousand or so years but can only continue to do so if we acknowledge our interdependence with her and her resources—and act accordingly.

Part II: Valuing Differently

Challenging Work and Business as Usual

The Homemaker as Worker

Second Wave American Feminist Campaigns to Value Housework

KIRSTEN SWINTH

> There has been a revolution in the kitchen, and like it or not, there is a new force and a determined new worker who will no longer work unreasonable hours under unreasonable conditions for unjust wages, some leftover food and a worn-out garment.
>
> —Edith Barksdale Sloan, National Committee for Household Employees, 1974

> Everybody's in favor of equal pay, but nobody's in favor of doing the dishes.
>
> —Mary Jo Bane, Wellesley Women's Research Center, 1977

Teacups shattered rather than washed. Shirts left "wrinkling in laundry baskets." Housework boycotted for a day. Women were on strike for equality. On August 26, 1970, American women gathered in the largest women's rights march since the suffrage demonstrations in the early twentieth century. Protesters across the country held aloft signs with pointed messages like "Oppressed Women: Don't Cook Dinner Tonight! Starve a Rat Today!!" and "Housewives are Unpaid Slave Laborers! Tell Him What to Do with the Broom!!" In Los Angeles, marchers responded to heckling men by chanting, "Go do the dishes, go do the dishes." Cooking, cleaning, and laundry were everywhere in a day of protest whose slogan was, "Don't Iron While the Strike is Hot!"[1]

1. This chapter contains verbatim text excerpts from Kirsten Swinth, "Housework," *Feminism's Forgotten Fight: The Unfinished Struggle for Work and Family* (Cambridge, MA: Harvard University Press, 2018), 97–133. Copyright © 2018 by Kirsten Swinth.
   "Women Arise: The Revolution That Will Affect Everybody," *Life*, September 4, 1970, 16; "Women on the March," *Time* 96, September 7, 1970, 20; Lee Dye, "L.A. 'Women's Lib' Marchers Greeted by Cheers and Jeers," *Los Angeles Times*, August 27, 1970, 1; Linda

The strike was conceived as a revolt from women's daily second-class status—in dead-end, low-paying jobs; in lack of childcare; and in housework that was wholly women's domain. As feminist leader and founder of the National Organization for Women (NOW), Betty Friedan told the assembled crowd, "All of us are housewives, but from now on it shouldn't be housewives—'housespouses' is a better word. Both of us will share the world inside the home and walk equally in the world outside the home." Calling the lack of economic value granted to women's work in the home the "unfinished business" of the women's revolution, Friedan asked, "What will happen to architecture, to city planning, when women are no longer the unpaid free servants of the home?"[2]

Second-wave American feminists launched an array of campaigns to redistribute and revalue household labor between 1963 and 1978. Movement activists critiqued the male prerogative that made housework women's work and challenged the advertisers and moral authorities who romanticized cooking and cleaning as natural female labors of love. Feminists led a movement to upgrade the status of paid household workers like domestics, nannies, and housecleaners, pursuing labor protections and professional respect. Other activists demanded proper economic valuation of household labor and acknowledgement of housewives' contribution to family well-being at divorce and in social security benefits. In telling men to "go wash the dishes," in other words, American feminists sought to alter fundamental economic practices and demand recognition of household labor as work with economic and social value.

This essay takes up two dimensions of second-wave feminists' sweeping activism on the question of household labor: domestic workers' campaign to amend the Fair Labor Standards Act (FLSA) and secure a minimum wage for household employees, and liberal and radical

---

Charlton, "Women March down Fifth in Equality Drive," *New York Times*, August 27, 1970, 30. See also Betty Friedan, *It Changed My Life: Writings on the Women's Movement* (New York: Dell, 1977), 185–206; Bonnie J. Dow, *Watching Women's Liberation, 1970: Feminism's Pivotal Year on the Network News* (Urbana: University of Illinois Press, 2014), 144–67; Susan J. Douglas, *Where the Girls Are: Growing up Female with the Mass Media* (New York: Times Books, 1994), 177–86.

2. Friedan, *It Changed My Life*, 205.

feminists' struggles to recognize housework as labor not love, worthy of fringe benefits awarded any other job, including most importantly, social security.[3] In both these areas, feminists struggled to achieve two central goals: accounting for the economic value of household labor and eradication of the assumption that such labor was unskilled or uncompensated work that should be assigned to women alone. By the end of the 1970s, feminist housework activism expanded domestic worker rights, forced social security reform, and changed divorce law. Housework itself became part of an ongoing struggle between partners. And feminists successfully shifted the ground under the presumption that housecleaning was women's work. By altering the valuation of household labor and fighting for its status as work, feminists of the era put forward successful working alternatives to conventional economics. The value system anchoring feminists' alternative economics was gender justice. In bringing such a competing value structure to bear on familiar market logics, feminists shared common ground with the critiques put forward by the social gospelers and Catholic social tradition discussed elsewhere in this volume.

Despite the gains feminists made, gaps in their achievements apparent today reveal much about resistance to altering economic practices tied to the domestic sphere. Devaluation of both paid and unpaid caretaking and household labor remains a constant, as does ambivalence about conceptualizing labor in the home as waged work rather than loving care. With neoliberal values dominating the United States in the last forty years, policies that awarded economic value to household labor through the market had greater purchase than the redistributive ones also proposed by feminists. Those dreams of connecting state benefits to the paid work of domestic employees and the unpaid service of homemakers laboring in the nation's homes remain incomplete.

3. Other scholars have begun to trace and connect these movements as well. See Lisa Levenstein, "'Don't Agonize, Organize!': The Displaced Homemakers Campaign and the Contested Goals of Postwar Feminism," *Journal of American History* 100 (March 2014): 1114–38; Mary Ziegler, "An Incomplete Revolution: Feminists and the Legacy of Marital-Property Reform," *Michigan Journal of Gender and Law* 19 (2013): 259–92; Premilla Nadasen, *Household Workers Unite: The Untold Story of African American Women Who Built a Movement* (Boston: Beacon Press, 2015), 124–47.

A Revolution in the Kitchen

Domestic workers did their jobs in a kind of netherworld of employment. In mid-century America their labor remained invisible by its location in the private home and its association with housewives' work. But it was also invisible in law. While other workers had acquired protections and benefits over the course of the twentieth century, domestics remained largely outside labor law. Minimum wages, unemployment benefits, workers' compensation, limits on hours worked, and overtime regulations—none applied to domestics. A workforce of mostly African-American women by the 1960s, domestics faced the added stigma of work associated with racial minorities.[4]

In the mid-1960s, a surge of domestic worker organizing began to challenge such injustice. "We won't go in the back door any more," vowed Jessie Williams, a member of the Auburn, Alabama, affiliate of Household Technicians of America (HTA), the organization fighting for the household workers' rights. "We won't be told to eat scraps in the kitchen and stay out of the living room except when we are sweeping," Williams declared, "We feel domestic work is just as professional as any other job. If people go on making it degrading, there won't be any workers doing it much longer." Williams's militant warning had roots in the revival of the National Committee on Household Employment (NCHE) by the Women's Bureau of the US Department of Labor. A longstanding network of feminists within the government, along with Dorothy Height, the president of the National Council of Negro Women, backed this renewed attention to household employees. The NCHE sought to upgrade the status of domestic work, to provide training to domestic workers, to educate employers about the skills involved in household work, and to advocate for decent employment conditions. The committee issued a voluntary code of standards for employers that included a minimum wage, social security contributions, overtime, sick days, and vacation benefits.[5]

4. Premilla Nadasen, "Power, Intimacy, and Contestation: Dorothy Bolden and Domestic Worker Organizing in Atlanta in the 1960s," in *Intimate Labors: Cultures, Technologies, and the Politics of Care*, ed. Eileen Boris and Rhacel Salazar Parreñas (Stanford: Stanford University Press, 2010), 208–10.

5. Phillip Shabecoff, "To Domestics: A Minimum Wage is a Raise," *New York Times*, June 6, 1973, 30, qtd. in Premilla Nadasen, "Citizenship Rights, Domestic Workers, and the Fair Labor Standards Act," *Journal of Policy History* 24 (2012): 90; Nadasen, *Household*

The NCHE supported domestic worker organizations that sprang up across the country in the late 1960s. In Atlanta, for example, Dorothy Bolden mobilized domestic workers into the National Domestic Workers Union of America beginning in 1968. Elsewhere, Mary McClendon led Detroit domestics in the Household Workers Organization starting in 1969, and Geraldine Miller brought Bronx household workers together in the Bronx Household Technicians and the New York State Household Technicians in 1971.[6] Recognizing the momentum behind these budding groups, the NCHE shifted direction at the end of the 1960s. Under its new leader, Edith Barksdale Sloan, NCHE spun off the Household Technicians of America (HTA) in 1971 to unite and represent the burgeoning movement. An activist in her thirties, Barksdale Sloan had graduated from Hunter College, served in the Peace Corps, and had worked for the US Commission on Civil Rights. Barksdale Sloan redirected the NHCE's energies toward more militant objectives. No longer would the group focus on providing "better" maids for employers and training mothers on public assistance to be domestics; instead they would rally household workers for decent wages and benefits and educate employers about domestic workers' rights and fair employment conditions. Without change in domestics' working days, warned Barksdale Sloan, to raucous cheers from the women gathered at the HTA organizing conference, "'Madame' is going to have to clean her own house, and cook and serve her own meals, because *everyone* is going to quit."[7]

Workers Unite, 61–71. See also Phyllis Palmer, "Outside the Law: Agricultural and Domestic Workers under the Fair Labor Standards Act," *Journal of Policy History* 7 (1995): 416–40; Eileen Boris and Premilla Nadasen, "Domestic Workers Organize!," *Working USA: The Journal of Labor and Society* 11 (2008): 413–37; Eileen Boris and Jennifer Klein, *Caring for America: Home Health Workers in the Shadow of the Welfare State* (New York: Oxford University Press, 2012); Dorothy Sue Cobble, "'A Spontaneous Loss of Enthusiasm': Workplace Feminism and the Transformation of Women's Service Jobs in the 1970s," *International Labor and Working-Class History* 56 (1999): 23–44; Evelyn Nakano Glenn, *Forced to Care: Coercion and Caregiving in America* (Cambridge, MA: Harvard University Press, 2010).

6. Boris and Nadasen, "Domestic Workers Organize!," 423; Nadasen, *Household Workers Unite*, 104–5.

7. Edith Barksdale Sloan, keynote address, July 17, 1971, National Committee on Household Employment (NCHE) Records, Landover, MD, qtd. in Nadasen, *Household Workers Unite*, 78. On Sloan and the HTA, see Nadasen, *Household Workers Unite*, 58–61, 71–73, 77–79; Boris and Klein, *Caring for America*, 127–28; "Of Note—Edith Barksdale Sloan," *Washington Post*, February 15, 2012, B7.

Before a crowd of more than a thousand equally enthusiastic delegates, Shirley Chisholm, the black feminist congresswoman from Brooklyn, New York, declared at HTA's 1972 national conference a year later, "We want equal pay for equal work, decent working conditions and respect for the long, hard hours we work." The mostly female and black attendees understood the message loud and clear. HTA, Chisholm explained, "is symbolic of what the Women's Movement is about." She had insisted the year before, "We want our piece of the American Dream," neatly linking women's claims for equality with the workers' and civil rights consciousness of the organization. With thirty-seven affiliates, and twenty-five thousand members in more than a dozen states at its high point in 1974, HTA was a thriving black feminist organization.[8]

Momentum for this domestic workers' movement came from a number of sources—civil rights struggles and the rising militancy of service workers, among them—but the women's movement gave its arguments renewed urgency and impact. In its organizing, the movement helped shape feminist arguments about the value of household labor and the necessity to make the home a decent workplace for those working in it—whether paid or unpaid. Josephine Hulett, a domestic worker activist from Ohio, made the point clearly that their movement was a feminist one. "After all," she told an interviewer for *Ms.* magazine, "there's a sense in which *all* women are household workers. And unless we stop being turned against each other, unless we organize together, we're never going to make this country see household work for what is really is—human work, not just 'woman's work.'"[9]

Domestic worker leaders forged a strategic alliance with the broader feminist movement. The ties between HTA and mainstream liberal feminism were varied and deep. NOW, the National Women's Political Caucus, the National Federation of Business and Professional Women's Clubs, and even New York Radical Feminists supported the domestic

8. "Domestics at Session Ask Gains," *New York Times*, October 10, 1972, 47; keynote address by Congresswoman Shirley Chisholm, 1972, NCHE Records, qtd. in Boris and Nadasen, "Domestic Workers Organize!," 423; "Domestics Fight for New Way of Life," *Chicago Defender*, August 21, 1971, 14. On HTA membership, see Nadasen, *Household Workers Unite*, 79; Boris and Klein, *Caring for America*, 127.

9. Josephine Hulett, interview by Janet Dewart, "Household Help Wanted: Female," *Ms.*, February 1973, 46. See also Nadasen, *Household Workers Unite*, 73–77, 139.

workers' cause, testifying in congressional hearings, organizing fund-raisers and speak outs, and serving on the board of the NCHE. Gloria Steinem, in particular, was a vocal and strong supporter of HTA. The black feminist leaders Shirley Chisholm and Eleanor Holmes Norton also both identified the household workers' cause as a priority and a women's issue.[10]

Activists in HTA participated in major feminist events and rallies. Geraldine Miller of the Bronx Household Technicians joined the Women's Strike for Equality; at the mass International Women's Day Rally in New York in 1975, Caroline Reed, leader of the Progressive Household Technicians of America, read out the workers' demands one by one. New York Radical Feminists co-organized a speak out in October 1973 with the Professional Household Workers Association. Later in the decade, Reed joined representatives from Black Women for Wages for Housework, Wages Due Lesbians, *Ms.* magazine writers, and professors from the women's studies program at Sarah Lawrence College outside New York at a conference on "The Future of Housework, the Role of the Housewife, and Sharing Arrangements for Child Care."[11]

Leaders of the domestic workers' movement had their own ties to other feminist organizations. Caroline Reed, for example, had leadership positions in the Women's Action Alliance and the National Women's Political Caucus, and she was also a founder of the National Black Feminist Organization. Geraldine Miller led both the Bronx chapter of the National Organization for Women and the NOW Women of Color Task Force in these years. She, too, became involved in the National Women's Political Caucus as a way to advance the household workers' agenda.[12] Reed's and Miller's activism reveals how domestic worker rights became a significant strand within black feminism. Shirley Chisholm spearheaded the campaign within Congress to amend the FLSA to include domestic workers, while Eleanor Holmes Norton used the platform of the New

10. Nadasen, *Household Workers Unite*, 128, 136, 138–39; Nadasen, "Citizenship Rights," 83–85; Palmer, "Outside the Law," 427–28; Anastasia Hardin, "Making the Dignity of Our Labor a Reality," Master's thesis (Rutgers University: 2013), 58–59.

11. Hardin, "Making the Dignity of Our Labor a Reality," 60, 62–65; Nadasen, *Household Workers Unite*, 136; Boris and Nadasen, "Domestic Workers Organize!," 423.

12. Nadasen, *Household Workers Unite*, 134; Nadasen, "Citizenship Rights," 84.

York City Human Rights Commission to speak out regularly on domestic workers' issues.

In 1971, Holmes Norton organized a conference, "Toward a Strategy for Solving the Problems of Household Employment in New York City," which brought NCHE and NOW leaders together with union representatives, city officials, and legislators. In her speech to conference attendees, Holmes Norton acknowledged the challenge in forging a coalition of women who employed domestic workers and the workers themselves, but emphasized the urgency of the alliance:

> That is why I have sought to highlight the plight of household workers as a question for the women's rights movement. . . . [O]nly the movement for women's rights embraces the entire affected group—those who work as household workers and those who need it most. . . . When the movement for women's rights can claim that it has done something concrete to change these conditions, such as winning legislative protection, it will have established itself as a serious movement that can deliver for all women and will lay to rest the foolishness about black women not having a stake in the fight for women's rights.

In her speech and elsewhere, Holmes Norton emphasized that domestic workers shared common interests with other women. Household labor attracted the same low wages and lack of respect of other jobs dominated by women. Moreover, as Carolyn Reed pointed out to the *New York Times*, men's presumption that they could get housework done for free by wives and girlfriends kept domestics from getting their "rights as a paid person in the labor force." To Reed, it was obvious: "This is a gut woman's issue."[13]

To resist such treatment, HTA adopted the strategy of emphasizing the value and skill of the labor of domestic workers. "If you still want an underclass to do your bidding," Barksdale Sloan proclaimed to employers of domestics in 1971, "you had better start building robots, because we refuse to play the part any longer. We refuse to be your mammies,

---

13. Edith Lynton, "Toward Better Jobs and Better Service in Household Work," New York Commission on Human Rights, 1972, qtd. in Hardin, "Making the Dignity of Our Labor a Reality," 59–60; Boris and Klein, *Caring for America*, 137; Nadine Brozan, "Bargaining Legislation for Domestics May Have Wide Impact," *New York Times*, April 28, 1975, 48.

nannies, aunties, uncles, girls and handmaidens any longer. What we will be are skilled, professional household technicians." The title "technician" was intentional. The Bronx HTA leader Geraldine Miller despised the word *domestic*. "We felt as though technicians were people that did something and were supposed to be great at it," she stressed. "We household workers were great people as technicians." Skilled at many tasks, HTA members demanded "the Three P's: pay, protection, and professionalism." Their fundamental goal: to be treated like real workers.[14]

Ensuring that domestic workers would receive the minimum wage through the requirements of the FLSA became the vehicle through which HTA sought recognition of household laborers' skills and professionalism, and they waged an extended battle from 1971 to 1974 to extend FLSA protections to domestic workers. Passed initially as a raft of legal protections for workers in the New Deal in 1938, the FLSA had excluded domestics, in part because of the work's location in the home and in part because of maneuvering by some in the Roosevelt administration who were nervous about placating legislators from the south, where large numbers of African-American domestics labored.[15]

In a series of congressional hearings on the FLSA amendments between 1971 and 1973, supporters reiterated the movement's feminist demands to uncouple housework from women's work, and to understand it as demanding labor, not selfless love. Domestic workers and their allies insisted that housework was skilled employment and that the home was a workplace. Barksdale Sloan told legislators that domestic work was "a demanding occupation requiring a variety of skills." A young NOW speaker emphasized that women understood that housework was "dirty, tedious work." "They," she continued, were "willing to pay to have it done because they more than anyone else, know what it is worth." Although both Barksdale Sloan and her NOW ally understood the labor involved in

14. Edith Sloan, keynote address, *NCHE News* 2 (July 1971), qtd. in Hardin, "Making the Dignity of Our Labor a Reality," 23; Hardin, "Making the Dignity of Our Labor a Reality," 27, 42; Geraldine Miller, interview by Loretta J. Ross, October 14, 2004, transcript, p. 30, Voices of Feminism Oral History Project, Sophia Smith Collection, Smith College, Northampton, MA. See also Nadasen, *Household Workers Unite*, 82–103; Cobble, "Spontaneous Lack of Enthusiasm," 34–35.

15. Palmer, "Outside the Law," 419; Nadasen, *Household Workers Unite*, 125–29.

domestic work, their differing descriptions of housework—"dirty, tedious work," rather than "demanding occupation"—reveal the challenges of maintaining coalitions among feminists very differently situated by race and class. Nevertheless, Hall echoed Barksdale Sloan's bottom line: having experienced workplace exploitation outside the home, she knew that without fair pay, domestic workers faced similar abuse. The esteemed labor organizer and NOW founder Dorothy Haener reiterated the organization's absolute support for the legislation. Its passage, she told legislators, was NOW's number one legislative priority.[16]

During their testimony, domestic worker leaders also challenged dismissive congressmen who brushed off the need for a minimum wage for domestic work as upsetting to their wives and disruptive to the comfortable, familial nature of domestic employment. Congressmen claimed, for example, that housewives could not manage complex paperwork or deal with federal bureaucracy in their homes. Supporters angrily called them out, pointing out that the idea that women couldn't add or subtract or organize the necessary forms was insulting to women. The deeper challenge to male prerogative became clear in a back-and-forth between Secretary of Labor Peter Brennan and Senator Pete Dominick as they fretted over the implications of higher valued—and higher cost—household labor. "Your wife will want to get paid," worried Brennan. "That means that you or I or we have to pay her. So we have to be very careful unless we are ready to do the dishes."[17]

Finally, advocates for domestic workers called for both respect and dignity for their work—and decent pay and benefits to match. For them, a legally mandated minimum wage was a first step toward such recognition. Senator Harrison Williams of New Jersey captured the arguments made by domestic workers and feminist allies when he commented that "many domestics are treated just as they were 150 years ago—as slaves. . . . They are called 'girl' and by their first names while they, themselves, must still address their employers and employers' children as 'ma'am' or

16. Gen. Subcomm. on Labor of the Comm. on Educ. and Labor, *Fair Labor Standards Amendments of 1973, H.R. 4757 and H.R. 2831*, 93d Cong. 208, 206, 242 (1973) (statements of Edith B. Sloan and Dorothy Haener and Kee Hall, National Organization for Women). For the hearings, see Palmer, "Outside the Law," 428–32; Glenn, *Forced to Care*, 139–42.

17. Palmer, "Outside the Law," 430–31; Brennan, qtd. in Nadasen, *Household Workers Unite*, 132.

'sir' or 'Miss Jane.'" Their average wages were less than one quarter of the minimum wage. "This hardly seems reasonable," he concluded with understated outrage. When Richard Nixon finally signed the amendments into law on April 8, 1974, the NCHE crowed in victory: "Minimum wage coverage for household workers gives to these one and a half million employees a legal mandate, a recognition of the value of their services and basic equality with other workers. . . . For the domestic worker, whether she is Black, White, Red or Brown, or lives in the North, East, South or West, it means a new respect—for her service and her person—and the ability to support herself and family."[18]

The domestic workers' movement brought a distinctive dimension to the second wave struggle to value housework. In important ways, it shaped the broader feminist view of housework as *work*—work that should be valued with social respect, legal rights, and decent treatment. Yet the alliance of domestic workers and mainstream feminist organizations was also fragile, partial, and complex. The portion of feminist rhetoric that painted housework as tedious, nasty work alienated many domestic workers, and the guilt many feminists felt employing domestics bemused domestic workers, who resented the implicit unwillingness of their feminist allies to make domestic work a good job with decent pay and treatment. When some women complained that they could not afford to pay a fair wage to a household employee, domestic workers argued that their employers had a responsibility to turn around and fight for better pay from their own bosses or greater contributions from their male partners.[19] HTA activists were clear-eyed about the larger problem: systematic devaluation and underpayment of women workers—inside the home, and outside of it.

The class and race differences among these feminist allies made sustaining common ground and shared goals over the long haul difficult. After the FLSA amendments passed, the struggle turned to enforcement, and a new invisibility pervaded domestic work, as responsibility for

18. The Subcomm. on Labor of the Comm. on Labor and Public Welfare, S., *Legislative History of the Fair Labor Standards Amendments of 1974 (Public law 93–259)* (Washington, DC: US Government Printing Office, 1976), vol. 2., 1818; NCHE, "Minimum Wage Coverage for Domestics: At Last!!!," press release, April 8, 1974, qtd. in Nadasen, *Household Workers Unite*, 142.

19. Nadasen, *Household Workers Unite*, 139–40.

adhering to the law returned to individual employers. The nature and site of domestic work shifted in the following decades as well. As the historians Eileen Boris and Jennifer Klein have shown, an expanding sector of care work produced more domestics working for multiple households and more working for contracting companies like maid services and home health-aide companies. By reshaping the employer-employee relationship, this restructuring shifted the ground for recognizing and valuing domestic labor.[20] Yet the enduring accomplishment of these insurgent years was to raise the status of the profession as a whole and to enshrine in law, for the first time, the labor rights of domestic workers. It gave tangible form to the feminist claim that housework was work.

"Washing Diapers Is Not Fulfilling"

For every glossied-up advertisement of dish soap, laundry detergent, or shirt-collar cleaner, for every smiling kitchen mopper in the movies, for every glowing extoller of Mr. Clean on television, many middle-class feminists had one answer: there was nothing glamorous or fun about housework. Unsparingly, women's liberationists stripped the glow from housework, and even childcare. A standard placard carried in the Women's Strike for Equality March read, "End Human Sacrifice! Don't Get Married!! Washing Diapers is Not Fulfilling." Radical feminist Pat Mainardi bluntly declared that the basic truth about housework is that "it stinks." Housework consisted of a series of "dirty chores" which had to be done, and done again, and had been routinely assigned to women of all races—but especially to African-American women.[21]

When feminists called household labor toil rather than love they reversed assumptions in place since the early 1800s when an idealized middle-class home became increasingly devoid of labor. Historian Jeanne Boydston has shown that prescriptive writers, ministers, and novelists pastoralized housework and sanctified the home "as an emanation of Woman's nature." In the process, says Boydston, nineteenth-century

---

20. Boris and Klein, *Caring for America*; Glenn, *Forced to Care*, 174–82.

21. Pat Mainardi, "The Politics of Housework," in *Sisterhood Is Powerful: An Anthology of Writings from the Women's Liberation Movement*, ed. Robin Morgan (New York: Vintage, 1970), 506, 502–3.

writers disguised the physical activity of household labor. Wifely devotion and motherly love—of white, middle-class women in particular—became a veneer covering up the demanding work involved. Sullivan-Dunbar's essay in this volume elaborates on the Catholic versions of this phenomenon, in particular, the idea of gender complementarity so dear to much papal writing about the economy. Second-wave feminists subjected such mystification of domestic labor to relentless debunking.[22]

This strand of the movement was led largely by white, middle-class feminists, and although their analysis overlapped with that of domestic workers' black feminism, its primary thrust was to challenge society's valorization of, and expectation for, full-time, unwaged female homemaking. It had four central aims. The first was to give unpaid household labor the value historically accorded to paid work. Second, these housework activists wanted to end the inequality of women's disproportionate burden of family work by compensating and supporting housewives who had devoted themselves to home and family. Such support, they believed, should also be available to spouses—whether male or female. Third, movement supporters argued that social benefits such as social security and tax deductions should be distributed by role and contribution rather than by marital status. And, finally, feminists fought for recognition that years of homemaking diminished opportunities for women in the larger society. They strove to facilitate movement between home and work in a variety of ways—from social security and other benefit credits for time out of the paid labor force to job-training programs for women with a long tenure in the home. In all of these cases, second-wave activism swirled around identifying a way to value housework so that it could be placed on a level playing field with waged work.

A concerted campaign to give dollar value to household labor was step one to this campaign. Feminists delighted in pointing out that, according to the Department of Labor, it would cost $8,000 to $9,000 a

22. Jeanne Boydston, *Home and Work: Housework, Wages, and the Ideology of Labor in the Early Republic* (New York: Oxford University Press, 1990), 149. For earlier efforts to value household labor, see Dolores Hayden, *The Grand Domestic Revolution: A History of Feminist Designs for American Homes, Neighborhoods and Cities*, rev. ed. (Cambridge, MA: The MIT Press, 1982); Glenna Matthews, *Just a Housewife: The Rise and Fall of Domesticity in America* (New York: Oxford University Press, 1987), 100, 113–14.

year—more than the annual income of nearly 40 percent of American households—to purchase all the services a housewife provided. One of Gloria Steinem's stock punch lines in her speeches on feminism introduced this staggering fact, although she coyly tweaked audiences by adding that the figures excluded "on and off prostitution."[23] The pressure of feminist activism was strong enough that several government agencies calculated housework's dollar value in the mid-1970s. In 1975, the Social Security Administration's Office of Research and Statistics performed its own calculations, a more modest $4,705 per year on average for a housewife's labor. The Bureau of Economic Analysis of the US Department of Commerce undertook an official effort to calculate "the dollar value of household work" in 1976. The goal was to provide a number to use in combination with more conventional calculations of the gross national product. Housework added $752.4 billion to the nation's economy, fully 44 percent of gross national product (GNP).[24] Although efforts to add housework to the GNP ultimately produced more discussion than action, the question of the dollar value of individual women's housework spawned efforts to secure wages for housework.

The demand for "wages for housework" had its roots in a critique of women's unrecognized contribution to capitalism. Socialist and radical feminists envisioned paying housewives as a provocative tactic toward the larger goal of revolution. Wages for housework would not end capitalist

23. US Department of Commerce, "Consumer Income," Current Population Reports, series P-60, no. 78 (May 20, 1971); Gloria Steinem, *ABC Nightly News*, January 25, 1972, qtd. in Susan J. Douglas and Meredith W. Michaels, *The Mommy Myth: The Idealization of Motherhood and How It Has Undermined Women* (New York: Free Press, 2004), 45. For a recent effort to calculate the value of household labor, see Nancy Folbre, "Valuing Care," in *For Love and Money: Care Provision in the United States*, ed. Nancy Folbre (New York: Russell Sage, 2012): 92–111.

24. Wendyce Brody, "Economic Value of a Housewife," Research and Statistics Note, US Department of Health Education and Welfare, Social Security Administration Office of Research and Statistics, Note No. 9–1975, August 28, 1975, Box 19, Folder 19, Catherine Shipe East Papers, 1941–1995, Schlesinger Library, Radcliffe Institute, Harvard University, Cambridge, MA (hereafter East Papers). Janice Peskin, "Measuring Household Production for the GNP," *Family Economics Review* 20 (June 1982): 17. The report considered several alternative methods to value household labor, ranging from $1,015.4 billion to $540 billion, and landed on the "specialist-cost valuation," which estimated the dollar value of hiring replacement labor to complete the work at the going wage rate.

exploitation, but its advocates believed paid homemaking provided a tool to raise consciousness about productive work long invisible even in Marxist analyses. Although the idea percolated among American feminists starting in the late 1960s, the movement was international in origins and had outgrowths in Europe as well as the United States in the early 1970s.[25] Vivien Leone first heard about the idea of wages for housework at meetings of her Older Women's Liberation group in New York in 1969. In the same year, Linda Gordon, writing for Bread and Roses, the Boston socialist women's group, argued that the work of housewives deserved "a salary just as much as that of their husband in the office or factory."[26]

The New York Wages for Housework Committee was founded in 1973 and opened a storefront office in Brooklyn not long afterward. Similar groups emerged in places as diverse as Los Angeles, Philadelphia, San Francisco, and Tulsa, Oklahoma. Sometimes they organized jointly as Black Women for Wages for Housework (New York and Los Angeles) and Wages Due Lesbians (Philadelphia and San Francisco). Members of wages-for-housework committees participated in women's movement demonstrations, provided speakers, led discussion groups, and distributed videotapes, cassettes, and pamphlets.[27]

The Marxist-feminist Silvia Federici summed up the campaign's argument in her 1975 treatise, "Wages Against Housework": "They say it is

25. Maud Anne Bracke, "Between the Transnational and the Local: Mapping the Trajectories and Contexts of the Wages for Housework Campaign in 1970s Italian Feminism," *Women's History Review* 22 (2013): 626–30; Ellen Malos, ed., *The Politics of Housework* (London: Allison and Busby), 21–24; Mariarosa Dalla Costa and Selma James, "The Power of Women and the Subversion of the Community," in *The Politics of Housework*, 160–95; Silvia Federici, *Wages against Housework* (Bristol, UK: Power of Women Collective and Falling Wall Press, 1975). For earlier incarnations, see Nancy F. Cott, *The Grounding of Modern Feminism* (New Haven, CT: Yale University Press, 1987), 77–78.

26. Vivien Leone, "Domestics" (1970), in *Radical Feminism: A Documentary Reader*, ed. Barbara A. Crow (New York: New York University Press, 2000), 519; "Leone, Vivien," in *Feminists Who Changed America, 1963–1975*, ed. Barbara J. Love (Urbana: University of Illinois Press, 2006), 276; Linda Gordon, "Functions of the Family" (1969), in *Voices from Women's Liberation*, ed. Leslie Barbara Tanner (New York: Signet, 1971), 184.

27. "Federici, Sylvia," in *Feminists Who Changed America*, ed. Love, 142; Alison Lefkovitz, *Strange Bedfellows: Marriage in the Age of Women's Liberation* (Philadelphia: University of Pennsylvania Press), 27–29; Silvia Federici and Arlen Austin, eds., *Wages for Housework: The New York Committee, 1972–1977—History, Theory, and Documents* (Brooklyn, NY: Autonomedia, 2017).

love. We say it is unwaged work." Indeed, Wages for Housework activists argued that government-paid wages for housework supported the feminist goal of disassociating housework from women's nature. "To say that we want money for housework is the first step toward refusing to do it," Federici pointed out, "because the demand for a wage makes our work visible, which is the most indispensable condition to begin to struggle against it."[28] Highlighting the connections between women's unpaid labor in the home and their status in the workforce, the movement reasoned that as long as women had no meaningful choice but to be housewives, they remained second-class citizens. Adding paid employment made no difference. The right to "refuse the double shift of a second job" complemented these activists' call to provide a wage for homemaking.[29]

Radicals were not alone in promoting wages for housework. Writing for *Ms.* in the summer of 1972, Ann Crittenden Scott noted that paying a housewife for her work was an idea in the air. "This salary," she observed, "would reflect the value of her individual services, what she could be earning in the labor market, or the official minimum wage. She could receive a percentage of her husband's salary to be paid by him or paid directly by his employer in the same way as the military sends allotment checks to the wives of servicemen who are stationed overseas."[30] Various

28. Federici, *Wages against Housework*, 1, 5.

29. New York Wages for Housework Committee, "Wages for Housework: From the Government. For ALL Women," 1975, in *Wages for Housework*, 54. It should be noted that significant conflict raged among radical feminists about the wages for housework campaign. Critics feared waged housework would legitimate keeping women in the home and continue to consign occupations dominated by women to low status. Wages for housework supporters countered that adding a wage to household labor would stimulate broader questions such as the real length of the working day for both men and women (once housework was added into the calculus); the limited benefit of a "second job" for women if housework is still their unpaid labor; and the psychological costs of women's dependency and lack of options. See Carol Lopate, "Pay for Housework?," *Social Policy* 5 (September/October 1974): 27–31; Heidi I. Hartmann, "The Unhappy Marriage of Marxism and Feminism: Toward a More Progressive Union," *Capital and Class* 3 (1979): 5–7; Malos, *The Politics of Housework*, 35–38; Lefkovitz, *Strange Bedfellows*, 29; Nicole Cox and Silvia Federici, *Counter-Planning from the Kitchen: Wages for Housework—A Perspective on Capital and the Left* (New York: New York Wages for Housework Committee and Falling Wall Press, 1975), 9. See also Betsy Warrior and Lisa Leghorn, *Houseworker's Handbook*, 3rd ed. (Cambridge, MA: Woman's Center, 1975).

30. Ann Crittenden Scott, "The Value of Housework—For Love or Money," *Ms.*, July 1972, 57.

schemes to "trade-a-maid" pointed out the ironies of the current system. Homemakers could hire each other, clean each other's homes, and pay each other a daily wage from their husbands' earnings. In the process, they would make social security payments, and as workers would qualify as well for disability and other employment benefits. As Jessie Hartline, a Rutgers University economist who proposed such a scheme, pointed out, "This isn't a gimmick at all. If I put an ad in the paper to hire a house-cleaner, and it turns out that the lady across the street answers the ad, that's fine, right?"[31]

The idea had surprisingly broad appeal for a position developed by radicals. One quarter of Americans surveyed in 1976 agreed that home-makers should earn pay for their work. A Connecticut homemaker told Crittenden Scott in *Ms.* that "it's not just the money. It's what it would mean psychologically. It would put a value on your work and make it clear that you've earned part of the family salary—that he's not just *giving* it to you." Other homemakers emphasized the humiliation factor: their husbands constantly questioned their use of money, and they repeatedly had to *ask* him for more. As feminist debate spread nationally, the topic of wages for housework became a focus for discussion. A 1974 Wisconsin conference on the homemaker generated a vigorous back-and-forth about paying a housewife, who would do it, and its potential risks and rewards. Mary Lou Munts, a leader of the discussion, suggested that a guaranteed income might better solve the problem. At a minimum, she concluded, a new model of social insurance based on need, not workforce participa-tion, seemed necessary. "The more we can do that—making old age and medical insurance, for example, the right of everyone—the more we can solve some of the problems of the homemaker."[32] Much liberal feminist energy would go into to these very efforts.

Three major attempts to modify law and policy exemplify this activ-ism by liberal feminists—social security reform, equalizing marital prop-erty division at divorce, and "displaced homemaker" legislation. Social security reform became a focus of feminist activism from the earliest

31. Hartline, qtd. in Rae André, *Homemakers: The Forgotten Workers* (Chicago: University of Chicago Press, 1981), 171; André, *Homemakers*, 171–76.

32. American Council of Life Insurance survey, cited in André, *Homemakers*, 112; Crittenden Scott, "Value of Housework," 58; Louise Kapp Howe, *Pink Collar Workers* (New York: Putnam, 1977), 211.

days of the second wave. The 1963 President's Commission on the Status of Women had recognized the need to provide homemakers with independent benefits beyond those they received as dependents of their husbands. Because social security payments were tied to employment-based contributions, housewives who had largely been out of the paid labor force had little entitlement in their own rights. Even when they worked, their pay was so low that they often received a better benefit as a spousal dependent. As one feminist analyst explained in 1977, "The social security system promotes dependency by defining women as family members rather than as individuals, by ignoring the prevalent phenomenon of the working wife and by failing to recognize the value of housework."[33]

Proposed plans ranged widely. In 1965, Congress had made an early change in the law and provided a divorced woman the social security benefits she would have received as a married wife as long as she had been married twenty years and not remarried before eligibility. The limits of this legislation were patently clear: a woman married nineteen years and eleven months received no benefits; those eligible had to wait until a former husband drew benefits, and then he received 100 percent of his benefit and she received 50 percent, rather than splitting the 150 percent total allowance between them. In response, feminists systematically put forward proposals to lower the number of years of marriage necessary for eligibility. Their demands were reflected in legislation that NOW member and US Representative Bella Abzug of New York introduced in Congress as early as 1971.[34] In 1977, the law finally required just ten years of marriage to be eligible for benefits due to an ex-spouse.

NOW also argued that employers should pay on husbands' earnings to build up a homemaker's benefits. Others proposed giving credits for years spent outside the labor force to give birth or care for children. Representative Abzug introduced additional legislation to pay for homemaker benefits from the general tax fund, a back door way to award homemakers

---

33. Susan Kinsley, "Women's Dependency and Federal Programs," in *Women Into Wives: The Legal and Economic Impact of Marriage*, ed. Jane Roberts Chapman and Margaret Gates (Beverly Hills: SAGE Publications, 1977), 89.

34. Suzanne Kahn, "Valuing Women's Work in the 1970s Home and the Boundaries of the Gendered Imagination," *Harvard Journal of Law and Gender* (2013): 3–5; Kinsley, "Women's Dependency," 89.

recognition for their labor while also acknowledging their work's import for the national economy. In 1974, Congresswomen Martha Griffiths of Michigan and Barbara Jordan of Texas proposed a bill to provide eligibility for homemakers as the equivalent of self-employed workers. Feminist lawmakers, with the support of activists, repeatedly introduced such legislation in a flurry of creative proposals through the 1970s.[35]

They ran into considerable opposition from those who would have had to pay. Some were angered by the prospect of adding to a husband's social security taxes. Others pointed out new contradictions in the program that the proposals would create, such as a working married woman's additional social security tax burden to cover homemakers, especially when their own husbands could not receive dependent benefits since married men were not eligible. Efforts to ensure that the proposals would not unfairly burden single earners, particularly lower-paid women, with social security taxes that would then be distributed to homemakers also raised concerns about the plans benefitting wealthier households. Although feminists pointed out that welfare recipients *were* homemakers deserving of similar benefits, the proposals were oriented to married housewives with wage-earning partners. They did little to grapple with the long-term disadvantages the system created for poor, single mothers on public assistance.[36]

Modest changes emerged, however. In 1977, in addition to the reforms in divorced women's eligibility, Congress granted remarried women the right to retain benefits from a previous spouse and made it possible for homemakers to establish Individual Retirement Accounts, which allowed them to build up independent retirement savings. More substantive proposals toward disentangling government-provided benefits from marital status and, alternatively, toward awarding them based on shared contribution to the couple's well-being—whether paid or unpaid labor—did not succeed. A system of earnings sharing in benefits has remained a

35. Kahn, "Valuing Women's Work," 6; André, *Homemakers*, 215.

36. Kahn, "Valuing Women's Work," 7; Nancy M. Gordon, "Institutional Responses: The Social Security System," in *The Subtle Revolution: Women at Work*, ed. Ralph E. Smith (Washington, DC: Urban Institute Press, 1979), 231–43; *Hearings Before the Subcomm. on Ret. Income and Emp't of the Select Comm. on Aging, H.*, 96th Cong., 108–10 (1979) (prepared statement of Eleanor Cutri Smeal).

feminist aspiration, with ongoing efforts to advance it over subsequent decades.[37]

Reform of the division of marital property at divorce emerged from a similar desire by liberal feminists to redress homemaker vulnerability. A NOW spokeswoman was explaining to a reporter as early as 1970 that "many housewives who don't work outside the home are shocked to discover that they are not automatically entitled to half the property." As divorce rates spiked in that decade, feminist groups from NOW to the Older Women's League shed light on the lack of protections for divorcing women and the economic difficulties they faced. NOW even went so far as endorsing "end of marriage" insurance to provide a measure of financial security for divorcing women. Feminists in NOW, the Older Women's League, and the League for Women's Rights put forward a number of proposals to secure women's access to marital property at divorce, from establishing defined shares of property to a divorce pension plan that would take annual payments during marriage for benefits payable if a marriage dissolved.[38]

Feminists also devised several more pragmatic strategies to count homemaker contributions in property distributions in divorce settlements. In states where state-level Equal Rights Amendments had passed, courts increasingly required that a homemaker's contribution be calculated. The Pennsylvania Supreme Court, for example, ruled in 1975 that property belonged to divorcing spouses equally regardless of who was the family provider, observing, "We can not accept an approach that would base ownership of household items on proof of funding alone, since to do

37. Spencer Rich, "Hill Widens Old-Age Aid for Women," *Washington Post*, January 10, 1978, A8; André, *Homemakers*, 213–14, 216–17; Gordon, "Institutional Responses," 239–43, 255; Kahn, "Valuing Women's Work," 8–9; Patricia A. Seith, "Congressional Power to Effect Sex Equality," *Harvard Journal of Law and Gender* 36 (2013): 22, 27–28, 57.

38. Enid Nemy, "Almost All Agree—Women Marrying Should Know Their Rights," *New York Times*, August 10, 1973, 33; Betty Berry, "Report of NOW–NY Marriage and Divorce Committee" [1970] (box 25, folder 3), East Papers; "Now, Homemaker's Insurance," News for and from Housewives for ERA, 4, no. 3, October–November 1976 (box 46, folder 40) National Organization for Women Records, 1959–2002, Schlesinger Library, Radcliffe Institute, Harvard University, Cambridge, MA (hereafter NOW Records). On NOW's divorce reform activism, see also "NOW Task Force on Marriage, Divorce and Family Relations," November 1973 (box 30, folder 54) NOW Records; Judy Klemesrud, "'Obsolete' Divorce Laws Assailed at NOW Conference Here," *New York Times*, January 21, 1974, 32; Ziegler, "An Incomplete Revolution."

so . . . would fail to acknowledge the equally important and often substantial non-monetary contributions made by either spouse." Feminist
lawyers often framed such arguments for courts, contributing to a series
of influential law review articles and the model Uniform Marriage and
Divorce Act.[39] In states without state-level Equal Rights Amendments,
feminists also found ways to advance recognition for homemakers' labor
in reformed divorce law. In Connecticut, for example, the State Commission on the Status of Women and NOW both pressed strongly for including homemaker labor in determining equitable division of property at
divorce, successfully influencing legislation passed in 1978. By the beginning of the 1980s, over half of the cases involving marital property distribution recognized the contribution of homemakers. By 1983, forty-two
states had laws to consider homemakers' labor at divorce—up from none
in 1968. The trend was unmistakably in this direction. As legal historian Mary Ziegler has observed, all of the demands put forward by the
NOW Task Force on Marriage and Divorce in 1975 "had either been
adopted at the federal level or had passed in more than twenty states"
within a decade.[40]

Housework's value drew feminist energies in one additional area:
addressing the needs of older women who had expected to spend their
lives as housewives but now found themselves "displaced" when their
husbands died or their marriages ended. The realities of widowhood
compounded by a surge in separation and divorce left more than four
million women in limbo by 1977, with many millions more facing such a
prospect. Bereft of the support they presumed they would receive from
husbands, they faced discrimination and limited opportunities when
they tried to get a job. One California divorcée stressed her narrow
options: after thirty-eight years as a homemaker, the only work she could
get was babysitting for seventy-five cents an hour. A job counselor told

39. DiFlorido v. DiFlorido, 459 Pa. 650, 331 A.2d 179 (1975), qtd. in Lefkovitz, *Strange Bedfellows*, 61; Lefkovitz, *Strange Bedfellows*, 59–61; Ziegler, "An Incomplete Revolution."

40. Lefkovitz, *Strange Bedfellows*, 33, 68–69; Fern Schumer, "Fairness New Byword," *Chicago Tribune*, March 24, 1981, C1, cited in Lefkovitz, *Strange Bedfellows*, 65; Ziegler, "An Incomplete Revolution," 278, 282–83. Lefkovitz offers a more equivocal assessment of the long-term outcome of feminist legal and legislative efforts to reform marriage and divorce; see Lefkovitz, *Strange Bedfellows*, 65–74.

her, "She hated to have to say it but that they just don't want older women on the job market."[41]

In 1974, feminist activist Tish Sommers coined the term *displaced homemaker* to describe these women; in her eyes, displaced homemakers were similar to the displaced persons of war or disaster. "A whole generation of women caught in the 1970s," she argued, was "'forcibly exiled,' displaced from a role, an occupation, dependency status, and a livelihood."[42] Displaced homemaker programs got their start in 1975, with legislation passed in California. In 1978, with the backing of Representative Yvonne Burke, a civil and women's rights supporter and the first African American woman elected to the House of Representatives from California, the movement secured national funding through the Comprehensive Education and Training Act. At that point, twenty-eight states had considered similar legislation in the previous year. Displaced homemaker programs did much the same thing as displaced worker supports, offering services including counseling, education, job seeking skills, job training, and preparation for nontraditional employment.[43]

The displaced homemaker movement had the needs of middle-aged and older women at its heart. By the last years of the decade, this single-minded focus ran up against other currents of the feminist movement. Rising attention to single mothers and the growing feminization of poverty raised questions about making older homemakers a sole priority. As public opposition to welfare grew, moreover, displaced homemaker activists played up the difference between themselves and poor women on public assistance. This approach angered antipoverty and welfare rights activists. In 1979, Beulah Sanders, a longtime welfare-rights leader, attacked the displaced homemaker movement for failing to deal with "poor Third World women, as usual." "They are creating a constituency of middle-class White women with whom they can relate most comfortably," she went on, "but how many minority women will reap any

---

41. Beverly Cederberg, "Displaced as Homemaker, She Builds New Life," *Valley News*, August 22, 1976, 4, qtd. in Levenstein, "Don't Agonize, Organize!," 1119; Levenstein, "Don't Agonize, Organize!," 1117–19. See also Laurie Shields, *Displaced Homemakers: Organizing for a New Life* (New York: McGraw-Hill, 1981).

42. Shields, *Displaced Homemakers*, ix.

43. Shields, *Displaced Homemakers*, 62–64; Levenstein, "Don't Agonize, Organize!," 1122–24, 1130.

benefits?"[44] In the face of that criticism, and with changing realities in female employment, programs funded originally for displaced home-makers alone came to include younger "women in transition," and the constituency served expanded to include poor mothers on assistance.

Feminism's Legacies: Valuing Housework and Care Labor Today

Feminist housework activism challenged the mid-century's conventional economic wisdom that designated work in the home as love and work outside it as labor. Second wavers showed how idealization of housework had generated a low status and racialized workforce, both paid and unpaid, that left women vulnerable. They struggled to make household labor visible and valued. Their efforts resulted in new domestic worker rights, significant social security reform, changed divorce law, and dis-placed homemaker supports. Unpaid housework itself became part of an ongoing struggle between partners. Feminists successfully shifted the ground under the presumption that housecleaning was women's work.

Yet the movement had critics. In part, the feminist orientation to valu-ing housework in dollar terms implicitly devalued not only the profes-sional pride of domestic workers but also the emotional satisfaction some experienced doing it. In seeking to break the link between womanhood and housewifery, many feminists also underplayed the devotion tied to some household work, particularly that connected to caring for children and other family members. Critics among the 1974 Wisconsin home-maker conference attendees voiced such sentiments. It was all fine and good for professional women to want to abandon housework, but, as one housewife pointedly noted, "For the average woman that's a lot of balo-ney" since everyday jobs for women were not so great. This homemaker felt keenly a feminist presumption that economic independence was the necessary goal to achieve equality and secure women's self-preservation. Women like her experienced pressure, even if they had small children, or

---

44. Shields, *Displaced Homemakers*, 112; Jill Nelson, "Displaced Homemakers: Who's Displacing Whom?," *Encore American and Worldwide News*, April 16, 1979, 18–19, qtd. in Levenstein, "Don't Agonize, Organize!," 1131–32; Levenstein, "Don't Agonize, Orga-nize!," 1131–34.

wished to be caretakers, to be employed in the paid labor force. "I got the feeling, you know, that women shouldn't want to be dependent," she commented, "that we're fools if we do, that we're stupid. But the fact is many of us, maybe most of us, like leaning on our husbands—he leans on us, too, you know—and we don't like to be told we're fools."[45] In spite of these doubts, some also praised the feminist desire to create real choices between homemaking and paid employment.

In the long term, feminists had the greatest success when their proposals shifted the burden of women's dependency in the home onto the wage labor market, as in displaced homemaker programs, or continued to link revised social benefits to marital status, as in broadening divorced women's eligibility for social security. Efforts to provide homemakers benefits as individuals in order to produce security regardless of marital or employment status stalled out, as did radical proposals for homemaker wages. Economic pressures that pushed more and more women into paid jobs compounded the limits of feminist successes in securing benefits for homemaking. In the process, the second wave unintentionally reinforced a solution distinctive to liberal feminism— eradicating dependency. Although the displaced homemaker movement, for example, had broad aims of emotional support and social recognition for homemakers, its programs were oriented toward economic self-sufficiency and employment. The impact of domestic worker activism was more complex. It, too, challenged female economic dependency. Yet, in demanding that household employment be a *good* job, these organizers represented the vanguard of a growing and diversifying labor force of nannies, household employees, home-healthcare aides, and eldercare workers.

Today, women remain saddled with the bulk of unpaid household labor, and although men's attitudes have changed substantially, little change in their actions has occurred. A slight recent increase in men's time devoted to household and family labor has leaned heavily toward childcare rather than housework. Women in this country still spend on average an hour more than men in caring for children each day, and they

45. Howe, *Pink Collar Workers*, 200. On this point, see also the essay by Sullivan-Dunbar in this volume.

pay the price in a variety of ways, from the "motherhood penalty" in wages to greater stress.[46]

Paid domestic labor continues, taking on new form: the number of in-home domestic and childcare workers has declined, while those employed as home health aides and personal attendants have risen. Nancy Folbre and Julie Nelson documented that by 1998, "professional care services" employed nearly 20 percent of all workers (rising from 4 percent in 1900; and 12 percent in 1960); women dominated such professional care industries, forming the large majority of workers in sectors such as "Other Health Services" and "Social Services." These occupations are some of the fastest growing jobs today, with no letup in sight.[47] Feminist insight that such labor should be recognized, accurately counted, and properly valued has been partially realized as feminist economists and sociologists have developed increasingly powerful analyses of this care sector and its place in the nation's economy. Deepening understanding of how the paid care sector today contributes to job polarization, to income inequality, to growth of a low-paid and racialized labor force, and to continued devaluation of unpaid domestic labor remains essential to any true working alternative to our current economy.[48]

Making paid domestic work a "good job" is central to constructing such a working alternative that is just and equitable. Enforcement of domestic workers' rights has been spotty, and despite some expansion of

46. Suzanne Bianchi, Nancy Folbre, and Douglas Wolf, "Unpaid Care Work," in *For Love and Money*, 47, 54, 58; Suzanne M. Bianchi, John P. Robinson, and Melissa A. Milkie, *Changing Rhythms of American Family Life* (New York: Russell Sage Foundation, 2006), 136–37.

47. Mignon Duffy, *Making Care Count: A Century of Gender, Race, and Paid Care Work* (New Brunswick, NJ: Rutgers University Press, 2011), figure 2.2, p. 25 and figure 2.5, p. 32; US Census Bureau, "Employment by Industry: 2000 to 2010," *Statistical Abstract of the United States: 2012* (Washington, DC: GPO, 2012), table 620, p. 339; Heidi Shierholz, *Low Wages and Scant Benefits Leave Many In-Home Workers Unable to Make Ends Meet* (Washington, DC: Economic Policy Institute, November 25, 2013), table 1, p. 4 and table 11, p. 22; Nancy Folbre and Julie A. Nelson, "For Love or Money—Or Both?," *Journal of Economic Perspectives* 14, no. 4 (Fall 2000): 126–27.

48. Rachel E. Dwyer, "The Care Economy? Gender, Economic Restructuring, and Job Polarization in the US Labor Market," *American Sociological Review* 78 (June 2013): 390–416; Glenn, *Forced to Care*.

their rights in recent years, many providing care still lack basic labor protections. Because many federal labor laws cover only those who work for an employer with multiple employees, for example, domestic workers still lack protections like those offered by the Family and Medical Leave Act. Other laws, like the Occupational Safety and Health Act and the National Labor Relations Act, continue to exclude household workers despite the victories of 1974. The workforce draws heavily on nonwhite and immigrant women; wages continue to be low, well below those of similar workers in other occupations. Immigrant status, including lacking papers, leaves many vulnerable to exploitation. Feminist sociologists and domestic-worker activists have also pointed to the elevation of some domestic labor as "spiritual"—an expression of caring—and other parts of it as "menial"—dirty housecleaning. That artificial divide further degrades some paid domestic labor. The second wave analysis that assigning women household and family labor contributes to the systematic devaluation of women's labor—unpaid and paid, inside and outside the home—continues to be necessary to resist rewarding and recognizing some types of family and domestic work over other forms.[49]

Beginning in the 1990s, feminists renamed household labor "care work" and began to advocate for a right to care, and renewed pressure to recognize the dignity and value of domestic and caring labor. By 2000, sociologist Deborah Stone was rallying a feminist movement on new terms: "We have the Bill of Rights and we have civil rights. Now we need a Right to Care, and it's going to take a movement to get it."[50] Silvia Federici has continued to advocate for valuing and recognizing household labor, writing about elder care and the global inequalities in care work. Selma James, another leader of the 1970s wages for housework movement, has been the moving force behind Global Women's Strike, a

49. Nadasen, "Citizenship Rights, Domestic Workers," 88; Shierholz, "Low Wages and Scant Benefits," 2; Pierrette Hondagneu-Sotelo, "Domésticas Demand Dignity," in *Women's America: Refocusing the Past*, 8th ed., ed. Linda K. Kerber, Jane Sherron De Hart, Cornelia Hughes Dayton, Judy Tzu-Chun Wu (New York: Oxford University Press, 2016), 759–75; Dorothy E. Roberts, "Spiritual and Menial Housework," Faculty Scholarship, Paper 1282 (Penn Law: Legal Scholarship Repository, 1997).

50. Deborah Stone, "Why We Need a Care Movement," *The Nation*, March 13, 2000, 13.

contemporary incarnation of the wages for homemakers movement.[51] A surge in labor organizing by paid care workers began again in the late twentieth century as well and lent renewed energy to domestic workers' rights campaigns. Today, groups like Domestic Workers United in New York and the Domestic Workers' Association in Los Angeles, as well as a new national organization, the National Domestic Workers Alliance founded in 2007, fight for domestic worker rights and enforcement of new state-level bills of rights for domestic workers. Home health care workers—such as health and personal care aides—have reshaped the fight for household workers' rights, leading unionization drives and gaining FLSA minimum wage and overtime protections in 2015.[52] Such campaigns to value caregiving in all its forms embody the latest frontier in campaigns pioneered by second-wave activists more than fifty years ago and are essential steps.

51. Silvia Federici, *Revolution at Point Zero: Housework, Reproduction, and Feminist Struggle* (Oakland, CA: PM Press, 2012); "Housework as Work: Selma James on Unwaged Labor and Decades-Long Struggle to Pay Housewives," *Democracy Now!* (April 16, 2012), www.democracynow.org/2012/4/16/housework_as_work_selma_james_on.

52. On domestic workers, see Shierholz, "Low Wages and Scant Benefits," 22; Hondagneu-Sotelo, "Domésticas," 772–74; Domestic Workers United, www.domestic workersunited.org/index.php/en/; National Domestic Workers Alliance, www.domestic workers.org. On home health care aides, see US Department of Labor, "Home Care: US Court of Appeals Unanimously Upheld DOL Rule" (2016), www.dol.gov/whd/home care/litigation.htm; Boris and Klein, *Caring for America*.

Curing the "Disease" in Corporatized Higher Education

Prescriptions from the Catholic Social Tradition

GERALD J. BEYER

Higher education in the United States has a "disease." As critical pedagogy expert Henry Giroux correctly maintains, "Many universities and colleges have become unapologetic accomplices to corporate values and power."[1] The corporatization of the university has infected higher education with hyper-individualistic practices and models imported from the business world, modern economics, and, more broadly, neoliberal capitalism. I argue that a vision of the human person as selfish, hyper-competitive, solipsistic, and unwilling to sacrifice for the common good undergirds these practices and models. In this paradigm, members of the university community, including entire programs or departments, who are perceived to be inferior are treated as drags on the system or instruments to be exploited. The corporatized university also sharply reifies hierarchical structures, which tend to disempower faculty and contravene the notion of shared governance. These hierarchical structures of the corporatized university also denigrate an important feature of the human person according to Catholic thought, namely her natural inclination to participation in the shaping of those structures that affect her life and those around her most significantly.

I contend that the Catholic social tradition and its underlying social anthropology offer one possible "antidote." I will thus employ the Catholic social tradition and Catholic understandings of the human person, as well as some insights from other disciplines, to propose "cures" for the

1. I am grateful to John Seitz, Christine Firer Hinze, and other contributors to this volume for feedback on this chapter. In addition, I am indebted to Dr. Mary Beth Yount of Neumann University for helpful suggestions for refining my arguments.

Henry A. Giroux, *Neoliberalism's War on Higher Education* (Chicago: Haymarket Books, 2014), 22.

"disease" of corporatized higher education. In doing so, I aim to reenvision just work at universities. This project has specific relevance to Catholic institutions of higher learning, as the Catholic social tradition provides a normative framework that should inform their policies and practices. However, the diagnosis of the problem, as well as the proposed solutions, can be applied to higher education generally, as the neoliberal corporatized university has proliferated across the globe.[2] I am not arguing that universities were once purely egalitarian and virtuous communal structures. I am aware, for example, that US higher education was created on the backs of slaves for white males only.[3] I only argue that corporatization has exacerbated and accelerated certain negative traits and tendencies.

My argument unfolds in several stages. First, I briefly describe the corporatized university and its general practices. Next, I examine one of the most pernicious "symptoms" of the corporatization of higher education, namely, the casualization (or "adjunctification") of the academic workforce.[4] A larger project would take up other deleterious consequences of the dominance of the neoliberal ethos and norms, stressing for example particularly harmful effects on people of color and women.[5]

The discussion then turns to infiltration of *homo economicus* as one of the most plausible root causes of both the "symptom" and "disease" of the corporatized university. I contend that the embrace of this flawed vision of human person at least partially explains why decision-makers at universities have largely accepted abusive practices associated with corporatized higher education such as adjunctification. I do not contend that decision-makers always act in accordance with *homo economicus*, nor

2. See Giroux, *Neoliberalism's War*; Willem Halffman and Hans Radder, "The Academic Manifesto: From an Occupied to a Public University," *Minerva* 53, no. 2 (2015); Lawrence D. Berg, Edward H. Huijbens, and Henrik Gutzon Larsen, "Producing Anxiety in the Neoliberal University," *The Canadian Geographer / Le Géographe canadien* 60, no. 2 (2016).

3. See Craig Steven Wilder, *Ebony & Ivy: Race, Slavery, and the Troubled History of America's Universities* (New York: Bloomsbury, 2013).

4. For example, "Resisting the Increase in Contingent Appointments," The American Association of University Professors, https://www.aaup.org/resisting-increase-contingent-appointments, uses the term "adjunctification."

5. I treat these issues in Gerald J. Beyer, *Just Universities: Catholic Social Teaching Confronts Corporatized Higher Education* (New York: Fordham University Press, forthcoming).

do I suggest that this mode of thinking is always conscious, even though it may be evident from the outside. Moreovever, decision-makers sometimes act altruistically and for the sake of the common good in admirable ways, at the expense of "rational self-interest."[6] Rather, I argue they unjustifiably act in accordance with *homo economicus* often enough to afflict the human dignity and well-being of those affected by these decisions.

In this section, I discuss economic theory, US business school training, and neoliberal capitalism as "conduits" through which *homo economicus* has penetrated universities. Drawing on the works of Michael Pirson, Rakesh Khurana, and others, I highlight business school training as a conduit for *homo economicus* to universities. However, I argue that all stakeholders at US universities (administrators, faculty, staff, board members, and students) have embraced *homo economicus* to some degree. This embrace of *homo economicus* manifests detrimental behaviors to the university community. Next, I treat two management practices at universities undergirded by the vision of *homo economicus*, namely, responsibility centered management (RCM) and the so-called Dickeson model. Having diagnosed some of the "symptoms" and the "disease" of corporatized higher education, I will turn to the Catholic social tradition to prescribe some possible "cures" in the second half of my essay. This section aims to spark further discussion of *Working Alternatives* to the corporatized university occupied by *homo economicus*.

Diagnosing the Symptoms and Disease of the Corporatized University

The Corporatized University Defined

According to Henry Steck, the corporatized university is "an institution that is characterized by processes, decisional criteria, expectations, organizational culture, and operating practices that are taken from, and have their origins in, the modern business corporation."

---

6. For example, many university leaders have recently declared their campuses to be "sanctuary campuses" for undocumented immigrants, perhaps risking the loss of federal funding.

Corporatized universities are "characterized by the entry of the university into marketplace relationships and by the use of market strategies in university decision-making."[7] These strategies include the following, among others: viewing students as customers and emphasizing "customer satisfaction"; responsibility-centered management; heavy reliance on quantitative metrics to measure performance; hierarchical organizational structures, downsizing or elimination of departments (especially in the humanities) because they fail to generate revenue; the marketing and "branding" of the institution; the increasing number of managers and administrators; and accepting funds from corporations in exchange for influence over research and academic programming.[8]

The corporatization of the university runs so deep at this point that many students and their parents now choose majors based on potential earnings data.[9] Studying a field to follow a passion or become an educated citizen—hallmarks of a liberal education—is passé.[10] Faculty members are often seen as "cashiers" who should above all strive for the "consumer satisfaction" of their high-paying customers, that is, students and their parents.[11] Some university presidents now see endowments not as "rainy-day" funds to buoy essential academic programs in times of need but rather as funds to be raised to boost their own resume for their next job, a phenomenon called "endowment hoarding."[12]

7. Henry Steck, "The Corporatization of the University: Seeking Conceptual Clarity," *Annals of the American Association of Political Science* 585 (2003): 74.

8. I draw here on Steck, "The Corporatization of the University," 75–76 and Andrew Delbanco, *College: What It Was, Is, and Should Be* (Princeton, NJ: Princeton University Press, 2012), 140–143. See also Joe Berry, *Reclaiming the Ivory Tower: Organizing Adjuncts to Change Higher Education* (New York: Monthly Review Press, 2005), 3–4.

9. Douglas Belkin, "Using Salary Prospects to Choose a College Major," *Wall Street Journal*, March 17, 2014. For a broader assessment of why students choose particular colleges, see Rachel Fishman, "College Decisions Survey: Deciding to Go to College," *New America*, last modified May 28, 2015, https://www.newamerica.org/education-policy/edcentral/collegedecisions/.

10. See Andrew Delbanco, *College: What It Was, Is, and Should Be*.

11. David M. Perry "Faculty Members Are Not Cashiers." *The Chronicle of Higher Education*, March 17, 2014.

12. Jeffrey R. Brown, "How Endowment Hoarding Hurts Universities," *The Chronicle of Higher Education*, last modified March 17, 2014, https://www.chronicle.com/article/How-Endowment-Hoarding-Hurts/145343.

A veteran of several different academic institutions, Marc Bousquet has also described the "corporate welfare university."[13] He points to the various ways in which "corporate shareholders" benefit from high-priced higher education and the simultaneous "faculty proletarianization." In the last thirty years of "managed higher education," the corporate class has also benefited from a growing number of well-paying managerial posts. Administrators have hired more administrators, while reducing the amount of tenure-track faculty positions and decreasing the pay of many campus workers. As Bousquet puts it, "the university under managerial domination is an accumulation machine. If in nonprofits it accumulates in some form other than dividends, there's all the more surplus for administrators, trustees, local politicians, and a handful of influential faculty to spend on a discretionary basis."

Benjamin Ginsburg also bemoans the "all-administrative university."[14] Administrators have largely wrested the responsibility of setting institutional priorities from the faculty. Ginsburg and others thus deplore the evisceration of shared governance, which "is supposed to characterize academic decision making" and requires "academic administrators share power over important decisions."[15] Thus, universities have come to more closely resemble a "bureaucratic or orthodox organization." This type of "formal hierarchy" is "an official system of unequal person-independent roles and positions which are linked via lines of top-down command-and control." All orders flow downward, while information flows upward.[16]

According to Bousquet, administrators have hired more and more administrators, while the number of tenure stream professors has waned significantly, because university management wants to "remake

13. Marc Bousquet, *How the University Works: Higher Education and the Low-Wage Nation* (New York: New York University Press, 2008), 20–22.

14. See Benjamin Ginsberg, *The Fall of the Faculty: The Rise of the All-Administrative University and Why It Matters* (New York: Oxford University Press, 2011).

15. Ibid., 15. On the erosion of shared governance, see also Giroux, *Neoliberalism's War*, 110–11.

16. Thomas Diefenbach and John A. A. Sillince, "Formal and Informal Hierarchy in Different Types of Organization," *Organization Studies* 32, no. 11 (2011): 1517–18. I am not arguing that all forms and degrees of hierarchy are illegitimate, but this type is inimical to shared governance. My understanding of workplace hierarchy is also informed by Jacob Morgan, *The Future of Work: Attract New Talent, Build Better Leaders, and Create a Competitive Organization* (Hoboken, NJ: Wiley, 2014).

competing campus cultures in its own image."[17] Swelling their own ranks has enabled administrators to dictate many, if not most, key decisions.[18] In 1975 roughly two hundred and fifty thousand administrators and professional staff worked at universities. That number grew to over seven hundred fifty thousand by 2005, far surpassing the number of professors on the tenure track.[19] In a 2014 report, the American Association of University Professors (AAUP) noted that from 1975 to 2011 the rate of growth for full-time nonfaculty professional positions was 369 percent, compared with just 23 percent for tenure and tenure track academic appointments.[20]

Casualization of the Academic Workforce as a Symptom and a Means

The casualization of the academic workforce represents one of the most pernicious consequences of the corporatization of university. The adjunctification of the faculty is both a means to and symptom of the corporatized university. Budget models such as RCM "create powerful incentives" to employ much cheaper labor, for example, adjunct (part-time) faculty, as the savings enables academic units to generate more revenue from tuition.[21] This has created a situation in which some administrators, athletics personnel, and distinguished full-time faculty make handsome salaries. At the same time, many adjunct faculty earn poverty wages, have no health or retirement benefits, and work as "temps" with no job security.[22]

17. Bousquet, *How the University Works*, 23. See also Ginsberg, *The Fall of the Faculty*, 20–27.

18. Bousquet, *How the University Works*, 26–28. See also Ginsberg, *The Fall of the Faculty*, 3.

19. James F. Keenan, *University Ethics: How Colleges Can Build and Benefit from a Culture of Ethics* (Lanham, MD: Rowman & Littlefield, 2015), 67.

20. John Curtis and Saranna Thornton, "Losing Focus: The Annual Report on the Economic Status of the Profession, 2013–14," *Academe* (2014): 8.

21. John G. Cross and Edie N. Goldenberg, *Off-Track Profs: Nontenured Teachers in Higher Education* (Cambridge, MA: MIT Press, 2009), 91–92.

22. See Ken Jacobs, Ian Perry, and Jenifer MacGillvary, "The High Public Cost of Low Wages: Poverty-Level Wages Cost U.S. Taxpayers $152.8 Billion Each Year in Public Support for Working Families," PDF File, (UC Berkeley Center for Labor Research and Education, 2015), http://laborcenter.berkeley.edu/pdf/2015/the-high-public-cost-of-low-wages.pdf; House Committee on Education and the Workforce, "The Just-in-Time Professor," PDF File, Washington, DC: United States House Of Representatives, 2014,

Women and people of color are disproportionately affected by this "bargain," as they are overrepresented among the adjunct faculty ranks.[23] As Swinth and Sullivan-Dunbar maintain in this book, the notion that women are doing their work "out of love" is often used to justify exploitation in the workplace. The same can be said of the gendered exploitation of adjunct faculty.[24]

Like Waddock's argument in this volume regarding the anthropology of current business models, I contend that ultimately this unjust situation is a symptom of the flawed anthropological vision undergirding corporatized higher education.[25] At present, many full-time professors and administrators aim to maximize their own salaries and benefits, while failing to see their complicity in unjust social structures that degrade other university workers. In the language of Catholic moral theology, maintaining a system that abuses university workers, by constructing, enacting or benefitting from it, amounts to cooperation in evil.[26] Those who cooperate in this evil often fail to see their obligations to others in the university community.

Homo Economicus *in the University*

How can it be that board members, administrators, and tenure-track faculty members allow colleagues to teach for poverty wages? How can so

---

http://democrats-edworkforce.house.gov/imo/media/doc/1.24.14-AdjunctEforum Report.pdf. I discuss the situation of adjunct faculty in greater detail in Beyer, *Solidarity or Status Quo?*

23. See Mary Ann Mason, Nicholas H. Wolfinger, and Marc Goulden, *Do Babies Matter? Gender and Family in the Ivory Tower* (New Brunswick, NJ: Rutgers University Press, 2013); Colleen Flaherty, "Study Finds Gains in Faculty Diversity, but Not on the Tenure Track," *Inside Higher Ed*, last modified August 22, 2016, https://www.insidehigh ered.com/news/2016/08/22/study-finds-gains-faculty-diversity-not-tenure-track.

24. See Maria Maisto, "Taking Art, Taking Part: New Faculty Majority and the Praxis of Contingent Faculty Activism," in *Embracing Nontenure Track Faculty: Changing Campuses for the New Faculty Majority*, ed. Adrianna J. Kezar (New York, Routledge, 2012).

25. See below contra the "financial exigency" argument.

26. I spell this argument out in Gerald J. Beyer, "Advocating Worker Justice: A Catholic Ethicist's Toolkit," *Journal of Religious Ethics* 45, no. 2 (2017).

many of us ignore Kant's categorical imperative, enjoining us not to deny the humanity of others by using them as a means (cheap academic labor) to an end (college education for our students)? What about The Golden Rule, expressed in the world's religions? Is adjunctification necessary to keep exorbitant tuition from spiking more? I cannot fully address the complex economic questions here, but doing so may not be necessary for the sake of my argument.[27] Economist and director for the Center for the Study of Academic Labor Steven Shulman has shown that the costs of improving the lot of adjuncts are not nearly as high as some have proposed. Rather, "Colleges and universities often claim that they are unable to afford certain expenditures when they simply are choosing other expenditures instead. The problem is not their overall financial capacity so much as it is their priorities."[28] If Schulman is correct, his study supports my contention that another cause of adjunctification remains more plausible than the financial exigency explanation. The fact that presidents and chief academic officers average $334,000 and $213,000 in salaries, respectively, whereas other employees endure poverty, attests to Shulman's claim.[29] Moreover, many colleges and universities prioritize spending exorbitant amounts of money on "non-educational spending" (luxury dormitories, fitness centers, homes for presidents, six and seven figure coaches' salaries, etc.) tangential to the institution's mission.[30] Claiming these are necessary expenditures lacks compelling evidence.[31] I argue that the sometimes tacit, sometimes explicit acceptance of a distorted, atomistic understanding of human personhood and community appears to be the more plausible explanation for universities' failure to prioritize just compensation for adjunct faculty. In other words, *homo*

27. I take up this issue more fully in Beyer, *Just Universities*.

28. Steven Shulman, "The Costs and Benefits of Adjunct Justice: A Critique of Brennan and Magness," *Journal of Business Ethics* (2017): 5.

29. Data taken from https://www.aaup.org/file/FCS_2016-17_nc.pdf.

30. Shulman, "The Costs and Benefits of Adjunct Justice: A Critique of Brennan and Magness," 6.

31. See Donna M. Desrochers, "Academic Spending Versus Athletic Spending: Who Wins?," Delta Cost Project at American Institutes for Research, 2013; Jeffrey Selingo, "Forget the Marketing Gimmicks. It's Time for Colleges to Cut Costs," *Washington Post*, May 17, 2017.

economicus (and other similar anthropologies) has infiltrated the academy.[32] The problem of the corporatized university runs deep, as deep as the understanding of what it means to be human. I will discuss several conduits through which *homo economicus* has arrived at the university.

The dominant approaches to modern economics, management theory, and US business education tend to emphasize the anthropology of *homo economicus* (see Pirson's contribution to this volume).[33] This reductionistic anthropology holds that humans always act "rationally," construed as acting to maximize economic self-interest.[34] *Homo economicus* "is utterly self-serving and only interested in maximizing his immediate utility. Economic man [sic] is therefore only engaging in transactional, short-term oriented encounters with others."[35] According to business education experts Michael A. Pirson and Paul R. Lawrence, this view informs much of current management theory and practice, and leads to leadership and organizational culture that is adversarial, competitive, "efficiency oriented" and "centered on hierarchies and top-down decision-making."[36] In a similar vein, Ginsberg contends that "all management theories attempt to "impose order and hierarchy on an institution."[37] Even if heterodox management models (e.g., "flatarchy" and "holacracy") have gained some traction in both

32. Resemblances exist between *homo economicus*, Hobbesian psychological egoism, selfish gene theory, etc. Space requires me to limit myself to considering *homo economicus* explicitly. See Andrew Michael Flescher and Daniel Worthen, *The Altruistic Species: Scientific, Philosophical, and Religious Perspectives of Human Benevolence* (Philadelphia: Templeton Foundation Press, 2007), 57–90.

33. See also Michael Pirson, "A Humanistic Perspective for Management Research: Protecting Dignity and Promoting Well Being," *Humanistic Management Association, Research Paper Series* No. 17–18 (February 13, 2017); Gabelli School of Business, Fordham University Research Paper No. 2916445, http://dx.doi.org/10.2139/ssrn.2916445.

34. See Amartya Sen, *On Ethics and Economics*, (New York: Wiley, 1987), 19. F. B. M. de Waal, *The Age of Empathy: Nature's Lessons for a Kinder Society*, (New York: Harmony Books, 2009), 162–63.

35. Michael A. Pirson and Paul R. Lawrence, "Humanism in Business—Towards a Paradigm Shift?," *Journal of Business Ethics* 93, no. 4 (2010): 554.

36. Ibid., 557–58. Tarak Barkawi, who has been on the faculty at US and British institutions, characterizes higher education in this manner. See Tarak Barkawi, "The Neoliberal Assault on Academia," *Al Jazeera*, April 25, 2013.

37. Ginsberg, *The Fall of the Faculty*, 208.

theory and the corporate world, formal hierarchy remains regnant.[38] Universities are no different: the exceptions do not disprove the rule.

Research demonstrates that students who are predominantly exposed to the individualistic anthropology of *homo economicus* in economics and business courses tend to behave as self-interest maximizers and see human beings as fundamentally in competition with one another.[39] Furthermore, in his acclaimed and exhaustive study, Rakesh Khurana of Harvard Business School argues that US business schools were originally characterized by the "ideal of professionalism," which included a commitment to "service and calling."[40] However, by the 1970s, they became dominated by "a market logic that . . . rests on a unique normative structure in which 'the only moral obligation of any enterprise is to maximize its economic well-being.'"[41] Khurana's description of contemporary US business education is disheartening. He maintains that "the dominance of market logic" largely eschews "discussion of education as a mission, management as a profession, or the risk to the integrity of university business schools from an uncritical adoption of the commercial self-conception." This model envisions selling a product, the MBA, to its "customers." The primary value of this product resides in its ability to "signal" to prospective employers that graduates will be productive

38. Morgan, *The Future of Work: Attract New Talent, Build Better Leaders, and Create a Competitive Organization* and Jacob Morgan, "The Complete Guide to the 5 Types of Organizational Structures for the Future of Work," *Forbes* (2015), https://www.forbes.com/sites/jacobmorgan/2015/07/22/the-complete-guide-5-types-of-organizational-structures-for-the-future-of-work/#228562de7705. See also Diefenbach and Sillince, "Formal and Informal Hierarchy in Different Types of Organization" and Michael Pirson's contribution to this volume, where he discusses a shift toward "bounded humanism" displayed by some companies.

39. F. B. M. de Waal, *Our Inner Ape: A Leading Primatologist Explains Why We Are Who We Are* (New York: Riverhead Books, 2005), 243; Stephen J. Pope, *Human Evolution and Christian Ethics* (Cambridge: Cambridge University Press, 2007), 214; Luigi Zingales, *A Capitalism for the People: Recapturing the Lost Genius of American Prosperity* (New York: Basic Books, 2012), 175.

40. Rakesh Khurana, *From Higher Aims to Hired Hands: The Social Transformation of American Business Schools and the Unfulfilled Promise of Management as a Profession* (Princeton, NJ: Princeton University Press, 2007), 19, 291.

41. Ibid., 343.

employees.[42] Khurana indicts US business education for "providing both the ideological justification and the revolutionary cadres for the overthrow of the old managerialist order, with its preference for consensus, compromise and stability, and its replacement by a neoliberal utopianism that valued what were taken to be historically ineluctable market processes over the contingent concerns and decisions of human actors, including managers and their constituents other than shareholders."[43]

Khurana debunks the fallacy that business school professors do not "teach values." In this regard, he cites research that shows during the course of an MBA program, students increasingly embrace the view that the "rights" of shareholders trump those of "employees, customers, and the larger community."[44] In his view, teaching that managers act in accordance with the values of *homo economicus* bears some responsibility for corporate scandals that harmed investors, employees and "undermined public trust in managers and corporations."[45] Luigi Zingales of the University of Chicago Booth Business School goes further. He argues that business schools' "amoral culture" generates corruption and crimes in the financial sector, some of which led to the global financial crises.[46] Citing a significant body of literature, Claus Dierksmeier contends, "In traditional classes, students are being instructed along the lines of the neoclassical economics, that is within a paradigm that prescribes profit maximization in such a manner as to offer little to no leeway for alternatively oriented decision-making, for example, in favor of morals." He maintains that when confronted with ethical theory, students "object,

42. Ibid., 343–48.

43. Ibid., 363.

44. Ibid., 370.

45. Ibid., 375.

46. Luigi Zingales, "Do Business Schools Incubate Criminals?," Bloomberg Opinion, last modified July 16, 2012 https://www.bloomberg.com/view/articles/2012-07-16/do -business-schools-incubate-criminals. See also Asher Schecter, "Are Business Schools Responsible For Strengthening Ethical Norms Among Students and Alumni?," last modified May 26, 2016, https://promarket.org/are-business-schools-responsible-for-strength ening-ethical-norms-among-student-and-alumni/. For evidence supporting his argumentation, see Zingales, *A Capitalism for the People: Recapturing the Lost Genius of American Prosperity*, 179–81.

for instance, the dog eat dog reality of business would not allow for any or much decent behavior."[47]

In light of this situation, Pirson, Lawrence, Dierksmeier, and others have argued for eschewing the "economism paradigm" of business education, leadership, management theory, and corporate governance structures in favor of a "humanistic paradigm." The latter adopts an anthropology based on a "renewed Darwinian theory" in light of contemporary neuroscience, behavioral economics, and evolutionary psychology, which posit that human beings are not simply self-interested maximizers. Rather, humans have four basic drives: to acquire, to bond, to comprehend, and to defend. According to the humanistic paradigm, human beings are "intrinsically motivated to self-actualize and serve humanity through what they do."[48] As Pirson and Lawrence point out, this understanding of the human person has much in common with Aristotle's notion of *zoon politikon*, which sees human beings as social by nature (like the Catholic social tradition, as I will discuss). This humanistic model must displace *homo economicus* in order to prevent crises like that of 2008 from happening again, and to promote "the sustainable development of business in the future."[49]

This challenge to *homo economicus* resembles recent work by ethologists such as Frans de Waal and evolutionary biologist D. S. Wilson, both of whom claim that experiments with humans and primates (and field observation in the latter case) demonstrate that we are much more community-oriented and capable of empathy and altruism than the

---

47. Claus Dierksmeier, *Reframing Economic Ethics: The Philosophical Foundations of Humanistic Management*, Humanism in Business Series (Switzerland: Palgrave Macmillan, 2016), 2.

48. Pirson and Lawrence, "Humanism in Business," 554–55.

49. Ibid., 563. On this problem in business schools and suggested solutions, see Wolfgang Amann, Michael Pirson, Claus Dierksmeier, Ernst Von Kimakowitz, and Heiko Spitzeck, eds., *Business Schools under Fire: Humanistic Management Education as the Way Forward* (Houndmills, Basingstoke, Hampshire: Palgrave Macmillan, 2011). The assumption here, not unfounded, is that the financial crisis of 2008 was largely rooted in greed that generated destructive behaviors. On this, see Simon Johnson and James Kwak, *13 Bankers: The Wall Street Takeover and the Next Financial Meltdown* (New York: Pantheon Books, 2010), 113.

notion of *homo economicus* would allow.[50] As De Waal maintains, "the danger of thinking that we are nothing but calculating opportunists is that it pushes us precisely toward such behavior."[51] Jeffrey Skilling, for example, created Enron based on his reading of Richard Dawkin's *The Selfish Gene*: a company should "mimic nature" by "instigating cutthroat competition."[52] Gordon Gecko's famous "greed is good" speech in *Wall Street*, along with characters in novels such as *Liar's Poker*, *Den of Thieves*, and Ayn Rand's *The Fountainhead* and *Atlas Shrugged* shaped the psyche and behavior of avaricious bankers, traders, business people, and politicians who put individual gain over the common good.[53] The "rugged individualism" of Ayn Rand's *The Fountainhead* and *Atlas Shrugged* has deeply shaped the psyche and behavior of myriad business people and politicians.[54] In other words, the stories we tell about ourselves often become self-fulfilling prophecies; narratives help determine whether we act on our inherent empathic or selfish tendencies.

Although neoclasscial economic theory and US business education may be particular "conduits" for *homo economicus* into the university, this view of human personhood underpins the entire global economic order, neoliberal capitalism, which in turn propagates it. In Henry Giroux's words, "neoliberalism as a form of economic Darwinism attempts to undermine all forms of solidarity capable of challenging market-driven values and social relations, promoting the virtues of an unbridled individualism, almost pathological disdain for community, social responsibility, public values and the public good."[55] Neoliberal culture, writes Jeremy Gilbert, sees economic "self-interest to be the only motivating force in life." It aims to foster the "acquisitive" and "entrepreneurial

50. See de Waal, *Our Inner Ape*, 228–34; David Sloan Wilson, *Evolution for Everyone: How Darwin's Theory Can Change the Way We Think About Our Lives* (New York: Delacorte Press, 2007), 228–34.

51. de Waal, *The Age of Empathy*, 162–63.

52. Ibid., 38–39.

53. See Johnson and Kwak, *13 Bankers*, 113–14; Juan M. Floyd-Thomas, Stacy M. Floyd-Thomas, and Mark G. Toulouse, *The Altars Where We Worship: The Religious Significance of Popular Culture* (Louisville, KY: Westminster John Knox, 2016), 41–48.

54. See Floyd-Thomas, Floyd-Thomas, and Toulouse, *The Altars Where We Worship*, 45–47.

55. Giroux, *Neoliberalism's War*, 2. See also Jeremy Gilbert, "Neoliberal Culture," *New Formations: a Journal of Culture/Theory/Politics* 80, no. 80 (2013): 9.

behavior" natural to the human condition, free from the interference of government.[56] Christian ethicist Keri Day correctly contends neoliberalism represents a "cultural project in that it distorts what it means to be responsible moral agents in our globalizing world today." According to Day, "neoliberalism is a market rationale that orders people to live by the generalized principle of competition in *all* social spheres of life, making the individual herself or himself an enterprise (and reducing social relations to monetary relations)."[57] The conception of freedom—neoliberalism's most cherished value—eschews solidarity while affirming "negative freedom," or freedom from coercion, particularly in the economic sphere.[58]

Virtually no arena of life remains devoid of neoliberalism's influence.[59] Pope John Paul II, Pope Benedict, and Pope Francis recognized the dangerous tendency of market economies to commodify everything.[60] Philosopher Michael Sandel adduces a plethora of examples to demonstrate that market values and mechanisms have infiltrated almost every aspect of modern life. Just about everything can be bought and sold: driving in carpool lanes for a fee, being paid to advertise on one's forehead, paying women halfway around the world to carry surrogate pregnancies, and buying admission to American universities. Sandel argues the United States no longer simply has a market economy, but has become "a market

56. Gilbert, "Neoliberal Culture," 8.

57. Keri Day, *Religious Resistance to Neoliberalism: Womanist and Black Feminist Perspectives* (New York: Palgrave Macmillan, 2016), 4, 8–9. Day provides a robust discussion of the "neoliberal subject," which resonates with the discussion here. She also recognizes that neoliberalism manifests itself in the social, economic, and political sphere in myriad, diverse, and sometimes contradictory ways.

58. See Gerald J. Beyer, *Recovering Solidarity: Lessons from Poland's Unfinished Revolution* (Notre Dame, IN: University of Notre Dame Press, 2010).

59. See the spectrum of essays introduced by Gilbert in this special journal issue on neoliberal culture: Jeremy Gilbert, "What Kind of Thing is Neoliberalism?," *New Formations: a Journal of Culture/Theory/Politics* 80, no. 80 (2013).

60. John Paul II, *Centesimus Annus*, Vatican Website, 1991, w2.vatican.va/content/john-paul-ii/en/encyclicals/documents/hf_jp-ii_enc_01051991_centesimus-annus.html, 40–41; 34–35; Benedict XVI, *Caritas in Veritate*, Vatican Website, 2009, http://w2.vatican.va/content/benedict-xvi/en/encyclicals/documents/hf_ben-xvi_enc_20090629_caritas-in-veritate.html, 35–36; 69; Francis, *Evangelii Gaudium*, Vatican Website, 2013, http://w2.vatican.va/content/francesco/en/apost_exhortations/documents/papa-francesco_esortazione-ap_20131124_evangelii-gaudium.html, 55.

society."[61] Advertising and branding tell us that "to have" possessions is "to be" a person.[62] Although a communitarian spirit has existed in certain eras of US history, and imbues some segments of contemporary society, hyper-individualism pervades our contemporary culture, political discourse, and the economy.[63] Religions have not remained unscathed, as the logic of market relations and consumerism has produced a distorted, individualistic, and self-serving understanding of their tenets among adherents.[64] Thus, all inhabitants of the cultural, political, and economic space of neoliberalism have encounters with the anthropology of *homo economicus* and are deformed by its seductive ethos to one degree or another. "Market fundamentalism," or the uncritical embrace of certain dogmas of neoliberalism, such as *homo economicus*, heralds the market as both the means and the end of human existence, thereby eroding the sense of meaning and purpose found in relationship with God, other human beings, and the natural world.[65] In fact, some observers maintain, like Francis, the market has been "deified."[66]Far too many people

61. Michael J. Sandel, *What Money Can't Buy: The Moral Limits of Markets* (New York: Farrar, Straus and Giroux, 2012), 10, 37–39, 48–51.

62. See John Paul II, *Sollicitudo Rei Socialis*, Vatican Website, 1987, http://w2.vatican.va/content/john-paul-ii/en/encyclicals/documents/hf_jp-ii_enc_30121987_sollicitudo-rei-socialis.html, 28; John Paul II, *Centesimus Annus*, 41; Tom Beaudoin, *Consuming Faith: Integrating Who We Are with What We Buy* (Lanham, MD: Sheed & Ward, 2003), 3–13, 43–60. Beaudoin trenchantly discusses brands doing "identity work for us."

63. See E. J. Dionne, *Our Divided Political Heart: The Battle for the American Idea in an Age of Discontent* (New York: Bloomsbury, 2012); Angus Sibley, *The "Poisoned Spring" of Economic Libertarianism* (Washington DC: Pox Romana, 2011). I recognize the long history and variegated cultural influences (literature, art, etc.) that have shaped American "rugged individualism," separate from but related to the economic sphere. See, for example, Floyd-Thomas, Floyd-Thomas, and Toulouse, *The Altars Where We Worship*, 41–47.

64. See Maria Teresa Davila, "The Role of Latina/o Ethics in the Public Square: Upholding and Challenging 'the Good' in a Pluralistic Society," in *Wading through Many Voices: Toward a Theology of Public Conversation*, ed. Harold J. Recinos (Lanham, MD: Rowman & Littlefield, 2011), 83; Alan Wolfe, *The Transformation of American Religion: How We Actually Live Our Faith* (New York: Free Press, 2003), 2–3; Joerg Rieger, *No Rising Tide: Theology, Economics, and the Future* (Minneapolis: Fortress Press, 2009).

65. I am indebted here to Stan G. Duncan, *The Greatest Story Oversold: Understanding Economic Globalization* (Maryknoll, NY: Orbis Books, 2010), 44; Rieger, *No Rising Tide*, 14–24.

66. Pope Francis, *Evangelii Gaudium*, 56.

blindly trust that the God of the Market will provide the answers to life's problems, meaning, and personal satisfaction, while in fact it often wreaks havoc.[67] As Harvey Cox contends, "the fact that acolytes of market faith do not formally acknowledge it as a religion does not change this reality."[68]

If the anthropology of *homo economicus* looks starkly different than Aristotle's zoon politikon, it clashes even more so with the Catholic social tradition's social anthropology. Space permits only a brief summary here. The Catholic social tradition sees the human person as a member of an interdependent family; the person's nature and calling is fulfilled in solidarity with others and through sustained commitment to the common good.[69] This theological anthropology is grounded in Christian claims about the nature of Jesus Christ and the Triune God.[70] As feminist theologians particularly have stressed, the doctrine of the Trinity grounds a relational anthropology that recognizes the obligation to promote mutuality, dignity, equality, and rights among all people.[71] In short, the Catholic social tradition holds that human beings most fully realize their God-given nature and freedom through love and solidarity with others, not through consumption, self-gratification, or individual achievement.[72]

Given the pervasive influence of the neoliberal self (*homo economicus*), many key decision-makers at universities, including but not only those trained in business schools and neoclassical economics, likely do not fully embrace the social anthropology that undergirds the Catholic social

---

67. Rieger, *No Rising Tide*, 60–88.

68. Harvey Cox, *The Market as God* (Cambridge, MA: Harvard University Press, 2016), 6.

69. See, for example, John Paul II, *The Acting Person*, trans. Anna-Teresa Tymieniecka (Dordrecht, Netherlands: D. Reidel, 1979); Jacques Maritain and John J. Fitzgerald, *The Person and the Common Good* (New York: C. Scribner's Sons, 1947); Michael J. Himes and Kenneth R. Himes, *Fullness of Faith: The Public Significance of Theology* (New York: Paulist Press, 1993), 56–61.

70. See, for example, John Paul II, *Sollicitudo Rei Socialis*, 40.

71. See Catherine Mowry LaCugna, *God for Us: The Trinity and Christian Life* (San Francisco: Harper SanFrancisco, 1991); Elizabeth O'Donnell Gandolfo, *The Power and Vulnerability of Love; a Theological Anthropology* (Minneapolis: Fortress Press, 2015); LaCugna, *God for Us*; Michelle A. Gonzalez, *Created in God's Image: An Introduction to Feminist Theological Anthropology* (Maryknoll, NY: Orbis Books, 2007).

72. Beyer, *Recovering Solidarity*, 105–12.

tradition and its claims about the common good and the duty of solidarity.[73] Rather, many have likely have absorbed, consciously or not, *homo economicus*. In addition, a considerable amount of money has been spent explicitly promoting neoliberal ideology at US universities, including Catholic institutions of higher education.[74]

Ginsberg maintains that, historically, university board members came from the "conservative business community" and attempted to impose "orthodox economic and social views" on faculty members.[75] He argues that administrators wield much more power today, and board members generally follow their lead. Some insiders disagree. A former president of two universities, Margaret McKenna contends that board members often lack expertise in academics but want to determine decisions about the life of the university too often. In her words, "shared governance is foreign to them." She adds that white, older, males still heavily dominate the membership of most boards of trustees, grossly underrepresenting the number of women, people of color, and students in higher education today.[76] A 2012 article in *Inside Higher Ed* agrees that "boards will become more involved in matters—particularly academics—they traditionally refrained from entering."[77]

Given that the majority of trustees hail from the corporate world, it is reasonable to ponder whether board members operate with models and mentalities from the business world and corporate capitalism that are

73. See Michael Pirson and Shann Turnbull, "Toward a More Humanistic Governance Model: Network Governance Structures," *Journal of Business Ethics* 99, no. 1 (2011).

74. See Jane Mayer, *Dark Money: The Hidden History of the Billionaires Behind the Rise of the Radical Right* (New York: Doubleday, 2016), 92–156.

75. Ginsberg, *The Fall of the Faculty*, 141.

76. Margaret McKenna, "The Changing Landscape has Created Ethical Challenges for Governing Boards Which Have Significant Impact on Culture, Values, and Priorities of the University," *Toward a Culture of University Ethics: A Interdisciplinary Conference*, April, 7, 2017, Boston College. The video of her lecture is available at http://www.bc.edu/centers/jesinst/toward-a-culture-of-university-ethics/speakers/day-three—wednesday.html.

77. Kevin Kiley, "What's up with Boards These Days?," *Inside Higher Ed*, last modified July 2, 2012, https://www.insidehighered.com/news/2012/07/02/trustees-are-different-they-used-be-and-uva-clashes-will-be-more-common.

foreign to the social anthropology of the Catholic social tradition.[78] In this vein, William Byron, SJ, who served as president of three universities and on ten boards, states that lay people now constitute 80 percent of board members at many Catholic institutions of higher learning. Therefore, although they bring valuable skills from the business world, board members need to be educated about the "Catholic identity of the institution." Two key elements of this identity directly challenge *homo economicus*: teaching students "that a good life is a life lived generously in the service of others" and "never justify board-approved bottom line strategies that deplete in a qualitative way the institution's human assets: its students, employees, and others."[79] David Hollenbach, SJ, maintains that board members, who often come "from the very top of the income ladder," and other university leaders may sacrifice "special concern for the poor" for the sake of "institutional advancement," which can devolve into a "tool serving the self-interest and privilege of the powerful."[80]

Succinctly stated, whether board members, administrators, or faculty members are making the decisions, many of them may hold a view of the human person antithetical to the anthropology of the Catholic tradition. A distorted understanding of human nature that depicts human beings as fundamentally in competition with one another and not capable of making compromises for the good of the community will not lead to a management style and policy decisions rooted in the Catholic social tradition.[81] This does not mean that all university leadership consciously embraces *homo economicus* and has conspired to advance the neoliberal agenda (though some may). Furthermore, colleges and universities certainly sometimes adopt practices and policies that contradict the spirit of *homo economicus*.[82] Nonetheless, well-intended decision-makers may

78. For data on board composition, see Ibid.

79. William Byron, "Essential Ingredients for Trusteeship at Today's Catholic Colleges," *Trusteeship*, September/October 2011, https://www.agb.org/trusteeship/2011/9.

80. David Hollenbach, "The Catholic University under the Sign of the Cross: Christian Humanism in a Broken World," in *Finding God in All Things*, ed. Stephen J. Pope (New York: Crossroads, 1996), 287–88.

81. For discussion of the concrete manifestations of the economistic paradigm in business and corporate governance, see Pirson and Lawrence, "Humanism in Business" and Pirson and Turnbull, "Toward a More Humanistic Governance Model."

82. For examples, see Susan Crawford Sullivan, *A Vision of Justice: Engaging Catholic Social Teaching on the College Campus* (Collegeville, MN: Liturgical Press, 2014).

import corporate models of financial and personnel management into higher education, while not contemplating how values such as solidarity, justice, human rights, the common good, and the option for the poor should shape the university's internal policies and structures. This creates a conundrum for Catholic institutions, which as I shall discuss, should be governed by the norms of the Catholic social tradition. Yet, as I have seen firsthand, those university leaders who conscientiously introduce concepts from the Catholic social tradition into conversations about university operations often meet strong resistance. However, the Catholic social tradition insists that these ideals serve as guiding principles for our institutions.

Responsibility Centered Management and the Dickeson Model: "We are NOT all in this Together"

According to John G. Cross and Edie N. Goldenberg, university administrators "tried to mollify the corporate members of their boards of trustees and convince donors and the public that higher education deserves their support and respect" by adopting corporate business models.[83] For the purpose of this essay, two of them are particularly noteworthy.

The Dickeson model of "program prioritization," named after former University of Northern Colorado President Robert Dickeson, has been adopted by numerous universities, including Catholic institutions.[84]

83. Cross and Goldenberg, *Off-Track Profs*, 86.

84. See Robert C. Dickeson, *Prioritizing Academic Programs and Services: Reallocating Resources to Achieve Strategic Balance*, rev. and updated. ed., The Jossey-Bass Higher and Adult Education Series (San Francisco: Jossey-Bass, 2010). See also http://www.academic impressions.com/PDF/PrioritizationMD-Print-0413.pdf?qq=17991v274891yT. The following articles indicate Dickeson's model has been adopted by Marywood University, College of Saint Rose, and Felician College: Jacob A. Bennett, "Reporting Back from the PA AAUP Annual Meeting," *Academe Blog*, last modified, October 10, 2015, https://academe blog.org/2015/10/10/reporting-back-from-the-pa-aaup-annual-meeting/?iframe=true& preview=true; "Academic Freedom and Tenure: College of Saint Rose," American Association of University Professors, https://www.aaup.org/report/college-saint-rose; Patrick Kernan and Rachel Onlooker, "A Closer Look: Goldstein's Strategic Resource Allocation Process," *The Wood Word: Marywood University's Online News Source*, last modified October 18, 2015, http://www.thewoodword.org/news/2015/10/18/a-closer-look-goldsteins -strategic-resource-allocation-process/; Peter Schmidt, "AAUP Blasts U. of Southern

Dickeson claims that more than 700 institutions of higher education have consulted him.[85]Although his model uses several metrics to evaluate academic programs and departments, this model ultimately proposes cutting those that generate the least revenue (or none). As such, programs such as fine arts, foreign languages, and philosophy—and their faculties, staff, and students—are often deemed dispensable from the university.[86] Some critics see the Dickeson model as a "fig leaf" for eviscerating tenure-track faculty by eliminating their programs. According to the AAUP, Dickeson terminated forty-seven tenured and tenure-track professors in 1984, his first year as president of University of Northern Colorado, which triggered censure by the AAUP.[87] Craig Heron contends that Dickeson seems to disdain faculty, quipping that professors often "scurry off campus" by 1:30 P.M. (insinuating they are not going to work at home, but perhaps enjoying a matinee instead).[88] The point to stress here is that the model is predicated on the assumption

Maine and Felician College for Handling of Faculty Layoffs," *The Chronicle of Higher Education*, May 13, 2015.

85. Peter Schmidt, "Meet the College Consultant the AAUP Seeks to Shame," *The Chronicle of Higher Education*, June 2, 2015.

86. See James Bradshaw, "No Department Is Safe as Universities Employ U.S. Cost-Cutting Strategy," *The Globe and Mail*, December 25 2012; Leo Groarke and Beverley Hamilton, "Doing the PPP: A Skeptical Perspective," *Academic Matters: OCUFA's Journal of Higher Education*, last modified January 13, 2014, http://www.academicmatters.ca/2014/01/doing-the-ppp-a-skeptical-perspective/. The model was explicitly used recently at Marywood University. See also Kernan and Looker, "A Closer Look," http://www.thewoodword.org/news/2015/10/18/a-closer-look-goldsteins-strategic-resource-allocation-process/.

87. See American Association of University Professors, "Academic Freedom and Tenure: National Louis University (Illinois)," April 2013, https://www.aaup.org/file/National_Louis.pdf, n. 2; cited in Nalinaksha Bhattacharyya, "Academic Prioritization—an Attack on Tenure," *CAUT Bulletin* (2014), https://www.cautbulletin.ca/en_article.asp?ArticleID=3784. See also American Association of University Professors, "Academic Freedom and Tenure: College of Saint Rose," December 11, 2015, https://www.aaup.org/report/college-saint-rose, n. 5.

88. Craig Heron, "Robert Dickeson: Right for Ontario? An Analysis of Program Prioritization by Craig Heron, York University," *Ontario Confederation of University Faculty Associations*, http://ocufa.on.ca/assets/Dickeson-Right-for-Ontario-Craig-Heron.pdf. On this, see Dickeson, *Prioritizing Academic Programs and Services*, 107.

that academic programs must be financially independent.[89] It is a "sink or swim" model of maintaining a university.

Another model that gained currency in higher education is RCM, known as "responsibility centered management" or "revenue center management."[90] Schools such as the University of Pennsylvania, Vanderbilt, and University of Illinois first implemented RCM in the 1970s. By 1997, 31 percent of private higher education institutions reported using some form of RCM.[91] Although more recent data show its usage decreased to 21 percent of all institutions, RCM still has strong advocates who want to adopt the model.[92] Moreover, many more institutions adopt "hybrid models," which incorporate RCM partially.[93]

David Kirp of University of California, Berkeley, encapsulates RCM as follows: "'each tub on its own bottom.' That is, each academic unit is expected to carry its own weight financially: expenses, including salaries, space, and such, cannot exceed income, whether raised through tuition, grants, or gifts."[94] According to the Rutgers University AAUP-AFT (American Association of University Professors-American Federation of

89. For more detailed analysis of the model, see "The Emperor Isn't Wearing Any Clothes: Intellectually Bankrupt Academic Prioritization," University of Saskatchewan: Faculty Association, last modified November 15, 2013, http://www.usaskfaculty.ca/2013/11/15/the-emperor-isnt-wearing-any-clothes-intellectually-bankrupt-academic-prioritization/.

90. For an overview of this budgeting model as well as others, see National Association of College and University Business Officers, "The Buck Stops Elsewhere," *Business Officer Magazine*, January 2013.

91. David L. Kirp, *Shakespeare, Einstein, and the Bottom Line: The Marketing of Higher Education* (Cambridge, MA: Harvard University Press, 2003), 115.

92. Scott Jaschik and Doug Lederman, "The 2016 Inside Higher Ed Survey of College and University Business Officers," *Gallup and Insider Higher Ed* (2016): 31, https://www.insidehighered.com/booklet/2016-survey-college-and-university-business-officers. See also Jack Stripling, "Your Tub or Mine," *Inside Higher Ed*, December 13, 2010, https://www.insidehighered.com/news/2010/12/13/your-tub-or-mine; National Association of College and University Business Officers, "The Buck Stops Elsewhere," (2016).

93. National Association of College and University Business Officers, "The Buck Stops Elsewhere."

94. David Kirp, "Outsourcing the Soul of the University" *Educause* (2002), https://library.educause.edu/~/media/files/library/2002/1/ffp0212s-pdf.pdf. Kirp aptly criticizes RCM and outsourcing at universities as "signs of the triumph of market values over the vision of the university as an intellectual commons where money isn't the principal metric of worth." See also Kirp, *Shakespeare, Einstein, and the Bottom Line*, 110–29.

Teachers), some faculty have characterized RCM as an "eat-what-you-kill" system.[95] Richard C. McCarty, a former dean and provost of Vanderbilt, lamented the "tension" among academic units for resources. He also admitted that the College of Arts and Sciences tried to thwart students from leaving for other schools within the university because the tuition dollars would leave with them. RCM discouraged people from seeing themselves as "university citizens." Rather, they see themselves as tenants "renting space on campus."[96]

Kirp levels a sustained and cogent critique against RCM in his book *Shakespeare, Einstein, and the Bottom Line: The Marketing of Higher Education.* In summary, he states: "The debate over the wisdom of running a university according to the principles of the corporate profit center is in essence a contest of worldviews. It is an argument between those who believe that the citizens of the University are members of the company whose chief mission is to maximize our profits and those committed to the idea of the University as a community in which 'gift relationships' are the norm."[97]

Succinctly stated, these models atomize the university into discrete elements that compete with one another rather than acknowledge their interdependence as part of a larger whole striving for a common good. They operate with the assumption that "we are NOT all in this together." Therefore, they contradict the Catholic vision of human personhood and community, as well as principles of the Catholic social tradition such as solidarity and subsidiarity. The pressure on departments to produce revenue engenders competition for "customers who want to have their preferences satisfied," rather than shaping the minds and hearts of students.[98] The Dickeson model and RCM oppose the understanding of the purpose of higher education in Catholicism, which, as will I discuss, entails working together for the common good.

95. See "RCM Budget Model," Rutgers AAUP-AFT, http://www.rutgersaaup.org/node/734.

96. Stripling, "Your Tub or Mine." See also the similar statements of former Boston University president Robert A. Brown.

97. Kirp, *Shakespeare, Einstein, and the Bottom Line,* 116. See also the similar critiques of RCM in Cross and Goldenberg, *Off-Track Profs,* 90–92.

98. Kirp, *Shakespeare, Einstein, and the Bottom Line,* 123.

University "Fiefdoms" and "Gated Intellectuals"

Administrators and board members may be responsible for policies, such as the casualization of the academic workforce and RCM, which are undergirded by a distorted vision of the human person. However, my argument above implies that as denizens of the corporatized university and neoliberal order, faculty too have embraced *homo economicus* even as their power has waned. Many academics have put their heads in the sand while "neoliberalism's war on higher education," has been occurring.[99] With some exceptions, they have often remained in their silos, churning out work in their disciplines rather than striving against corporatization.[100] Full-time faculty frequently remain complicit in the exploitation of part-time faculty, whose underpaid labor facilitates research leaves, lighter course loads, etc.[101]

Why do the supposedly progressive faculties at US universities tolerate this situation? For centuries, university culture and scholarly formation have been individualistic. As Keenan maintains, the long and lonely process of writing a dissertation initiates academics into the "isolationist culture" of the academy, which rewards individual toil and achievement much more than teamwork and contribution to the community.[102] Corporatization has exacerbated the problem. Sadly, faculty largely "adapted to the conditions of our profession by developing a culture as steeped in the ethos of productivity and salesmanship as one might encounter in the business world," as Frank Donoghue contends.[103] The corporatized university gives rise to a situation in which academics silo themselves in order to "produce more." They do so in order to measure up to the quantitative metrics used to evaluate them for annual raises, tenure, and promotions. Many academics encounter tremendous pressure to obtain grants, do research, publish, "churn out" graduate students, that is, to produce. Thus, the corporatized university signals to faculty, and to administrators who are similarly often assessed, that self-interest dictates behaving like

99. Giroux, *Neoliberalism's War.*

100. See Keenan, *University Ethics*, 57–64.

101. Jan Clausen and Eva Maria Swidler, "Academic Freedom from Below: Toward an Adjunct-Centered Struggle," *Journal of Academic Freedom* 4 (2013): 13.

102. Keenan, *University Ethics*, 57–64.

103. Donoghue, *The Last Professors*, 26.

homo economicus rather than *homo relationis*. There are of course, pockets of resistance, recently growing especially among adjunct faculty.[104] However, many faculty succumb to the ever-expanding assessment protocols that valorize producing individual "outcomes" rather than building solidarity and community within the university. Preserving self-interest first, faculty sometimes maintain that they will speak out after getting tenure, but by then they are often habituated to the ethos of the corporatized university.

Even worse, many academics function as "gated intellectuals," who legitimize the neoliberal global order by giving it intellectual "cover." As Giroux maintains, they eschew any responsibility for the hordes of marginalized people afflicted by neoliberalism.[105] Although Giroux mainly speaks of these intellectuals "walling themselves off from growing impoverished populations" in societies broadly, his critique can be applied specifically to faculty ignoring the plight of adjunct faculty and other mistreated university workers.

Even if some academics are discontent with the status quo of corporatized higher education and its deleterious consequences, many acquiesce due to fear and/or fatigue. Data has shown that the extreme emphasis on productivity at the corporatized university has led many academics to feel overworked, stressed out, and hopeless.[106] Evidence indicates a "culture of perfection" and job insecurity has led to an increase of anxiety and suicides on campuses, particularly among professors (revealing the title of this chapter is more than a metaphor).[107] One may thus reasonably ask, "Who has time to try to change the structure of the university?" Furthermore, as I mentioned earlier, the rise of the administrative class has made participation in shared governance a sham at many institutions, resembling "a sophisticated version of the familiar suggestion box" as the National Labor Relations Board claimed.[108] Keenan has argued that universities resemble "fiefdoms," in which "administrators function

---

104. See, for example, Maisto, "Taking Art, Taking Part."

105. Giroux, *Neoliberalism's War*, 89, 77–102.

106. See Maggie Berg and Barbara K. Seeber, *The Slow Professor: Challenging the Culture of Speed in the Academy* (Toronto: University of Toronto Press, 2016), 13. See also Berg, Huijbens, and Larsen, "Producing Anxiety."

107. Berg, Huijbens, and Larsen, "Producing Anxiety," 170.

108. Ginsberg, *The Fall of the Faculty*, 16. Cited in Keenan, *University Ethics*, 67.

like feudal lords."[109] These "feudal lords" rule over departments. This structure facilitates fragmentation, lack of transparency, ignorance and/or apathy toward the larger university.[110] Whatever the reason, many academics have long ignored the corporatization of the university and its nefarious consequences, such as adjunctification. The prevalence of decision-makers influenced by *homo economicus*, "gated intellectuals," and the university functioning as "silos" and "fiefdoms" undermines the solidarity necessary to overcoming the atomization of the modern university and resisting the corporatization of higher education. Faculty accepted, knowingly or unwittingly, the erosion of our solidarity.[111] In this situation, it is necessary to recall that the Catholic social tradition sees participation in building the common good in solidarity with others as both a right and a *duty*. As I will discuss below, this has significance for higher education.

Prescriptions for a "Cure": Re-envisioning Just Work at Universities

The Catholic Tradition on Higher Education and Participation in the Common Good

Having described the "illness," let me now turn toward some possible cures. I want to stress that these suggestions are by no means exhaustive. Other perspectives, such as critical pedagogy, feminist, and critical race theory analyses of neoliberal higher education, have yielded fruitful alternatives.[112] I offer but one set of possibilities here, rooted in Catholicism.

Catholicism holds that higher education has among its primary goals the integral development of individual persons and the promotion of the common good. By integral development, Catholic tradition means "the

---

109. Keenan, *University Ethics*, 65.

110. Ibid., 64–68. Keenan sees the problem of fiefdoms as "the most compelling of all challenges" universities face today (66).

111. See Bousquet, *How the University Works*, 23, 26–28, 34–35, 193.

112. See, for example, Giroux, *Neoliberalism's War*; Mason, Wolfinger, and Goulden, *Do Babies Matter?*; Kenneth J. Fasching-Varner, Katrice A. Albert, Roland W. Mitchell, and Chaunda M. Allen, eds., *Racial Battle Fatigue in Higher Education: Exposing the Myth of Post-Racial America* (Lanham MD: Rowman & Littlefield, 2015).

development of every person and the whole person."[113] Each person is born with a "set of aptitudes and qualities for him [or her] to bring to fruition."[114] Society has the duty of enabling this goal. Toward that end, Catholicism posits that societies must protect the dignity and rights of all people. Those rights, such as the right to education, adequate nutrition, health care, work, and just wages are necessary for the development of each person's God-given potentialities.

Educational institutions have a particular role to play, as they must ensure, in the words of Saint John Paul II, that "the entire educative process be directed towards the whole development of the person."[115] Furthermore, while Catholicism acknowledges the need for universities to equip students with vocational skills, universities are meant to foster the common good:

> A Catholic University, as any University, is immersed in human society . . . it is called on to become an ever more effective instrument of cultural progress for individuals as well as for society. Included among its research activities, therefore, will be a study of *serious contemporary problems* in areas such as the dignity of human life, the promotion of justice for all, the quality of personal and family life, the protection of nature, the search for peace and political stability, a more just sharing in the world's resources, and a new economic and political order that will better serve the human community at a national and international level.[116]

In what follows, I will argue that the very nature of a university, which entails a commitment to the common good, necessitates the protection of certain basic rights of those who work at them. In particular, I will

---

113. Pontifical Council for Justice and Peace, *Compendium of the Social Doctrine of the Church*, Vatican Website, 2006, http://www.vatican.va/roman_curia/pontifical_councils/justpeace/documents/rc_pc_justpeace_doc_20060526_compendio-dott-soc_en.html, 373; see also Paul VI, *Populorum Progressio*, Vatican Website, 1967, http://w2.vatican.va/content/paul-vi/en/encyclicals/documents/hf_p-vi_enc_26031967_populorum.html, 14. In addition, Benedict XVI, *Caritas in Veritate*, 11 is germane: "Integral human development is primarily a vocation, and therefore it involves a free assumption of responsibility in solidarity on the part of everyone."

114. Paul VI, *Populorum Progessio*, 15.

115. John Paul II, *Ex Corde Ecclesiae*, 20.

116. John Paul II, *Ex Corde Ecclesiae*, part 1, 32.

emphasize the Catholic social tradition's insistence on the right to participation as crucial to the mission of a Catholic university, and by extension, any university. I also will discuss the need to respect workers' rights, such as the rights to a just wage and to unionize in order for universities to fulfill their commitment to the common good.

THE RIGHT TO PARTICIPATION AND HIGHER EDUCATION

According to the Catholic social tradition, the common good is the "sum total" of material, spiritual, political, and cultural conditions that make it possible for women and men to fully flourish as human beings.[117] All human beings have a right to share in the common good and an obligation to contribute to it. Thus, the chief responsibility of a society is to ensure that individual rights are respected and "coordinated with other rights" so that each individual can fulfill her or his duties in society and promote the common good.[118] In Catholic doctrine, human rights demarcate "the minimum conditions for life in the community."[119] In other words, human rights are empowerments so that all persons can contribute to the common good. In turn, the common good enables all persons to enjoy these rights so that they may live a life of dignity. Human rights therefore have both intrinsic and instrumental value.

Among the rights of the human person, the right to participation holds particular significance. The Catholic social tradition sees the right to participation as the precondition of all other rights; without it, the realization of all other rights remains in jeopardy.[120] According to the Catholic social tradition, authorities should respect and protect the right and duty of participation of all to contribute to and benefit from the common good because "every person, family, and intermediate group has

117. Pontifical Council for Justice and Peace, *Compendium of the Social Doctrine*, 164–70.

118. John XXIII, *Pacem in Terris*, Vatican Website, 1963, http://w2.vatican.va/content/john-xxiii/en/encyclicals/documents/hf_j-xxiii_enc_11041963_pacem.html, 60. See also United States Conference of Catholic Bishops, "*Economic Justice for All: A Catholic Framework for Economic Life*," United States Conference of Catholic Bishops Website, http://www.usccb.org/upload/economic_justice_for_all.pdf, 17. This paragraph is drawn from Gerald J. Beyer, "Economic Rights: Past, Present, and Future," in *Handbook of Human Rights*, ed. Thomas Cushman (New York: Routledge, 2012), 298.

119. United States Conference of Catholic Bishops, "*Economic Justice for All*," no. 17.

120. David Hollenbach, *Claims in Conflict*, 86–87.

something original to offer to the community."[121] As John Paul II wrote repeatedly, the principle of solidarity seeks to empower all people to participate in the shaping of a just social order and the common good.[122] In the 1971 World Synod of Bishops document *Justitia in Mundo* and elsewhere,[123] the Catholic social tradition has maintained that all persons have the right and duty to become "principle architects of their own economic and social development" in "mutual cooperation with others." Toward this end, all people, "as active and responsible members of human society, should be able to cooperate for the attainment of the common good on an equal footing with other peoples."[124]

Participation in the Catholic social tradition denotes a *substantive* contribution to society; it is not just a formal, procedural task to be valued in abstract from the ends served by it. Authentic participation contributes to true human flourishing, "the fulfillment of the self," as John Paul II put it, and the flourishing of the community in concrete ways.[125] As members of a community, exercising this right and duty requires the willingness to cooperate with others, to make compromises when necessary, and to take seriously the expertise and wisdom of others.[126] The very nature and dignity of the human person mandates that persons share in the decisions that affect their lives and the good of the community.[127] A community that negates the right and obligation of participation is

121. *Compendium*, 187. I draw here from my discussion of participation in Beyer, *Recovering Solidarity*, 93.

122. See John Paul II, *Christifideles Laici*, 1988, http://w2.vatican.va/content/john -paul-ii/en/apost_exhortations/documents/hf_jp-ii_exh_30121988_christifideles-laici .html, 42 and discussion in Beyer, *Recovering Solidarity*, 90–94.

123. On solidarity promoting participation, see also John Paul II, *Laborem Exercens*, 1981, no. 14; John Paul II, *Sollicitudo Rei Socialis*, no. 27; John Paul II, *Centesimus Annus*, 1991, nos. 33, 34; Karol Wojtyła, *Osoba i czyn oraz inne studia antropologiczne* (Lublin: Towarzystwo Naukowe KUL, 2000), 323.

124. World Synod of Bishops, "Justitia in Mundo" in *Catholic Social Thought: The Documentary Heritage*, ed. David J. O'Brien and Thomas Shannon, (Maryknoll, NY: Orbis Books, 1997), 300.

125. See Karol Wojtyła, *Osoba i czyn*, 307.

126. See John XXIII, *Pacem in Terris*, 1963, no. 53.

127. John XXIII, *Mater et Magistra*, Vatican Website, 1961, http://w2.vatican.va/ content/john-xxiii/en/encyclicals/documents/hf_j-xxiii_enc_15051961_mater.html, 73; John XXIII, *Pacem in Terris*, 26; 31–34; John Paul II, "Respect for Human Rights: The Secret to World Peace," Vatican Website, 1999, http://w2.vatican.va/content/john-paul-ii/

a deformed community and "totalistic," in the words of John Paul II. It negates the person herself and her good.[128] More recently, Francis maintained "The future also demands a humanistic vision of the economy and a politics capable of ensuring greater and more effective participation on the part of the people, eliminating forms of elitism and eradicating poverty."[129]

The right to participation pertains to all levels of society, but it has particular relevance to the world of work. All workers must be treated with dignity and their work seen as valuable because, as John Paul II stated in *Laborem Exercens* (no. 6), Jesus the Worker revealed that all human labor is imbued with dignity. More concretely, social justice demands that all workers have the right to participate in the operations of their workplace in a "fully human way" and to participate in wage and benefit negotiations, as spelled out in *Centesimus Annus* and elsewhere.[130] Economic processes, including wage and price determinations, must not take place over the heads of workers, especially the poor, whose livelihood depends on them to the largest degree. In short, the right to participation, a requirement of solidarity and subsidiarity, calls for decisions to be made as much as possible by persons most directly affected by them in the workplace, while providing them the resources needed to implement these decisions.[131]

There are important implications for higher education. For example, the New Faculty Majority's advocacy for the right of all professors, regardless of rank and status, to participate equally in faculty governance

en/messages/peace/documents/hf_jp-ii_mes_14121998_xxxii-world-day-for-peace .html, 6.

128. See Beyer, *Recovering Solidarity*, 92.

129. Pope Francis, "Excerpts from Message for the World Food Day 2014," October 16, 2014, http://www.usccb.org/beliefs-and-teachings/what-we-believe/catholic-social -teaching/upload/pope-francis-quotes1.pdf.

130. John Paul II, *Centesimus Annus*, 15. See also John XXIII, *Mater et Magistra*, 77, 97; Paul VI, *Octogesima Adveniens*, 15; John Paul II, *Laborem Exercens*, 14; *Compendium of the Social Doctrine of the Church*, 307; United States Conference of Catholic Bishops, *Economic Justice for All*, 71, 72. For analysis of the right to worker participation in greater detail see Beyer, *Recovering Solidarity*, 90–94, 145–48.

131. On solidarity and subsidiarity, see Gerald J. Beyer, "What Ryan Missed: What Catholic Social Teaching Says About Solidarity and Subsidiarity," *America*, June 4, 2012.

reflects the "participatory self" of the Catholic social tradition and should be supported.[132] The AAUP's One Faculty campaign is laudable for likewise seeking to empower contingent faculty so they can have a voice in the academy.[133] As such, it represents an embodiment of solidarity as understood in the Catholic social tradition. An institution of higher learning shaped by the Catholic social tradition and its underlying anthropology should also practice the ideals of shared governance articulated by the AAUP. The AAUP's "Statement on Government of Colleges and Universities" rightly maintains that "the variety and complexity of the tasks performed by institutions of higher education produce an inescapable interdependence among governing board, administration, faculty, students, and others. The relationship calls for adequate communication among these components and full opportunity for appropriate joint planning and effort."[134] The AAUP statement spells out the modalities of cooperation necessary to embody the kind of community the Catholic social tradition's right to participation envisions. Although I do not have time to rehearse those intricacies here, I want to call attention to one particularly germane recommendation: "agencies for faculty participation in the government of the college or university should be established at each level where faculty responsibility is present. An agency should exist for the presentation of the views of the whole faculty."

Keeping the lines of communication open between faculty, staff, administration, and students is paramount. As the AAUP document states, the views of all stakeholders at the university, "including dissenting views," must be presented and openly discussed.[135] The Catholic social tradition sees this as dialogue in solidarity, which Saint John XXIII embodied par excellence in word and deed.[136] Theologian Joseph Curran explicitly contends that Francis's "commitment to dialogue in both teaching and

132. See http://www.newfacultymajority.info/equity/learn-about-the-issues/mission-a-identity/nfms-7-goals.

133. See "One Faculty," American Association of University Professors, https://www.aaup.org/get-involved/issue-campaigns/one-faculty.

134. "Statement on Government of Colleges and Universities," http://www.aaup.org/report/statement-government-colleges-and-universities.

135. Ibid.

136. See Gerald J. Beyer, "John XXIII and John Paul II: The Human Rights Popes," *Ethos*, 2 no. 106 (2014): 50–91.

governance offers guidance for Catholic higher education."[137] Curran concludes: "Francis's use of dialogue as a direct response to polarization also models for American Catholic universities the best way to respond to our own polarized society, a reminder to listen to and work with those with whom we disagree, not only out of civility, but also because this is the way that problems are solved and knowledge advances."[138]

Unfortunately, the 2015 crisis at Mount St. Mary's University in Maryland reveals what may occur when Francis's leadership model is eschewed, and the right to participation is not respected at a university. The president allegedly told faculty they should "drown the bunnies . . . put a Glock to their heads" when dealing with struggling students. Two professors were subsequently fired, and a provost was compelled to resign for criticizing policies that hurt and demean students.[139] Accounts of the situation indicate a complete lack of regard for the right of all faculty and staff to participate in the work of the university to ensure the good of the community in the way the Catholic social tradition envisages.[140] Thus, *The Chronicle of Higher Education* rightly dubbed the debacle at Mount St. Mary's "a corporate test case" that "failed miserably."[141] This situation, apparently extreme, did not arise *ex nihilo*. It is a consequence of the corporatization of the modern university that has been happening at an accelerated pace for decades. As the Mount St. Mary's example demonstrates, Catholic colleges and universities have not remained unscathed.

This brings me to the topic of academic freedom. Catholic teaching explicitly affirms academic freedom. As *Ex Corde Ecclesiae* states: "'academic freedom' is the guarantee given to those involved in teaching and research that, within their specific specialized branch of knowledge, and according to the methods proper to that specific area, they may search for the truth wherever analysis and evidence leads them, and may teach and publish the results of this search, keeping in mind the cited criteria,

137. Joseph Curran, "Teaching and Leading through Dialogue: Pope Francis and Higher Education," *Journal of Catholic Higher Education* 34, no. 2 (2015): 135.

138. Ibid., 149.

139. Jack Stripling, "The Mount St. Mary's Presidency Was a Corporate Test Case. It Failed Miserably," *The Chronicle of Higher Education*, March 2, 2016.

140. See the articles at "Uproar at Mount St. Mary's," *The Chronicle of Higher Education*, https://www.chronicle.com/specialreport/Uproar-at-Mount-St-Marys/30.

141. Stripling, "The Mount St. Mary's Presidency."

that is, safeguarding the rights of the individual and of society within the confines of the truth and the common good."[142] In my judgment, within the framework of the Catholic social tradition, academic freedom flows from the right to participate in and benefit from the common good. Those who work at Catholic universities are called to be prophetic by showing the academic industry in the United States and elsewhere that there is a more humane and just way of maintaining institutions of higher learning than the corporatized university, which prioritizes the bottom line and metrics over people and their dignity and commodifies education. As John Paul II stated, "If need be, a Catholic university must have the courage to speak uncomfortable truths which do not please public opinion, but which are necessary to safeguard the authentic good of society."[143]

The right to participation entitles professors to contribute in accordance with their abilities to shaping the minds and hearts of their students, and to contribute to advancing the mission of their Catholic university. That mission entails both teaching and modeling the Catholic social tradition in order to fulfill the university's evangelizing task. The university's task in evangelization is to be, according to *Ex Corde Ecclesiae*, "a living *institutional* witness to Christ and his message, so vitally important in cultures marked by secularism, or where Christ and his message are still virtually unknown."[144] Thus, an essential element of the mission of every Catholic university requires challenging the dominant paradigm of the corporatized university, in order to render the Gospel credible in a pervasive, institutionalized culture that rejects it. Therefore, the university must model policies, practices, and a community imbued with the values and principles of Catholic social tradition.[145]

Academics in the areas of finance, management, economics, and other fields can and should use their expertise to discern how to make Catholic institutions better conform to this vision while remaining financially viable. Trustees, administrators, faculty, staff, and students are tasked with creating an institution shaped by the norms and values of

142. John Paul II, *Ex Corde Ecclesiae*, 12, 29.
143. Ibid., 31.
144. Ibid., part 1, 49.
145. See Ibid., part 1, 21. See also part 2, 2.

the Catholic social tradition, of being a "sign of contradiction" in the corporatized higher education industry.[146]

The Catholic social tradition calls for building solidarity between all stakeholders in the academic community through real dialogue and collaboration. Solidarity should always entail dialogue first. Dialogue requires that we genuinely attempt to see things from the other's perspective and acknowledges that one side never monopolizes the truth.[147] However, when dialogue breaks down and blatant injustices persist, opposition can be, in the words of John Paul II, a "form of participation in the common good" so long as it strives at "attaining that which is true and just."[148] As *Solidarność* chaplain Józef Tischner stated, shaming, strikes, and "holding up a mirror for the oppressor" may be employed so that he or she may recognize their violations of justice and rectify them.[149] Conflict, as John Paul II argued in *Centesimus Annus*, may have a "positive role" when it is "takes the form of a struggle for social justice."[150] Of course, advocates of justice should not seek the destruction of the oppressor. Rather, they should ultimately seek the oppressor's conversion and the overturning of unjust social structures as Tischner contended.[151] Succinctly stated, the Catholic social tradition clearly supports the rights of students, faculty, staff, and administrators to express dissent and to protest nonviolently for the sake of the common good when necessary. Attempts to quell such action by appealing to blind "loyalty," as was the case at Mount St. Mary's, cannot stand scrutiny in the light of the Catholic social tradition.

For academics to undertake this critical function when necessary, their basic right to participation and the academic freedom that flows from it must be protected. Academic freedom is intrinsic to and necessary for the duty of participating in critique of one's own and other

146. See Luke 2:34; Acts 28:22; Karol Wojtyla, *Sign of Contradiction* (New York: Seabury Press, 1979), 108. According to Wojtyla, the church, like Jesus, must also be a "sign of contradiction" to "unjust structures, both social and economic."

147. Józef Tischner, *The Spirit of Solidarity*, trans. Marek B. Zaleski and Benjamin Fiore (San Francisco: Harper & Row, 1984), 11.

148. Karol Wojtyła, *Osoba i czyn*, 325.

149. Józef Tischner, *The Spirit of Solidarity*, 80–81.

150. John Paul II, *Centesimus Annus*, 14. See also *Laborem Exercens*, 20.

151. See Tischner, *The Spirit of Solidarity*, 10–12, 71–74, 79–82; John Paul II, *Laborem Exercens*, 20.

institutions when they fail to live up to its mission as a Catholic university. They are necessary bulwarks against the neoliberal university's erosion of their rights as workers.[152] Without participation, academics lose their voice and the ability to preserve their just due. Without academic freedom, they fight for their rights and resist the commodification of higher education at their peril.

Workers' Rights on Campus

Universities are obliged to protect the labor rights of their employees for two reasons. First, in order to participate in building the common good, workers must be able to meet their own basic needs. This simply means that for a person to fulfill her duty to the common good she must be able to avoid afflictions such as morbidity and early mortality and enjoy the basic protections needed for human flourishing such as a safe home, adequate nutrition, etc. If workers have dependents, they must be able to provide those basic needs for their family. Put another way, without basic rights, individual persons cannot contribute to their institutions and the common good to their fullest potential. In accordance with *Laborem Exercens*, the "direct employer," in this case the college or university, bears the primary responsibility for ensuring the rights of its workers.[153]

Second, as I mentioned earlier, Catholic universities must embody the Catholic social tradition in their institutional policies and procedures. This requirement stems from the need to be a credible witness to the Catholic social tradition in an economy and culture that lavishly rewards some while systematically marginalizing others and denying their basic rights.[154] Institutionally, if we fail to model what a community that fosters the common good looks like by denying basic rights of workers, we simply mirror neoliberal capitalism. As Francis put it, Catholic universities must serve as a "valuable resource for the evangelization of culture" and search for appropriate ways of undertaking this endeavor in situations where cultural currents and dominant trends oppose the values of

---

152. See, for example, Bousquet, *How the University Works*.

153. See John Paul II, *Laborem Exercens*, 19; see also John Paul II, *Laborem Exercens* 16–18.

154. See Francis, *Evangelii Gaudium*, 34.

the Gospel.[155] The success of our mission as Catholic institutions of higher learning depends on our willingness to practice what we teach. As our mission statements and *Ex Corde Ecclesiae* declare, we do not simply transmit knowledge. We strive to help shape the minds and hearts of our students so they can transform the world for the better. In other words, we should seek to aid them in the formation of their faith and their consciences. If teaching the Catholic social tradition is to have this kind of transformative effect on our students, Catholic educators and institutions must move from talk to action. Modeling the ideals of the Catholic social tradition is even more important than teaching them in the classroom. As Rick Malloy, SJ, of Scranton University has contended, if we fail to model the values of the Gospel, "we will be subtly communicating to our students that it makes more sense to 'Look out for Number One,' 'Grab All the Gusto You Can' and forget the poor and oppressed of our world."[156]

By spelling out the demands of the Gospel with greater specificity, the Catholic social tradition permits moving from more general biblical values and norms to actions, policies, and institutional priorities.[157] Catholic institutions of higher learning have a clear mandate to do this. As the United States Catholic Conference of bishops has maintained, "All the moral principles that govern the just operation of any economic endeavor apply to the Church and its agencies and institutions; indeed the Church should be exemplary."[158] Institutions that call themselves Catholic must heed the words of the 1971 World Synod of Bishops in *Justitia in Mundo* by attempting to be just before teaching about justice. In the United States, the bishops applied the Catholic social tradition on labor to their guidelines for Catholic hospitals in *Respecting the Just Rights of Workers*.[159] Although not having the same regulatory force, the Association of Catholic

155. Ibid., 134.

156. Rick Malloy, "Why Not Us? Making Our Jesuit Universities and Colleges Moral Institutions," in *Jesuit Education 21: Conference Proceedings of the Future of Jesuit Higher Education*, ed. Martin R. Tripole (Philadelphia: Saint Joseph's University, 2000), 214.

157. John Paul II, *Centesimus Annus*, 5, 56–57; USCCB, *Economic Justice for All*, 61–68; *Compendium of the Social Doctrine of the Church*, 62–67.

158. USCCB, *Economic Justice for All*, 347.

159. United States Conference of Catholic Bishops, *Respecting the Just Rights of Workers: Guidance and Options for Catholic Health Care and Unions*, 2009, http://www.usccb .org/issues-and-action/human-life-and-dignity/labor-employment/upload/respecting _the_just_rights_of_workers.pdf.

Colleges and Universities has formally recommended Catholic institutions "continue to strive to incorporate CST into all aspects of their institutional life."[160]

In the context of the modern corporatized university it is essential to start by implementing the rights of the workers according to the Catholic social tradition. As we see in *Laborem Exercens* (no. 19), in addition to the right to participation, official Catholic teaching posits the rights of workers to just wages, health care, and other benefits; safe working conditions; freedom from discrimination in the workplace; and formation of unions and to engage in collective bargaining. Unfortunately, the right to unionize has not always been respected at Catholic hospitals, schools, and Catholic universities in the United States.[161] Numerous Catholic universities in the United States have prevented their adjunct faculty from unionizing in recent years.[162] In addition, the right to a just wage for adjunct faculty is not always respected by Catholic institutional employers, as I discussed earlier. Other campus workers also earn below living wages in many cases.[163]

The corporatization of the modern university, including many Catholic institutions, lies at the root of such violations of the Catholic social tradition. I hope I have demonstrated clearly why all Catholic institutions of

160. See Association of Catholic Colleges and Universities, "Catholic Higher Education and Catholic Social Teaching: A Vision Statement," http://www.accunet.org/i4a/pages/index.cfm?pageid=3614.

161. See, for example, David L. Gregory and Charles J. Russo, "The First Amendment and the Labor Relations of Religiously-Affiliated Employers," *Boston University Public Interest Law Journal* 8 (1999) and Adam D. Reich, *With God on Our Side the Struggle for Workers' Rights in a Catholic Hospital* (Ithaca, NY: Cornell University Press, 2012).

162. Gerald J. Beyer and Donald C. Carroll, "Battling Adjunct Unions Fails Legal and Moral Tests," *National Catholic Reporter*, last modified April 5, 2016, https://www.ncronline.org/news/people/battling-adjunct-unions-fails-legal-and-moral-tests. See also Bill Schackner, "NLRB Upholds Order for Duquesne University to Recognize Adjunct Faculty Union," *Pittsburgh Post-Gazette*, last modified April 11, 2017, http://www.post-gazette.com/news/education/2017/04/11/NLRB-upholds-order-Duquesne-University-faculty-union/stories/201704110149. See also Law 360, "NRLB Says Most College Adjuncts Can Organize," *Law 360*, last modified April 21, 2017, https://www.law360.com/articles/915840/nlrb-says-most-manhattan-college-adjuncts-can-organize.

163. See Corey Payne, "The School of Subcontracting," *Jacobin*, October 25, 2016, https://www.jacobinmag.com/2016/10/universities-unions-low-wage-subcontracting-neoliberal/.

higher learning should abide by the ideals of the Catholic social tradition. Already, the 1967 Land' O Lakes statement, signed by representatives of several of the nation's most influential Catholic universities, reflected the need "to practice what we preach" regarding the right to participation and other basic rights: "The total organization should reflect this same Christian spirit. The social organization should be such as to emphasize the university's concern for persons as individuals and for appropriate participation by all members of the community of learners in university decisions. University decisions and administrative actions should be appropriately guided by Christian ideas and ideals and should eminently display the respect and concern for persons."[164]

To summarize, the Catholic tradition offers an antidote to the nefarious consequences of the commodification of education and the corporatization of the university. It remains to be seen how many universities will embrace the vision of the Catholic social tradition and promote justice and solidarity within their walls. Although some have already done so, at least partially, much work remains to be done to "cure the fever."

An Alternative Vision of Higher Education

For the remainder of this essay, I want to highlight an alternative way of envisioning the university and its work. I suggest that a social conception of the human person, which affirms that human dignity commands respect for and obligations toward others, operates in this case.

In 2005, Georgetown University adopted a just employment policy that it requires all subcontractors to uphold. The policy mandates that all workers be paid a living wage, whether subcontracted or directly employed by the university. It also identifies a number of other workers' rights, including the right to unionize and the right to a workplace free of safety hazards or harassment. In addition, the policy confers benefits, such as library privileges, access to English as a second language classes, and shuttle services.[165] Georgetown's Just Employment Policy (JEP) and

164. See the statement at http://archives.nd.edu/episodes/visitors/lol/idea.htm. A brief history of the statement and its influence can be found at http://www.bc.edu/content/dam/files/offices/mission/pdf1/cu7.pdf.

165. The policy and information regarding its implementation are available at "Advisory Committee on Business Practices," Georgetown University, http://publicaffairs.georgetown.edu/acbp/.

subsequent efforts on campus to enforce it are highly commendable.[166] As a result of its attention to workers' rights, the Catholic Labor Network appropriately honored Georgetown University in 2014 for modeling how Catholic institutions can implement employment policies rooted in the Catholic social tradition.[167] As was mentioned above, the JEP recently served its purpose by undergirding the unionization drive of adjuncts at Georgetown. For all its merits, however, the JEP does have a major flaw. The compensation policy has not been applied to adjuncts thus far.

However, the policy did serve the adjunct faculty during their unionization campaign in 2014. Unlike other Catholic universities that have prevented adjuncts from unionizing, the administration at Georgetown recognized the right of the adjunct faculty to unionize in accordance with the just employment policy.[168] Furthermore, the administration and union worked together amicably to recognize the union and begin the negotiation process. According to presidential advisor Lisa Krim, "taking a neutral position has actually served Georgetown very well. In subsequent dealings with the newly formed union, we brought a whole lot of good faith to the table, which really helps a lot."[169] A spokesperson for the union stated that the University's administration was "not just neutral but very cooperative throughout the entire process . . . They really upheld their social values."[170] The adjuncts and their union representatives from SEIU (Service Employees International Union) have since negotiated their first contract, belying the canard that the presence of a "third-party" union precludes collaboration between employer and employee.[171]

166. See Christopher Zawora and Annie Chen, "Activists March on Epicurean," *The Hoya*, last modified November 12, 2013, http://www.thehoya.com/activists-march-on-epicurean/.

167. Molly Simio, "Labor Network Honors GU for Fair Labor Practices," *The Hoya*, last modified February 28, 2014, http://www.thehoya.com/labor-network-honors-gu-for-fair-labor-practices/.

168. Zawora and Chen, "Activists March on Epicurean."

169. Peter Schmidt, "Union Efforts on Behalf of Adjuncts Meet Resistance Within Faculties' Ranks," *The Chronicle of Higher Education*, last modified April 9, 2014, http://chronicle.com/article/Union-Efforts-on-Behalf-of/145833/.

170. Peter Schmidt, "Georgetown U. Adjuncts Vote to Unionize," May 3, 2013, http://chronicle.com/article/Georgetown-U-Adjuncts-Vote-to/139069/. Lemoyne University has had an adjunct union since 2007. See http://lemoyne.edu/AZIndex/HumanResources/FacultyStaff/AdjunctFaculty/tabid/3036/Default.aspx.

171. Several Catholic university administrators have made this claim. See note 17.

Perhaps the most impressive aspect of this example is the solidarity, the sense of "being in this together" among members of the community from different spheres. Students, staff, and faculty engaged in a campaign for several years before the JEP's adoption in 2005 to urge the university to uphold its Jesuit, Catholic traditions in the treatment of its workers. Some of these actions were collegial, such as dialogue and personal testimonies of workers. Some were more confrontational, such as a hunger strike undertaken by twenty-six students for eight days.[172] During the protest, notable leaders such as Richard Trumka, head of the AFL-CIO, District Congressional Delegate Eleanor Holmes-Norton, and Jos Williams, President of the DC Central Labor Council, came to campus to express their support.[173] As John Paul II maintained, solidarity sometimes requires standing firmly in opposition to the status quo.

In 2011, Georgetown University community members stood in solidarity with campus dining hall workers. Students from the Georgetown Solidarity Committee, cafeteria workers, and faculty jointly supported the unionization effort of campus food service staff, who were directly employed by Aramark. These workers felt they were being mistreated and deserved better wages. The undergraduate students played a key role in helping to unionize the workers, creating the "One Georgetown" campaign (note the contrast with the anthropology of *homo economicus*)[174] In addition to the pressure and solidarity among these community

172. See Doug Lederman, "Compromise Ends Hunger Strike," *Inside Higher Ed*, March 25, 2005, http://www.insidehighered.com/news/2005/03/25/hunger#sthash. EWXOdQca.dpbs; Gavin Bade, "Workers Unite: GSC Organizes Around Labor Rights," *The Georgetown Voice*, last modified January 19, 2012, http://georgetownvoice.com/2012/01/19/workers-unite-gsc-organizes-around-labor-rights/.

173. Bade, "Workers Unite."

174. See Michael Kazin, "Labor Needs More Than Labor," *The New Republic* (2011). See also Bade, "Workers Unite." I personally heard his story and others at a meeting at Georgetown University in December 2012 of the Jesuit Just Employment Project and the Annual Conference of Catholic Scholars for Worker Justice at Georgetown University in June, 2012. This discussion of the Georgetown case is informed by conversations with students, food service workers, and faculty there as well as the accounts cited herein and two accounts by Clayton Sinai, Director of the Catholic Labor Network, at http://americamagazine.org/content/all-things/georgetown-models-catholic-social-teaching-during-food-service-workers%E2%80%99-union and http://americamagazine

members, the university administration stepped up by issuing a letter to Aramark's CEO, reminding him that the University's just employment policy guaranteed, among other things, the right to "freedom of association without intimidation." Moreover, the letter stressed that "Georgetown University's mission as a Catholic and Jesuit institution includes principles and values that support human dignity in work, and respect for workers' rights."[175] In April 2011 Aramark recognized the union chosen by the workers. Since then, their situation has substantially improved. Other cases of workers' rights violations have arisen, evoking a spirited response.[176] In 2014 the Catholic Labor Network honored Georgetown University for modeling how Catholic institutions can implement employment policies rooted in the Catholic social tradition.[177]

The Georgetown experience reveals that when enough people from various groups in the community form a critical mass behind a cause, it encourages decision-makers to move in the right direction. In this situation, decision-makers can confidently move forward knowing that not all members of the university community see it simply as a corporation governed solely by the laws of the market. In the future, it will be crucial for members of Catholic campuses to engage in sustained, thoughtful, and strategic campaigns to win the rights of all workers, including adjuncts. Thus far, efforts to promote a just employment policy on other Catholic campuses have not borne fruit.[178] However, there are some active campaigns ongoing at several institutions.

Catholic universities, and all universities, that rightfully commit themselves to sustainability and care of the environment must earnestly pursue

---

.org/content/all-things/georgetown-students-workers-administrators-explain-univ ersity%E2%80%99s-%E2%80%9Cjust-employment.

175. Letter of Margie A. Bryant and Lamar Q. Billips to Aramark CEO Joseph Neubauer, February 3, 2011, http://www.scribd.com/doc/49007133/Georgetown-s-Letter-to -Aramark-CEO-Joseph-Neubauer; cited in http://americamagazine.org/content/all-things/ georgetown-models-catholic-social-teaching-during-food-service-workers%E2%80%99 -union.

176. See Zawora and Chen, "Activists March on Epicurean."

177. Molly Simio, "Labor Network Honors GU."

178. Loyola University of New Orleans has a just employment policy, but it only applies to vendors.

a "social ecology of work"[179] that respects the rights to a living wage and freedom of association, education that empowers the marginalized, and a milieu that fosters equity for those historically oppressed in society broadly and at universities in particular. Doing so would provide a potent remedy for the "fever" afflicted higher education today.

179. John Paul II, *Centesimus Annus*, 38.

Working Alternatives

From Capitalism to Humanistic Management?

MICHAEL PIRSON

Capitalism has long had a questionable reputation, and not only in the former communistic countries. The public discourse in many countries in Europe, Latin America, and Africa has been very critical of Anglo-Saxon style business. The economist Jeffrey Sachs explains this dissatisfaction as arising partly from the British domination of global affairs in the nineteenth century and the US domination of global affairs in the twentieth century. What seems novel in the twenty-first century, however, is that the discontent with capitalism has reached even Anglo-Saxon countries, arguably the bastions of private property, free entrepreneurship, and deregulated markets. What has been termed shareholder capitalism has sparked widespread protests that unify such ideological foes as the Tea Party or the Occupy Wall Street movements, supporters of Donald Trump and Bernie Sanders, nationalists and socialists in various countries, including France, Greece, and Hungary. Whereas the political left blames current shareholder capitalism for creating an unfair and inequitable society, the political right blames crony capitalism and collusion of political and economic elites for the 2008 financial crisis and unsustainable levels of debt. In early 2014, even *The Economist*, a stalwart of economic liberalism and free markets, denounced current forms of capitalism on its front page and called for emerging-market "Roosevelts" to intervene. The global *status quo*, it appears, is untenable, a standpoint shared by religious figures including the Dalai Lama and Pope Francis (see the encyclical *Laudato Si*).[1]

---

1. Francis, *Laudato Si': On Care for Our Common Home*, encyclical letter, Vatican website, 2015, http://w2.vatican.va/content/dam/francesco/pdf/encyclicals/documents/papa-francesco_20150524_enciclica-laudato-si_en.pdf. Parts of this first section are adapted from Michael Pirson, Ulrich Steinvorth, Carlos Largacha-Martinez, and Claus Dierksmeier, eds., *From Capitalistic to Humanistic Business* (London: Palgrave Macmillan, 2014).

Capitalism: An Attempt at Definition Destined to Fail?

In a book on working alternatives, it may be helpful to clarify what we are trying to find alternatives to. In current academic and popular conversations, capitalism is often invoked as a problem to which society needs to find better alternatives. Although some conversations stop at the stale capitalism-socialism comparison, it may be useful to provide some general clarifications for a term that is so commonly used in public discourse. I will argue that capitalism, rather than denoting a specific system, is better viewed as a rhetorical device: a label for something people either like or dislike. This perspective has consequences for determining what we need to find working alternatives to: namely, I will argue, the narratives that currently shape and dominate economic understanding, policy, and practice.

Today, popular and academic understanding in Western cultures connects a capitalistic economic system with a free, democratic political system. However, societies without liberal, free, democratic political systems have arguably developed capitalistic economies, China being the most obvious example. To define the term more closely then, market principles are often held up as distinctive elements of capitalistic economies. It seems true that market economies in which private actors regulate supply and demand of products and services are different from centrally planned systems. However, highlighting private property and markets as *uniquely* capitalistic can also create confusion.

Markets and private property have been in existence since antiquity. In addition, in many countries that are considered to have capitalist economies, there is a strong, perhaps even domineering element of central planning (e.g., China) as well as highly visible state market activity (e.g., Saudi Arabia). To point to the elevated role of markets and the importance of private market actors may be helpful; yet, private trade and markets have long played a role in human history. Some anthropologists claim that trade and exchange is fundamental to *homo sapiens* and their survival over the last two hundred thousand years. To call capitalist systems merely market-based systems then may also qualify premodern economies capitalist and render the nomenclature useless.

Marxist thinkers have suggested that the main feature of capitalism versus any other economic arrangement stems from exploitation of labor.

But once again, exploitation of labor has consistently occurred across historical periods, such as during antiquity with slavery, in feudal times until deep into eighteenth century with serfdom (and in North America, chattel slavery that was legally abolished only in the mid-nineteenth century). Moreover, scholars like Sven Beckert argue that historically there have been a variety of capitalisms—from war capitalism to merchant capitalism to industrial capitalism to current day financial capitalism.[2] Witnessing this puzzle, James Fulcher argues that the only unifying aspect of "capitalist" economies lies in the role of "capital."[3] Fulcher suggests that despite their differences, what connects different forms of capitalism is essentially the expectation to turn a profit by way of investment under risk. Such a definition is open to a range of political systems, market or state operations, and exploitative or nonexploitative practices.

This definition strikes some as unduly general or abstract, and this may present yet another obstacle for thinking about working alternatives. Whereas in many systems capital was invested to achieve *subsistence*, in a capitalist system it is invested to gain *surplus*. This could be a useful distinction; however, it would be hard to argue that during Soviet communism "capital" was only invested to achieve subsistence; in fact trade, albeit centrally planned, was based on the assumption of surplus production (claims of over-fulfillment of the five-year plans come to mind). The fact that many centrally planned economies often failed to produce such surplus to the same extent as highly developed capitalist economies does not help with the attempt to delineate more clearly what capitalism is.

It may be helpful, then, to note that the word capitalism was and is predominantly used as an ideological and rhetorical device rather than a technical term of politics or economics. Arguably, Karl Marx introduced and popularized the term by describing the capitalist as a person who invests capital and uses the market to increase capital. This stood in contrast to the businessperson producing goods and services sold at a profit to reinvest in further production (using capital to invest in production). Capitalism as a term gained societal relevance and prominence in the

---

2. Sven Beckert, *Empire of Cotton: A Global History* (New York: Vintage Books, 2014).

3. James Fulcher, *Capitalism: A Very Short Introduction* (New York: Oxford University Press, 2015).

late nineteenth century, and it perhaps derived its usefulness more as an evaluative rather than a descriptive concept. Google N-Gram viewer suggests the word capitalism became widely used only in the 1920s, peaking in the 1980s at the height of the Cold War.

To showcase the benefit of understanding "capitalism" as a rhetorical device, I want to offer a personal experience from my teaching (which I think can be easily replicated by any reader). In a class titled "Capitalism and its Alternatives," I asked what students mean by capitalism and if they like capitalism or not. Although you could argue this was a leading question, almost half of the class said they liked capitalism and the other half did not (intensities of like and dislike varied of course). The students who liked capitalism said it represents freedom, opportunity, fairness, and democracy. The students who did not like capitalism said the opposite, that capitalism is oppressive, unfair, and undemocratic. My students' responses illustrate a wider point: when people like it, capitalism is identified with positive terms; when people do not like it, it is loaded with negative connotations. Following Georg Hegel loosely, we might conclude that a term that can be both thesis and antithesis at the same time represents its own contradiction, and is therefore useless for conceptual work on alternatives.

Another way to showcase the benefit of understanding capitalism as a rhetorical device rather than a clear descriptor of an economic system is to consider the multitude of attempts to qualify it. Beyond the aforementioned versions of capitalism, prominent authors argue that there is natural capitalism, regenerative capitalism, social capitalism, communitarian capitalism, autocratic capitalism, conscious capitalism, democratic capitalism, etc. I present this casual and nonexhaustive enumeration of descriptors of capitalism because it offers a window into the nondescript nature of capitalism itself. It is hard to talk and think about alternatives to capitalism when its precise nature is so disputed.

What seems clear though is that many people believe that there is both a need and a possibility for vastly improving the current system. It is increasingly obvious that the current economic system presents drastic challenges to our own way of life and to the welfare of future generations. This suggests that we need to reexamine the economic narrative embedded in the present system, and consider alternatives. Accordingly, I will outline what I think are alternative rhetorical devices or narratives of the economy. I will also propose that these narratives inform our thinking about business, the economy, and, more generally, how we organize ourselves and the institutions that make up society, possibly beyond the economic sphere.

Understanding the rhetorical nature of the term capitalism can then help us understand that capitalism in specific and economic systems more generally is malleable, context-dependent, and historically variable. Rather than focus on systems and organizations when we think of the economy or business, I propose to focus on the underlying narratives for organizing. Why use the word business organizing and not business organizations? Karl Weick suggests that using the terminology of organization, or nouns in general, narrows people's cognitive frameworks, in particular by decreasing the amount of agency humans perceive to change organizations. To expand beyond these limits, he suggests focusing on the practices, the doing, such as the organizing or the managing that occur within an organization and a system, as a starting point for understanding which alternatives can be mindfully developed.

Need for an Alternative Narrative

Einstein famously stated: "We can't solve problems by using the same kind of thinking we used when we created them.[4]" Thinking about working alternatives then would require us to question the basic premises of the predominant narrative currently employed within economics and management. For scholars in the social sciences and especially business economics, agency theory is a fundamental theoretical approach to understanding how we should manage and govern firms.[5] Agency theory holds that unaligned interests and information symmetry create governance risks. Those risks, such as those of corporate managers and their shareholder owners need to be managed by realigning manager and shareholder interests (arguably by making managers focus on shareholder value increases). This theory gives legitimacy to the assumption

4. Albert Einstein. BrainyQuote.com, Xplore Inc, 2016, accessed June 27, 2016, http://www.brainyquote.com/quotes/quotes/a/alberteins121993.html.

5. Michael Pirson, *Humanistic Management: Protecting Dignity and Promoting Well-Being* (New York: Cambridge University Press, 2017).

that firms need to maximize shareholder value, particularly so because managers cannot be trusted to act in the interest of owners without such an imperative. This perspective has become so dominant that William Allen, the former chancellor of the Delaware Court of Chancery, which has jurisdiction for more than 50 percent of US corporations notes that "[o]ne of the marks of a truly dominant intellectual paradigm is the difficulty people have in even imagining an alternative view."[6]

The Predominant Narrative: The Economistic Perspective

In the quest for working alternatives, I propose that we need to unearth some of the foundational assumptions of current management theory generally and agency theory specifically. I therefore suggest that one of the critical stepping stones toward alternative and possibly better management practice rests on a more accurate understanding of who we are as people.[7]

Several scholars have argued convincingly that business schools have embraced the assumptions about human nature presented by agency theory developed in the late 1960s and 1970s of the twentieth century. The predominant narrative, which I label "economistic," teaches a model of human nature that closely resembles an amoral actor. Michael Jensen and William Meckling, two of the most prominent and oft-cited management scholars, have specified their perspective on human nature, which underlies agency theory in a model they call REMM: the Resourceful, Evaluative, Maximizing Model. Jensen and Meckling suggest that REMM is the product of over two hundred years of research and debate in economics, the other social sciences, and philosophy. They provide a number of postulates that serve as a "bare bones summary of the concept":

Every individual is a rational evaluator.
There are no needs only wants that can be exchanged (i.e., no commitments).

---

6. W. T. Allen, "Contracts and Communities in Corporation Law," *Washington & Lee Law Review* 50 (1993): 1395–1407, 1401.

7. Pirson, *Humanistic Management*.

Human wants are insatiable.

Humans are very creative at maximizing wants.

They postulate that their understanding of human behavior is fundamental to understanding how organizations function, whether they are
profit-making firms, nonprofit enterprises, or government agencies. Jensen and Meckling not only had an enormous impact on management
theory but also on management practice. Based on their research on the
theory of the firm, corporate governance was redesigned, motivational
schemes were developed, and stock options created. Harvard University's
Rakesh Khurana describes an event in the early 1980s in which corporate
raiders linked to T. Boone Pickens provided regulators with copies of Jensen and Meckling's papers when they had to convince them that his proposed takeovers would be the best way to deliver shareholder value
maximization.[8] As such, by the 1980s, REMM thinking took a firm hold
on practice. REMM also became a cultural phenomenon when movie
director Oliver Stone portrayed corporate raiders in his movie "Wall
Street," and his main character Gordon Gekko uttered the famous line:
"Greed, for lack of a better word, is good." It is therefore difficult to
understate the impact of Jensen and Meckling's perspective on human
nature, as it percolates tacitly throughout the social sciences and business culture.[9]

To take the REMM perspective to its logical conclusion, let's consider
the example of Elisabeth. Elisabeth is a mother of two kids, married to a
husband who has to travel very often for his work. She works in hospital
administration and also needs to take care of her mother who lives in the
area. Her wish to be successful at her job, have a good relationship with
her spouse, provide a good education for her kids, and take care of her
mother's needs, defines her opportunity set. The REMM-type Elisabeth
could use her ingenuity to create a life situation in which she is best able

8. Rakesh, Khurana, *From Higher Aims to Hired Hands: The Social Transformation of
American Business Schools and the Unfulfilled Promise of Management as a Profession*
(Princeton, NJ: Princeton University Press, 2007).

9. It is important to note that in more recent work Michael Jensen has qualified his
perspective on human nature, arguing that personal integrity, i.e., commitments, are
critically important for successful business interaction.

to maximize all of these ambitions. Wanting to be successful at her job, she would need to spend more time and energy at the hospital. Because she hardly sees her husband, she decides (knowing no commitments and willing to substitute anything) to divorce her husband and marry her boss. At the hospital, they can spend more time together, while increasing her income. The additional income could be used to pay a tutor for her kids, allowing her to outsource their education. Spending that much time at work, she ingeniously suggests to her mother that she should (pretend to) become ill, which will mean that she too can be at the hospital. Although such behavior may be ingenious and creative, it is also rather absurd. It is far more likely that Elisabeth will simply decide to spend just enough time at the hospital to ensure she does not lose her job, spend quality time with her current husband and not get divorced, take care of her kids when she can in order to personally provide educational experiences, and look after her mother in her home when she is able to. In the latter case, Elisabeth is balancing creatively rather than ingeniously maximizing options within her opportunity set.

I argue that it is helpful to provide an alternative narrative on human nature that can explain human behavior better and therefore create a more solid foundation for working alternatives. The REMM model's influence on business management theory, practice, pedagogy, and policy is difficult to overstate. Yet, to explore working alternatives to current shareholder maximizing entities, we need to shift the underlying narrative, beginning with our account of what makes people tick and better explain our human nature.

A Humanistic Alternative Narrative

I argue that an alternative perspective on human nature, informed by scientific evidence along with wisdom from the humanities, can provide a critical stepping stone for a "humanistic" narrative.[10] In particular, evolutionary biology, neuroscience, and quantum physics provide very interesting insights that support the quest for a more accurate perspective on human nature.

---

10. The following section is adapted from Pirson, *Humanistic Management*.

According to the biologist E. O. Wilson, human beings have survived because they are truly social beings, for better or worse. As such, they developed ways to keep their basic emotions in check by developing their brain (i.e., prefrontal cortex) and developed morality as a set of guidelines for general survival in communities and societies. These moral guidelines require commitments beyond libertine pleasure seeking in the moment. They allow human beings to foresee conflicts and build lasting relationships. To build environments where human beings can flourish, a dignity threshold (meeting basic needs) needs to be established. When humans can build capabilities to develop themselves and their communities to achieve higher levels of well-being, they create the conditions for flourishing.[11]

These various insights allow humanistic management theorists to recalibrate claims about human nature that dominate management theory:

First, humans are fundamentally social (eusocial).

Second, they are fundamentally emotionally driven, which enhances survival.

Third, reason and rationality act as a guide but are not exclusively in charge of decision-making.

Fourth, morality and ethical standards/commitments are crucial for eusocial beings.

Fifth, altruistic behavior makes sense in the context of group survival norms that interplay with individual survival norms.

Sixth, commitments such as unconditional respect for human dignity and the aspiration to promote human well-being are critical for good communities (eusocial beings).

Evolutionary biology increasingly supports the traditional philosophical perspective on human nature as a *zoon politikon*, a relational human being. According to that perspective, people materialize their freedom through value-based social interactions. When they engage well with people, they do so by protecting and enhancing their respective humanity and dignity; guided by the Golden Rule, they treat each other as a

---

11. See, for example, writings of E. O. Wilson, Hans Kueng, Steven Pinker, Donna Hicks, and Joshua Greene.

means but also as ends in themselves. Drawing on evolutionary biology, one can argue that this is not an idealistic vision of people as do-gooders but is the reason for *Homo sapiens* having survived. Moral behavior allows people to build better and longer lasting relationships that enhance mutual trust and well-being. When they thrive, they are intrinsically motivated to self-actualize and serve others through what they do. Humans do not predictably follow maximization strategies, nor do they have fixed, preconceived utility functions, but their interests, needs, and wants take shape through discourse and a continuous exchange with the outside world.[12] To thrive and be happy, such human beings balance their interests and, in accordance with general moral principles, align them with the interests of others (partners) and their community.[13] Respect for dignity and overall moral behavior are viewed as pathways to well-being and a higher common good.

Figure 1: Comparative Views on Human Nature

Human nature	Economistic View	Humanistic View
Foundation	Wants	Drives
Goal	Maximization	Balance
Operating Modes	Fixed Utility Curves/ Opportunity Sets	Routines, Learning, Practical Wisdom
Focal Point	Individual	Relational
Role of Dignity	Absent	Critical
Role of Morality	Amoral	Moral/Immoral
Aspiration	Wealth/Status/Power/Reputation	Well-being

To summarize, both views of human nature are based on some understanding of human agency and freedom. The economistic perspective highlights wants as the foundation of human agency, and argues that the maximization of wants is a fundamental human motivation. According to the economistic perspective, fixed utility functions, or opportunity sets

---

12. Claus Dierksmeier and Michael Pirson, "Freedom and the Modern Corporation," *Philosophy of Management* 9, no. 3 (2010).

13. Ibid.

centered on their individual benefit above all else, guide humans. The notion of human dignity as a moral cornerstone is absent, and humans are fundamentally considered amoral (not immoral). The highest aspiration for humans is therefore to achieve wealth, power, status, and reputation (see also Figure 1).

In the humanistic narrative, evolutionary drives are the foundational motivation, and achieving a balance is the goal.[14] In the humanistic perspective, humans operate according to routines, yet learn and adapt constantly. According to the humanistic perspective, the key reason for the survival of humans is their relational nature, for which dignity and morality are crucial. Their highest aspiration is to achieve a level of well-being and to flourish.

Dignity and Well-Being as Cornerstones of a Humanistic Narrative

When we employ this more humanistic perspective on human nature, our focal points shift. I suggest that two different concepts become part of the narrative for successful management. The first concept is the notion of human dignity as that which escapes price mechanism and has intrinsic value. The second concept relates to the purpose of management, which shifts from maximization of wants or profit maximization, to survival as baseline or flourishing, and well-being as the ultimate goal.[15]

Dignity is what distinguishes humanistic management from traditional economistic management. There are three relevant aspects of dignity: dignity as a general category encompassing that which has no price, human dignity as inherent and universal, and human dignity as conditional and earned. Similarly, the humanistic perspective suggests that welfare and utility should not be seen as material wealth only but rather understood as well-being. In short, humanistic management suggests a return to the foundational Aristotelian concept of well-being as flourishing (Eudaimonia).

14. For further elaboration, see Pirson, *Humanistic Management*.

15. The following taxonomy is adapted from Michael Pirson and Claus Dierksmeier, "Reconnecting Management Theory and Social Welfare: A Humanistic Perspective," *Academy of Management Proceedings* 2014, no. 1, (2017): 550–55.

Max Weber, one of the founding fathers of sociology, suggested that social science depends on the construction of abstract, hypothetical concepts. He proposed that social scientists focus on the formation of ideal types or, as I will call them, archetypes. Weber wrote: "An ideal type is formed by the one-sided accentuation of one or more points of view and by the synthesis of a great many diffuse, discrete, more or less present and occasionally absent concrete individual phenomena, which are arranged according to those one-sidedly emphasized viewpoints into a unified analytical construct. . . ."[16]

I am proposing a framework of such ideal types of management. As good theories are parsimonious, I propose two dimensions along which alternative forms of organizing and management can be conceptualized. The first dimension, *the input dimension*, relates to the role dignity is playing as a foundational assumption regarding human nature. The second dimension, *the output dimension*, relates to the ultimate goals of organizing.[17]

Input Dimension: The Role of Dignity

The role that dignity plays within a number of different management approaches is crucial for an understanding of the input dimension. A first distinction can be drawn according to whether organizing is mainly a function of exchange, or whether non-exchange goods and activities play a role as well. A second distinction can be drawn with regard to the role of human dignity within an organization. If the foundational assumption is that humans are *unconditionally* endowed with dignity, then organizing practice should reflect that by aiming to *protect* it. If, in addition, there is a concern for the *conditional* aspects of human dignity, then organizational practices should aim to *promote* such dignity.

16. Max Weber, *The Methodology of the Social Sciences*, trans. and ed. Edward A. Shils and Henry A. Finch (New York: Free Press, 1997), 90.

17. According to Weber, an ideal type is formed from characteristics and elements of the given *phenomena* (e.g., dignity and well-being), but it is not meant to correspond to all of the *characteristics* of any one particular case. It is not meant to refer to perfect things, *moral* ideals, nor to *statistical averages* but rather to stress certain elements common to most cases of the given phenomena.

As a consequence, the input dimension is measured according to the relevance of dignity within an organization, that is, whether it is neglected, protected, or promoted.

Output Dimension: The Ultimate Goal of Organizing

The output dimension, as well, can be categorized according to whether the ultimate goal of organizing is wealth or well-being. These two concepts refer to differing notions of utility. These differences are reflected in the proposed alternative management archetypes in Figure 2.

Figure 2: Economistic vs. Humanistic Archetypes of Management

	Role of Dignity (Input)		
Output	Neglected	Protected	Promoted
Wealth Creation	Pure Economism	Bounded Economism	Enlightened Economism
Well-being Creation	Bureaucratic Paternalism	Bounded Humanism	Pure Humanism

As shown in Figure 2, these two dimensions result in six archetypes: three economistic and three humanistic management approaches. The economistic management archetypes are all focused on wealth creation. Management practices within that economistic approach may 1) neglect dignity, as in *Pure Economism*, 2) protect dignity as in *Bounded Economism*, or 3) promote dignity as in *Enlightened Economism*. However, the humanistic management archetypes are all focused on well-being creation. Management practices within a humanistic approach may 1) neglect dignity, as in *Bureaucratic Paternalism*, 2) protect dignity as in *Bounded Humanism*, or 3) promote dignity as in *Pure Humanism*.[18]

---

18. The following discussion is building on Pirson and Dierksmeier, "Reconnecting Management Theory and Social Welfare"; Pirson, *Humanistic Management*.

Each of these archetypes represent a normative stance and reflect an ideal type: a mindset with which people can engage in management practice.[19]

Archetype 1: Pure Economism

In the *Pure Economism* archetype, human beings are viewed as homo economicus or REMM. As outlined before, assumptions regarding human nature center on insatiable wants. Humans in this context always want more and aim to maximize their utility. Utility in this context is understood as wealth and money. In the context of *Pure Economism*, concerns for other evolutionary needs, such as bonding, comprehension, or safety, are moot; everything is up for exchange, there are no protected values, and commitments do not count. As Henry Mintzberg paraphrases, humans are practically whores, willing to trade anything.[20]

In *Pure Economism*, humans are seen and studied in the context of market engagement only, for example, as participants in the labor or consumer market. Considerations outside the exchange paradigm, such as love, trust, or care, are considered irrelevant. Rational behavior is based on cost-benefit calculations, and any notions of fairness are considered irrational.[21]

In *Pure Economism*, organizations are treated as a nexus of contracts in which rationally maximizing agents negotiate their respective benefits, often at the expense of others. An example of this type of economistic practice can be found in the financial markets, in which commitments do not matter, and where "exchange" is the dominant logic. At the extreme end, *Pure Economism* is represented by psychopaths engaging with each other.[22]

19. There has been a long discussion in the literature about science being nonnormative and purely descriptive. The author subscribes to the view that even a position about management science as nonnormative is a normative stance.

20. Henry Mintzberg, *Managers Not MBAs: A Hard Look at the Soft Practice of Managing and Management Development* (London and New York: Financial Times Prentice-Hall, 2004).

21. Noreena Hertz, *Eyes Wide Open: How to Make Smart Decisions in a Confusing World* (New York: HarperBusiness, 2013).

22. Clive R. Boddy, "The Corporate Psychopaths Theory of the Global Financial Crisis," *Journal of Business Ethics* 102 (2011): 255–59.

In *Pure Economism*, the market becomes *the* organizing mode above all others, including community, family, or hierarchy. The ideal society within this archetype is represented by a market society.[23] The ultimate goal of a market society is to create efficiencies and increase wealth. Developments such as the financialization and marketization of organizations, from Uber to Airbnb, to freelance websites such as Huffington Post, are a witness to the marketization logic.[24] In this organizing perspective, human dignity is not a relevant category and human beings are typically referred to as "human resources" or "human capital."

The *Pure Economism* archetype of management can be found in a number of management practices. Clearly, the use of slave labor and sweat shops denies universal human dignity, and most large corporations dealing with global supply chains seem to engage in some form of dignity violation, whether they are aware of it or not. The most prominent cases of *Pure Economism* in practice are represented by the large investment banks that were in part responsible for the financial crisis of 2008. Banks, once iconic, such as Lehman Brothers, Bear Stearns, and Merrill Lynch, engaged in economistic practices in the purest sense in the run-up to the financial crisis. They behaved opportunistically in order to maximize short-term profits, in some cases only to be saved from the market system that would have destroyed them.

Bear Stearns, for example, developed mortgage-backed securities that focused on value extraction and monetization. It also developed several highly leveraged hedge funds trading with asset-backed securities. These products were sold to oftentimes unsuspecting customers without concern for their actual risk.[25] Lehman Brothers was similarly notorious for its fixation on profit maximization. To support their profit maximization strategy, Lehman's CEO Dick Fuld focused on high-risk investments. The bankruptcy report suggests that the internal leadership and culture of the bank were so focused on money making that they neglected the risk

23. Michael J. Sandel, *What Money Can't Buy: The Moral Limits of Markets* (New York: Macmillan, 2012).

24. Gerald Davis, *Managed by the Markets: How Finance Re-shaped America* (New York: Oxford University Press, 2009).

25. Michael Pirson, Anuj Gangahar, and Fiona Wilson, "Humanistic and Economistic Approaches to Banking–Better Banking Lessons from the Financial Crisis?," *Business Ethics: A European Review* 25 (2016): 400–15.

of their investments; poor risk management and fraud led to Lehman's downfall. Merrill Lynch followed a similar management logic.[26] Behavioral economist Hersh Shefrin comments that in 2004, "the five major Wall Street investment banks successfully petitioned the Securities and Exchange Commission (SEC) to raise leverage limits dramatically, from 12 to 40! Not all banks increased their leverage as high as 40, although one did—Merrill Lynch."[27]

Observers argue that investment banks had turned into casinos, and never particularly cared about the actual societal value of their products.[28] Although not all investment banks failed, other banks like Deutsche Bank, UBS, and JP Morgan were caught up in a litany of scandals.[29] Even post-financial crisis, fraudulent behavior seems commonplace, and fines are a calculated business risk. As one might expect from *homo economicus*, opportunism is truly part of business strategy.[30]

Archetype 2: Bounded Economism

The *Bounded Economism* archetype represents very similar ideas to the *Pure Economism* archetype, yet there is an intentional limit on the reach of marketization. Human beings are viewed in a more enlightened way. Equally, the commodification of human beings is bounded by legal strictures, norms, and attitudes. Human beings are viewed as human resources *with rights*. Sometimes people use the term "human capital" to denote the increased respect for the value that human beings bring to the production system. Greed, as the character Gordon Gekko suggests, is still viewed as a central feature of human aspiration, yet needs to be curbed and controlled. Opportunism is not wholeheartedly endorsed, and "cheating behavior" requires punishment. Dignity, as a

26. Ibid.

27. Hersh Shefrin, "Ending the Management Illusion: Preventing Another Financial Crisis," *Ivy Business Journal* (July 2009).

Pirson, Gangahar, and Wilson, "Humanistic and Economistic Approaches to Banking."

28. M. Taibbi, *Griftopia* (New York: Spiegel & Grau, 2010).

29. Luigi Zingales, *Does Finance Benefit Society?* National Bureau of Economic Research, 2015, https://www.nber.org/papers/w20894.

30. Zingales, *Does Finance Benefit Society?*

category of intrinsicallyvaluable traits, including trust, wisdom, or respon-sibility, can play a role. Yet these traits enter the fray as a means to the end of wealth creation, so that trust and wisdom enter the conversation mostly to facilitate performance. A typical statement to demonstrate *Bounded Economism* would be: "Corporate Social Responsibility is good *because* it adds to the bottom line."

The *Bounded Economism* archetype of management is common in much of management practice and would seem to represent the majority of practice within Western economies. The use of slave/child labor and sweat shops is illegal in this archetype; laws protecting human rights, worker rights, consumer rights, etc., exist and are typically enforced. These laws and norms provide the frame for "bounded economistic" practice, which still focuses on the goal of profit maximization. On the global level, however, such rules and legislation are difficult to enforce, so that many Western companies that behave legally within their home country do not do so overseas. Examples within the textile industry, such as the 2013 Rana Plaza incident in Bangladesh that killed more than one thousand workers in a building collapse,[31] showcase such problems. More enlightened practitioners understand that their legitimacy depends on protecting human dignity at some basic level. Many of these practitioners sign voluntary compacts to ensure practices that aim to protect dignity.

Among the various global initiatives, the United Nations Global Compact established in 2000 is worth highlighting. The Global Com-pact was cocreated by business practitioners and public policymakers who understood the need to fill a void for the protection of human dig-nity as well as environmental protection (with dignity as a category). As the current website states, the Global Compact is "a call to companies to align strategies and operations with universal principles on human rights, labor, environment and anti-corruption, and take actions that advance societal goals."[32]

Many global companies have signed the Global Compact, but its crit-ics claim that they often do so out of expedience rather than true ethical

---

31.   http://www.globallabourrights.org/campaigns/factory-collapse-in-bangladesh, accessed May 24, 2018.

32.   "Who We Are," United Nations Global Impact, accessed May 23, 2016, https://www.unglobalcompact.org/what-is-gc.

commitment.[33] Instances of companies such as Siemens or Volkswagen fundamentally violating the Global Compact are common, as the compliance standards are rather low and enforcement is weak.

Within this ideal type, the rationale that companies give for joining such efforts is often couched in economistic logics that present concerns for dignity as a benefit that contributes to the business case for earning more profit. Even the reasons given to encourage companies to join the Global Compact are couched in an economistic language of cost and benefit. Again, the website states that the Global Compact is[34]:

> A win-win for business and society. The connection between the bottom-line and a company's environmental, social, and governance practices is becoming clear:
>
> **How will I benefit?**
>
> **It's good for business.** Corporate and organizational success requires stable economies and healthy, skilled and educated workers, among other factors. And sustainable companies experience increased brand trust and investor support.
>
> **It's good for society—and business really *can* make a difference.** Companies offer fresh ideas and scalable solutions to society's challenges—exactly what we need to create a better world. More than 8,000 business participants and 4,000 non-business participants in the UN Global Compact are already changing the world. They're helping alleviate extreme poverty, address labor issues, reduce environmental risks around the globe, and more.

Although the case for societal well-being is made, it is interesting to note that the ultimate reasoning here is the contribution of such dignity-protecting practices to the financial bottom line. The results of a study are shown prominently: "CEO's agree that sustainable practices matter: 93% say it is important to the future success of their business, 80% see it as a route to competitive advantage in their industry and 78% view it as

33. G. Knight and J. Smith, "The Global Compact and its Critics: Activism, Power Relations, and Corporate Social Responsibility, in *Discipline and Punishment in Global Politics* (New York: Palgrave Macmillan: 2008), 191–213.

34. "Participation," United Nations Global Impact, accessed May 23, 2016, https://www.unglobalcompact.org/participation/join/benefits.

an opportunity for growth and innovation."[35] Practice within *Bounded Economism* aims to protect dignity, in order to ensure profitability.

Archetype 3: Enlightened Economism

In the *Enlightened Economism* archetype, human beings are viewed as endowed with dignity. In addition, the guiding assumption is that human beings wish to promote their dignity through personal development. A central focus in organizing practice rests on the development of faculties that are intrinsically valued, such as aesthetic and artistic dexterity, or wisdom, trustworthiness, and character. However, the ultimate objective is to increase performance and wealth. Melé therefore calls this archetype "Masked Economism," where protecting and promoting people's dignity serves as a means to higher financial gains.[36]

The *Enlightened Economism* archetype of management can be found in an increasing number of businesses. "Conscious business," "conscious capitalism," or business with purpose" are only a few of the ever more popular labels. It seems that many business practitioners have understood that human beings are not only human resources but they are their most "important assets." For that reason, people need to be engaged, trained, and developed. Clearly the notion of human beings as assets is meant to highlight the value of human beings to the business but also connotes that the main purpose of a human being is to service the wealth creation of the organization.

The dominant discourse for promoting practices of *Enlightened Economism* revolves around the business case. The business case for sustainability, for example, attempts to put the appreciation of the intrinsic value of a healthy environment into the language of cost-benefits.[37] Similarly, corporate social responsibility is hailed as a means of boosting

35. Ibid.

36. D. Mele, "Current Trends of Humanism in Business" in *Humanism in Business: Perspectives on the Development of a Responsible Business Society*, ed. H. Spitzeck, M. Pirson, W. Amann, S. Khan, and E. von Kimakowitz (Cambridge: Cambridge University Press, 2009), 170–84.

37. T. Dyllick and K. Hockerts, "Beyond the Business Case for Corporate Sustainability," *Business Strategy and the Environment* 11, no. 6 (2002): 30–141.

employee engagement.[38] Studies show that employees enjoy volunteering and appreciate a company more if it is engaging in corporate social responsibility activities. The reason many companies now do so is partly to regain lost legitimacy but also to increase performance as well as bottom-line results.

Archetype 4: Bureaucratic Paternalism

In the *Bureaucratic Paternalism* archetype, the organizing objective shifts toward well-being. Wealth creation can play a role in that it becomes a *means* to achieve well-being. Nevertheless, in *Bureaucratic Paternalism* well-being is achieved without particular consideration to human dignity. It is thus conceivable that in the name of "well-being," individual dignity is neglected. It has been argued with good reason that in the guise of welfare or well-being, human liberty and dignity can be abused.[39] Therefore, *Bureaucratic Paternalism* provides room for authoritarian and possibly even totalitarian organizational forms. Even in its more benign forms, *Bureaucratic Paternalism* can be authoritarian and undermine respect for human dignity.

Bureaucratic Paternalism in practice can be found in public administrations, including the military and government bureaucracies. These organizational forms use command and control structures to create what those in control deem to be well-being. The *Bureaucratic Paternalism* archetype can also be found in various organizational practices of the nineteenth and early twentieth centuries in Western Europe and the United States. Companies led by strong founders like Werner von Siemens, Robert Bosch, or Henry Ford were concerned for their workers' welfare, and built housing for their employees, as well as entire cities. These businessmen often acted like statesmen rather than profit maximizers. The Tata Group in India is also credited with working toward the

---

38. Roy Saunderson, "Top 10 Ways to Use CSR to Motivate Employess," last modified March 8, 2012, http://www.incentivemag.com/Strategy/Ask-the-Experts/Roy-Saunderson/Top-10-Ways-to-Use-CSR-to-Motivate-Employees/.

39. M. Friedman, *Capitalism and Freedom* (Chicago: University of Chicago Press, 1962); F. Hayek, *Constitution of Liberty* (Chicago: University of Chicago Press, 1970).

well-being of its country,[40] and is building a state within the state for its workers. *Bureaucratic Paternalism* practices are often rooted in larger cultural practice. Businesses in many geographic and cultural areas have been run "like a family."[41] As a result, a "strong" leader or a benevolent dictator is an acceptable and often desirable leader, and hierarchical practices in which men more frequently than women making key decisions are justified.

Archetype 5: Bounded Humanism

In *Bounded Humanism*, the organizing objective remains well-being, yet there is a central focus on valuing human dignity to prevent autocratic and paternalistic practices. Human beings are valued in themselves, which reflects on organizational practices in terms of decision-making, governance, and strategy. As with the previous model, scholars suggest that the metaphor of community and family are helpful to an understanding of organizing practices within this archetype. Yet the distinction between *Bureaucratic Paternalism* and *Bounded Humanism* rests in the accordance and protection of individual freedom and autonomy. Transcending the individual, *Bounded Humanism* also embraces the practices that are intrinsically valuable for the creation of a functioning community. Such practices can relate to building and maintaining social trust, responsibility, and wisdom.

Bounded Humanism practice can be witnessed in many nongovernmental organizations, churches, and some family-run businesses that wish to contribute to the community. For-benefit corporations (B Corps) and social enterprises similarly reflect *Bounded Humanism*, as they aim to protect human dignity while contributing to the common good. These organizations recognize the intrinsic value of human beings; that is why they are in existence. Grameen Bank, for example, is an organization that

40. R. R. Sharma and S. Mukherji, "Can Business and Humanism Go Together? The Case of the Tata Group with a Focus on Nano Plant," in *Humanistic Management in Practice* (London: Palgrave Macmillan, 2010), 247–65.

41. See, for example, N. E. Thornberry, S. R. Rangan, and D. Wylie, "Casa Pedro Domecq" Harvard Business School Publishing (June 1999), https://hbsp.harvard.edu/product/BAB004-PDF-ENG?Ntt=BAB004-PDF-ENG&itemFindingMethod=Search.

set out to decrease poverty through microloans. Starting in Bangladesh, Grameen Bank gave out small loans mainly to women so they could buy the equipment, such as sewing machines, necessary to launch businesses. Before Grameen Bank, these women had no access to loans other than through loan sharks. Grameen Bank founder Muhammad Yunus considers credit a fundamental human right and he therefore worked tirelessly to ensure that that right was protected. Another example of *Bounded Humanism* in practice is an organization of lawyers in New York City that helps minorities to understand their legal rights. This organization even sponsors legal action in cases of discrimination. In both cases, organizational practices focus on protecting the dignity of the poor and minorities. Wealth creation is not the main point, even though wealth creation can be used to promote well-being, such as in the case of Grameen Bank.

Archetype 6: Pure Humanism

In the *Pure Humanism* archetype, the organizing objective is still well-being, and dignity in its various forms is protected. The difference between *Bounded Humanism* and *Pure Humanism* is the latter's focus on promoting dignity through organizing practices. This may seem a small difference, yet it highlights an important aspirational shift. Within *Pure Humanism*, the formal protection of human dignity through the application of human rights is insufficient on its own; it is important to allow space for the cocreation of human development so that all people can flourish.

Pure Humanism practices are reflected in some form of cocreation and self-management that advance the common good. Organizational researcher Frederic Laloux calls these humanistic practices "teal" practices.[42] Building on Ken Wilber's integral theory, he suggests that some organizations achieve a higher level of consciousness that allows for organic self-organization and personal development. These organizations are organically organizing communities that are guided by a higher purpose than wealth creation. These practices reflect a higher level of consciousness, and promote the full human development of all people

42. F. Laloux, *Reinventing Organizations: A Guide to Creating Organizations Inspired by the Next Stage in Human Consciousness* (Brussels: Nelson Parker, 2014).

affected by the organization. Social enterprises, in many ways, embody such practices.

Moving toward Bounded Humanism

In the following section, I wish to highlight how a shift in underlying narrative about who we are as people and what we organize for can provide "working alternatives" for business practice.[43] None of the below-mentioned case studies suggest a perfect adherence to any of the above-mentioned archetypes. Yet, I argue that they represent significant shifts in management practice that highlight how organizations can move from traditional, economistic practices toward more humanistic practices. By no means, however, should their more humanistic practices be seen as "ideal." There remains much room for improvement with regard to the protection of dignity and the promotion of the common good.

Unilever: The World's Largest Nongovernmental Organization?

In 2009, Paul Polman became CEO of Unilever, one of the largest consumer goods providers in the world. At the time, Unilever had already begun to embrace sustainable business practices. In 2000, it had acquired Ben and Jerry's, an ice cream company known for its socially conscious business practices, and in 2007 Unilever committed to having all its Lipton Tea products harvested sustainably. Unilever, a conglomerate of food, health, and beauty products, was traded on the public stock exchange and played by market rules. When Polman took over, however, he suspended some of those rules, including quarterly reporting, and refused to give financial analysts earnings estimates.

Boynton and Barchan reported on his first day in the CEO position in *Forbes Magazine*[44]:

---

43. The following discussion is building on Pirson and Dierksmeier, "Reconnecting Management Theory and Social Welfare" and Pirson, "Humanistic Management."

44. Andy Boynton, "Unilever's Paul Polman: CEOs Can't Be 'Slaves' to Slaveholders," Forbes, last modified July 20, 2015, http://www.forbes.com/sites/andyboynton/2015/07/20/unilevers-paul-polman-ceos-cant-be-slaves-to-shareholders/#22cb060240b5.

Immediately, the Dutch-born Polman put his shareholders on notice. [. . .] Unilever, he explained, was now taking a longer view. The CEO went a step further, urging shareholders to put their money somewhere else if they don't "buy into this long-term value-creation model, which is equitable, which is shared, which is sustainable." "I figured I couldn't be fired on my first day," Polman quipped later on.

He added: "I don't have any space for many of these people that really, in the short term, try to basically speculate and make a lot of money." He said his responsibility is to multiple stakeholders, among them, consumers in the developing world and climate-change activists. Regarding shareholders, Polman said, "I'm not just working for them." On that note, he added this zinger—"Slavery was abolished a long time ago.[45]"

He launched an ambitious reorientation to make Unilever a company that provides solutions to global problems. Starting in 2010, the leadership developed a sustainable living plan that set out to impact the "well-being of one billion people in the next 5 years."[46] Again Boynton and Barchan share: "Soon after he became CEO, Polman spearheaded the 10-year Unilever Sustainable Living Plan, which seeks to decouple the company's growth from its environmental footprint. The ambitious goals include doubling Unilever's revenue while slashing the footprint by 50%; sourcing 100% of its raw materials sustainably (meaning that the supply chain is managed according to environmental, social, and ethical principles); and helping more than a billion people improve their health and well-being."[47]

Many companies may make such general statements, but as Rick Wartzman of the Drucker Institute comments in *Fortune*[48]: "Unilever [. . .] rigorously measures and reports its progress against three ambitious goals it aims to reach by 2020: helping more than a billion people across the globe improve their health and well-being; halving the environmental footprint of its products; and sourcing 100% of its agricultural raw

45. Ibid.
46. Ibid.
47. Ibid.
48. Rick Wartzman, "What Unilever Shares with Google and Apple," *Fortune*, last modified January 7, 2015, http://fortune.com/2015/01/07/what-unilever-shares-with -google-and-apple/.

materials sustainably while enhancing the livelihoods of those working across its supply chain. What's more, the company has committed to doing all this while doubling the size of its business, to about $100 billion. (Unilever derives nearly 60% of its sales from emerging markets.)[49]

Unilever aims to do so by reengineering its various brands to address social and environmental concerns by finding their true purpose. Ben and Jerry's was one of the first certified B Corporations, and Polman and his colleagues thought hard about Unilever becoming a for-benefit corporation. So far, they have not found how to do this amid the tangle of international laws, but they are working on it.

Again Rick Wartzman comments:

> On the ground, these objectives manifest themselves in many ways, like the recent launch of the Toilet Board Coalition, a cross-sector group that is trying to find scalable, market-based solutions to what it calls "the sanitation crisis." Could this Unilever-led effort make a difference in the lives of the 2.5 billion people around the world who lack access to a safe, clean toilet? Quite possibly. Could it also help Unilever sell more bottles of Domestos, its bathroom germ killer? Definitely.
>
> Using the same logic, Unilever is trying to position Knorr bouillon as a weapon to combat food insecurity; Lifebuoy, a vehicle to promote good hygiene.
>
> Making this tangible for those on the front lines isn't easy. So, in late 2013, Unilever launched an online "Social Impact Hub" for its 174,000 employees to learn more about its myriad initiatives in this area. Unilever has also augmented its training programs so that workers at all levels can understand the company's commitment to sustainability and how their own jobs fit in.[50]

Although many of these activities could be labeled as mere marketing, they show how a different narrative is being employed. The impact of this more humanistic narrative so far has been that employees have become very motivated, making Unilever an employer of choice for many graduates. Just how serious the Unilever leadership is about the transition toward *Humanism* can be seen from their statements regarding the role of their institution. Rather than being simply a better business (i.e.,

49. Ibid.
50. Ibid.

conscious business), they describe their organization as a force that shapes the common good. Kees Kruythoff, CEO of Unilever North America, views himself as working in one of the largest social enterprises, and Paul Polman states that they are working for the largest nongovernmental organization in the world. Their leadership is attracting a great deal of attention, and they are credited with leading the business community in pushing for a binding climate agreement at the United Nations Climate Change Conference in Paris in December 2015. That level of political ambition shows the active role Unilever wishes to take in creating a better, not only richer, world, world. Nevertheless, it remains to be seen whether that shift in narrative translates into sustained action. One test has been a 2017 takeover attempt by highly economistic private equity companies, which was thwarted due to a lack of cultural fit and alignment.

Elon Musk and Tesla Motors

The story of Tesla Motors describes another organization that is shifting toward *Humanism*. Elon Musk, a software engineer, made his fortune by selling his shares in the company Paypal to Ebay. With that money, he bought into Tesla Motors, a company that was attempting to build fully electric vehicles. In 2008, Musk took on the role of CEO, and Tesla's mission ever since has been to accelerate the advent of sustainable transport.

With this mission and its strategic approach, Tesla Motors has taken on one of the biggest global and social challenges confronting humanity—climate change. *New York Times* columnist Tom Friedman suggests that our future will be decided by whether we are willing to tackle these massive global challenges. Tesla Motors is hailed as a pioneer in creating a better future for humanity and thus in creating higher levels of well-being.

Musk elaborates on the firm's strategy:

> Our mission from day one has been to accelerate the advent of sustainable transport by bringing compelling mass market electric cars to market as soon as possible. If we could have done that with our first product, we would have, but that was simply impossible to achieve for a startup company that had never built a car and that had one technology iteration and no economies of scale. Our first product was going to

be expensive no matter what it looked like, so we decided to build a sports car, as that seemed like it had the best chance of being competitive with its gasoline alternatives.[51]

He then explains that the revenue from the sales of the sports car and the expertise gained were critical to the development of the Model S, as well as future models that would lead to a mass market car. It is obvious that Musk uses the market as a tool for advancing societal well-being. Further demonstrating how the company is defying economistic logics, he waived all patent rights in the hope that other established car makers would adopt Tesla Motors's technologies. The ultimate goal is not necessarily to make Tesla Motors the dominant company but to solve the problem of carbon-based transportation. Musk states: "Tesla Motors was created to accelerate the advent of sustainable transport. If we clear a path to the creation of compelling electric vehicles, but then lay intellectual property landmines behind us to inhibit others, we are acting in a manner contrary to that goal. Tesla will not initiate patent lawsuits against anyone who, in good faith, wants to use our technology."[52]

Musk then explains how he used to think patents were useful but started to doubt this assumption.

At Tesla, however, we felt compelled to create patents out of concern that the big car companies would copy our technology and then use their massive manufacturing, sales and marketing power to overwhelm Tesla. We couldn't have been more wrong. The unfortunate reality is the opposite: electric car programs (or programs for any vehicle that doesn't burn hydrocarbons) at the major manufacturers are small to non-existent, constituting an average of far less than 1% of their total vehicle sales.

At best, the large automakers are producing electric cars with limited range in limited volume. Some produce no zero emission cars at all.

51. Elon Musk, "The Mission of Tesla," Tesla Motors, last modified November 18, 2013, https://www.teslamotors.com/blog/mission-tesla.

52. Elon Musk, "All Our Patent Are Belong to You," Tesla Motors, last modified June 12, 2014, https://www.teslamotors.com/blog/all-our-patent-are-belong-you.

Given that annual new vehicle production is approaching 100 million per year and the global fleet is approximately 2 billion cars, it is impossible for Tesla to build electric cars fast enough to address the carbon crisis. By the same token, it means the market is enormous. Our true competition is not the small trickle of non-Tesla electric cars being produced, but rather the enormous flood of gasoline cars pouring out of the world's factories every day.

We believe that Tesla, other companies making electric cars, and the world would all benefit from a common, rapidly-evolving technology platform.[53]

This is an unusual statement for a traditional, competitive-minded market player. In fact, it transcends the logic of competition, even that of conscious competition, and invites collaboration to tackle much larger challenges. Clearly, such behavior builds trust, and many people are willing to support the company despite its lack of profitability. This was highlighted by more than four hundred thousand people willing to pay a $1,000 deposit to reserve the new Model 3 car years ahead of its availability.

No one thought that this level of consumer trust was possible, but it showcases the power of a humanistic approach, with people willing to collaborate and solve large human problems. Tesla's experience suggests that when organizations sincerely aim to solve problems and not just make money from them, they will find a ready market for their products and services.

Moving Toward Pure Humanism

There are far fewer organizations that have made the leap to become truly humanistic. With that I mean that organizations and their leadership actively work to protect the dignity of all stakeholders and attempt to solve problems that affect society at large and therefore increase well-being. As Frederic Laloux suggests, many organizations need to reinvent themselves in order to reach what he calls a higher level of consciousness.[54] In this

---

53. Ibid.
54. Frederic Laloux, *Reinventing Organizations* (Belgium: Lannoo Meulenhoff, 2015).

section, a number of examples are provided that illustrate what it means to promote human dignity by organizing for well-being.

Grameen Bank

Grameen Bank is the result of economist Muhammad Yunus's search for a cure to poverty. In the later 1970s, when he returned from studies in the United States to a university position in Bangladesh, Yunus felt the urge to apply his knowledge to help his country. The then recently independent Bangladesh was the poorest country in the world. Although many traditional colonial institutions were in place, they were not functioning well enough to assure well-being.

Plagued by both government and market failure, Bangladesh lacked a functioning banking sector. Loan sharks, who imposed exorbitant interest rates, and traditional banks, which would not lend to poor people because they had no collateral, kept entrepreneurial people in poverty. To address this problem, after many iterations, Muhammad Yunus pioneered a microfinance business. The business model centered on lending small amounts of money (called microloans) primarily to poor women to allow them to earn a living through self-employment. No material collateral was required to apply for a loan; instead, a social form of collateral was required: Borrowers had to organize in groups of five, and each group member needed to repay his or her loan on time, while ensuring that the other group members did the same. The failure of just one borrower to meet a payment jeopardized the entire group's future borrowing opportunities. This model established a delicate dynamic between "peer pressure" and "peer support" among Grameen borrowers, and is credited with the high loan repayment rate of 95 percent. Despite the delicacy of the business model, the bank had signed up 8.35 million members (96 percent were women) in 81,379 Bangladeshi villages by 2011.

In a redesign of its original model, Grameen abolished the "peer pressure" model, and now provides credit without any collateral. The system is based on accountability, mutual trust, creativity, and participation. The ownership structure of Grameen Bank is a stabilizing feature of the business model. Like cooperative banks, the bank's poor borrowers (93–95 percent) largely own it, while a small minority (5–7 percent) remains in government hands.[55] The fact that the people formerly deprived of banking services now own their own bank strengthens their commitment to the bank, and helps explain its success. In this sense, the organizational model strengthens the business model.

When the business model is examined more closely, Grameen Bank provides four types of loans: income-generating loans with a 20 percent interest rate, housing loans with an 8 percent interest rate, higher education loans with a 5 percent interest rate, and a 0 percent interest loan for struggling society members (beggars). Although the last goes against traditional economic logic, Grameen Bank makes it work from the humanistic perspective (i.e., helps alleviate poverty).[56] Here is how: Each member receives an identity badge with a Grameen Bank logo to let everybody know that this national institution stands behind them. In addition, the members are covered free of charge by life insurance and loan insurance programs, and existing Grameen groups are encouraged to become their mentors. This form of social support is combined with favorable loan conditions, which only require the repayment of the principal in installments and in keeping with their repayment ability. More than ten thousand beggars have joined the program. Grameen maintains that of the more than $20 million disbursed, 80 percent has already been repaid. In addition, roughly twenty thousand have abandoned begging and are making a living in a sales profession. Among them, roughly ten thousand beggars have joined Grameen Bank groups as mainstream borrowers.[57]

This program shows that poor people can work themselves out of poverty and become bankable. Muhammad Yunus explains: "At Grameen Bank, credit is a cost effective weapon to fight poverty and it serves as a catalyst in the overall development of socio-economic conditions of the poor who have been kept outside the banking orbit on the ground that they are poor and hence not bankable."[58] Using innovative business models, Grameen Bank has shown that business can protect and increasingly advance human dignity to provide higher levels of well-being.

55. Grameen Bank, accessed May 12, 2016, www.grameen-info.org.

56. Ibid.

57. Ibid.

58. "About Us," Grameen Bank, accessed May 30, 2019, http://www.grameen-info.org/about-us/.

Grameen Danone

Inspired by Grameen's success, Franck Riboud, the Chairman and CEO of Groupe Danone, offered to collaborate with Muhammad Yunus to "do something good."[59] During their initial meeting in October 2005, Riboud told Yunus that Danone had a major presence in the developing markets, and wished to orient its business even more toward serving the very poor. Yunus recalls making Riboud an impulsive offer: "Your company is a leading producer of nutritious foods. What would you think about creating a joint venture to bring some of your products to the villages of Bangladesh? We could create a company that we own together and call it Grameen Danone. It could manufacture healthful foods that will improve the diet of rural Bangladeshis—especially the children. If the products were sold at a low price, we could make a real difference in the lives of millions of people."[60]

To Yunus's surprise, Riboud agreed. He also agreed to operate the project as a social business enterprise. Yunus explains: "It's a business designed to meet a social goal. In this case, the goal is to improve the nutrition of poor families in the villages of Bangladesh."[61] Grameen and Danone each own half of the social business enterprise Grameen Danone.

Danone found eradicating malnutrition attractive, but the approach was completely novel. According to Schneider, Danone management had to completely change its management style in order to do business the Grameen way. Danone's objective and mission had previously been to maximize shareholder value: "Now profit had to be a condition, a means—no longer the end and no longer the goal."[62] Having been conceived as a social business, Grameen Danone was free from shareholder pressure for quick returns. However, the project had to be self-supporting

59. D. John, "Grameen Danone," in *Humanistic Management in Action*, ed. E. von Kimakowitz, M. Pirson, H. Spitzeck, C. Diercksmeier and W. Amann (London: Palgrave Macmillan, 2010).

60. M. Yunus, "Social Entrepreneurs are the Solution," in *Humanism in Business: Perspectives on the Development of a Responsible Business Society*, ed. H. Spitzeck, M. Pirson, W. Amann, S. Khan, and E. von Kimakowitz (Cambridge: Cambridge University Press, 2009).

61. E. Schneider, "Muhammad Yunus Recounts Grameen Success Stories" (2008) H40 Berlin.

62. D. John, "Grameen Danone"; E. Schneider, "Muhammad Yunus Recounts."

to generate funds for its operations. At the same time, maximization of social goals had to be achieved.

The founding documents state that the mission of Grameen Danone is to reduce poverty through "a unique proximity business model that will provide daily healthy nutrition to the poor." The specific objectives are stated as:

> to develop a product (nutritional yoghurt) that has high nutritional value and is affordable for the poorest individuals;
>
> to improve the living conditions of the population: jobs, income level, enhancement of the social fabric; and
>
> to protect the environment and conserve resources, as well as
>
> to ensure a sustainable economic activity.[63]

According to Yunus, a social business is a business that pays no dividends. It sells products at prices that make it self-sustaining. The owners of the company can recover their investment in the company over a period of time, but no profit is paid to investors in the form of dividends. Instead, any profit made remains in the business, to finance expansion, to create new products or services, and to do the world more good.[64] He emphasizes that Grameen Danone's bottom line is the reduction of malnutrition while not incurring losses.

Such an innovative approach to creating higher levels of well-being through innovative organizational practices has been, not surprisingly, fraught with problems. It is, for example, unclear how many additional manufacturing plants will actually be implemented. Furthermore, partnerships between traditionally economistic and humanistic organizations are difficult to manage. Danone's shareholders are increasingly skeptical of the social business model as they do not receive dividends. However, no matter how successful this specific project is, the Grameen group as a whole symbolizes the various ways in which organizations are

63. D. John, "Grameen Danone"; E. Schneider, "Muhammad Yunus Recounts Grameen Success Stories," (2008) H40 Berlin.

64. M. Yunus, "Social Entrepreneurs are the Solution" in *Humanism in Business: Perspectives on the Development of a Responsible Business Society*, ed. H. Spitzeck, M. Pirson, W. Amann, S. Khan, and E. von Kimakowitz (Cambridge: Cambridge University Press, 2009).

moving toward *Pure Humanism*. By addressing social problems entrepreneurially, they are protecting and promoting dignity, and creating higher levels of well-being.

Concluding Remarks

Many people are yearning for working alternatives to the current predominant model of shareholder-value maximizing corporations. It seems obvious that our species must find new ways of management to ensure survival. I have argued here that such alternatives can be more easily created when we understand the roots of the current dominant narrative of business. This narrative is rooted in an ontology of people as greedy, amoral, utility maximizers. I briefly outline how a different ontology can give birth to a different narrative for management, rooted in the need to protect human dignity and the aim to contribute to the common good. The examples I outline above are illustrations of working alternatives that fit in what I label a humanistic narrative. The transition toward more humanistic "working alternatives" is, however, still at the experimental stage. Many humanistic practices still need to be established. Better products and services need to be created to address the various global challenges. Better practices to protect dignity of employees and other stakeholders need to be developed. Novel strategies need to be devised to enable more legitimate organizations. A pathway needs to be set forth for guiding a company in a transition from capitalistic/economistic management to humanistic management. No doubt this requires almost an entirely novel societal operating system as well as commitments and policies that enable dignity and well-being not only for a few but, as Buckminster Fuller said, for 100 percent of humanity.

Part III: Practicing Differently

Creating Alternative Ways of Working

The "Dignity of Motherhood" Demands Something Different

A Catholic Experiment in Reproductive Care in New Mexico

KATHLEEN HOLSCHER

In 1953 Helen Perry came to Santa Fe to learn nurse-midwifery from the Medical Mission Sisters (MMS). Perry was an obstetrical nurse, and she was disillusioned with the US health care industry. Working in hospitals, she had assisted physicians who—like so many American obstetricians of that era—routinely administered scopolamine, morphine, and other drugs to laboring patients to produce a "painless" childbirth.[1] The memory of one woman in Santa Monica, California, haunted her. She was "clothed in a scanty hospital gown," the nurse later recalled, "crouched in a corner completely out of it!"[2] Perry expected to find something different in New Mexico. Enrolling as a student at the Catholic Maternity Institute (CMI), she began to shadow nurse-midwives who traveled to women's homes in Santa Fe and throughout surrounding villages to attend their deliveries. Most of the women these midwives cared for were poor, and nearly all of them came from Spanish-speaking or *Nuevomexicano* families. Decades later, Perry remembered the first birth she witnessed in New Mexico, and the way it made her feel: "We arrived out in the country and entered a little adobe home. All was quiet, calm and peaceful. The room was all prepared and it seemed without any ado the baby was born to a mother quietly happy and very capable of fulfilling

1. For a comprehensive history of childbirth pain management in the United States, see Jacqueline H. Wolf, *Deliver Me from Pain: Anesthesia and Birth in America*, reprint ed. (Baltimore: John Hopkins University Press, 2012).

2. Helen Perry, CNM, "Years of Matriculation at CMI," in *CMI Graduates and Faculty Remember Nurse-Midwifery in Santa Fe, New Mexico*, ed. Rita A. Kroska and Sr. Catherine Shean, revised for Fox Chase Archives, August 1996, 45, Archives of the Medical Mission Sisters, Philadelphia, (cited hereafter as MMS archives).

her role. [. . .] I can remember driving back feeling so glad that such beautiful care was being made available to these people, so rich in dignity and so poor in material goods."[3] As Perry saw it, CMI midwives made it possible for economically disadvantaged women to maintain their dignity during childbirth—the same dignity more affluent (and white) women elsewhere in the country were routinely denied.

A decade before Perry's arrival in Santa Fe, the MMS began CMI as an experiment in health care for the poor. In 1944 two members of the Philadelphia-based, Roman Catholic religious order opened the institute to provide prenatal, birthing and postpartum services to *Nuevomexica-nos*—a population afflicted by pervasive poverty as well as the highest maternal and infant mortality rates in the nation.[4] These sisters and their successors came to Santa Fe to save lives, and they succeeded at that. Between 1944 and the institute's close in 1969, CMI nurse-midwives assisted in several thousand births.[5] In many cases they replaced traditionally trained *parteras* (local midwives). The sisters, along with lay nurse-midwives who worked alongside them, adhered to professional, US public health nursing standards of care. Steep declines in maternal and infant mortality in New Mexico were closely connected to their efforts (Santa Fe County alone saw a 75 percent drop in infant mortality between 1929 and 1959).[6]

When the MMS described the CMI as experimental—"a new experiment in organized maternity care," as one former CMI director put

3. Ibid.

4. As late as 1966, CMI categorized 261 of 296 patients as "Spanish American." Catholic Maternity Institute, *Annual Report*, 1966, p. 2, Folder 150, Santa Fe: Curriculum, CMI, MMS archives.

5. During the institute's first decade and a half, CMI nurse-midwives assisted 3,422 women with childbirth. By 1964 the institute reported that its midwives had made nearly 64,000 home visits (preparatory visits and births combined); Sr. Rosemary Smyth, SCMM, BSN, "History of the Catholic Maternity Institute, 1943–1958" (master's thesis, Catholic University of America, 1960), 26; "63,982 Home Visits in 20 Years," flier, n.d., Folder RG -3: Brochures, General Information, MMS archives.

6. Rita C.A. Kroska, *History of Nurse-Midwifery in Santa Fe, New Mexico* (n.p., 2012), 82, MMS archives. CMI also played a key role in the elimination of *parteras*; by the institute's close in 1969, traditional midwives were delivering only 1 percent of New Mexican babies. "Public Health Nursing Marks 50 Years," *Pasatiempo*, 19 October 1969, n.p., Folder: RG-3, Santa Fe: Newspaper Clippings, 1964–1969, MMS archives.

it—they were not thinking about the newness of their reproductive health care model in New Mexico communities, though the care they brought to New Mexico *was* new in important and sometimes difficult ways.[7] Rather, the sisters understood the CMI approach to women's health as an alternative to the dominant, medical model of pregnancy management in both Catholic and non-Catholic hospitals in the United States at mid-century. The institute's nurse-midwives encouraged patients to birth in their homes, in the presence of husbands and children. Within a few years, CMI also offered its patients use of an on-site homelike birthing center—the first non-hospital birthing center in the nation. In an era when nearly 90 percent of American women (and nearly all white women) delivered under the paid care of a physician at a hospital, and when laboring women regularly received spinal anesthesia, scopolamine, or similar drugs, the MMS acted from the countercultural assumptions that pregnancy and childbirth were normal rather than pathological processes.[8] Decades before "natural childbirth" became a movement in the United States, the MMS built CMI on the radical premise that the safest—and most *Christian*—way for a woman to deliver a baby was not alone in a hospital room but surrounded by family, "awake and alert, participating and cooperating."[9] When the MMS began the CMI, midwifery was legal in only three states—Kentucky, New York, and New Mexico.[10] Seventy years later, more than eleven thousand certified nurse-midwives practice in all fifty states, and attend approximately 8 percent of US births. In New Mexico, nurse-midwives or certified midwives now attend

7. Smyth, "History of the Catholic Maternity Institute," 1.

8. In 1900, almost all US women gave birth outside of hospitals. By 1935, just over a third of US births were happening inside hospitals. In 1950, 88 percent of US women and 93 percent of white women gave birth under a physician's care in a hospital (US Department of Health, Education, and Welfare, *Vital Statistics of the United States, 1950*, vol. 1, 95, Centers for Disease Control and Prevention, https://www.cdc.gov/nchs/data/vsus/vsus_1950_1.pdf); Mother Anna Dengel, SCMM, MD, "An Airplane View of Midwifery" *The Bulletin for Schools of Nursing of the Catholic University of America*, series vii, n. 4, May 1945, 3, Folder 1-04, Mother Anna Dengel Talks, 1945, MMS archives.

9. "Description of Service by Sister Mary Patrick, Director," n.d., Folder 150, Santa Fe: Curriculum, CMI, MMS archives.

10. Anne Zschoche Cockerham, "A Mission for Mothers: Nurse-Midwifery and the Society of Catholic Medical Missionaries in Santa Fe, New Mexico, 1943–1969" (PhD diss., University of Virginia, 2008), 5–6.

25 percent of all births (and an even higher portion of vaginal births). The CMI and its leadership helped lay the foundation for the rise of nurse-midwifery in New Mexico and around the nation.[11]

For the sisters who ran the CMI, their experiment was not a self-consciously "economic" one. It was, however, integral to anti-poverty work in New Mexico. From the vantage point of this volume, the CMI experiment speaks to the scope of Catholic anti-poverty efforts and also, more importantly, illuminates a mid-century Catholic perspective that—working from the understood dignity of the human person—approached poverty as a problem that was never only about money and not always best or most relevantly addressed in standard economic terms. This was especially the case when it came to supporting poor *women*. In this Catholic view, women suffered from economic disadvantages like men did, and like men they benefited from efforts at economic uplift. But support geared only toward uplift in the context of the money economy failed to address their unique dignity as women. In the mid-century Catholic understanding, a woman's dignity lay foremost in "the vocation of motherhood," and honoring that vocation entailed extra-economic—and by standard definitions, *noneconomic*—forms of support.[12]

11. "Essential Facts About Midwives," *American College of Nurse-Midwives*, http://www.midwife.org/Essential-Facts-about-Midwives; ACNM Department of Advocacy and Government Affairs, "State Fact Sheet: New Mexico," American College of Nurse Midwives, http://www.midwife.org/acnm/files/ccLibraryFiles/Filename/000000005600/ACNMStateFactSheets8-21-15.pdf. The numbers here are from 2014 and 2013, respectively. The American College of Nurse Midwives (ACNM) began in the parlor of CMI in 1955, and MMS sister and CMI founder Theophane Shoemaker served as the organization's second director, correspondence, n.s., 12 December 1955, Folder RG 3-05 b.12.f.11, CMI Family Values, MMS archives. Today the ACNM remains the professional association representing CNMs and certified midwives in the United States.

12. "Objectives of the Catholic Maternity Institute," n.d., Folder 150, Santa Fe: Curriculum, CMI, MMS archives. See also Smyth, "History of the Catholic Maternity Institute," 20. CMI had no formal statement of philosophy until 1959, and it is unknown whether "dignity of motherhood" was explicit to the mission of the institute at its founding. One sister who was part of the institute's earliest cohort of nurse-midwives recalled a founding mission of simply providing "good, safe maternity care and the kind of care they could afford." ("Oral History II: Sister Catherine Shean, MMS," *History of Nurse-Midwifery*, 1992, 63). That said, the dignity of motherhood was an organizing theme by the 1950s not only in the mission statement but in lesson plans and other CMI course material. It is likewise frequently mentioned in the recollections of former CMI

This is how the sister-midwives at CMI talked about their anti-poverty work; they answered the plight of New Mexico's poor in a way that recognized impoverished women's dignity and all that dignity demanded. If their work was self-consciously noneconomic as a result—driven by an ideology of domesticity that elevated the home as a space apart from the money economy and "sacred to family living," and motherhood as a vocation most fully realized in that sphere—the CMI experiment still does useful work here.[13] CMI's inclusion in this volume highlights the way in which Catholic attention to gender has historically informed church initiatives to support the poor, both in their material and nonmaterial needs. In particular, CMI sheds light on how Catholic ideas about femaleness informed a range of noneconomic initiatives aimed at the poor. In doing so it also pushes us to consider, alongside Sullivan-Dunbar in this volume, parallel ways that religious ideas about gender complementarity propelled Catholic attention to, and assumptions regarding, the money economy through the twentieth century and beyond. In a similar vein, CMI opens up space for considering historically gendered forms of living a dignified life that are obscured when the money economy is privileged as a framework for the promotion and the assessment of human flourishing. My purpose is *not* to diminish the importance of thinking about economic practice but rather to point to ways in which, in Catholic contexts, the economic has functioned as a gendered category, and to recall Catholic forms of living well in the world it excludes as a result. The CMI speaks to the inadequacy of "the economic" as an umbrella category for locating Catholic anti-poverty work and for talking about Catholic ways of flourishing as a human through much of the twentieth century.

In the eyes of the MMS, similar to the leadership of their church, poor people in New Mexico—like poor people around the world—found themselves in circumstances that denied their dignity as human beings. On a basic level, those circumstances were created by an unjust money economy, and the Catholic Church taught that honoring human dignity entailed working toward economic justice. When it came to poor *women,*

---

midwives. See Perry, "Years of Matriculation." See also, for example, Carol Dorey Hurzeler, CNM, "Memories of CMI," *CMI Graduates and Faculty Remember Nurse-Midwifery in Santa Fe, New Mexico,* 82.

13. "Class III: Baby's Birthday," 62, Folder 55: CMI, Santa Fe: Mother's Classes / Medical Records, MMS archives.

however, the church maintained that the dignity of women was substantively different than the dignity of men, that it made different demands, and that it was, at the end of the day, incommensurable with—or at least insufficiently addressed via—forms (good or bad) of economic practice. This is where the MMS stepped in. The sisters at CMI taught their impoverished patients that the "essence of female dignity is motherhood."[14] Although dignified motherhood required economic stability (and it's worth emphasizing that sisters cared a great deal about economic justice, and routinely distributed information about parish credit unions, cooperatives, and other economic initiatives to women as part of their work) it also depended on other things.[15] Those other things included good relations among family members and the home as a haven to grow those relationships. The right use—accompanied by knowledge and awareness—of one's body was important too. MMS told their patients that God designed the female body for motherhood, and "[He] expects you to use your body as He intended."[16] The sisters built an experiment that kept their patients safe, and supported their dignity by respecting these factors. They offered their service as an alternative to a health care industry that, in its pursuit of efficiency (and profit), dragged mothers out of the home and away from family, and, leaving them alone and "clothed in scanty hospital gown[s]," failed to recognize their dignity.[17]

The CMI experiment in home birthing replicated, in some ways, preexisting or "traditional" practices around childbirth in New Mexico. In other ways, the birthing model that CMI midwives introduced to honor the dignity of their patients was an intervention that reordered local knowledge and practice. The latter is most evident in efforts of CMI's women religious to include fathers as intimate participants in the births they attended. For the sisters, a man's involvement in childbirth was essential; it upheld both his dignity and that of his birthing partner. By

14. "Class I: Motherhood," 1, Folder 55: CMI, Santa Fe: Mother's Classes / Medical Records, MMS archives.

15. Catherine Shean, MMS, CNM, "Beginnings," *CMI Graduates and Faculty Remember*, 3; "Mothers Class Lesson VI: 'the Tree of Life,'" Folder 55: "CMI, Santa Fe: Mother's Classes / Medical Records," MMS archives.

16. "Class III: Baby's Birthday," 1, Folder 55: MMS archives.

17. Perry, "Years of Matriculation."

introducing men to the space and time of childbirth, however, the CMI model unsettled the *Nuevomexicano* understanding of childbirth as a female-populated process. Through their medical work, CMI staffers imposed a mid-century US Catholic model of family (husband, wife, children) upon an event that, in *Nuevomexicano* communities, had long reflected—and helped sustain—a different (female-centered, extended) family model. Even as CMI offered itself as a countercultural experiment, a working alternative to the medicalized and male-dominated culture of American childbirth at mid-century, it was also a participant in the century-old legacy of US imperialism in New Mexico, where it performed at the complex intersection of religion, biopolitics, and state power. Describing efforts of state health officials to replace *parteras* during the early twentieth century, Lena McQuade-Salzfass writes, "Midwifery in New Mexico was deeply intertwined with constructions of the state's racial difference and the legacies of colonialism that shaped public health."[18] So too became the sisters when they came to Santa Fe. In this sense, the CMI offers a lesson in the layered effects of historical experiments, economic or otherwise, to honor the "dignity of the poor," when those experiments happen—as they so often do—across lines of racial difference, and in the shadow of asymmetrical relations of political power.

New Mexico was a poor state in the 1940s, and its *Nuevomexicano* population was especially poor. Since the late nineteenth century, Spanish-speaking communities concentrated in the rural north of New Mexico had acutely felt their disenfranchisement within an Anglo-dominated regional economy—from the loss of land grants and the livelihoods they had made possible, and from a precarious, imposed economic system built on single-source, wage-dependent incomes.[19] This pattern persisted after New Mexico became a state in 1912. During the Great Depression, nearly two-thirds of *Nuevomexicanos* in the north fell reliant on government

18. Lena McQuade-Salzfass, "'An Indispensible Service: Midwives and Medical Officials after New Mexico Statehood," *Precarious Prescriptions: Contested Histories of Race and Health in North America* (Minneapolis: University of Minnesota Press, 2014), 115.

19. On the transformation of the New Mexico economy during this period and its effects on *Nuevomexicano* communities, including gender roles therein, see Sarah Deutsch, *No Separate Refuge: Culture, Class, and Gender on an Anglo-Hispanic Frontier in the American Southwest, 1880–1940* (New York: Oxford University Press, 1987).

aid.[20] New Mexico was also a dangerous state to give birth, and to be born, into the 1940s. Statewide and across ethnic groups, New Mexico had the highest infant mortality rate and the second highest maternal mortality rate in the nation. Moreover, the death rate of *Nuevomexicano* infants was nearly three times that of Anglo infants in New Mexico. The mortality rate among *Nuevomexicano* infants eclipsed even that of African Americans in every state in 1940.[21]

New Mexican health officials recognized a correlation between poverty and maternal and infant mortality in *Nuevomexicano* communities, and so did the Catholic women religious who came to provide prenatal care. As Sister Rosemary Smyth, who directed the CMI in the late 1950s, would later put it, "An unsound land system creat[ed] acute poverty which in turn caused serious health [. . .] conditions."[22] Early efforts by the New Mexico Health Department to improve maternal and infant outcomes did not address poverty directly, however, but instead focused on eliminating—or in lieu of eliminating, at least licensing—the *parteras* who assisted most rural women during childbirth.[23] Anglo health officials, concerned about establishing an American health care model in their new state, cast *parteras* as backward and "superstitious." Explaining this urgent push for *partera* regulation, McQuade-Salzfass writes: "In the [. . .] post-statehood period, *parteras* [. . .] played a key discursive role in the production of New Mexico as a racially distinct and suspect political space."[24] The MMS arrived in New Mexico as part of the push to replace

20. Deutsch, *No Separate Refuge*, 167.

21. Laura Ettinger, "Mission to Mothers: Latino Families, and the Founding of Santa Fe's Catholic Maternity Institute," in *Women, Health and the Nation: Canada and the United States Since 1945*, ed. Georgina Feldberg, Molly Ladd-Taylor, Alison Li, and Kathryn McPherson (Montreal: McGill-Queen's University Press, 2003), 146; Sr. M. Lucia Van der Eerden, SCMM, "Maternity Care in a Spanish-American Community in New Mexico," (PhD diss., Catholic University of America, 1948), vii–viii. According to data provided by Van der Eerden, "Spanish-Americans" in New Mexico had an infant mortality rate of 114.7 per 1,000 births during 1940–1942, compared with a rate of 38.5 for Anglos in the state. The highest infant mortality rate for African Americans, by state, was in Virginia (between 75 and 80 deaths per 1,000 births).

22. Smyth, "History of the Catholic Maternity Institute," 7–8.

23. On efforts to restrict *parteras* in New Mexico during this era with attention to the racialization of *Nuevomexicanos*, see McQuade-Salzfass, "An Indispensible Service."

24. McQuade-Salzfass, "An Indispensible Service," 115, 116.

unlicensed *parteras*.[25] The community came at the invitation of Archbishop Rudolph Gerken of Santa Fe in 1943, but it began its work with
financial support from both the state health department and the Maternal-
Child Health Division of the US Children's Bureau.[26]

All of these parties—the archbishop, the state and federal government
agencies, and the women religious—shared a vision of sisters providing
"scientifically sound" midwifery services to New Mexico's people.[27] From
the perspective of government officials, professional nurse-midwives—
women who were trained in medicine, and who worked under the
watchful eyes of doctors—were efficient, if temporary, replacements for
parteras. In 1943 the state health department approved nurse-midwives
as a "sound public health procedure" for "women unable to secure medical care at time of child-bearing." But such professionals should only be
used (the board was careful to stipulate) "until such time as adequate
medical care can be made available to replace all midwifery."[28] The Archbishop of Santa Fe, for his part, agreed with health officials that nurse-
midwives would save lives. In addition, from the prelate's perspective, a
community of Catholic sisters doing this work offered a critical, moral

25. In 1937 the health department began a program for re-educating and licensing
the local women they called "granny midwives." Despite this initiative, unlicensed
parteras remained the norm in many communities through the early 1940s. Between
1938 and 1944 in Taos County, for example, 70 percent of *Nuevomexicano* women still
gave birth at home attended by traditional midwives. Taos County alone had more than
fifty *parteras*. Statewide, a quarter of all women were attended by midwives in 1942, and
the majority of those women remained traditionally trained and unlicensed. Edwin F.
Daily, Director, Division of Health Services, US Dept. of Labor, Children's Bureau to
James R. Scott, Director, New Mexico State Dept. of Public Health, personal correspondence, 1 September 1942, Folder 150, Santa Fe: Curriculum, CMI, MMS archives; Van
der Eerden, "Maternity Care," 12, 50; Mother Anna Dengel, SCMM, "An Airplane View
of Midwifery," *The Bulletin for School of Nursing of the Catholic University of America*,
series 7, n. 4 (May 1945), 4.

26. Cockerham, "A Mission for Mothers," 124–27. At CMI's founding, the state
health department supplied personnel for consultation and essential equipment, and
the US Children's Bureau provided additional subsidies. The health department also
underwrote the salary of its clinical director (Smyth, "History of the Catholic Maternity
Institute," 17–18).

27. Smyth, "History of the Catholic Maternity Institute," 1.

28. Stuart W. Adler to Frances C. Rothert, personal correspondence, 19 February 1943,
Folder 150, Santa Fe: Curriculum, CMI, MMS archives. See also Daily correspondence.

alternative to another Anglo reproductive-care initiative already at work in the region. A decade earlier, the Santa Fe Maternal Health Clinic had opened its doors to local women. Although its staff provided a wide range of reproductive services, the Maternal Health Clinic had benefited from early sponsorship from Margaret Sanger's Birth Control Clinical Research Bureau, and it infuriated the archbishop with its ongoing policy of making contraception available to patients.[29]

For the MMS, the timing of Archbishop Gerken's invitation to Santa Fe was providential. Since the community's founding in 1925 the MMS had pursued a global mission, dedicating themselves, in the words of their physician-founder Anna Dengel, to providing "skilled medical care [. . .] to the sick and poor [. . .], as a means of relieving their physical suffering and of bringing them to a knowledge and appreciation of our Faith." From the start, the professional expertise of its religious, as nurses, physicians, and also midwives, was an essential part of the congregations's mission. "Unscientific methods and care by untrained people," Dengel explained in 1945, "no longer suffice."[30] Women's health was an MMS specialty, and until the 1940s, its missions were exclusively international, focused in India and Africa.[31] Archbishop Gerken's request for MMS help came just as a US prohibition on international travel, prompted by the nation's entry into World War II, was forcing Dengel to consider domestic missions for the first time.[32] The archbishop helped

29. On the Santa Fe Maternal Health Clinic, see Michael Anne Sullivan, "Walking the Line: Birth Control and Women's Health at the Santa Fe Maternal Health Center, 1937–1945" (master's thesis, University of New Mexico, 1995). The Santa Fe Maternal Health Clinic did not offer delivery or postpartum care (Cockerham, "A Mission for Mothers," 154).

30. Anna Dengel, *Mission for Samaritans: A Survey of Achievements in the Field of Catholic Medical Missions* (Milwaukee: Bruce Publishing Company, 1945), 1–2. The Medical Mission Sisters were founded as a "pious society" rather than an official religious order, due to the Vatican's then-prohibition on women religious practicing medicine, surgery, and obstetrics. The community became an official order, with its members taking public vows, immediately after the Vatican removed its prohibition in 1936 (Cockerham, "A Mission for Mothers," 107, 114–16).

31. Of particular concern to Dengel were lower caste women in India and Muslim women who did not receive adequate medical care due to prohibitions against women interacting with male physicians (Cockerham, "A Mission for Mothers," 101–2).

32. Ibid., 124.

Dengel obtain the necessary ecclesial permission for work inside the United States, and five months later the superior sent her first religious, Sisters Theophane Shoemaker and Helen Herb, to New Mexico.[33]

Sister Theophane was thirty years old when she came to Santa Fe in November of 1943, and Sister Helen was sixteen years her senior. In line with their congregations's expectations, both women had training and experience as nurses. In addition, both had recently completed a specialized program in nurse-midwifery at the Lobenstine Clinic in New York City.[34] Less than a year after their arrival, the sisters opened the CMI in an adobe building near the city's main plaza, with space for classrooms, offices, a chapel, a clinic, and a dormitory for sisters.[35] A local female obstetrician stepped in as the institute's first medical director, and within a few months other sisters began arriving to join the CMI staff.[36] Sisters Theophane and Helen worked with other early CMI leaders to implement the institute's two objectives: 1) to provide "an urgently needed obstetric service, scientifically sound, and keyed into a specific health problem," and 2) to train nurses from across the nation—and around the world—in nurse-midwifery.[37]

In line with the first objective, CMI began to offer care that was both comprehensive and affordable. For a one-time fee of $10, a woman who registered with the institute could expect ongoing support from CMI midwives, from the first trimester of her pregnancy, through labor and delivery, and for the first month of her infant's life.[38] In contrast to *Nuevomexicano* custom, which placed little weight on the special supervision of women during pregnancy, CMI required all its patients to attend regular prenatal checkups at the institute's clinic. During these prenatal visits, nurse-midwives drew samples for lab work, monitored fetal

33. Ibid., 129–31.

34. Kroska, *History of Nurse-Midwifery*, 8; Cockerham, "A Mission for Mothers," 148–51.

35. Kroska, *History of Nurse-Midwifery*, 16.

36. Cockerham, "A Mission for Mothers," 161.

37. Smyth, "History of the Catholic Maternity Institute," 1.

38. "Memories of Agnes Shoemaker Reinders (Sr. Theophane Sheomaker, MMS)," in Kroska, *History of Nurse-Midwifery*, 29. By the late 1960s the fee had increased to $210 but was reduced in accordance with a patient's ability to pay (Sr. Mary Patrick, "Description of Service," n.d., Folder 150, Santa Fe: Curriculum, CMI, MMS archives.

development and position, and kept tabs on a patient's diet.[39] Although not required, patients were also encouraged to attend biweekly "mother's classes" at the institute, designed to "prepar[e] them for labor, delivery and deeper understanding of their own and baby's care."[40]

By confirming an uncomplicated pregnancy, and by preparing the patient intellectually, spiritually, and physically for childbirth, this prenatal regimen laid groundwork for the CMI model of home and home-like births that, though normal (at least in terms of setting) for *Nuevomexicano* women, were a radical departure from the hospital-based US health care industry. During the institute's early years, all CMI births took place inside the homes of patients or their close relatives. CMI policy stipulated that nurse-midwives would attend births within a thirty-mile radius—an area that covered not only Santa Fe and its outlying villages but also places as far north as Española and Chimayó.[41] Travel to more remote locations often meant using dirt roads, crossing arroyos, and searching for unmarked addresses, and so CMI midwives always made a preparatory home visit late in a woman's pregnancy, "to ascertain the home conditions, to instruct the patient regarding the arrangement of equipment in the home for delivery," and also "to be sure of the location of the home."[42] During that visit, midwives instructed the expectant mother how to prepare the space for childbirth, by putting clean sheets on the bed, assembling a basin and other basic supplies, and assembling sanitary pads or "Kelly pads" out of clean newspaper.[43]

At the onset of labor, a nurse-midwife returned to her patient's home with medical kit in tow. Although CMI delivery kits included medicines for pain management, former CMI staffers recall proudly "little or no pain medication was used."[44] In lieu of administering medicine, CMI

39. Van der Eerden, "Maternity Care," 34, Cockerham, "A Mission for Mothers," 189; Sr. Mary Patrick, "Description of Service."

40. Sr. Mary Patrick, "Description of Service."

41. Catholic Maternity Institute, *Annual Report*, 1966.

42. "Narrative recording the overall plan of the training program conducted for nurse midwives," 1946, 8, Folder 150, Santa Fe: Curriculum, CMI, MMS archives.

43. "Mothers Class: Lesson II: Preparation of a Christian Family," Folder 55, Santa Fe: Mother's Classes / Medical Records," MMS archives. See also Cockerham, "A Mission for Mothers," 157.

44. Sr. Patricia Elder, DC, CNM, "Memories of Catholic Maternity Institute," *CMI Graduates and Faculty Remember*, 60.

nurse-midwives preferred to assist their patients with breathing and relaxation techniques that would enable them to remain "awake and alert" and "fully participating" throughout the birth process.[45] Midwives encouraged fathers to be present during labor and delivery, and older children were invited into the bedroom immediately following a birth, to "look at the baby, touch it and then with the help of their parents decide on a name for it."[46] Following a successful delivery, it was standard procedure for the midwife to place the infant in the arms of its father for a blessing, and join the gathered family members in a prayer of thanksgiving. "We would kneel down at the foot of the bed and recite the Our Father," remembered Rita Kroska (formerly Sister Judith Kroska).[47] "We would form a prayer circle around the bed of the mother and following the example of the father we would all bless this new life with the sign of the cross," Sister Mary Simpson recalled.[48]

The CMI care cycle concluded with a series of postpartum visits to the home, during which the nurse-midwife measured the infant's weight, checked in on the mother's recovery, and offered support with breastfeeding and baby care.[49] This model of exclusively home-based care changed only after CMI opened "La Casita," its on-site birthing center, in 1951. Decorated "attractively with chintz curtains, white wicker furniture and pictures," La Casita quickly became the preferred childbirth option for CMI patients, in part because expecting mothers came to recognize that giving birth at the center meant time away from the care work comprised of "household responsibilities."[50] Though CMI's staff continued to encourage and support home births, by 1956, births at La Casita had begun to outnumber births inside patients' home. A few years later, CMI home births ended altogether.[51]

45. Ibid.; Sr. Mary Patrick, "Description of Service."

46. Sr. Mary S. Simpson, DC, CMN, "Family as One," *CMI Graduates and Faculty Remember,* 55.

47. Kroska, *History of Nurse-Midwifery,* 21.

48. Simpson, "Family as One," 55.

49. Cockerham, "A Mission for Mothers," 158, 197.

50. Sr. Catherine Shean, "Beginnings," 2; Cockerham, "A Mission for Mothers," 234.

51. Smyth, "History of the Catholic Maternity Institute," 27; Kroska, *History of Nurse-Midwifery,* 8. On the continuing preference of CMI midwives for home births, and the pushback they received from their patients, see Cockerham, "A Mission for Mothers," 234–39.

In addition to offering health care, CMI also trained nurse-midwives. Despite the state health department's early initiative to license local *parteras*, CMI's nurse-midwifery program was designed for women who were already nurses and who had acquired prior experience in public health nursing. In practice it was a program for Anglo women who traveled to Santa Fe from other parts of the country to enroll.[52] When CMI began its certification program in 1944, it became the third nurse-midwifery school for white women in the United States (two other schools offered training to African American nurses).[53] Within a few years, the institute had built an affiliation with Catholic University of America to offer the nation's first graduate degree in nurse-midwifery.[54] Students enrolled in classes (often team taught by resident sisters and affiliated lay obstetricians) on topics like "Midwifery Techniques" and "Public Health Nursing in Obstetrics," and they assisted CMI staff during childbirths.[55] Between 1945 and 1958, fifty-six students—including twenty-two Catholic women religious—completed training at CMI.[56] The institute also regularly hosted international visitors, from places like Burma, Liberia, and the Philippines, who had interest in replicating parts of the CMI experiment in their own countries.[57]

Midwife care and home childbirths made sense to CMI's staff for several reasons. Given a patient population with limited means to pay medical professionals, nurse-midwives offered quality care at an affordable cost. Attending births at home allowed them to assist rural patients for whom travel could be difficult, and to do so (at least initially) without the costs involved in maintaining a permanent birthing facility. Moreover, in New Mexico, home childbirths reassuringly mimicked—in some ways, at least—the birthing customs of *Nuevomexicano* communities. For the

52. Cockerham, "A Mission for Mothers," 165. Despite CMI's de facto training of Anglo women, program leaders were explicit that African Americans with the appropriate credentials were permitted to enroll (Cockerham, "A Mission for Mothers," 182).

53. Daily correspondence; Gerald R. Clark to Seth L Evans, personal correspondence, 14 October 1953, Folder 150, Santa Fe: Curriculum, CMI, MMS archives.

54. Kroska, "Memories of Agnes Shoemaker Reinders," *History of Nurse-Midwifery*, 30.

55. Cecilia Buser, CNM, "How I Came to Become a Nurse-Midwife and Came to Love It," *CMI Graduates and Faculty Remember*, 11; Smyth, "History of the Catholic Maternity Institute," 45.

56. Smyth, "History of the Catholic Maternity Institute," 48.

57. "Oral History I—Sr. Catherine Shean, MMS," *History of Nurse-Midwifery*, 47.

women religious who staffed CMI, however, midwife care and home births represented more than pragmatism. By the 1950s, the MMS were emphasizing that their health care experiment was a meaningfully *Catholic* enterprise. For the sisters, home birthing and other aspects of midwife-assisted care were practices that, in contrast to the health care provided by US hospitals, elevated the dignity of women. As the CMI's 1959 statement of philosophy put it, the institute's aim was "to provide a maternity service which recognizes and responds to the dignity of motherhood. By this it seeks to restore the family to God who created it. [. . .] The essentially normal character of obstetrics is emphasized. Physical, spiritual, social, educational and economic aspects are given due consideration and every attempt is made to make the mother aware of her own significance and true worth."[58]

When MMS talked about the "dignity of motherhood" in the 1950s, they participated in a well-established Catholic discourse on the dignity of the human person. The same discourse on human dignity underpinned Catholic social teaching, which in turn underpinned Catholic experiments in economic uplift and calls for economic reform through the first part of the twentieth century. Unlike the dignity of the working person, however, responses to the dignity of the mother—as the sisters articulated it here—emphasized forms of support that happened mainly (though not entirely) away from the market. Their Catholicism taught them that, whether poor or not, women (men too, but women especially) required more than a living wage to live lives reflective of their "true worth."

In his book *Dignity: Its History and Meaning*, Michael Rosen charts the historical development of dignity as a concept in western thought, including within the Catholic tradition. As early as the thirteenth century, Thomas Aquinas defined dignity as "something's goodness on account of itself," or as Rosen explains it, "the value that it has by occupying its appropriate place in God's creation, as revealed by Scripture and by natural law."[59] In later centuries, the Catholic Church continued to talk about human dignity in these terms—as premised on a person successfully

58. "Statement of Philosophy," n.d., Folder 150, Santa Fe: Curriculum, CMI, MMS archives.

59. Michael Rosen, *Dignity: Its History and Meaning* (Cambridge, MA: Harvard University Press, 2012), 16–17.

occupying his or her "appropriate place." This Catholic take on dignity not only allowed for but *required* different humans to live in different ways—ways "appropriate" to each. By the early twentieth century, human dignity had emerged as a core value in a new body of Catholic social teaching with a focus on the well-being of the laboring class. In *Rerum Novarum* (1891), Pope Leo XIII called on employers "not to look upon their employees as bondsmen, but to respect in every man his dignity as a person ennobled by Christian character."[60] In *Quadragesimo Anno* (1931), Pope Pius XI praised labor laws created "to protect vigorously the sacred rights of the workers that flow from their dignity as men and as Christians."[61] Even when invoked by the popes on behalf of labor, however, human dignity continued to imply difference rather than equality. Different classes of men, treating each other justly, was essential so that all might play, in Rosen's words, "the role that is appropriate to their station within a hierarchical social order."[62]

Just as Catholic teaching, well into the twentieth century, held that human dignity was honored in situations where social classes, acting justly to one another, were free to fulfill their (different) purposes, the church instructed that the dignity of the sexes, male and female, also emerged from difference. In his 1880 encyclical on Christian marriage, Leo had declared that "Woman [. . .] must be subject to her husband and obey him; not, indeed, as a servant, but as a companion, so that her obedience shall be wanting in neither honor nor dignity." Here as Rosen explains it, a woman's dignity "is not an attribute of an individual person" but emerges out of a rightly lived social relationship—a relationship between husband and wife characterized by the latter's correctly performed subordination to the former.[63] This dignity of woman-as-wife/

60. Pope Leo XIII, "Rerum Novarum," *Online Archive of the Vatican*, http://w2.vatican.va/content/leo-xiii/en/encyclicals/documents/hf_l–xiii_enc_15051891_rerum-novarum.html.

61. Pope Pius XI, "Quadragesimo Anno," *Online Archive of the Vatican*, http://w2.vatican.va/content/pius-xi/en/encyclicals/documents/hf_p-xi_enc_19310515_quadragesimo-anno.html.

62. Rosen, *Dignity*, 49.

63. Pope Leo XIII, "Arcanum" (1880), *Online Archive of the Vatican*, http://w2.vatican.va/content/leo-xiii/en/encyclicals/documents/hf_l-xiii_enc_10021880_arcanum.html; Rosen, *Dignity*, 49.

mother remained intact a half century later, in Pius's encyclical *Casti Connubii* (1930), although the theme of subordination was diminished. A wife's "subjection" to her husband, Pius explained, "does not deny or take away the liberty which fully belongs to the woman [. . .] in view of her dignity as a human person." Nevertheless, the encyclical went on to denounce "exaggerated" claims to equality between the sexes—including economic parity, "whereby the woman even [. . .] against the wish of her husband may be at liberty to conduct and administer her own affairs, giving her attention chiefly to these rather than to children, husband and family."[64] Equality of this sort could only lead, Pius warned, to "the debasing of the womanly character and the dignity of motherhood." "This [. . .] unnatural equality with the husband is to the detriment of the woman herself," the pope explained. "For if the woman descends from her truly regal throne to which she has been raised within the walls of the home [. . .], she will [. . .] become [. . .] the mere instrument of man."[65]

In *Casti Connubii* Pius also addressed, as he would in *Quadragesimo Anno* a year later, "the duty of the public authority" to aid families in economic need. Here the pope emphasized that men and women required adequate support, economic and otherwise, to be able to perform the different, dignified forms of labor appropriate to each: "If the husband cannot find employment and means of livelihood [. . .]; if even the mother of the family to the great harm of the home, is compelled to go forth and seek a living by her own labor; if she, too, in the [. . .] labors of childbirth, is deprived of proper food, medicine, and the assistance of a skilled physician, it is patent to all to what an extent married people may lose heart, and how home life and the observance of God's commands are rendered difficult for them."[66] Throughout this period, as the Catholic Church put forth calls for economic justice, it did so with the understanding that human dignity demanded men and women labor differently. As Deborah Figart, Ellen Mutari, and Marilyn Power describe Catholic teaching of

---

64. Pope Pius XI, "Casti Connubii," *Online Archive of the Vatican*, https://w2.vatican.va/content/pius-xi/en/encyclicals/documents/hf_p-xi_enc_19301231_casti-connubii.html.

65. Ibid.

66. Ibid.

the period: "In general, [it] promoted the view that a family wage enabled women to concentrate on their work, and their duty, in the home."[67]

During the 1950s, Pius XII focused directly on the significance of women's reproductive labor, in a pair of speeches before professional associations of European midwives (1951) and gynecologists (1956).[68] In these talks, the pope expanded on his predecessors' articulations of the relationship between reproductive labor and female dignity, by explicitly taking up the question of pain management during childbirth. Although approving of pain-alleviating interventions that allowed women to retain "full consciousness," the pope reminded his audiences both of the religious merits of pain and the importance of a woman retaining her faculties throughout a process so central to her purpose. In his speech to gynecologists (later distributed in pamphlet form to an American audience by the National Catholic Welfare Conference), Pius extolled "the assistance afforded the mother in childbirth opportunely to collaborate with nature, to remain tranquil and under self-control; an increased consciousness of the greatness of motherhood in general, and particularly of the hour when the mother brings forth her child." Such approaches to the birthing process, the pope explained, "fully conform to the will of the Creator."[69]

When the MMS said that the "primary aim" of their Santa Fe experiment was to offer care that "would recognize and respond to the dignity of motherhood," and in particular (though they did not make it explicit in their statement) the dignity of *poor* mothers, they carried forward their church's teachings on dignity and gender. They performed their work from the understanding that, in line with God's design, women inhabited different social roles than men.[70] Though circumstances might

67. Deborah M. Figart, Ellen Mutari, and Marilyn Power, *Living Wages, Equal Wages: Gender and Labour in the Market Policies in the United States* (New York: Routledge, 2005), 42.

68. "Address to Midwives on the Nature of their Profession," 29 October 1951, Papal Encyclicals Online, http://www.papalencyclicals.net/Pius12/P12midwives.htm; "Psychological Method of Natural Painless Childbirth," Pius XII addressing audience of gynecologists, 8 January 1956, Washington, DC: National Catholic Welfare Conference.

69. Pius XII, "Psychological Method of Natural Painless Childbirth," 8–9.

70. Smyth, "History of the Catholic Maternity Institute," 20.

require a woman to labor in the workplace, and she deserved just treatment there, her highest purpose was the other labor of motherhood. Her dignity had its roots, as Pius XII and the sisters all understood it, in her body's reproductive capabilities: its ability to conceive, to grow a fetus, to birth, and to nurture a newborn. Recognizing a woman's dignity therefore required more than economic uplift; it required the medical support that would make her body strong and healthy, and allow it to accomplish its purpose.

From the MMS's vantage point, the dignity of motherhood also demanded other things in addition to good medical care. For one, it required that each mother be made "aware of her own significance." And so, in contrast to a medical industry that restricted what women knew or experienced of their own reproductive bodies, CMI midwives made priorities of patient knowledge and participation. The sisters also followed their church in the understanding that human dignity—that of a man or a woman—existed only in the context of social relationships, particularly relationships between family members. Responding to dignity also therefore required the building up of family units "broken" (as the CMI leadership understood it) both by economic hardship and by cultural mores. With this in mind, staff encouraged family members, and especially fathers, to be present—not only in attendance, but emotionally and spiritually participating—at CMI births. Prioritizing family in this way likewise required abandoning the "cold and distant" hospital in favor of the space of the home. Because the "home is sacred to family living," CMI midwives taught their patients, it is "only fitting that birth should occur there."[71] Dignified maternity care, Sister Rosemary Smyth concluded in 1960, required both "technical proficiency" and "a manifest appreciation of the family and its true purpose."[72]

At the CMI, educating women as mothers included lessons in church doctrine alongside lessons in physiology. Sisters understood the latter as essential; after all the dignity of motherhood, while recognizable only in relation to God's plan for humanity, was demonstrated in "the structure, resiliency, adaptability and purposefulness of woman's body." All CMI patients were encouraged to complete a series of six mothering classes,

71. "Class III: Baby's Birthday," n.d., 2, Folder 55, MMS archives.
72. Smyth, "History of the Catholic Maternity Institute," 20.

offered biweekly by institute staff. Each class covered a different stage in the process of becoming a mother (from conception to newborn care), and each included a mixture of catechetical lessons (relaying church teachings related to marriage, sexuality, family relations, etc.) with instruction in anatomy, hygiene, and "good body mechanics." As one curricular outline explained it, all classes included "discussions on what happens within the mother's body from the beginning to the end of labor, how she can know what is happening by the way she feels and what she can do about it."[73]

The first in this series of classes—over the years it was titled "A Christian Mother" as well as simply "Motherhood"—offered patients instruction both on "the mother's attitude toward marriage and motherhood" and on "the normal bodily changes of pregnancy."[74] Students learned the Catholic Church's take on the purpose of marriage—"To sanctify family life, by giving the spouses [the] grace of absolute abiding fidelity"—and on the roles of the sexes therein, including that "every woman [is] made to be a mother [as well as a] helpmate to man in participation in Divine Plan."[75] During the same class, patients also learned the locations and functions of reproductive organs, including uteruses, ovaries, and fallopian tubes, and, at the instructor's encouragement, "stood and felt their own boney pelvis," in order to understand how their infant would enter the world.[76] In subsequent classes, students studied the various changes their bodies were undergoing, and how to cope with symptoms from nausea to constipation and hemorrhoids. They received coaching on different breathing techniques, breast care, and postpartum abdominal tightening exercises, as they digested lessons like "No accomplishment of man can ever approach in importance the growth and development of

73. "CMI: Mothers' Class Outline," n.d., 3, Folder 55, Santa Fe: Mother's Classes / Medical Records," MMS archives. Attendance at parenting classes varied; one undated photograph shows eighteen mother's class graduates ("Sr. Helen, Sr. Patrick, Santa Fe," photograph, n.d., MMS archives), whereas a CMI newsletter from May 1952 reports just two women awarded diplomas for attending all six meetings ("CMI Family News," 1, no. 6 [18 May 1952], Folder RG 3-05 b.12.f.11, CMI: Family Values, MMS archives).

74. "Lesson One: A Christian Mother," n.d., 36, Folder 55, Santa Fe: Mother's Classes / Medical Records, MMS archives.

75. "Class One: Motherhood," n.d., 52–53, Folder 55, Santa Fe: Mother's Classes / Medical Records, MMS archives.

76. "Lesson One: A Christian Mother," 37.

another human being," and also that "Willing acceptance [of] God's plan for you will help to make you a more complete and happy woman."[77]

Just as a woman came to know her dignity though knowing her body and its place in God's plan, she came know it too through participation in her own childbirth. Through CMI's prenatal classes, midwives hoped to prepare each patient "to accomplish labor and delivery unafraid, experiencing the birth of her baby in consciousness [. . .] with full awareness of the part she is privileged to play in this creative act of God."[78] As we have seen, although CMI midwives made pain medicine available to patients in labor, they discouraged its use.[79] In its stead they coached patients on avoiding pain "by relaxation and proper breathing techniques."[80] Midwives also sometimes instructed women on the spiritual merit of any pain they did experience. "The truly Christian mother will offer up any discomfort she will feel in Thanksgiving for the privilege that is being given her," advised one lesson plan.[81] Another lesson plan upped the ante for women anticipating labor pain. Pain could be powerful penance: "There will be some pain. Don't merely endure it. Embrace your cross courageously, even joyfully. What a power you have now to repair all wrongs, to make reparation for your sins and those of others, to make right what the first woman made wrong. Man's punishment—sweat, fatigue; woman's—pain and inconvenience of childbirth."[82]

CMI midwives admired their patients' ability to birth without medication. "We were so amazed at [. . .] the ability of these Spanish women to tolerate this discomfort and go through it without anesthesia," one CMI alumna later remembered.[83] "To the Spanish American women childbearing was a natural experience," Sister Rosemary Smyth recalled.[84] These local women—as the sisters saw it—had an extraordinary capacity

77. "Class II: Preparation," 56–59; "Class III: Baby's Birthday," 65; "Class IV: Mother's Care," 68, Folder 55, Santa Fe: Mother's Classes / Medical Records, MMS archives.

78. "CMI: Mothers' Class Outline," 3.

79. "Class III: Baby's Birthday," 65.

80. Ibid.

81. Ibid.

82. Untitled teaching notes, n.d. 2, Folder 55, Santa Fe: Mother's Classes / Medical Records, MMS archives.

83. Cecilia Buser, CNM, "How I Came to Become a Nurse-Midwife and Came to Love It," CMI Graduates and Faculty Remember, 13–14.

84. Smyth, "History of the Catholic Maternity Institute," 9.

for managing pain. This sort of racialized framework for interpreting women's birthing bodies—in particular, the assumption that nonwhite women, whether by virtue of physiology or temperament, were better equipped to endure childbirth than their more "delicate" white counterparts—was shared by other early Anglo proponents of what eventually became known as the "natural" childbirth movement.[85] For the sisters, race was a durable register (though it was never the only one) for evaluating patients' experiences and for explaining their ability to birth with dignity, in a way that remained elusive for hospital-reliant Anglo women in the 1940s and 1950s.

Talking about their work at CMI, former staffers also moved easily between the categories of woman-centered and family-centered care. Recalling her time at CMI, Sister M. Paula D'Errico recounted sisters "who had this [. . .] wonderful vision of women delivering women." Sister Catherine Shean recalled the institute was founded out of a "deep concern for all women."[86] "We experienced true family-centered maternity care at CMI," remembered alumna Carol Dorey Hurzeler. "CMI taught me [. . .] care with a family-centered focus," explained Sister Patrica Elder.[87] For CMI's leadership, statements like these would have followed naturally from one another, since a woman's dignity was most realizable in the context of her family. CMI leaders had this truth in mind when they plotted the institute's mission of family-centered care. They worked too from the assumption that New Mexican families were damaged and required "restoration." "Help us to restore the family to Christ!" a CMI newsletter appealed to its readers during the early 1950s.[88]

85. British obstetrician Grantly Dick-Read, who introduced the term "natural childbirth" in 1944, wrote: "The more cultured the races of the earth have become, so much more dogmatic have they been in pronouncing childbirth to be [. . .] painful" (Grantly Dick-Read, *Childbirth Without Fear: The Principles and Practices of Natural Childbirth* [New York: Harper and Brothers, 1944], 5).

86. Sr. M. Paula D'Errico, MMS, CNM, "Original Call—To Become a Nurse-Midwife," *CMI Graduates and Faculty Remember*, 38; "Oral History II—Sister Catherine Shean, MMS" (1992)," in Kroska, *History of Nurse-Midwifery*, 63.

87. Sr. Patricia Elder, DC, CNM, "Memories of Catholic Maternity Institute"; Carol Dorey Hurzeler, CNM, "Memories of CMI," *CMI Graduates and Faculty Remember*, 59, 82.

88. "CMI Family News," 1, no. 1 (Easter 1952), Folder RG 3-05 b.12.f.11 CMI: Family Values, MMS archives.

American Catholic calls for restoring the family were not reserved for *Nuevomexicanos* during this era; from the Christian Family Movement to Father Patrick Peyton's Family Rosary Crusade, the US Catholic Church abounded with initiatives to bring the nuclear family closer to God, and family members closer to one another, at mid-century.[89] But even in this climate the MMS understood New Mexican families as facing extraordinary challenges. Fathers were a special concern for them. The sisters recognized an exploitative regional economy that removed laboring men from home, sometimes for extended periods of time. They also worried over a local culture that encouraged what Hurzeler referred to as "macho Hispanic males" to purposely absent themselves from key events in the life of the family.[90] The sisters imagined their own experiment in home birthing as a family-affirming corrective on both these accounts. Ensuring the father's involvement in the birth experience quickly became a CMI priority.[91]

Sisters knew the hospital-birthing model that dominated elsewhere in the United States, with its emphasis on treating female patients in sterile isolation, was inadequate for addressing the challenge of New Mexican fathers. One sister, who had begun her medical work as an obstetrical nurse in a hospital, recalled "rushing [a] mother into the labor room and the father into the waiting room, which offered little consolation to either of them." "I don't want to imply we didn't have feeling," Sister Mary Simpson reflected on her hospital career, "We had plenty of that

---

89. CMI's leadership was explicit that its objectives included "to cooperate with family life programs," including the Christian Family Movement ("Objectives of the Catholic Maternity Institute," n.d., n.p., Folder 150, Santa Fe: Curriculum, CMI, MMS archives). On the emergence of the post-World War II "family apostolate" in the US Catholic Church, see Kathryn Johnson, "A Question of Authority: Friction in the Catholic Family Life Movement, 1948–1962," *The Catholic Historical Review* 86, no. 2 (April 2000): 217–41. For a brief overview of the Christian Family Movement, see also James O'Toole, *The Faithful: A History of Catholics in America* (Cambridge, MA: Harvard University Press, 2010), 171–75.

90. Hurzeler, "Memories of CMI," 82.

91. The terms "father" and "husband" might be used interchangeably in discussing male participation in most, but not all, CMI births. In 1966, for example, sixty-two of 296 registered patients were "out of wedlock." It is doubtful but unknown whether unmarried fathers-to-be were ever welcomed to the birthing process. CMI, *Annual Report*, 1966, 2, Folder 150, Santa Fe: Curriculum, MMS archives.

but it was focused more on our professional performance than on the families that we were serving."[92] By contrast, CMI nurse-midwives worked to involve fathers at different stages of pregnancy and childbirth. They encouraged expectant fathers to attend parenting classes along with their partners. During these classes, instructors reminded attendees: "Having a baby is the most important event that can happen in a family. It can help the family grow more close together."[93] Students also received coaching on ways fathers might assist in preparing for the birth, including by "making supplies available," by "understanding paternity and maternity," and by "aid[ing] in preparation of other children."[94]

Nurse-midwives also went to lengths to ensure a father was present throughout the birth itself. Sometimes this meant dealing with his employer. "I remember giving grown men a note to their boss verifying that they had missed work to be at home for the delivery of their baby," remembered Sister Catherine Shean.[95] Once labor commenced, midwives encouraged the father to offer direct support to his partner by applying pressure on her lower back ("Husbands can be very good at this," one lesson plan offered encouragingly).[96] Immediately following the birth, it was CMI practice for the attendant midwife to invite older children into the room to join their newly expanded family, and then to give the newborn directly to the father so that he might take the infant in

92. Sr. Mary S. Simpson, DC, CMN, "Family as One," *CMI Graduates and Faculty Remember*, 55.

93. "Class III: Baby's Birthday," 62. In addition to involving family members in the pregnancy and birthing processes, sisters also endeavored to build family in a variety of other ways. Lesson plans, for example, instructed students on the importance of praying the Family Rosary during the pregnancy ("Class II: Preparation," 60). The institute's briefly circulated newsletter, sent home with patients, offered advice on everything from teaching children to say grace before meals to teaching how to save money through local parish credit unions, all with the aim of enabling patients "to help us more directly in the work of bringing Christ back into the hearts of our families!" ("CMI Family News," 1, no. 1 [Easter 1952], 1; "CMI Family News," 1, no. 2 [20 April 1952], 1; "CMI Family News," 1, no. 3 [27 April 1952], Folder RG 3-05 b.12.f.11, CMI: Family Values, MMS archives).

94. "Class II: Preparation," 60.

95. Sr Catherine Shean, MMS, CNM, "Beginnings," *CMI Graduates and Faculty Remember*, 4.

96. "Class III: Baby's Birthday," 64.

his arms and bless it. While one CMI alumna understood this father's blessing as a moment at which he "acknowledged responsibility for the child," Agnes Shoemaker Reinders (formerly Sister Theophane Sheomaker) recalled it as an act that helped "the father to focus on his dignity and his place in the family."[97] Interactive births built good family relationships, as the sisters saw it, and those relationships in turn enabled women—and men too—to know their own dignity.

On some occasions, expectant fathers surprised sisters with their enthusiasm. Sister M. Paula D'Errico recalled a birth at the La Casita birthing center that—at least as she remembered it—was a model for the CMI vision. The expectant father had accompanied the expectant mother to all the parenting classes, she recalled. When labor began, "he helped her with the breathing, the pushing, and the encouragement she needed, to which she responded so peacefully. This went on, and suddenly the head was crowning [. . .]. Well, before I knew it he was standing right behind me, [and] took a photos [sic] of the infant's head as it was crowning and all the way through the complete birth of his child. So Junior will be able to see where he came from [. . .]. The family will always have first-hand information about Mom and Dad's role in procreation with God."[98]

On the whole, however, there isn't sufficient evidence—nor does it lie within the scope of this study—to determine how men felt about CMI's invitation to participate in the birthing process. It *is* worth noting that the CMI vision of "family-centered" childbirth, and its corresponding initiative to "restore the family to Christ," intervened in and reshaped longstanding, gendered practices surrounding childbirth in northern New Mexico. Before the arrival of CMI's nurse-midwives, it was typical for *Nuevomexicano* mothers to give birth exclusively in the company of other women—both *parteras* (who were always female) and female family members. Well into the twentieth century, childbirth in rural *Nuevomexicano* villages "was restricted to the women's community, the knowledge and the personnel were defined and controlled by women alone."[99] Although men were permitted in the home during childbirth,

97. Hurzeler, CNM, "Memories of CMI," 88; Kroska, "Memories of Agnes Shoemaker Reinders," *History of Nurse-Midwifery*, 55.

98. Sr. M. Paula D'Errico, "Original Call," 39.

99. Deutsch, *No Separate Refuge*, 46–47.

sources from the period suggest that a father's attendance at the birth itself was uncommon and could be construed as distracting or otherwise problematic.[100]

The nurse-midwives who worked at CMI recognized this pattern, and they were explicit about their desire to change it. "Culturally men were expected to be at home in case of an emergency," explained Sister Catherine Shean, "[but] usually they were not at the delivery. Gradually we learned the advantage of including them in every aspect of maternity care."[101] "Our sister midwives were [. . .] strong women, able to persuade many macho Hispanic males to stay with and support their wives, despite the near absence of this practice in their traditional culture," remembered Carol Dorey Hurzeler. "We were not just about birthing, but about building stronger marriages and families.[102] In addition to strengthening the Christian family (or at least the Christian family model celebrated at CMI), a father's presence during childbirth in lieu of female relatives could make it easier for the nurse-midwife to manage the details of the process, and to limit the introduction of "undesirable" birthing practices. In addition to the custom of fathers' nonattendance, there were other New Mexican birthing customs, from the wearing of full clothing, including stockings and shoes during childbirth, to the practice of birthing in a kneeling position, that were at odds with CMI's approach to reproductive care. Sisters found that fathers, when present, generally submitted to sisters' efforts to introduce new protocols—unlike, as Sister Catherine

100. In her 1948 study of traditional birthing practices in Taos County, Sr M. Lucia van der Eerden (SCMM) mentions expectant fathers only twice. In both instances she relays cases as recounted by a *partera* she interviewed, and in both cases the *partera* represented fathers as introducing negative psychology into the birthing space. One father was sent to buy groceries and returned "far from sober." "This fact upset the woman and it made her very angry. She died two days after childbirth." The second husband interrupted his wife's labor to announce his own father's death. "The midwife deeply regretted that she had been unable to keep the husband out of the mother's presence until he was able to hide his sorrow." (Van der Eerden, SCMM, "Maternity Care," 17).

101. Sister Catherine Shean, MMS, CNM, "Beginnings," *CMI Graduates and Faculty Remember*, 3.

102. Carol Dorey Hurzeler, CNM, "Memories of CMI," 82.

recounted, "the woman or grandmother [. . . who] always had her own ideas which were really different from yours."[103]

It is inaccurate to say that by introducing New Mexican fathers to the birthing process, CMI nurse-midwives were imposing an Anglo-American norm on a non-Anglo population. After all, the family-centered childbirth that sisters celebrated was also a radical departure from Anglo birthing practices in the United States. More accurately, CMI midwives enacted a distinctly (and also counter-culturally) *Catholic* vision of women's dignity and the Christian family in New Mexico. Theirs was a vision informed by their church's teaching on labor, gender, and marriage, even as it was also a vision that participated in the celebration of the nuclear family in full swing across the Anglo-America they came from—in Catholic circles and also outside of them—during the middle decades of the twentieth century. That the sisters were themselves Anglo mattered too insofar as it granted them access, authority, and material resources to do their work in New Mexico—including the support of the archbishop, the approval of the state board of health, and the public funds they depended on. And so the CMI was different things at once: it was an experiment that challenged the boundaries of an Anglo-centric US health care model, and it was a public health intervention that saved the lives of economically disadvantaged women and infants; it was also a beneficiary of, and a participant in, the long shadow of US imperialism in New Mexico.

The CMI is testament to the twists and turns, and the layered effects of Catholic experiments to honor the "dignity of the poor." CMI is a reminder too, in this volume, of the historical actors and perspectives that are easily overlooked when human flourishing is cast in terms of the money economy. Through much of the twentieth century, the fight for economic justice within the Catholic Church proceeded hand in hand with Catholic teachings about gender, the differences between men and women, and the different sorts of labor that honored the dignity of each. Because the dignity of women emerged first and foremost in the space of the home, through the relational identities of wife and mother, the money economy is not always a salient category for assessing Catholic

103. "Oral History I—Sister Catherine Shean, MMS" (1988), in Kroska, *History of Nurse-Midwifery*, 55.

efforts to honor the dignity of poor women. The MMS's CMI was such an effort. Through their experiment in nurse-midwifery, through their confidence that New Mexican women could know and do childbirth better than their affluent Anglo counterparts, and through their insistence that New Mexican homes were spaces sacred to family living, the MMS enacted a distinctly Catholic form of anti-poverty work; a Catholic response to everything the dignity of motherhood demanded.

Southern Christian Work Camps and a Cold War Campaign for Racial and Economic Justice

ALISON COLLIS GREENE

Nelle Morton stepped into leadership in the Fellowship of Southern Churchmen in 1945 determined to turn the decade-old organization into more than "a statement making group."[1] In late January, just three weeks after she took office as the Fellowship's general secretary, Morton approached her friend Eugene Smathers at a planning meeting. A founding member of the Fellowship and a fellow Presbyterian, Smathers was minister of Calvary Church in the tiny Cumberland community of Big Lick, Tennessee, where he had slowly introduced cooperative farming and health initiatives, worked with his parishioners on the construction of a new church building with a recreation hall and an adjacent House of Health, and welcomed into fellowship black guest speakers and missionaries from around the world. Morton admired his work, and she told Smathers that she thought his little all-white Appalachian community would be an ideal location for a new Fellowship initiative: the south's first interracial work camp. Smathers consulted his parishioners, and in a special session on March 4, 1945, they approved the camp, which would convene for six weeks that summer.[2]

The Fellowship of Southern Churchmen was an interdenominational and interracial coalition of southern Protestants who first gathered in

1. Nelle Morton to David Burgess, June 1, 1945, Folder 9, Box 1, Fellowship of Southern Churchmen Records #3479, Southern Historical Collection, Wilson Library, University of North Carolina (hereafter FSC Records); Howard Kester to Members and Friends of the Fellowship of Southern Churchmen, November 21, 1944, Folder 9, Box 1, FSC Records.

2. Mike Smathers, *Adventurers in Faith: Memoirs of an Appalachian Ministry: Two People—One Vision—Faith, Practical Action, and a Farm* (Bloomington, IN: Xlibris, 2014), 113–17; Eugene Smathers, "I Work in the Cumberlands," *Prophetic Religion* 3, no. 4 (November 1939): 5–10.

1934 to translate radical egalitarian theologies into action in the Jim Crow south. The religious activists who formed the Fellowship had supported striking workers and investigated lynchings, launched projects across the south to support organized labor and racial equality, published a magazine denouncing economic and racial injustice as anathema to biblical Christianity, and released regular statements denouncing the south's white supremacist capitalist order. Yet the organization itself operated more as a support network for often lonely southern activists than as an activist organization in its own right. Morton saw untapped potential in the Fellowship of Southern Churchmen. If Fellowship members claimed a prophetic Christianity, she determined, then they must not only promote radical Christian work across the region but also must also collectively model Christian action. The Fellowship of Southern Churchmen must present a working alternative to the south's unjust racial and economic order.[3]

The Big Lick camp of 1945, and additional camps in subsequent summers, provided one model. Morton also worked to develop relationships with other communities where the Fellowship might engage. She worked with Fellowship member Clarence Jordan to send members to his Georgia religious community and farm, Koinonia, and sponsored joint camps with the American Friends Service Committee. She also contacted an

---

3. David Burgess, "The Fellowship of Southern Churchmen: Its History and Promise," n.d., 1–3, Folder 40, Box 3, Charles M. Jones Papers #5168, Southern Historical Collection (UNC). On the Fellowship of Southern Churchmen's history and work, see Paul Harvey, *Freedom's Coming: Religious Culture and the Shaping of the South from the Civil War through the Civil Rights Era* (Chapel Hill: University of North Carolina Press, 2007), 92–106; John A. Salmond, "'Flag-Bearers for Integration and Justice': Local Civil Rights Groups in the South, 1940–1954," in *Before Brown: Civil Rights and White Backlash in the Modern South*, ed. Glenn Feldman (Tuscaloosa: University of Alabama Press, 2004): 222–37; Salmond, "The Fellowship of Southern Churchmen and Interracial Change in the South," *The North Carolina Historical Review* 69, no. 2 (April 1992), 179–99; Robert Francis Martin, *Howard Kester and the Struggle for Social Justice in the South, 1904–77* (Charlottesville: University of Virginia Press, 1991); Robert F. Martin, "Critique of Southern Society and Vision of a New Order: The Fellowship of Southern Churchmen, 1934–1957," *Church History* 52, no. 1 (March 1983), 66–80; Robert F. Martin, "A Prophet's Pilgrimage: The Religious Radicalism of Howard Anderson Kester, 1921–1941," *Journal of Southern History* 48, no. 4 (November 1982), 511–30; Anthony P. Dunbar, *Against the Grain: Southern Radicals and Prophets, 1929–1959* (Charlottesville: University of Virginia Press, 1982).

advocate of economic cooperatives among African American communities in North Carolina and the head of one of those cooperatives in remote Tyrrell County, on the eastern edge of the state. Together, they organized a two-week interracial Workshop on Cooperative Living with guest speakers from around the country, which convened in June 1945. Two summers later, Tyrrell County hosted another Fellowship camp.[4]

In the interim summer, in addition to Fellowship camps, Morton recruited thirty-two youth, two clergy, and two veterinarians from across the south to board a cattle boat for Europe, sponsored by the United Nations Relief and Rehabilitation Administration (UNRRA). The trip was UNRRA's first interracial relief voyage, and proved such a success that the organization agreed to desegregate its relief trips. Morton organized some of the youth work herself, but she also established a series of Fellowship commissions—on labor, race, and rural reconstruction. They organized a regional conference for labor leaders and ministers, convened regular interracial gatherings of college students across the south, and reported on the region's shortcomings and plans for addressing them.[5]

The work camps in Big Lick, Tennessee, and Tyrrell County, North Carolina, and the UNRRA trip are particularly noteworthy, both because Morton saw them as the heart of the Fellowship's work, and because they represent most clearly the way Fellowship members understood the relationship between economic and racial justice. At first modeled on camps run by Quakers and other peace churches during the interwar and war years, the Fellowship camps put strong emphasis on interracial cohabitation and the cultivation of Christian community. They also explicitly supported economic cooperatives and other programs designed to circumvent or undermine the Jim Crow capitalist economy of the south. The work camps were supposed to transform their participants, but also, and more importantly, to embody an egalitarian racial and economic

4. Nelle Morton to Howard Kester, March 30, 1974, Box 24, Folder 277, FSC Records; Fellowship of Southern Churchmen Newsletter, August 1945, 1–4, Folder 12, Box 1, FSC Records.

5. Nelle Morton to Howard Kester, March 30, 1974; William Howard Deihl, "Heifers for Europe," a report, Folder 276, Box 9, Howard Kester Papers #3834, UNC; Fellowship of Southern Churchmen Newsletter, November 1947, Box 10, Folder 105, FSC Records; David Burgess, "The Fellowship of Southern Churchmen," 6–7.

model that Fellowship members deemed an essential feature of genuine Christian community and a blueprint for a more just economic system.[6]

Remarkably, Morton launched these economic and racial experiments in the remotest corners of the rural south. A native of East Tennessee, her own connections to the rural south shaped her commitment to rural communities, as did those of many other Fellowship members. Many of the organization's members also had roots in the broader rural church movement, a mainline effort to rehabilitate rural landscapes and remake country churches. They had worked with coal miners in Tennessee, aided the Southern Tenant Farmers Union in rural Arkansas in the 1930s, and helped support the Delta and Providence Cooperative Farms in Mississippi. Although many Fellowship members lived and worked in southern cities, they shared a sense that the rural south could stand at the leading edge of the region's social and economic transformation. It was no mere coincidence that the Fellowship's most daring experiments in racial and economic justice began in some of the south's most out-of-the-way places.[7]

Those rural places and the people who inhabited them had endured a difficult few decades, so much so that it may have seemed before 1930 that things could not get worse—until they did. In the aftermath of the Civil War and the first years of Reconstruction, formerly enslaved people and poor black and white farmers had fought to control their own fate on the land. Elite whites who owned large swaths of southern farmland were determined to hold onto that land, however. Wealthy farmers negotiated from a position of power a system of sharecropping and tenant farming that poor farmers hoped would allow them to save up enough to buy their own small plots of land. The capitalist plantation economy

6. For Morton's perspective on the camps, see Nelle Morton to David Burgess, June 1, 1945 and Nelle Morton, *The Journey Is Home* (Boston: Beacon Press, 1985), 188–91. On the longer history of work camps among the peace churches, see Gregory A. Barnes, *A Centennial History of the American Friends Service Committee* (Scotts Valley, CA: CreateSpace Independent Publishing Platform, 2016); Allan W. Austin, *Quaker Brotherhood: Interracial Activism and the American Friends Service Committee, 1917–1950* (Urbana: University of Illinois Press, 2012).

7. Morton, *The Journey Is Home*, 183–91. On the range of backgrounds of Fellowship members, see Dunbar, *Against the Grain*. On distinct forms of racism in the rural south, see Mark Schultz, *The Rural Face of White Supremacy: Beyond Jim Crow* (Urbana: University of Illinois Press, 2007).

prospered from a large and marginalized workforce, however, and in the first thirty years of the twentieth century, the plantation system pushed tenant farmers and sharecroppers down the economic ladder rather than boosting them up it. A brief boom in cotton and crop prices during and after World War I gave way to wildly fluctuating prices in the 1920s. By 1935, 46 percent of white southern farmers and 77 percent of black farmers in the region had no land of their own.[8]

Rural industrial and mine workers fared no better. In the years after the Civil War, southern industrialists touted a New South primed for development in large part because of its low-wage, racially divided workforce. Workers in the mines and mills of the south, and sometimes farmers as well, sought repeatedly to organize labor unions to fight for better wages and hours, safer working conditions, and protection against retaliation from employers. At the same time, the white elites who had lost the Civil War fought to restore their control over the region. When black and white farmers or workers allied together—in the Populist Party of the 1890s, for instance—white elites recognized the threat to their power and responded with violent repression that targeted African Americans and anyone who allied with them. In Wilmington, North Carolina, for instance, white Democrats launched a violent coup to overthrow the city's elected Fusionist government—an interracial alliance between Populists and Republicans—and install a white supremacist Democratic regime.[9]

8. On tenancy rates, see H. A. Turner, *A Graphic Summary of Farm Tenure* (Washington, DC: United States Department of Agriculture, 1936), 2–3; On the South's farm economy from Civil War to Great Depression, see Adrienne Monteith Petty, *Standing Their Ground: Small Farmers in North Carolina Since the Civil War* (New York: Oxford University Press, 2013); Jack Temple Kirby, *Rural Worlds Lost: The American South, 1920–1960* (Baton Rouge: Louisiana State University Press, 1986); Pete Daniel, *Breaking the Land: The Transformation of Cotton, Tobacco, and Rice Cultures Since 1880* (Urbana: University of Illinois Press, 1985); Gilbert Courtland Fite, *Cotton Fields No More: Southern Agriculture, 1865–1980* (Lexington: University Press of Kentucky, 1984).

9. The literature on this period and these themes is extensive. On Reconstruction, redemption, and racial violence, see Nicholas Lemann, *Redemption: The Last Battle of the Civil War* (New York: Farrar, Strauss, & Giroux, 2007). On labor organization, see Jarod Roll, *Spirit of Rebellion: Labor and Religion in the New Cotton South* (Urbana: University of Illinois Press, 2010). On populism and race, see David S. Cecelski and Timothy B. Tyson, *Democracy Betrayed: The Wilmington Race Riot of 1898 and Its Legacy* (Chapel Hill:

As white elites reclaimed dominance in the region, they also cemented the system of Jim Crow segregation that excluded black southerners from the basic rights of citizenship, including the right to vote, run for office, and appear before a jury of their peers. Jim Crow capitalism depended on a divided labor force and an unequal wage system that kept both black and white workers poor and without recourse. Progressive reforms that established public education, public health programs, and basic sanitation often bypassed the rural south, and even when present, they disproportionately served whites and often reinforced white supremacist systems. Many white leaders chose to forego reforms that would benefit both races. For instance, notorious South Carolina Governor Benjamin Tillman convinced Thomas Green Clemson to endow an agricultural school for white South Carolinians. But when federal legislation in the 1890s granted funds to agricultural schools, Tillman rejected all such funds for South Carolina because they would benefit not only Clemson but also Claflin College, the black agricultural school.[10]

The Great Depression devastated the southern economy, and as working men and women faced homelessness and starvation by the tens of thousands, southerners of all classes and across racial and ethnic lines welcomed Franklin Roosevelt's New Deal. Southern congressmen dominated the Democratic Party, however, and they worked to ensure that the New Deal's relief and rehabilitation efforts, from works programs to organized labor protections, adhered to the dictates of Jim Crow. Although the Federal Emergency Relief Administration provided direct relief to those most devastated by the Depression, many of the first New Deal programs of 1933 and 1934, including the National Recovery Administration and the Agricultural Adjustment Act, prioritized businesses and

---

University of North Carolina Press, 1998); Stephen Kantrowitz, *Ben Tillman and the Reconstruction of White Supremacy* (Chapel Hill: University of North Carolina Press, 2000).

10. On southern progressivism and race, see Glenda Elizabeth Gilmore, *Gender and Jim Crow: Women and the Politics of White Supremacy* (Chapel Hill: University of North Carolina Press, 1996); William A. Link, *The Paradox of Southern Progressivism, 1880–1930* (Chapel Hill: University of North Carolina Press, 1997). On class divisions among white southerners, see Keri Leigh Merritt, *Masterless Men: Poor Whites and Slavery in the Antebellum South* (Cambridge, MA: Cambridge University Press, 2017). On Tillman, see Kantrowitz, *Ben Tillman*, 127-128, 217-218.

large-scale farmers. Most significantly, congressmen ensured the administration of New Deal programs on the state and local level, rather than at the federal level. They thus privileged local administrators who generally worked to preserve existing racial and economic hierarchies. On the one hand, the New Deal provided southern liberals and even radicals, women, and African Americans access to the federal government that they had long been denied; on the other hand, its structures preserved a white supremacist, patriarchal, capitalist social order.[11]

The group of liberal and radical clergy who would later call themselves the Fellowship of Southern Churchmen first gathered in an attempt to respond to both the Great Depression and to the New Deal from the perspective of southern Christians engaged in a broader campaign for racial and economic justice in the region and across the nation. Grounded in southern Protestantism, their work grew from a broader effort in the United States and around the world to address the inequalities and injustices of industrializing and capitalizing economies. Fellowship members had roots in the rural church movement, which sought to restore rural places through their churches, and they forged connections with Catholics and Protestants around the world who advocated for worker-led economic cooperatives. They joined forces with Dorothy Day and the Catholic Worker around the abuses of rural landscapes and people, and they learned from cooperative economic models across Europe and in Japan and Canada. Yet they struggled from the start to marshal an adequate, unified theological and social response to the segregated, class-riven southern landscape they inhabited.[12]

The Conference of Younger Churchmen in the south first convened in May 1934 in Monteagle, Tennessee, in response to a call from Methodist

11. Ira Katznelson, *Fear Itself: The New Deal and the Origins of Our Time* (New York: W. W. Norton, 2013); Harvard Sitkoff, *A New Deal for Blacks: The Emergence of Civil Rights as a National Issue: The Depression Decade*, 2nd ed. (New York: Oxford University Press, 2009).

12. Dunbar, *Against the Grain*, 114–15; Dorothy Day, "Sharecroppers," Reel A, *Southern Tenant Farmers Union Scrapbook and Newspaper Clippings, 1934–1970* (Chapel Hill: University of North Carolina, 1971–1973); "The Tiller's Rights and Duties," reprinted in *Prophetic Religion* 6, no. 3 (Winter 1945): 70; Sam Franklin, "The Growth of a Cooperative Mustard Seed," *Prophetic Religion* 5, no. 2 (April-May 1941): 3. See also Nicholas Rademacher's essay in this volume.

minister and labor advocate James Dombrowski. A graduate of Union Theological Seminary, Dombrowski gathered a group of colleagues at Highlander Folk School, an adult labor education facility that he had established two years earlier with fellow activists Myles Horton and Don West. Horton, West, Dombrowski, and their colleagues had developed their radical perspectives as they worked to help southern miners, farmers, and industrial workers form unions in the 1920s. As a result, they were particularly committed to the rights of organized labor. Interracial but predominantly white and male, those gathered at Monteagle had concluded long since that southern capitalism was an economic system that depended on white supremacy. There would be no economic justice without racial justice.[13]

Many of these young southern clergy found in Christian socialism the clearest expression of their beliefs. In particular, many had connections to Reinhold Niebuhr, either as his students at Union or as members of the pacifist, socialist Fellowship of Reconciliation. Dombrowski invited him to the meeting in Monteagle to address the several dozen gathered clergy and activists on the theme "Religion and the New Social Order." Niebuhr's speech set the tone for the meeting, as attendees discussed how "to set the redemptive gospel of Christ to work in the midst of a society floundering in economic chaos, political uncertainty, and spiritual dry-rot."[14]

Niebuhr's influence on the Fellowship of Southern Churchmen proved so powerful that a decade later, members still called him their "spiritual godfather." They drew particularly on his *Moral Man and Immoral Society*, which—as its title indicates—drew a distinction between the moral possibilities of individuals and the inherent sinfulness of human institutions. As Niebuhr explained, "Human society will never escape the problem of the equitable distribution of the physical and cultural goods which provide for the preservation and fulfillment of human life." Christians must recognize that any political system was necessarily flawed. They should push nonetheless for "the most rational possible social goal, that of equal

13. Burgess, "The Fellowship of Southern Churchmen," 1; Martin, *Howard Kester and the Struggle*, 114–16.

14. Burgess, "The Fellowship of Southern Churchmen," 1; Don Donahue, "Prophets of a New Social Order: Presbyterians and the Fellowship of Southern Churchmen, 1934–1963," *American Presbyterians* 74, no. 3 (Fall 1996): 209–21.

justice." For many of those gathered in 1934, as for Niebuhr, socialism represented the best way toward that goal. Other attendees aligned more generally with the 1930s political left but stopped short of advocating socialism.[15]

If they could not agree on a clear path forward, those gathered at Monteagle could agree that the New Deal, as it stood in May 1934, was inadequate and even wrongheaded. "We approve of the objectives of the New Deal, in so far as they seek to abolish poverty, end child labor, recognize the right of the workers to bargain collectively, move in the direction of a planned economy (as, for example, in the T.V.A. development), and provide a more equitable distribution of wealth," they reported in a statement of the meetings findings. They further applauded the New Deal's effect of "creating a mental background destructive of the previous individualism." But they went on to enumerate ten ways that the New Deal either underserved those who needed it most or reinforced existing racial and class inequities, concluding that "the objectives of the New Deal cannot be achieved under the profit economy, and that these short-comings of the New Deal are inherent in the capitalistic system."[16]

The southern churchmen condemned systematic racial discrimination and—in one of only two references to religion in the document—declared, "We call upon church groups to make the principle of brotherhood concrete in the relationships between the races, especially in the economic area." In the only remotely prescriptive part of the document, those gathered agreed, "We are convinced of the need of developing a radical political party of all races, composed of farmers, industrial workers, and members of the middle class." This party would advocate "the socialization of natural resources, the principal means of production and distribution, including the nationalization of land, with the clear

15. Reinhold Niebuhr, *Moral Man and Immoral Society; a Study in Ethics and Politics* (New York: Charles Scribner's Sons, 1932), 82, 169–74 (quotations on 170–71). For an astute reading of Neibuhr's early 1930s theology, the effects of *Moral Man and Immoral Society*, and its particular appeal in the south, see Joseph Kip Kosek, *Acts of Conscience: Christian Nonviolence and Modern American Democracy* (New York: Columbia University Press, 2009). See also Reinhold Niebuhr, "Is Peace or Justice the Goal?," *The World Tomorrow*, September 21, 1932, 275–77.

16. "Findings," Conference of Younger Churchmen of the South, Monteagle, Tennessee, May 27–29, 1934, Folder 328, Box 9, Kester Papers.

understanding that the farmer retains possession of the land he uses." Finally, it should "recognize the revolutionary tradition of America, and the higher values of patriotism and religion."[17]

Both in its condemnation of capitalism and its demand that communities of faith challenge social injustice through political avenues, the statement echoed Niebuhr's positions. Its final words demonstrate that the Conference of Younger Churchmen also drew deeply on the rural church movement. Several attendees, including Howard Kester and Eugene Smathers, had close connections not only to Niebuhr but also to Alva Taylor of Vanderbilt, Warren Wilson of the Presbyterian Department of Church and Country Life, and a cohort of leaders both within and without the south who argued that the salvation of the countryside lay in the rural church.

One of the most understudied Social Gospel efforts, the Protestant rural church movement and its Catholic counterpart, the Catholic Rural Life Council, tried to address a sense of environmental, social, and religious crisis in rural communities as the nation industrialized. Its most vocal participants argued that country churches of various denominations should serve as social and community centers, and that rural clergy should take the lead both in agricultural and theological modernization. Although most rural church reformers did not advocate the socialization of natural resources and land, southern reformers who confronted the rise of farm tenancy and the exploitation of landless rural workers increasingly advocated labor-based claims to land. The southern reformers' emphasis on the particular problems of the rural south comes through clearly in their first collective statement.[18]

17. Ibid.

18. On the rural church movement, see Larsen Plyler, "Fertilizing Faith: Religion and Rural Reform in the Deep South, 1908–1945" (PhD diss., Mississippi State University, 2019); Kevin Lowe, *Baptized with the Soil: Christian Agrarians and the Crusade for Rural America* (New York: Oxford University Press, 2015). See also Merwin Swanson, "The 'Country Life Movement' and the American Churches," *Church History* 46, no. 3 (September 1977): 358–73; Leigh Eric Schmidt, "From Arbor Day to the Environmental Sabbath: Nature, Liturgy, and American Protestantism, *Harvard Theological Review* 84, no. 3 (July 1991): 299–323. The best insider account of the rural church movement's history is Mark Rich, *The Rural Church Movement* (Columbia, MO: Juniper Knoll Press, 1957), 133–34. On Kester and Smathers, see Martin, *Howard Kester and the Struggle*, 17–60; Smathers, *Adventurers in Faith*, 33–42, 211–19. On the National Catholic Rural

The group gathered again later that year but only formally organized as the Fellowship of Southern Churchmen in 1936. They welcomed supporters like Niebuhr and activists Sherwood Eddy and Kirby Page but only allowed southerners to join. The membership included a sprinkling of white women and black men, as did the executive committee, but the two key leaders were white men: the group elected Thomas B. "Scotty" Cowan, a Scottish-born Presbyterian minister in Chattanooga, Tennessee, and a fierce advocate for organized labor, as president, and Kester as general secretary—the group's only paid leadership position. Cowan proved an able theologian for the group, whose purpose he deemed akin to the prophets of ancient Israel. He described it the Fellowship's task "with Christian critical insight" to "look into the dark whirling hell-broth and proclaim upon it the judgment of God and how redemptive changes can be wrought by way of repentance and restitution." Cowan took his own charge seriously, and he hosted interracial meetings in his churches and fought from the pulpit for the rights of workers.[19]

Kester was the primary force behind the Fellowship of Southern Churchmen in the 1930s, however. A Christian socialist who had investigated lynchings for the NAACP and worked alongside striking miners in Wilder, Tennessee, Kester saw the Fellowship as a support network for Christian activists doing work across the south. Its annual interracial meetings and its journal, *Prophetic Religion*, provided interpersonal and intellectual sustenance to often lonely and isolated southern radicals. Members like labor advocate Lucy Randolph Mason, writer and activist Lillian Smith, Highlander founders Dombrowski and Horton, Howard University President Mordecai Johnson, Morehouse College President Benjamin Mays, and Koinonia farm founder Clarence Jordan worked to connect their grassroots initiatives to one another and to supporters across the south. Members joined efforts to protect workers of both races through labor unions, worker education, and cooperative enterprises. In addition to Highlander, they supported the Southern Tenant Farmers

Life Council, see Christopher Hamlin and John T. McGreevy, "The Greening of America, Catholic Style, 1930–1950," *Environmental History* 11, no. 3 (July 2006): 464–99.

19. T. B. Cowan, "The Need for Prophets," printed in *Prophetic Religion* 1, no. 7 (December 1938): 6; Donahue, "Prophets of a New Social Order," 212.

Union in Arkansas and the Delta and Providence Cooperative Farms in Mississippi.[20]

By the late 1930s, however, some of those alliances began to fray. The ramifications of New Deal policies on rural life sparked debates among rural church reformers, the Catholic Worker, and other back-to-the-land efforts. Likewise, the dissolution of the Popular Front, which had united the liberal, socialist, and communist left in the early 1930s, played out in broken relationships among Fellowship members. Kester grew disillusioned as his activist efforts seemed to bring little change, and he also grew paranoid that Communists in the Fellowship sought to manipulate its work. By 1938 he encouraged Fellowship members to agree that religious people and churches, rather than political organizations, must lead the way toward economic and racial justice. "Let me assure you," he wrote in 1940, "that the Fellowship of Southern Churchmen is just exactly what it purports to be; namely, a movement of Christian men and women of known Christian faith and character who reside in the South and whose basic motivation in life is religious and Christian and who seek to give expression to this faith in all human relationships." Furthermore, "The Fellowship is not open to persons whose primary loyalty is outside religion." The message was clear: those who prioritized political over religious action were no longer welcome. The Fellowship had not conducted collective actions; now it withheld support from individuals whose actions it deemed either insufficiently religious or excessively activist.[21]

Kester distanced the organization from Dombrowski, Horton, and Claude Williams, his former ally in the Southern Tenant Farmers Union. By 1940, Kester, like his mentor Reinhold Niebuhr and many other Depression radicals, also parted ways with Socialism and political radicalism. Soon World War II captured Fellowship members' attention and

---

20. The most accessible primary source on the Fellowship's theology and work in the 1930s is its journal, *Prophetic Religion*, published quarterly. See also Burgess, "The Fellowship of Southern Churchmen," 1–6; Salmond, "The Fellowship of Southern Churchmen," 179–82.

21. Unaddressed letter from Howard Kester, apparently to potential Fellowship of Southern Churchmen members, December 12, 1940, Folder 2, Box 1, FSC Records.

their energy, and the organization's efforts languished. In 1943, Kester stepped down as general secretary.[22]

Just as the Fellowship of Southern Churchmen seemed poised to fade away, its executive committee recruited longtime member Nelle Morton to step into Kester's position. Most recently an associate director of youth work for the southern Presbyterians, Morton had a degree in religious education from Biblical Seminary of New York and held several national committee positions in youth education. She had demonstrated a deep commitment to racial and economic justice in her work, but she expressed more interest in practical action than in prophetic denunciations. Kester himself seemed to recognize this difference when he said in announcing Morton's leadership, "How to make flesh the creative word of prophetic faith is our urgent concern."[23]

Morton wasted no time addressing that concern. She immediately revived the defunct Fellowship publication, *Prophetic Religion*, and expanded its distribution around the country. She organized a conference of southern labor leaders and ministers—two forces whose mutual antagonism she was determined to heal—and she began to seek out locations for interracial work camps. Where Kester had limited the Fellowship's reach in previous years, Morton sought to expand it. Though the Fellowship navigated the Cold War years as a firmly anticommunist organization, Morton showed no interest in religious or political tests for membership. Instead, she wanted the Fellowship as an organization to set a Christian example of racial and economic justice, and she set out to show that work camps were one powerful way to do that.[24]

The work camps apparently evolved from Morton's education work in the 1930s and her activism during the war years. Morton graduated from

22. Nelle Morton, interview by Dallas Blanchard, June 25, 1983, transcript, 34–36, interview F-34, Southern Oral History Program, UNC; Martin, *Howard Kester and the Struggle*, 109–25; Erik S. Gellman and Jarod H. Roll, *The Gospel of the Working Class: Labor's Southern Prophets in New Deal America* (Urbana: University of Illinois, 2011), 105; Kosek, *Acts of Conscience*, 147–53.

23. Kester to Members and Friends of the Fellowship of Southern Churchmen, November 21, 1944.

24. "1945 Almanac of Fellowship of Southern Churchmen Activities," Folder 7, Box 1, FSC Records; Fellowship of Southern Churchmen Newsletter, February 1945, Folder 7, Box 1, FSC Records.

seminary in 1931, and after a few years of parish work, she became an assistant director of youth work for the Board of Christian Education for the southern Presbyterian church.

In that position, Morton organized interracial youth camps and conferences. White Presbyterian youth gathered at Montreat, the church's western North Carolina retreat center, each year. Black students could attend "if they secured jobs of menial labor that provided housing space in shacks on the side of the hill," and could only participate in workshops "if work permitted." Both black and white Presbyterian youth protested the injustice, but the church stonewalled.[25]

In her memoir, Morton wrote of a young black woman drowning in Montreat's picturesque Lake Susan, an event Morton recalled as a suicide that resulted from the despair of white supremacy but that the church chalked up to a pregnancy and kept quiet. Morton recalled that only the youth at the conference protested, vowing with her "that this young woman's death would not have been in vain." Morton concluded then what she had suspected before: that young people represented the south's best hope, that they "stood on the edge of the times, where a new reality was trembling to break into the human experience—making visible the transcending nature of faith."[26]

Almost unique among southern Presbyterians, Morton was also a pacifist through the Depression and World War II. During the war, she contributed a portion of her salary to peace organizations rather than buying war bonds, and she supported the three young men in the denomination who registered as conscientious objectors. The peace churches, led by the American Friends Service Committee, had established the first work camps in the United States in 1934. Soon allied with the Federal Council of Churches, those camps brought together young people of all major Protestant denominations, as well as Catholic and Jewish youth, to labor on projects to rebuild and support rural communities—most famously including the New Deal Subsistence Homesteads community

25. Morton, *The Journey Is Home*, 184–88; Elaine Magalis, "Nelle Morton: A Woman for All Seasons," *Response*, November 1972, Box 6, Nelle Morton Papers, Montreat College, Black Mountain, North Carolina (Morton's papers have been expanded and are currently being recatalogued).

26. Morton, *The Journey Is Home*, 184–88; Morton interview, 66–67. I have yet to find corroboration of this event in the documentary record.

of Arthurdale, West Virginia. Morton's close personal and spiritual connections to youth work and to the peace churches are clear in her work with the Fellowship.[27]

Likewise, Morton's decision to approach Smathers about the first Fellowship work camp may have grown at least in part from their mutual familiarity. Morton grew up in Kingsport, Tennessee, and as an adult she visited her father regularly on his farm outside town. Morton and Smathers had mutual acquaintances among southern Presbyterians and in the activist communities of the Tennessee Appalachians, and if she had not known of Smathers's work before rural church advocates began to feature him in national publications, she certainly learned of it then.[28]

When Smathers moved to Big Lick to serve as its resident minister in 1932, the fifty white farm families who occupied its rolling hills had little money left for their crumbling church. Most owned some land and scratched a living from it; few had any other income to speak of—on average, $50 a year. For half the year, the fourteen-mile drive to the nearest town was impossible on snow- or mud-ruined dirt roads. Influenced by the rural church reformer Wilson, Smathers hoped to rehabilitate and expand the small church into a social center for this isolated community, but he wanted local people to lead the effort. After a few false starts, Smathers adopted a strategy pioneered by Catholic priest Moses Coady among fishermen in Nova Scotia and popular among rural activists: he organized community study clubs in which local people would identify a problem and meet regularly to discuss its sources and possible solutions.

The study clubs proved a success. Big Lick residents discussed their lack of tools and supplies, and within a year organized a local consumer cooperative, pooling money to purchase farm machinery and mix fertilizer. They established a farmers association and saved funds to build a workshop. They soon decided to build a church, and as they raised funds locally, Smathers persuaded an outside donor to help with additional materials. It took the community just 180 days to build its own sturdy wood and stone structure, with space for community gatherings and a school and library. The church also began a demonstration farm on a plot

27. Morton, *The Journey Is Home*, 188; Barnes, *A Centennial History of the American Friends Service Committee*, 91–102.

28. Smathers, *Adventurers in Faith*, 112–14; Morton interview, 3–4.

of adjacent land. With the help of local physicians, Big Lick soon organized a medical cooperative, hired a nurse, hosted classes for expectant mothers, and offered inoculations. In 1938, an additional donation helped the community build the Warren H. Wilson House of Health, the community's only building with electricity and running water.[29]

Fellowship members and rural church advocates alike held up Smathers and his church as a model of rural rehabilitation, applauding the Big Lick community for its cooperative economic efforts. Smathers's son Mike—who became the minister of Big Lick after his father and lives there still—later recalled that his father, like Moses Coady, "believed fervently that is was the right and responsibility of common people to initiate and control the economic structures that shape their lives." Cooperatives seemed to offer a way between capitalism and socialism, a path increasingly popular among southern radicals who had begun to distance themselves from socialism but continued to believe "that any method of economic development had to be based on Christian ethics and social justice."[30]

By 1945, although the Soviet Union remained a United States ally, it was increasingly clear to many on the left that any economic critique of capitalism would meet with charges of un-Americanism and communism. Members of the Fellowship continued to fight for economic justice but no longer as radicals. The Big Lick model exemplified their new approach: it elevated self-help and community-led cooperative economic efforts that softened or even circumvented Jim Crow capitalism but did not directly challenge it.

Morton surely saw Big Lick as an ideal place to pioneer a southern interracial work camp: a rural community committed to shared decision-making, experienced in economic cooperation, and supported by a committed member of the Fellowship. A work camp at Big Lick would allow Morton to test out her hope that southern youth, living together in Christian interracial community and working alongside poor people in their own communities, could model precisely the kind of Christian economic

29. Eugene Smathers, "I Work in the Cumberlands," *Prophetic Religion* 3, no. 4 (November 1939): 5–10; Ralph Felton, "The Church at the Center," in *One Foot on the Land: Stories of Sixteen Successful Rural Churches* (New York: Home Missions Council of North America, 1947); Mike Smathers, *Adventurers in Faith*, 55–78.

30. Smathers, *Adventurers in Faith*, 83–84.

and racial justice work that would remake, and perhaps even redeem, the south. This rural Appalachian community would be a laboratory for a working Christian alternative to Jim Crow capitalism.

Smathers too seemed excited by the idea when Morton proposed it in January 1945, but he wanted his community to take the lead. He wrote to Morton in early February about the camp's potential structure and leadership, the work students might do in leading a vacation (Bible) school, and the possibility that they could stay together in the House of Health. "I feel that we could have the group interracial," he wrote, "but I would want to discuss it with the community . . . If there could be more than two races, it would be simpler. I would like to have it interracial." In early March, church members met and agreed unanimously to host an interracial camp. For her part, Morton agreed on the strategy to confuse the Jim Crow binary by including campers of other ethnicities.[31]

Morton and Smathers recruited eight students for the six-week camp: four whites, two African Americans, one Cuban American, and one Japanese American recently released from internment. Divided by neither race nor gender, the campers conducted a vacation school, helped with a community canning project, and cleared land for a new cemetery. They cooked, ate, and lodged together in the House of Health and also held periodic study sessions on economic and social issues. Smathers reported enthusiastically, "The group was in no sense an outside element, but the members were participants in our life; in the church, in recreation, in work, and in neighborly relationships."[32] Big Lick parishioners welcomed them in church on Sundays and—still more significantly—in church socials on Friday evenings, where local and Fellowship youth together played "singing games" and "folk games," a euphemism for dancing.[33] They joined locals at a swimming hole after work, and in their homes in the evenings. One of the young women enjoyed the experience so much that she stayed on that fall as a teacher in Big Lick's small school.[34]

31. Eugene Smathers to Nelle Morton, February 21, 1945, Folder 8, Box 1, FSC Records; Smathers, *Adventurers in Faith*, 112–17.

32. Eugene Smathers, "Big Lick Work Camp," in Fellowship of Southern Churchmen Newsletter, August 1945, 4–5, Folder 12, Box 2, FSC Records.

33. Smathers, *Adventurers in Faith*, 116.

34. Jack Anderson, "A Study in Reconversion," *Prophetic Religion* 6, no. 3 (Winter 1945), 85; Smathers, "Big Lick Work Camp," 4.

The participants agreed with Smathers's assessment. In an extensive report afterward, a white woman named Garland Worsley wrote, "Our relationship with the community was very genuine, sincere, and natural. We ceased to be outsiders very quickly."[35] Another white camper, Jack Anderson, was "surprised to find that our outlook on life had been reinterpreted, that our goals had been subtly modified, and that our kinship with people, bursting the bonds of race and culture, had been broadened."[36] Just one event gave the campers pause. In their last week, Anderson recalled, a group of people from a neighboring community "withdrew from the games of the Friday night social because their sense of fellowship did not include Negroes and Nisei." Despite those individuals' "empty threats," no one seemed alarmed.[37] Morton, Smathers, and the residents of Big Lick deemed the camp such a success that they began to plan for another the following summer.

If the Big Lick camp in the summer of 1945 seemed to confirm Morton's belief that small-scale models of alternative southern economies and communities might portend a broader change in the region, the 1946 camp dashed that hope. Six campers, only one of them black, gathered at the end of June that summer. Mike Smathers reports that his father wrote in his journal after the first social that there was "some flare up of racial prejudice." Smathers discussed his concerns with parishioners after church on Sunday, July 7, and seemed reassured. The following week went well, and a local family hosted a party for the campers. That Friday, July 12, campers and locals gathered for a social, this time with the protection of half a dozen Big Lick men just home from the war. Half a mile away another dozen or so men—most of them from neighboring communities, a few from Big Lick—gathered. They got drunk, burned a cross in a field, and then rode their horses to the social, where they shouted racial slurs and threatened the only black camper. The Big Lick veterans put themselves between the night riders and the campers, and after a forty-five minute standoff, the night riders departed. Smathers

35. Garland Worsley, "Evaluation of Work Camp," September 10, 1945, Folder 12, Box 2, FSC Records.

36. Anderson, "A Study in Reconversion," 85.

37. Ibid., 87.

consulted local law enforcement and an attorney that week, and on their advice he closed the camp.[38]

That was Big Lick's last Fellowship camp. Smathers continued his work in the community, with the strong support of locals, one of whom wrote a letter to the local paper asking, "Is this free America? . . . NO, not as long as American citizens are treated as this Negro boy was in our county or any other place in the U.S.A. . . ." The response of Big Lick citizens seemed to affirm Morton's faith in the power of local rural communities to embrace racial and economic justice, but it also called into question whether their model could expand beyond the borders of one community.

Another project in the summer of 1946 more successfully built on Morton's hope in rural people, economic cooperation, and interracial models for justice. In April of that year, an agent from the Church of the Brethren Service Committee's Heifer Project Committee wrote to Morton to ask for help organizing an interracial, interfaith relief trip to Europe under the auspices of UNRRA. One of the peace churches with which Morton had worked during the war, the Brethren had begun the Heifer Project before the war ended. In the war's aftermath, UNRRA expanded the operation with its own ships. Heifers for Europe shipped livestock to war-ravaged countries, most of them in southern and eastern Europe. The Brethren recruited the ships' attendants and continued to contribute livestock, about four thousand animals in all. Between June 1945 and August 1947, UNRRA's fleet of seventy-two livestock ships made at least 360 livestock shipments of between two hundred and fifty thousand and three hundred thousand animals.[39]

---

38. Smathers, *Adventurers in Faith*, 118–22.

39. Peggy Reiff Miller keeps a thoroughly sourced and well-documented blog that is at present the best resource on the seagoing cowboys. See "UNRRA and the Brethren Service Committee Partner Up," https://seagoingcowboysblog.wordpress.com/2014/11/. See also *The Story of U.N.R.R.A.* (Washington, DC: United Nations Relief and Rahabilitation Organization, 1948), 30–31; George Woodbridge, *UNRRA: The History of the United Nations Relief and Rehabilitation Administration* (New York: Columbia University Press, 1950); Leslie Eisan, *Pathways of Peace: A History of the Civilian Public Service Program, Administered by the Brethren Service Committee* (Elgin, Illinois: Brethren Publishing House, 1948), 313–32.

Led by a pair of veterinarians and a pair of supervisors, the seagoing cowboys, as they called themselves, were young men who had farm experience and could handle livestock. Some were members of the peace traditions; many more were either too young to have served in the military or had received deferments for farm work or college. For the first year, all the trips were segregated, and even as it faced a shortage of cattle attendants, UNRRA turned away black attendants or delayed their assignments until they had enough for a segregated cohort. Leaders of the Heifer Project Committee objected, but as Charles Brashares of the Brethren Service Committee explained to Morton of the Fellowship of Southern Churchmen regarding his interest in recruiting black youth, we "know of no sure prospective cowboys."[40] Furthermore, they worried of "possible friction with southern captains," even though many of the ships' seafaring crews were unionized and interracial. Brashares wanted Morton's help recruiting an interracial crew. UNRRA provided its cautious support, promising that if the trip were a success, they would integrate all relief trips.[41]

Morton wasted no time. In just two months, she recruited thirty-two black, white, Latino, and Japanese-American southerners with farming backgrounds to staff the ship. She also drafted two veterinarians and two ministers—one of each black and one white—to lead them. Work campers paid their own way when they could, but cattle boat attendants received $150 for the four- to six-week trip, with no expenses during the trip itself. So many young southerners proved willing to staff the ship that Morton asked about staffing a second trip.[42]

Morton had not sought out the UNRRA cattle boat work as she had the work camps, but that project allowed her to build on the Fellowship's work in building relationships with rural people and rural communities.

40. Charles Brashares to Nelle Morton, April 26, 1946, Folder 29, Box 3, FSC Records.

41. Brashares to Morton, April 26, 1946; Martin Cohnstaedt to Nelle Morton, April 15, 1946, Folder 272, Box 9, FSC Records; Nelle Morton to William Lloyd Imes, May 2, 1946, Folder 30, Box 3, FSC Records.

42. Brashares to Morton, April 26, 1946; "Heifers for Relief Application Blank," completed by Talmage Gordon Hiebert, Folder 29, Box 3, FSC Records; Elizabeth Taylor to Charles Brashares, May 3, 1946, Folder 30, Box 3, FSC Records; Nelle Morton to Charles Frantz, May 25, 1946, Folder 33, Box 3, FSC Records; Nelle Morton to Martin Cohnstaedt, June 6, 1946, Folder 34, Box 3, FSC Records.

Furthermore, this was an effort that could lead to a major policy change for international relief work. Rather than a model to a local community, the cattle boat attendants represented the United States in Europe. They were a test case for future relief trips, and perhaps too for the still-segregated United States military. Significantly, both the organizers and participants in the trip came from the Jim Crow south. This was an opportunity for precisely the kind of broader witness that Morton had sought, and rural southern youth led the way.

The selected attendants gathered at Hampton Institute, a black college on the Virginia coast, and on July 4, 1946, they loaded 214 horses and 590 cattle onto the *SS Creighton* and pushed off from Newport News for Danzig, Poland. They cared for the livestock on the trip out, enjoyed three days in port, and then boarded for the leisurely return. The Brethren Service Committee and Morton arranged a shipboard schedule that included shared leisure time as well as programs designed to build community and to introduce attendants to some of the Fellowship's ideals. As one ebullient attendant recalled in his post-trip report, the group engaged in lively conversations on: "What can we do toward world peace; the ecumenical church movement; the influx of labor unions into the South and their influence on rural communities; problems of rural and urban educational systems; problems of minority groups in the United States." By all accounts, the trip was a smashing success. The crew and the attendants got along well with one another even in the midst of a storm and subsequent rash of seasickness, and they lost fewer livestock than the average relief trip. Pleased, UNRRA officials applauded the crew's good rapport and good work, and they upheld their commitment to integrating subsequent trips.[43]

Heartened by UNRRA trip's success and hopeful that the Big Lick camp breakup was an isolated event, Morton and the Fellowship planned four work camps for the summer of 1947. One of those represented the culmination of another relationship Morton had worked to build since she began work with the Fellowship. In early February 1945, as she worked

43. William Howard Deihl, "Heifers for Europe," a report, Folder 276, Box 9, Kester Papers; Nelle Morton to Howard Kester, May 1, 1946, Folder 30, Box 3, FSC Records. Additional trip details collected from Fellowship of Southern Churchmen files, Folders 28–39, Boxes 3–4, FSC Records; and from Peggy Reiff Miller's blog devoted to the Church of the Brethren's "Seagoing Cowboys," https://seagoingcowboys.com.

with Smathers on the Big Lick camp, Morton also introduced herself to Nathan Pitts, a researcher and supporter of black credit unions and cooperatives, and to Simpson P. Dean, head of the Light of Tyrrell Credit Union in rural Tyrrell County, on the swampy northern coast of North Carolina. She hoped to learn more about their work, and to connect the Fellowship with what she saw as one of the state's most important grassroots economic efforts.[44]

As principal of Tyrrell County's black high school in the town of Columbia and a former student of rural life educator and cooperatives advocate Mabel Carney, Dean had taught the high school's faculty and students about cooperative economics. Together, they then organized study clubs in which black residents of Tyrrell County could discuss the economic and social problems they deemed most pressing in their communities. Although African Americans represented 36 percent of the county's population, they owned only 10 percent of its farmland. Black farm owners lacked ready access to credit and disproportionately faced usurious lending rates that made it hard to hold onto a farm in a bad crop year. With Dean's encouragement, the study clubs agreed that a credit union that could make loans to members would give them the best chance at holding onto and improving their land.[45]

Dean had other local models to lean on for support. Black North Carolinians had begun to organize credit unions and cooperative purchasing groups during the 1910s as an alternative to discriminatory lending and pricing practices. Credit unions made savings accounts accessible and offered reasonable credit. They built on longstanding models of segregated self-help, and thus gained widespread support. They also encouraged other forms of economic cooperation. Members

44. Fellowship of Southern Churchmen Newsletter, February 1947, 2–3, Folder 61, Box 6, FSC Records; Nelle Morton to Nathan Pitts, February 8, 1945, Folder 7, Box 1, FSC Records; Nelle Morton to S. P. Dean, February 24, 1945, Folder 8, Box 1, FSC Records.

45. Nathan Alvin Pitts, *The Cooperative Movement in Negro Communities of North Carolina* (Washington, DC: The Catholic University of America, 1950), 26–31, 86–87, 101-3; United States Bureau of the Census, 1940, 382. "Tyrrell" is pronounced with a short "y" and emphasis on the first syllable: "-ul." I have written more extensively about this camp in "Radical Christianity and Cooperative Economics in the Post World War II South," in *Between the Pew and the Picket Line: Christianity and the American Working Class*, ed. Christopher Cantwell, Heath Carter, and Janine Giordano Drake (Urbana: University of Illinois Press, 2016), 167–91.

could take out group loans for bulk purchases or to establish businesses that provided discounted goods and services to other members. Some credit unions also provided financial management programs. In North Carolina, a state credit union law passed in 1915 encouraged the growth of credit unions and even provided training and support for local people who organized them.[46]

The Light of Tyrrell began with twenty-five members who each made a $25 investment. It obtained a state charter in January 1939 and grew to 187 members by the end of that year. During World War II, when farmers benefited from the increased prices of a wartime economy and observed restrictions on purchasing, the credit union flourished. Several families took out a group loan, bought a farm and machinery, and built a cooperative sawmill that provided low-cost lumber and materials used to repair or rebuild housing for twenty-five more members. Other new cooperative groups organized to purchase farm supplies, livestock, and machinery, allowing farm owners and sharecroppers direct access to equipment otherwise unavailable. Local women headed up a health care cooperative that would cover hospitalization and maternity expenses, and a cooperative grocery store. By 1945, the Light of Tyrrell had made 528 loans for a total of $67,461 and boasted assets of $43,456.[47]

For members of the Fellowship of Southern Churchmen, the Light of Tyrrell represented the very best of what southern rural communities might become. It was a grassroots initiative with roots in the rural life and rural church movements. Despite its implicit critique of Jim Crow capitalism, the credit union was an expression of African American economic independence that also won support from white community members. The Light of Tyrrell was not an explicitly religious effort, but Fellowship members nonetheless saw it as a model of Christian community, and a way to work toward the dual goals of economic and racial justice in the years after the war.

46. Pitts, *The Cooperative Movement*, 21–23. On the broader history of credit unions in the United States, see J. Carroll Moody and Gilbert C. Fite, *The Credit Union Movement: Origins and Development, 1850–1980* (Lincoln: University of Nebraska Press, 1971).

47. Pitts, *The Cooperative Movement*, 21–31, 36–39; Roy Bergengren, *I Speak for Joe Doakes: For Co-operation at Home and Among Nations* (New York: Harper & Brothers, 1945), 93–95, 106–7; Nelle Morton, "The Light of Tyrrell," *Prophetic Religion* 6, no. 1 (Summer 1945): 23–25.

Morton first spoke of developing a relationship between the Fellowship and the Light of Tyrrell with Nathan Pitts, a social scientist and educator who hoped to organize a summer workshop on cooperatives with Dean. Morton wrote to Dean in February 1945 to introduce the Fellowship's work. She visited Tyrrell County that spring, and reported in *Prophetic Religion* that its work was well-established, and that despite the Light of Tyrrell's origins in the local school, it had also transformed local churches. Credit union members told Morton that they had "practically eliminated fights between church and school and the jealousies between various churches." Furthermore, "the ministers now talk of co-ops from their pulpits and relate their sermons more to the daily living of the people."[48]

Morton initially proposed a work camp in Tyrrell County but quickly agreed to help Pitts and Dean with the Workshop on Cooperative Living, an interracial training to be held for ten days in June 1945, just before the first Big Lick work camp. That summer, more than sixty black and white North Carolinians gathered at the Tyrrell County Training School. Those who attended stayed in segregated housing, but they joined together each day for sessions led by Dean, state and national credit union officials, representatives from the Federal Council of Churches, and faculty of several North Carolina universities. Attendees also toured credit unions and cooperatives nearby.[49]

For the next year and a half, the Fellowship worked with the Light of Tyrrell as Dean transitioned into a state-level credit union leadership position and continued to juggle his local commitments. Then, in early 1947, Dean invited Morton to send some Fellowship members to help the credit union build its new cooperative store. Delighted, Morton handselected a group of college and seminary students for an eight-week summer work camp. They would stay with Dean and his wife Lily and prepare their shared meals next door in the kitchen of the Tyrrell County Training School. She invited John Anderson and Garland Worsley, who had participated in the first Big Lick camp and had recently married, to lead the students.[50]

48. Pitts, *The Cooperative Movement*, 31–34, 89–91, 109–110, 135–38; Fellowship Newsletter, November 1947: 3.

49. Nelle Morton to Nathan Pitts, February 8, 1945, Folder 7, Box 1, FSC Records; Morton, "The Light of Tyrrell."

50. "Six Living with Negro Are Ousted," *Charlotte Observer*, August 19, 1947; Fellowship Newsletter, November 1947, 3.

Signs of trouble emerged a month before the camp began, when Dean asked Morton not to include white women in the camp. She agreed, but this acknowledgement of white anxieties about interracial sex, particularly between white women and black men, raised concerns for some of Dean's supporters. Morton reassured one concerned colleague that he would "find the setup too natural to bring about any problems of antagonism, and the students of such high calibre that they will avoid any incidents which might lead to misunderstanding."[51] Morton's phrasing was not accidental. Morton chose her words carefully when she characterized integration as "natural." Even as she implied that these "high calibre" students would not engage in sex, she also dismissed the white supremacist claim that segregation represented a biological imperative or even an inviolable norm. Morton was hopeful that Fellowship members' model of interracialism could reach white southerners by "loving them into understanding."[52]

The Andersons arrived in the town of Columbia at the end of June, along with four young men: two white, one Lebanese American, and one African American; and two young women: one Japanese American and one African American. The campers were dismayed to find a disordered worksite, with neither tools nor building supplies, and an unanticipated degree of skepticism from local whites. They also detected an undercurrent of discontent in the credit union, apparently related to Dean's dual state and local roles. Still, they settled into a summer of work and group living at the Deans' house. Twice work stalled, and local hostility almost persuaded the campers to leave. They voted to stay, but the young men moved from the Deans' house to an old chicken house on the credit union farm to defuse tensions. Still, the campers hosted games of softball, met with local community members of both races, and in the evenings gathered—often joined by local youth of both races—on the Deans' screened porch to discuss "cooperatives and the freedom of man."[53]

51. Nelle Morton to Roy Bergengren, June 13, 1947, Folder 83, Box 8, FSC Records.

52. Nelle Morton to Gertrude Bullock, June 7, 1947, Folder 81, Box 8, FSC Records; Roy Bergengren to Nelle Morton, June 11, 1947, Folder 82, Box 8, FSC Records; Nelle Morton to Roy Bergengren, June 13, 1947, Folder 83, Box 8, FSC Records; Zan Harper to Nelle Morton, June 26, 1947, Folder 85, Box 8, FSC Records. *Misspelling in the original.*

53. Jack Anderson to Nelle Morton, July 19, 1947, Folder 89, Box 8, FSC Records; Bob Wherritt to Nelle Morton, July 16, 1947, Folder 88, Box 8, FSC Records; Mounir Khouri to Nelle Morton, September 19, 1947, Folder 97, Box 9, FSC Records; Kay Kaneda to

Just over a month after the work camp began, the campers welcomed members of another Fellowship camp in Phoebus, Virginia, for a picnic and day of recreation. This camp included the white women excluded from Columbia. The night after they left, local whites arrived at the Deans' house to warn the campers of trouble. The campers decided to segregate for the evening, sending white members to the farm while the nonwhite students remained with the Deans. No sooner had the white campers begun to settle in at the farm than they noticed "the whole road ablaze with headlights." They fled for the cornfields and dropped to the ground as roughly three hundred men armed with knives, guns, and farm tools jumped out of their cars and gave chase. Three hours later, the sheriff arrived. He dispersed the mob and instructed the students to pack their bags. The work campers took the first bus out of Columbia the following morning.[54]

The breakup of the Tyrrell camp made national news, in part because the interracial arrangement in rural eastern North Carolina seemed a curiosity, and in part because the mob's targets were white students. It also exacerbated existing tensions within the Light of Tyrrell and aggravated an ongoing breakdown in Dean's health. The Light of Tyrrell did not survive the decade.[55]

Morton and the Fellowship of Southern Churchmen ran two more work camps the following summer, and one of those, in Atlanta, also

Nelle Morton, September 9, 1947, Folder 97, Box 9, FSC Records; Evangeline Royall to Nelle Morton, September 5, 1947, Folder 96, Box 9, FSC Records; "Six Living with Negro Are Ousted," *Charlotte Observer,* August 19, 1947.

54. Kay Kaneda to Nelle Morton, September 16, 1947, Folder 97, Box 9, FSC Records; A. M. Rivera Jr., "Mob Runs Mixed Student Group Out of Town," *Pittsburgh Courier,* 30 August 1947: 1, 4; Fellowship newsletter, November 1947: 6–7. Estimates ranged from two to four hundred men. Some reports say they were armed; others insist they were not. The first report, from the local sheriff, counted three hundred men, some of whom he claimed to have disarmed at the Deans' house. He would later report that none of the men had been armed.

55. "Columbia Mob Orders Students from Negro Home," August 18, 1947; "Ordered to Leave Town," *New York Times,* August 19, 1947; "Wife of Tyrrell Negro Tells How Inter-race Student Group Came to and Left Columbia," *Elizabeth City (NC) Daily Advance,* August 19, 1947; Zan Harper to Cornelia Lively, August 1947, FSC Records, Box 9, Folder 92; Cornelia Lively to Nelle Morton, August 19, 1947, FSC Records, Box 9, Folder 94; "Prominent Carolinian Asked to Leave Town," *Atlanta Daily World,* September 10, 1947; Pitts, *The Cooperative Movement,* 34.

ended when hostile whites—this time including local police—intervened. Morton continued to work for the Fellowship despite a cancer diagnosis and treatment but left in 1949 to return to East Tennessee, where she slowly recovered. Kester soon returned to leadership, and he focused the Fellowship's energies on building a conference center for its interracial meetings and retreats. Members disagreed about the strategy: some agreed that they needed a safe place to gather in the south; others argued that the Fellowship's most important work required it to engage with southern communities, not retreat from them.[56]

The work camps represented Morton's greatest hope for modeling racial and economic justice in the south, and indeed many of those students who participated in them went on to lives in ministry and activism. Yet their model of an alternative southern economy, their examples of racial and economic justice, proved neither persuasive nor replicable in the south's entrenched Jim Crow economies. Even as members of the Fellowship of Southern Churchmen recognized that southern communities must play a role in their own transformation and worked toward that end, their membership—always predominantly white, male, middle-class, and Protestant—replicated the south's white supremacist hierarchy. At the same time, Morton and others in the Fellowship nurtured relationships across lines of race, class, gender, and community, and they learned over time to hear more fully those with whom they worked. The organization disintegrated, but many of its members moved into the civil rights movement and the women's movement, or refocused their efforts on their own local communities. Their example might now serve both as a model and a note of caution as southern communities look once again— or still—for working alternatives to a racialized capitalism that privileges the few at the expense of the many.

56. Morton interview, 1, 37–38; Burgess, "David Burgess, "The Fellowship of Southern Churchmen," 6–8.

Meaningful Work in a Time of Crisis

VINCENT STANLEY

I am by vocation a writer but didn't set out to make my living that way (or by teaching English). In 1973, shortly before I turned twenty-one, I went to work at what was then Chouinard Equipment at the river's edge in Ventura, California, a town otherwise noted for its oil patch, lemon packing plants, and great surf. I found the work culture of climbers and surfers at the "shop" egalitarian, relaxed, and congenial. I thought what we made—mountain climbing equipment, and later, high-quality clothes for outdoor use—honorable. Because I was not a surfer, I stayed behind to answer the phones when the waves were firing, and so was dubbed, after a few months, "sales manager." I hired our original sales reps, and scrambled and learned on the job as the little company, now Patagonia, quadrupled its sales in four years. I left twice. At age forty, I found satisfaction working alone, sitting in my study, its light filtered through the leaves of a wizened cork oak tree, teaching myself how to write fiction and poems. But after a while I also realized that there were things I had learned how to do with others at Patagonia that I could not do anywhere else. So I started going into the office again.

I became involved in sharing some of the company's environmental storytelling, then came back inside as half-time manager of the editorial department. There I had the happiest work years of my life. I helped develop the *Footprint Chronicles*, the company's Common Threads program (urging customers to buy less, repair what's broken, recirculate what's fallen out of use, and recycle what's worn out), and Patagonia Books. Having been involved with the company so long, I began to derive meaning from the accumulated, accreted richness of my experience and my usefulness to newcomers but, more importantly, from the work we were doing to minimize our environmental impact, and communicating that to others.

I derived meaning from my work because the *company* was doing more meaningful work. I found common ground with other employees who felt the same way.

Some further background: Yvon Chouinard and I told the story of Patagonia's switch to organic cotton in our book, *The Responsible Company*.[1] We first discovered the toxicity of conventional cotton in 1988 when we opened our Boston store. Within days, employees started to call in sick, with headaches and stomachaches. We closed the store, had the air tested, and discovered that the problem was formaldehyde off-gassing from cotton sportswear stored in the basement. That got our attention: we had understood, as a climbing-equipment company, the environmental impacts of steel and aluminum. We understood that polyester and nylon both derive from oil (and we had already begun working with a supplier on producing recycled polyester from plastic soda bottles). But we had thought of cotton as a benign, natural fiber until our employees took sick.

We commissioned a study of the four major fibers we used—nylon, polyester, wool, and cotton—and discovered that cotton was the worst, not only because of the formaldehyde. Here's what we reported in *The Responsible Company*:

> It's a horrific story. To prepare soil for planting cotton, workers spray organophosphates (which can damage the human central nervous system) to kill off all other living organisms. The soil, once treated, is doornail dead (five pesticide-free years have to pass before earthworms, an indication of soil health, can return). Such soil requires intensive use of artificial fertilizers to hold the cotton plants in place. Rainwater runoff from cotton fields contributes significantly to the growth of ocean dead zones. Cotton fields, representing 2.5 percent of cultivated land, ingest 15 percent of chemical insecticides used in agriculture and 10 percent of pesticides. About one-tenth of 1 percent of these chemicals reach the pests they target . . .
>
> Cotton fields contribute 165 million metric tons of greenhouse gas emissions every year. A conventional cotton field stinks; its chemicals

1. Yvon Chouinard and Vincent Stanley, *The Responsible Company: What We've Learned from Patagonia's First 40 Years* (Ventura, CA: Patagonia Books, 2012).

burn the eyes and nauseate the stomach. Before harvesting in non-frost regions like California, cotton has to be sprayed by a cropduster with the defoliant Paraquat, about half of which hits its target. The rest settles over the neighbors' fields and into our streams.

When we first started looking for alternatives, organic cotton was available from a few family farmers in California and Texas. We experimented. At first we made only T-shirts with organic cotton. Then, after several trips to the San Joaquin Valley, where we could smell the selenium ponds and see the lunar landscape of cotton fields, we asked a critical question: How could we continue to make products that laid waste to the earth this way? In the fall of 1994, we made the decision to take our cotton sportswear 100 percent organic by 1996.

We had eighteen months to make the switch for sixty-six products, and less than a year to line up the fabric. There simply wasn't enough organic cotton commercially available to buy through brokers, so we had to go directly to the few farmers who had gone back to organic methods. We had to talk to the certifiers so that all the fiber could be traced back to the bale. And then we had to go to the ginners and spinners and persuade them to clean their equipment before and after running what for them would be very low quantities. The spinners in particular objected to organic cotton because it was full of leaves and stems and sticky from aphids. Our most creative partner, in Thailand, solved the problem by freezing the cotton before spinning. Due to the resourcefulness and open-minded of our new partners, we succeeded. Every Patagonia garment made of cotton in 1996 was organic and has been ever since. Our cotton odyssey taught us our responsibility for what happens in Patagonia's name at every step in the supply chain.[2]

What we didn't explain in *The Responsible Company* is the bad impact the switch had on our employees. People who worked in design and production faced the same work they had to do every season: design, color, spec the line, order the samples, etc., but now found themselves in the position of having to develop an entirely new infrastructure for cotton sportswear. Because the cotton could not be purchased from a broker (through the sewing factory) and because farmers had no experience dealing with spinners, it was our people who had to work to solve the problems. Many of them weren't happy about the extra demand on their

2. Chouinard and Stanley, *The Responsible Company*, 46-48.

time—and for what? Customers weren't asking for organic, and the prices would have to go up $2 to $5 for a pair of shorts or pants or shirt. Why risk the business for a benefit you couldn't see or feel in the final product?

Yet the people familiar with how conventional cotton was grown knew just how serious it was. So we decided to take employees, forty at a time, in buses to the San Joaquin Valley to first visit a conventional farm, then an organic farm. At the conventional farm the first thing they noticed when the bus door opened and they stepped out was the chemical smell. Then they noticed the absence of birds anywhere nearby, then the lack of earthworms or vegetal matter. One woman, who still works in our child care center and had just had her first child, asked the ginner (who separates the fiber from the seed and the oil) what he did with the oil: Did he throw it away? "Oh no," he said, he captured more value from the oil than from the fiber. And where does the oil go? He said that it was a key ingredient in all kinds of processed food—mayonnaise, potato chips.

Then the bus would drive around to the organic farm, which didn't smell like an outdoor chemical factory, where there were birds and earthworms, and where the cotton actually grew in the soil, rather than being held mechanically in place while fed fertilizer.

No one ever came back from one of these trips saying the effort wasn't worthwhile. The switch to organic cotton was a royal pain, *but* people now said the company was doing the right thing. Our employees supported the switch with enthusiasm. They made it happen.

That we made it happen was a turning point for the company; our success became a source of confidence and pride that permeated the business culture. Facing similar challenges, like the problem of neoprene in wetsuits, we developed a habit of tackling these problems rather than shying away from them.

Others have had similar experiences in business. Fred Keller is a second-generation entrepreneur from Grand Rapids, Michigan, who founded, among other companies, Cascade Engineering, a manufacturer of injection-molded recycling carts and bins.[3] Years ago, Keller decided to do something for his community by hiring the poor—just out of prison or

---

3. Fred S. Keller, "Rings of Impact: Opportunities for Business," unpublished.

still on welfare. Two attempts quickly failed; the new hires couldn't adjust to working life and Keller's managers had no practice dealing with the problems of workers without transportation or who had domestic complications that called them out during working hours. For his third attempt, Keller persuaded the state to put a social worker on the factory floor, who, unlike the managers, was experienced in the problems of transition. After two years, Cascade's culture learned how to train every-one—managers and new hires alike—to deal with all the now-familiar challenges without the help of a social worker. Cascade's retention rate of workers out of poverty rose to 95 percent. A Stanford Graduate School of Business study estimated Cascade's five-year savings from lower contract costs and tax credits to be $502,000. The savings to Michigan, in lower welfare costs and a fattened tax base, was more than $900,000.

Keller has engaged the local business community, nongovernmental organizations, and governments in other programs that benefit Grand Rapids. He has also developed a simple classification device of four rings to describe the varying impacts of different kinds of business.[4]

The first ring comprises profit maximizers, those who follow the immensely influential admonition from Milton Friedman that, "[t]he sole purpose of the firm is to maximize profit for its shareholders." For such companies, the quality of their product or service is secondary to their defining product, the company stock price, which for most mature businesses is determined by earnings per share. Such companies game their taxes sharply and work ruthlessly to reduce costs progressively, quarter by quarter.

The second ring belongs to companies, often family owned, whose primary purpose is to earn its shareholders profits but "give back" to the community, often in the form of support for local hospitals, schools, and cultural institutions.

The third ring includes companies that want to "do well by doing good," and define themselves by long- rather than short-term goals for business health. These businesses tend to be good employers and good citizens in their communities. For most of their histories both Patagonia and Cascade have belonged to this circle.

4. Ibid., 6–12.

In the fourth ring are businesses working "to solve some of the world's toughest problems," those that actively examine what those problems are, environmentally and socially, and engage their employees in that work. There is no excuse, for instance, for two major causes of misery among the poor, absence of water filtration for drinking or stoves that generate indoor pollution. Businesses that focus on solving big problems are businesses we need more of.

There are many individuals, and businesses, eager to join Keller's fourth ring. They row against the tide. The economy—and essentially, the social contract—based on cheap and disposable goods has generated a dysfunctional politics; both realms in turn need to sustain mass illusion, worthy of Oz the Magnificent, to hold onto power. That illusion is now dissolving into inchoate but growing dissent on both the left and the right, among the less economically rewarded of all races in their various hollowed-out communities. The illusion has been a massively expensive proposition and not just for our dispossessed, or Asian laborers, or the earth's atmosphere. As the right points out, arcane, complex, and contradictory regulations choke and restrict small businesses that could be a source of employment and healthy rather than cancerous economic growth. As the left points out, the United States spends as much as Scandinavian countries on social welfare, but the money goes disproportionately to health care as a percentage of gross domestic product. We also have, in the United States, the burden of an outsized defense budget. And worldwide, a full third of the global economic pie consists of commissions taken from financial transactions—a slice here for buying, a slice there for selling—that feed only the very few.

In recent years, we have seen glimmers of the way forward that emerge from a more ambitious vision of the human project. Norway has invested its North Sea oil money in an intelligently managed, broadly beneficial sovereign fund that mimics university endowments more than it does traditional, raidable national treasuries. We have seen and experienced the moral force of Pope Francis's *Laudato Si*.[5] John Fullerton, a former JP Morgan Chase banker, has developed a framework, called regenerative

5. Pope Francis, "Laudato Si: On Care for Our Common Home," Encyclical Letter, 2015. Vatican City: 2015.

capitalism,[6] that calls for a whole-systems approach to rebalance and reshape the flow of the economy (through both centralized and distributed means) by identifying and learning to apply principles common to the health and vibrancy of all natural (including human-created) systems.

In *The Well-Tempered City*, Jonathan F. P. Rose, a New York-based developer of green, low-cost housing, examines what a happy city might look like, feel like, and what it would be like to work in were it to be redesigned as a cradle for opportunity for all and serve as a buffer to and support for the natural world.[7] He describes "nodes of multiple benefit," what others might traditionally call leverage points or catalysts, where one blow of the hammer drives five nails into the board. An example: tree planting. Tree-lined urban blocks are six degrees cooler during the summer than equivalent blocks without trees. Trees reduce pollution from passing traffic. They are beautiful, *and* it has been demonstrated that people are happier and experience better mental health when they live with trees in sight rather than without.

I cite personal happiness and mental health, reflexively, as benefits more significant than beauty. But the devaluation of beauty in the built world attends the devaluation of all that is sublime. In the rough and tumble of our day-to-day secular culture, philosophy is for after six o'clock, religion for Sunday, humility and reverence for the gap year, compassion is for girls of all ages and both genders. This cultural loss and coarsening we must not get used to. Rose derives the title of his book from *The Well-Tempered Clavier*, Bach's demonstration that with astute tuning all the major and minor keys can be aired harmoniously in one piece and played on one instrument.[8] That is an apt metaphor for the meaningful work to be done in our time—to fully face our crises, act, change, and in doing so, restore our humanity and bring along with us all

6. John Fullerton, "Regenerative Capitalism: How Universal Principles and Patterns Will Shape Our Economy," http://capitalinstitute.org/wp-content/uploads/2015/04/2015-Regenerative-Capitalism-4-20-15-final.pdf.

7. Jonathan F. P. Rose, *The Well-Tempered City: What Modern Science, Ancient Civilizations, and Human Nature Can Teach Us About the Future of Urban Life* (New York: Harper-Collins, 2016).

8. Richard Florida, "How to Tune a City," https://www.citylab.com/equity/2016/09/how-to-tune-a-city/501776/, interview with Jonathan F. P. Rose.

of the planet's creatures and flora so that the web of life can continue to create and evolve new life.

We have work to do over the next three decades or so—to slow the rate of climate change and adapt to it, and to save as many other species as possible or risk the life of our own, and in the process learn how better to get along with one another. As yet we are distracted, as a species, by the effort to make our living and by the fact and prospect of war or terror. We see the crisis of the environment and its intertwined human crisis as one among many, and not the most urgent. Those of us who might yearn with William James for a moral equivalent to war to address the twinned social and economic crisis with unity of purpose and resolve know that in human history we have never seen such a thing without mass violence. Yet we can see that many great civilizations blinded by the magnitude of their problems and contradictions have walked headlong and heedless over the edge of the cliff into oblivion, unaware that the ground that had always been there no longer held.

It is probably good that we will never experience that yearned-for moral equivalent of war and its totality of action. It may be more important to learn how to both borrow from nature and repay her, so that she can regain some of the wealth she has lost to our agriculture and industry. Large-scale, top-down directed change may be less useful to our future than many local efforts to recover for human communities the sense of place and attendant responsibility to each community's social and natural ecosystem. It is vitally true that we need to learn to trade more fairly with one another (including for our labor) and adapt the remarkable human capacity to mobilize, organize, and dominate the movement of capital, resources, and fellow beings in order to serve human and natural needs rather than continue to turn nature upside down and ourselves inside out in service to an unhealthy economy and in exchange for an uncertain paycheck.

The work that needs to be done will require, paradoxically, as Andrew Revkin has described, both urgency and patience.[9] We must counter our

---

9. Andrew C. Revkin, "On Issues Like Climate Change, Can Urgency and Patience Coexist?," https://dotearth.blogs.nytimes.com/2012/12/24/urgency-and-patience-required-when-dealing-with-wicked-issues-like-climate-change/.

tendency toward quick technological fixes that hammer in one nail while popping out of place the heads of five others. And although we need to be far more judicious about our use of human energy, capital, and natural resources, we also need to be far more creative in the service of our highest and most necessary goals. As Francis puts it, presently, "we have too many means and only a few insubstantial ends."[10]

To help explore the nature of the work to be done, and why it needs to be done, I'll respond to the call of two papal encyclicals, *Laudato Si* on the environmental crisis, and Pope Leo XIII's *Rerum Novarum* (1891) on work and the dignity of the human person.[11] Written 125 years apart, both propound a critique of secular culture that is at once conservative and radical, moral and worldly, in a way that can help all of us, believers and nonbelievers alike, identify what meaningful work can be for our time.

I draw from these encyclicals as a nonbelieving birth Catholic who holds humanistic views influenced by, indeed steeped in, the church's social teaching, and by my own four decades at Patagonia and the experience of my colleagues' and my own process of discovery of the environmental and social harm we do directly or that is done in our name throughout the supply chain. Over the years, I have seen us scramble to right wrongs where we can, including the switch to organic cotton, or as another example, the work to stop indentured servitude in fabric mills that supply us. I have seen us struggle to understand how, fifteen or twenty years from now, we might bring our own company to live within the planet's boundaries,[12] or find bio-based materials to substitute for fossil fuels in the polyester and nylon fabrics that constitute half our product line, or even to secure a living wage, 125 years after *Rerum Novarum*, for the ill-paid women who sew our clothes.

Laudato Si has made many ex-Catholics proud to be connected to the church. No one else with the moral authority of Francis has told the story of the environmental crisis with such eloquence or linked it so well, as it should be, to the human prospect. Francis puts it neatly when he says the

10. Pope Francis, "Laudato Si," 223.

11. Pope Leo XIII, "Rerum Novarum," Encyclical Letter on the Condition of Labor, Vatican City: 1891.

12. "Planetary Boundaries," University of Stockholm, Stockholm Resilience Centre, https://www.stockholmresilience.org/research/planetary-boundaries.html.

"earth herself, burdened and laid waste, is among the most abandoned and maltreated of our poor."[13] And he creates a new, necessary, larger context for the environmental crisis by stating, "We are faced not with two separate crises, one environmental and the other social, but rather with one complex crisis which is both social and environmental."[14]

It is indeed one crisis, one yarn spun from interwoven environmental and social strands. At the risk of oversimplifying, I'll quickly identify the most critical fibers within each strand, beginning with five key problems comprising the environmental crisis.

What scientists call an extinction crisis, the sixth mass wave of species extinction since the formation of the planet and the first since the loss of the dinosaurs sixty-five million years ago.[15] This has evolved slowly since the introduction of agriculture ten thousand years ago but is now quickening in pace. It is the most critical element of the environmental crisis because a mass die-off of plant and animal species thins and weakens the web of life in ways that humans don't understand and can't predict. To lose the honeybee is to threaten a third of the human food supply. The solution to the slow-brewing extinction crisis is long-term, through restoration of quality of habitat.

The threat of greenhouse gases to the atmosphere and resulting climate change.[16] The atmospheric concentration of carbon dioxide is the highest it has been in six hundred thousand years. Climate change caused by carbon dioxide and other greenhouse gas emissions, primarily methane, disrupts the habitat for plants and animals, raises sea levels and threatens coastal cities, and increases the intensity and frequency of storms. Consider the impacts of hurricanes Katrina, Irene, and Sandy during one decade. The solution lies in reduced emissions and increased carbon sequestration.

Ocean acidification that threatens the chain of life in the seas by preventing the smallest, most basic life forms to calcify and develop shells. The oceans, which have been our friend for the past two hundred years, absorbing

13. Pope Francis, "Laudato Si," 2.

14. Ibid., 139.

15. See Elizabeth Kolbert, *The Sixth Extinction: An Unnatural History* (New York: Henry Holt, 2014), among other publications.

16. Paul Hawken, ed., *Drawdown: The Most Comprehensive Plan Ever Proposed to Reverse Global Warming* (New York: Penguin Books, 2017) is an excellent resource.

the extra carbon released into the air by our factories, can no longer do so without acidifying further. The solution for climate change—reduced emissions and increased carbon absorption—also reduces acidification.

Acute loss of freshwater, both above ground in rivers and lakes and below in slow-to-recharge aquifers.[17]As more of the earth's rivers fail to meet the seas year-round, wetlands shrink and ocean dead zones expand. What water we have is polluted with runoff from sewage and fertilizers; the nutrients from increased nitrogen and phosphorus create algae blooms in rivers that choke oxygen and kill fish. The solution lies in better agricultural practices, especially the radically reduced use of dangerous chemicals.

The loss and degradation of farmland. It takes nature from one hundred to five hundred years to create an inch of topsoil; today, the rate of loss in the American Midwest is one inch a year. Our practice of industrial farming, including excess plowing, monocultural planting, and use of synthetic fertilizers and pesticides, contributes to topsoil loss (as does erosion and development). This also degrades the soil, depriving it of micronutrients.[18] Crops grown in degraded soil require, in general, two-thirds more water and a third more fertilizer (whether natural or synthetic) than they do in healthy soil. This problem can be addressed through the adoption of regenerative, organic practices that may also help farmland gain the capacity to sequester the carbon our oceans can no longer absorb.

These five problems lead us in one direction—toward the world becoming a desert. The economic globalization of the past fifty years (a doubled worldwide population, an economy quintupled in size) has been largely responsible for the *speed* at which life is now turning to sand, and we now have little time left to slow the process. To do so will require employment of globalization's singular virtue: the speed at which ideas can travel and be tested. It will also require humility, compassion, and the will to learn to take from nature only what we can repay.

On the social side, principal problems include the following:

17. See annual publications from the World Resource Institute.
18. See Karen Ohlsen, *The Soil Will Save Us* (Emmaus, PA: Rodale Books, 2014).

Inequality of income, opportunity, and power between the global north and south and industrial/postindustrial and traditional agricultural economies, and within cities from neighborhood to neighborhood.[19] Gross inequality and attendant, justifiable, resentment threaten the peace across the globe. There is less social solidarity now than there was in Leo's time, especially along class lines. Moreover, poverty is more disjointed and less immediately apparent than it used to be: a family that has a television and cell service may not have enough money to pay its electric bill—or enough to eat. Across the globe, 20 percent of human beings still do not get enough to eat to be able to thrive physically and mentally. An end to poverty requires a concerted effort of all elements of society: government, nongovernmental organizations, businesses, faith leaders, and the poor themselves, who tend not to be consulted about decisions made in or against their interests.

Heavily armed states, large and small, on a permanent war footing. An outsized military, especially of a nuclear-armed state, eats a large portion of national wealth, deflecting resources from other uses and often requiring spurred economic growth—specifically exports—to pay the bills, regardless of the environmental or social impact of that growth.

A global economic model that relies on rapidly accelerating personal consumption, concentration of capital, and reduction of costs in favor of maximal shareholder return. This model suppresses rates of employment and pay; minimizes, delays, and obstructs environmental protection; and, to increase sales by making disposable products cheaper, drives down the quality of goods (including food) and services, except for luxuries. This model disrupts local economies, displaces whole communities and regions, and sacrifices the human sense of place (or even citizenship) to the global economic juggernaut. The resulting economy, of unprecedented size, scale, and speed, is controlled by a few but requires passive service from the many and from nature itself. We need to rebalance economic power and redefine healthy growth. Scaling business is not always desirable; replication can be a better alternative, with individuation to meet local and regional needs.

19. See Thomas Piketty, *Capital in the Twenty-First Century*, trans. Arthur Goldhammer (Cambridge, MA: Harvard University Press, 2014).

Political power in thrall to a global economic model dominated by finance capital's outsized relation to the productive economy and driven by continuously accelerated production of cheap, disposal goods.[20] Even politicians who step back from advocating the global model describe economic growth, regardless of social or environmental cost, as a good, an engine of wealth creation necessary for the success of either a right-wing small government/low-tax or left-wing welfare-state vision of government. The politicians may not be wrong in the short term: Economic stimulus, especially in infrastructure, helps people back on their feet when the economy tanks. But the prospect of desertification is also real. Our failure to realign the economy—in any frame of time, short, medium, or long—to serve rather than master humanity and nature in a time of environmental crisis has an accelerating negative impact.

Elected public servants who understand the existence of the crisis in its twin from need to help their donors, constituents, and colleagues expand the idea of the politically possible, to lead with vision rather than follow the wind.

The moral anomie of the global consumer culture except at its dissenting margins.[21] This culture has universalized human recognition of the Mercedes-Benz, Apple, and Nike logos to the level of myth and meme but fails to identify, let alone live by, values common to humanity's major religions and moral philosophies: respect for the dignity of the individual, love of justice and of the greater good, compassion, humility, and stewardship of nature among them.

This double crisis, environmental and social, could be described as a process of *deserting*—as well as desertifying—nature, of denying our own natural being as well as nature's intrinsic value and, in its place, deifying the technological paradigm as its replacement. But we are a part of nature and cannot survive should nature lose her capacity to support life.

To interrupt the process, we need learn to use fewer means to pursue more substantial ends. We need a systems approach equal to the complexity of the problem.

20. See Piketty, *Capital in the Twenty-First Century*, and Fullerton, "Regenerative Capitalism," among others.

21. This has been discussed by writers of both secular and religious orientation and from the left, right, and center of political conviction.

Francis illustrates usefully in one passage of *Laudato Si* what we at Patagonia have learned almost accidentally and over time in the course of our work to reduce the environmental harm we do:

> Ecological culture cannot be reduced to a series of urgent and partial responses to the immediate problems of pollution, environmental decay and the depletion of natural resources. There needs to be a distinctive way of looking at things, a way of thinking, policies, an educational programme, a lifestyle and a spirituality which together generate resistance to the assault of the technocratic paradigm. Otherwise, even the best ecological initiatives can find themselves caught up in the same globalized logic. To seek only a technical remedy to each environmental problem which comes up is to separate what is in reality interconnected and to mask the true and deepest problems of the global system.[22]

A second passage is critical for both business and policymakers if we are to make the economy both more responsive and responsible:

> Environmental impact assessment should not come after the drawing up of a business proposition or the proposal of a particular policy, plan or programme. It should be part of the process from the beginning, and be carried out in a way which is interdisciplinary, transparent and free of all economic or political pressure. It should be linked to a study of working conditions and possible effects on people's physical and mental health, on the local economy and on public safety. Economic returns can thus be forecast more realistically, taking into account potential scenarios and the eventual need for further investment to correct possible undesired effects.[23]

Laudato Si adds a significant moral voice to these social and environmental wake-up calls. Other trends now at work help amplify that voice, including a disenchantment and disbelief among the dispossessed of the developed world that a global economy modeled on consumerism and driven by finance capital will provide them a steady income or dignified work; a recognition in newly enriched nations of the social inequity and ecological destruction wrought by the global

22. Pope Francis, "Laudato Si," 111.
23. Ibid., 183.

consumerist model; unfolding advances in scientific understanding of how nature works and thrives; the adoption in 2015 by 183 countries of the United Nations Sustainable Development Goals; the growing capacity of business to mobilize people, money, and resources to substantial as well as insubstantial ends; a heightened awareness of the social and environmental crises within the generation now coming of age; and a recognition, in some quarters, that the way forward requires a holistic approach, one that engages us not from the top down but from inside out, and the development on both large and small scales of more regenerative or restorative models for both rural and urban economic activity.

As Francis points out:

> In some places, cooperatives are being developed to exploit renewable sources of energy which ensure local self-sufficiency and even the sale of surplus energy. This simple example shows that, while the existing world order proves powerless to assume its responsibilities, local individuals and groups can make a real difference. They are able to instil a greater sense of responsibility, a strong sense of community, a readiness to protect others, a spirit of creativity and a deep love for the land. They are also concerned about what they will eventually leave to their children and grandchildren. These values are deeply rooted in indigenous peoples. Because the enforcement of laws is at times inadequate due to corruption, public pressure has to be exerted in order to bring about decisive political action. Society, through non-governmental organizations and intermediate groups, must put pressure on governments to develop more rigorous regulations, procedures and controls. Unless citizens control political power—national, regional and municipal—it will not be possible to control damage to the environment. Local legislation can be more effective, too, if agreements exist between neighbouring communities to support the same environmental policies.[24]

This is as good a description as any of the way forward and one that might provide meaningful work.

Here might be a useful place to turn for a study of the nature of work, to *Rerum Novarum*, a declaration of the obligations of capital to labor (not to keep people in misery) and labor to capital (to work in good faith and

---

24. Ibid., 179.

not to revolt). Leo makes a moral argument, in the face of the modernity of his time, for limits to the rights of the powerful and for the dignity of the human person. He argues for social solidarity and supports unionization as a principle. He rues, as did Marx, the collapse of the guilds in the eighteenth century that had protected urban working men. He laments, in words any socialist of his day would have found sympathetic, that the "hiring of labor and the conduct of trade are concentrated in the hands of comparatively few; so that a small number of very rich men have been able to lay upon the teeming masses of the laboring poor a yoke little better than that of slavery itself."[25]

Leo argues, too, the Catholic social principle of subsidiarity, which holds that the power of decision should rest primarily with those who most closely feel the impact. Subsidiarity argues that society functions not top down but inside out, from the individual first, then the family, what Leo refers to as a "society, a very small, one must admit, but nonetheless a true society, and one older than any State. Consequently, it has rights and duties peculiar to itself which are quite independent of the State."[26] This inside-out view of rights and responsibility extends from the family to the community, the community to the state, and the state to global economic forces.

Leo strongly defends property rights, especially against state confiscation, on several grounds. (He does not directly defend the right of the church to own property.) He considers the right to own property, in particular, land, a source of dignity for working people that enables them to rise in the world on the basis of thrift and industry independent of their jobs. He states that:

> It is surely undeniable that, when a man engages in remunerative labor, the impelling reason and motive of his work is to obtain property, and thereafter to hold it as his very own. If one man hires out to another his strength or skill, he does so for the purpose of receiving in return what is necessary for the satisfaction of his needs; he therefore expressly intends to acquire a right full and real, not only to the remuneration, but also to the disposal of such remuneration, just as he pleases. Thus, if he lives sparingly, saves money, and, for greater security, invests his

25. Pope Leo XIII, "Rerum Novarum," 3.
26. Ibid., 12.

savings in land, the land, in such case, is only his wages under another form; and, consequently, a working man's little estate thus purchased should be as completely at his full disposal as are the wages he receives for his labor.[27]

There was no perceived environmental crisis in 1891, though the as-yet-unseen Extinction Crisis was well underway, and greenhouse gases had begun their rate of increase with the onset of the Industrial Revolution. But one finds in Leo's letter this haunting reference to nature as the source of all sustenance: "Man's needs do not die out, but forever recur; although satisfied today, they demand fresh supplies for tomorrow. Nature accordingly must have given to man a source that is stable and remaining always with him, from which he might look to draw continual supplies. And this stable condition of things he finds solely in the earth and its fruits. There is no need to bring in the State. Man precedes the State, and possesses, prior to the formation of any State, the right of providing for the substance of his body."[28] This reminds us that the way we practice agriculture no longer produces a "stable condition" nor is nature any longer a reliable source from which we can draw "continual supplies," because we are drawing on them faster than the rate of natural replenishment.

Leo twins his strongest case against state ownership of productive property with a protest against displacement of the family by the state as the principal source of authority and wealth:

> In addition to injustice, it is only too evident what an upset and disturbance there would be in all classes, and to how intolerable and hateful a slavery citizens would be subjected. The door would be thrown open to envy, to mutual invective, and to discord; the sources of wealth themselves would run dry, for no one would have any interest in exerting his talents or his industry; and that ideal equality about which they entertain pleasant dreams would be in reality the levelling down of all to a like condition of misery and degradation. Hence, it is clear that the main tenet of socialism, community of goods, must be utterly rejected, since it only injures those whom it would seem meant to ben-

27. Ibid., 5.
28. Ibid., 7.

efit, is directly contrary to the natural rights of mankind, and would introduce confusion and disorder into the commonweal.[29]

This is the universally held position of conservatives today, whether Christian Democrat or secular: that property held in common results in the tragedy of the commons, discourages the ambition that leads to creation of wealth, and ultimately gnaws away the sources of wealth or, as a widely circulated paraphrase of Margaret Thatcher goes, "The problem with socialism is that you eventually run out of other people's money."[30] There is enough truth to this, based on a century's experience of all kinds of socialism—from Stalinist to South American to Scandinavian—to compel the left to at least give a nod to the risks, the "moral hazard," of the advanced welfare state and its mixed economy. Everywhere, large sections of the population still hold to Leo's conservative definition of the principal use and meaning of a state: "We have said that the State must not absorb the individual or the family; both should be allowed free and untrammelled action so far as is consistent with the common good and the interest of others. Rulers should, nevertheless, anxiously safeguard the community and all its members; the community, because the conservation thereof is so emphatically the business of the supreme power, that the safety of the commonwealth is not only the first law, but it is a government's whole reason of existence."[31]

At the same time, Leo also holds to the liberal, not the socialist, principle of assistance to the poor, who were the majority in his time, when he says: "The richer class have many ways of shielding themselves, and stand less in need of help from the State; whereas the mass of the poor have no resources of their own to fall back upon, and must chiefly depend upon the assistance of the State."[32]

No form of capitalism and no form of politics, whether left or right, has as yet created an economy of "stable condition." And lest one be tempted to cite Leo as an advocate for unrestricted capitalism, he puts us

29. Ibid., 15.

30. Margaret Thatcher interviewed on "This Week," Thames TV, February 5, 1976. She actually said, "Socialist governments traditionally do make a financial mess. They always run out of other people's money."

31. Pope Leo XIII, "Rerum Novarum," 35.

32. Ibid., 37s.

off the scent by quoting Aquinas: "Man should not consider his material possessions as his own, but as common to all, so as to share them without hesitation when others are in need."[33]

Leo and Aquinas describe here a moral rather than a political imperative for the wealthy, one that presupposes our modern practice of philanthropy but not of redistribution. But what of those in need? What are their rights?

> The members of the working classes are citizens by nature and by the same right as the rich; they are real parts, living the life which makes up, through the family, the body of the commonwealth; and it need hardly be said that they are in every city very largely in the majority. It would be irrational to neglect one portion of the citizens and favor another, and therefore the public administration must duly and solicitously provide for the welfare and the comfort of the working classes; otherwise, that law of justice will be violated which ordains that each man shall have his due.[34]

And Leo has this to say about the nature of their work:

> Social and public life can only be maintained by means of various kinds of capacity for business and the playing of many parts; and each man, as a rule, chooses the part which suits his own peculiar domestic condition. As regards bodily labor, even had man never fallen from the state of innocence, he would not have remained wholly idle; but that which would then have been his free choice and his delight became afterwards compulsory, and the painful expiation for his disobedience. "Cursed be the earth in thy work; in thy labor thou shalt eat of it all the days of thy life."[35]

In this language one can read the shame of original sin associated in most of Western thought with any human labor and the idea of *uncompelled* work as "free choice and . . . delight." Leo associates, as often do we, our *need* to work with our loss of innocence and expulsion from Eden and subsequent indignity. It has become Western tradition that the indignity of compulsory labor be *temporary* and relieved at some point in this

33. Ibid., 22.
34. Ibid., 33.
35. Ibid., 17.

life (childhood, old age) or in the next world or generation. The necessity of labor is to be transcended in the future. "Exclude the idea of futurity, and forthwith the very notion of what is good and right would perish; nay, the whole scheme of the universe would become a dark and unfathomable mystery. The great truth which we learn from nature herself is also the grand Christian dogma on which religion rests as on its foundation—that, when we have given up this present life, then shall we really begin to live."

This overtly religious lesson can be translated into an insight palatable to nonbelievers as well, concerning the limits to our rights as individuals to interfere with those of future generations, a recognition that as part of life we are individually born, blossom, fade, and die—and are replaced.

Societies die too, though first they become endangered. Leo here refers to what he sees as the loss of his own world:

> When a society is perishing, the wholesome advice to give to those who would restore it is to call it to the principles from which it sprang; for the purpose and perfection of an association is to aim at and to attain that for which it is formed, and its efforts should be put in motion and inspired by the end and object which originally gave it being. Hence, to fall away from its primal constitution implies disease; to go back to it, recovery. And this may be asserted with utmost truth both of the whole body of the commonwealth and of that class of its citizens—by far the great majority—who get their living by their labor.[36]

Leo could not have foreseen the conditions of relative material abundance enjoyed by Western societies of all classes over the last half of the twentieth century, but he was familiar with the materialism and display that has plagued every society when it first comes into wealth, an excess still held up as a birthright attendant to industrialization:

> Christian morality, when adequately and completely practiced, leads of itself to temporal prosperity, for it merits the blessing of that God who is the source of all blessings; it powerfully restrains the greed of possession and the thirst for pleasure—twin plagues, which too often make a man who is void of self-restraint miserable in the midst of abundance; it makes men supply for the lack of means through economy, teaching them to be content with frugal living, and further,

36. Ibid., 27.

keeping them out of the reach of those vices which devour not small incomes merely, but large fortunes, and dissipate many a goodly inheritance.[37]

One of the saddest things to read in *Rerum Novarum* is Leo's words about what we would call now the living wage:

> Let the working man and the employer make free agreements, and in particular let them agree freely as to the wages; nevertheless, there underlies a dictate of natural justice more imperious and ancient than any bargain between man and man, namely, that wages ought not to be insufficient to support a frugal and well-behaved wage-earner. If through necessity or fear of a worse evil the workman accept harder conditions because an employer or contractor will afford him no better, he is made the victim of force and injustice . . .[38]
>
> If a workman's wages be sufficient to enable him comfortably to support himself, his wife, and his children, he will find it easy, if he be a sensible man, to practice thrift, and he will not fail, by cutting down expenses, to put by some little savings and thus secure a modest source of income. Nature itself would urge him to this. We have seen that this great labor question cannot be solved save by assuming as a principle that private ownership must be held sacred and inviolable. The law, therefore, should favor ownership, and its policy should be to induce as many as possible of the people to become owners.[39]

For Leo, a living wage is one sufficient for one worker to support a family— a larger family than is common now. Although current definitions of a living wage vary, most now assume *two* earners supporting a family of four people. Most people in the world do not earn such a wage, not even in wealthy nations. Nearly two-thirds of American families have set aside savings less than $1,000. There can be no culture of ownership without savings, nor a culture that honors the commons. Let us shift away from Leo now to look at meaningful work through another lens.

There is on the other side of this crisis the seemingly odd prospect of a new Eden, not the garden of our expulsion, but one in which we can once

37. Ibid., 28.
38. Ibid., 45.
39. Ibid., 46.

again exercise free choice and take delight. We don't yet know how to tune an economy that works for all of us and for nature, but we do have a glimmer of what we need to do to reverse and resolve the ecological crisis: to reserve (as E. O. Wilson suggests[40]) large swaths of land from commercial use to recover biodiversity, to recover the health of our soil through regenerative organic agriculture so that we may not only reduce emissions but draw carbon back out of the air and firmly into the soil (as Paul Hawken and colleagues have shown in *Drawdown*).[41] Most of this work is the province of communities, civil society, and small- to medium-sized businesses. We do not need to wait for renewed sanity in Washington to begin. We do know from Paul and Percival Goodman[42] and Jane Jacobs,[43] and now from Jonathan Rose, how cities can be remade more conducive to human life. Emerging technologies like 3-D printing promise a radically more efficient use of material resources. A switch to energy sources produced with zero or minimal marginal cost (over the initial capital investment) will make a world cheaper to run, as would a world that uses less water and generates far less waste than 50 percent of its food and nearly all of its used-up consumer goods. So would a world that requires far less unnecessary labor to meet regulations and codes that require work be done in one way that could be better done differently. Finally, we live in a world in which far more local jobs are hived off by machines than by offshoring. In the foreseeable future, we face the prospect of service work (cab, bus, and truck driving, housekeeping, copywriting) being done by robots at minimal marginal cost and at a scale that effectively decouples human labor from measures of productivity.

It may be possible, through a guaranteed basic income that increases as the economy becomes more productive, for human beings to settle into work we most love to do and that most needs to be done. There is

40. Edward O. Wilson, *Half-Earth: Our Planet's Fight for Life* (New York: Liveright, 2017).

41. Paul Hawken, ed., *Drawdown: The Most Comprehensive Plan Ever Proposed to Reverse Global Warming* (New York: Penguin Books, 2017).

42. Percival Goodman and Paul Goodman, *Communitas: Means of Livelihood and Ways of Life* (New York: Vintage, 1960).

43. Jane Jacobs, *The Death and Life of Great American Cities* (New York: Random House, 1961).

much good, paid work to be done in traditionally low-paying agriculture (60 percent of American farmland is planted in soy, corn, and wheat, when there exist forty thousand grains that could be potentially adapted specifically to local soil and climate).[44] There is much important, unpaid work to be done in cities.

So, finally, what does it mean to work meaningfully? After working for paychecks or freelancing by the hour for five decades, I can speak for myself (and counsel graduate students!): Meaningful work expresses and makes use of an individual's gifts and strengths, feels useful to others, serves a purpose one can honor, and, if one is lucky, earns a measure of appreciation and recognition.

One prescription for meaningful work, as good as any I've read, comes from Jean-Francois Zobrist, who runs FAVI, a French supplier of metal parts to the automotive industry: "To be happy, we need to be motivated. To be motivated, we need to be responsible. To be responsible we must understand why and for whom we work, and be free to decide how."[45]

I've heard Chouinard, who worked for years as a blacksmith, say, "Anyone who works with his hands knows he can effect change." I would add that anyone who has effected change has the confidence to do so again, and that this confidence applies to groups as well as individuals.

This leads me to draw one last distinction: between work that respects the dignity of the person and *good* work that respects the dignity of the human person. Respectful, humanistic management must replace command-and-control forms of management (borrowed by the industrial world from the military—and the Catholic Church) if we are to do the work that needs to be done to restore our social and natural ecology. But humanely, intelligently managed work will not *a priori* accomplish moral ends. A land mine factory that treats its people as fully useful, creative individuals, pays well, provides on-site child care, and

---

44. "About the Bread Lab," Washington State University, http://thebreadlab.wsu.edu/about-the-bread-lab/.

45. Frederic Laloux, *Reinventing Organizations: A Guide to Creating Organizations Inspired by the Next Stage of Human Consciousness* (Brussels: Nelson Parker, 2014).

engages in innovative design practices, still offers work that *does* no more good than a traditionally run land mine factory.

Meanwhile, the work we now do in our time of crisis—including the work we do to learn to get along with one another and make critical decisions together—defines and forms, for good or ill, the world coming into being.

Contributors

GERALD J. BEYER is Associate Professor of Christian Ethics at Villanova University. He has published *Recovering Solidarity: Lessons from Poland's Unfinished Revolution* (University of Notre Dame Press, 2010) and articles in *Journal of Catholic Social Thought, Political Theology, Heythrop Journal, Journal of Religious Ethics, Huffington Post, National Catholic Reporter* and *America*. Beyer co-edited and contributed a chapter to the critical edition of Karol Wojtyła, *Katolicka etyka społeczna* (Wydawnictwo KUL, 2018). His forthcoming book is entitled *Solidarity or Status Quo? Catholic Social Teaching and Higher Education in the Age of the Corporatized University* (Fordham University Press). Beyer is vice president of the Villanova University AAUP chapter and executive committee member of Catholic Scholars for Worker Justice.

ALISON COLLIS GREENE is Associate Professor of American Religious History at Emory University's Candler School of Theology. She is author of *No Depression in Heaven: The Great Depression, the New Deal, and the Transformation of Religion in the Delta* (Oxford University Press, 2016), which won the Charles S. Sydnor Award of the Southern Historical Association and was named a CHOICE Outstanding Title.

CHRISTINE FIRER HINZE is Professor of Christian Ethics and Director of the Curran Center for American Catholic Studies at Fordham University. Her research focuses on foundational and applied ethical issues, with special emphasis on the dynamics of social transformation, Catholic social thought, and economic and work justice for women, families, and marginalized groups. Recent publications include *Glass Ceilings and Dirt Floors: Women, Work, & the Global Economy* (2015), and essays in *Theological Studies, Journal of the Society of Christian Ethics, Proceedings of the Catholic Theological Association of America,* and *The Journal of Catholic Social Thought,* along with a forthcoming monograph on economic livelihood and work justice.

KATHLEEN HOLSCHER is Associate Professor of American Studies and Religious Studies, and holds the endowed chair in Roman Catholic Studies at the University of New Mexico. She is the author of *Religious Lessons: Catholic Sisters and the Captured Schools Crisis in New Mexico* (Oxford University Press, 2012).

DR. MICHAEL NAUGHTON is Director of the Center for Catholic Studies at the University of St. Thomas where he holds the Koch Chair in Catholic Studies and is a full professor in the department of Catholic Studies. Author, co-author, and co-editor of ten books and over fifty articles, he also serves as board chair for Reell Precision Manufacturing.

MICHAEL PIRSON is the Loschert Chair of Social Entrepreneurship and Associate Professor of Leading People and Organizations at The Gabelli School of Business at Fordham University. He co-founded the Humanistic Management Network, the International Humanistic Management Association, and is the editor of the *Humanistic Management Journal*. Pirson is a full member of the Club of Rome, chair of the Academy of Management MSR interest group, chair of the Leading People and Organization Area, and leads a number of initiatives to transform business and management to protect dignity and promote well-being.

NICHOLAS RADEMACHER is Professor of Religious Studies at Cabrini University. He is co-editor of *American Catholic Studies* and founding co-editor of *Praxis: An Interdisciplinary Journal of Faith and Justice*. His book *Paul Hanly Furfey: Priest, Scientist, Social Reformer* (Fordham University Press, 2017) will provide readers with a more comprehensive treatment of many of the themes that he addresses in his essay in the present volume.

JOHN C. SEITZ is a scholar of US religion. He serves as Associate Professor in the Department of Theology and as Associate Director for the Curran Center for American Catholic Studies at Fordham University. He is the author of *No Closure: Catholic Practice and Boston's Parish Shutdowns* (Harvard University Press, 2011) and of academic articles about the Roman Catholic priesthood in the United States, US Catholics in the Second World War, and about theoretical questions in the study of religion. He is working on a book about priesthood.

VINCENT STANLEY, co-author with Yvon Chouinard of *The Responsible Company*, has been with Patagonia on and off since its beginning in 1973, for many of those years in key executive roles as head of sales or marketing. He currently serves as the company's director of philosophy, is a resident fellow at the Yale Center for Business and Environment, and a visiting executive at INSEAD in Fontainebleau. He is also a poet (*Paid Notices*) whose work has appeared in the *Best American Poetry* series.

SANDRA SULLIVAN-DUNBAR is Associate Professor of Christian Ethics at Loyola University Chicago, where she specializes in feminist ethics and Christian social ethics. She is the author of *Human Dependency and Christian Ethics* (Cambridge University Press, 2017).

KIRSTEN SWINTH is Professor of History and American Studies at Fordham University. She is the author of *Feminism's Forgotten Fight: The Unfinished Struggle for Work and Family* (Harvard University Press, 2018) and *Painting Professionals: Women Artists and the Development of Modern American Art, 1870–1930* (University of North Carolina Press, 2001). Recipient of Mellon, ACLS, and Getty fellowships, Swinth is currently at work on a new book, *The Rise of the Working Family: A Story of Promise, Peril, and Working Mothers at the Breaking Point, 1975–2020.*

SANDRA WADDOCK is Galligan Chair of Strategy, Carroll School Scholar of Corporate Responsibility, and Professor of Management at Boston College's Carroll School of Management. Winner of numerous awards, including a 2017 PRME Pioneer Award, she has published over 150 papers and 13 books, including *Healing the World* (Routledge/Greenleaf, 2017) and *Intellectual Shamans* (Cambridge University Press, 2014).

Index

Note: Figures are indicated by page numbers in *italics*.

CATHOLIC PRACTICE IN NORTH AMERICA

James T. Fisher and Margaret M. McGuinness (eds.), *The Catholic Studies Reader*

Jeremy Bonner, Christopher D. Denny, and Mary Beth Fraser Connolly (eds.), *Empowering the People of God: Catholic Action before and after Vatican II*

Christine Firer Hinze and J. Patrick Hornbeck II (eds.), *More than a Monologue: Sexual Diversity and the Catholic Church. Volume I: Voices of Our Times*

J. Patrick Hornbeck II and Michael A. Norko (eds.), *More than a Monologue: Sexual Diversity and the Catholic Church. Volume II: Inquiry, Thought, and Expression*

Jack Lee Downey, *The Bread of the Strong:* Lacouturisme *and the Folly of the Cross, 1910–1985*

Michael McGregor, *Pure Act: The Uncommon Life of Robert Lax*

Mary Dunn, *The Cruelest of All Mothers: Marie de l'Incarnation, Motherhood, and Christian Tradition*

Dorothy Day and the Catholic Worker: The Miracle of Our Continuance. Photographs by Vivian Cherry, Text by Dorothy Day, Edited, with an Introduction and Additional Text by Kate Hennessy

Nicholas K. Rademacher, *Paul Hanly Furfey: Priest, Scientist, Social Reformer*

Margaret M. McGuinness and James T. Fisher (eds.), *Roman Catholicism in the United States: A Thematic History*

Gary J. Adler Jr., Tricia C. Bruce, and Brian Starks (eds.), *American Parishes: Remaking Local Catholicism*

Stephanie N. Brehm, *America's Most Famous Catholic (According to Himself): Stephen Colbert and American Religion in the Twenty-First Century*

Matthew T. Eggemeier and Peter Joseph Fritz, *Send Lazarus: Catholicism and the Crises of Liberalism*

John C. Seitz and Christine Firer Hinze (eds.), *Working Alternatives: American and Catholic Experiments in Work and Economy*

Jill Peterfeso, *Womanpriest: Tradition and Transgression in the Contemporary Roman Catholic Church*

Lincoln Rice (ed.), *The Forgotten Radical Peter Maurin: Easy Essays from the Catholic Worker*

Lightning Source UK Ltd.
Milton Keynes UK
UKHW042222070620
364476UK00014B/292